SOFTWARE
REQUIREMENTS

2

Second Edition

Practical techniques for gathering and managing requirements throughout the product development cycle.

Karl E. Wiegers
Two-time winner of the Software Development Productivity Award

PUBLISHED BY
Microsoft Press
A Division of Microsoft Corporation
One Microsoft Way
Redmond, Washington 98052-6399

Library of Congress Cataloging-in-Publication Data
Wiegers, Karl Eugene, 1953-
    Software requirements / Karl E. Wiegers.-- 2nd ed.
      p. cm.
    Includes index.
    ISBN 0-7356-1879-8
    1. Computer software--Development.   I. Title.

  QA76.76.D47W517   2003
  005.1--dc21   2002045512

Printed and bound in the United States of America.

1 2 3 4 5 6 7 8 9   QWE   8 7 6 5 4 3

Distributed in Canada by H.B. Fenn and Company Ltd.

A CIP catalogue record for this book is available from the British Library.

Microsoft Press books are available through booksellers and distributors worldwide. For further information about international editions, contact your local Microsoft Corporation office or contact Microsoft Press International directly at fax (425) 936-7329. Visit our Web site at www.microsoft.com/mspress. Send comments to *mspinput@microsoft.com*.

Acquisitions Editor: Danielle Bird
Project Editor: Devon Musgrave

Body Part No. X08-99937

For Chris, again

Contents at a Glance

Table of Contents

Preface

Despite some fifty years of industry experience, many software development organizations struggle to gather, document, and manage their product requirements. Lack of user input, incomplete requirements, and changing requirements are the major reasons why so many information technology projects fail to deliver all of their planned functionality on schedule and within budget.[1] Many software developers aren't comfortable or proficient at gathering requirements from customers. Customers often don't have the patience to participate in requirements development, or they have the wrong people supply the requirements. Project participants often don't even agree on what a "requirement" is. As one writer observed, "Engineers would rather decipher the words to the Kingsmen's 1963 classic party song 'Louie Louie' than decipher customer requirements." [2]

Software development involves at least as much communication as computing, yet we often emphasize the computing and neglect the communication. This book offers dozens of tools to facilitate that communication and to help software practitioners, managers, marketers, and customers apply effective requirements engineering methods. Newly added to this second edition are chapters on the role of the requirements analyst; the importance of business rules; and ways to apply requirements engineering to maintenance projects, package solutions, outsourced projects, and emergent projects. Numerous sidebars present stories—all true—that illustrate typical requirements-related experiences. Also, look for the "true stories" icon, like the one to the left, next to real examples drawn from many project experiences.

The techniques presented here are mainstream "good practices" for requirements engineering, not exotic new techniques or an elaborate methodology that purports to solve all of your requirements problems. Since I wrote the first edition of this book in 1999, I have taught more than 100 seminars on software requirements to people from corporate and government organizations of all types. I've learned that these practices apply to virtually any project, including those following incremental delivery approaches, both small projects and large-scale endeavors, and both new development and maintenance projects. Nor are the techniques limited to software projects, being applicable to

---

1. The CHAOS Report. The Standish Group International, Inc., 1995.

2. Peterson, Gary. 2002. "Risque Requirements." *CrossTalk* 15(4):31.

hardware and systems engineering as well. As with any other software practice, you'll need to use common sense and gain some experience to learn how to make the methods work best for you.

Benefits This Book Provides

Of all the software process improvements you could undertake, improved requirements engineering practices will likely provide the greatest benefits. I focus on describing practical, proven techniques that can help you to

- Improve the quality of your project's requirements early in the development cycle, which reduces rework and improves productivity.

- Meet schedule objectives by controlling scope creep and requirements changes.

- Achieve higher customer satisfaction.

- Reduce maintenance and support costs.

My objective is to help you improve the processes you use for gathering and analyzing requirements, writing and validating requirements specifications, and managing the requirements throughout the product development cycle. I hope you will actually implement improved practices, not just read about them. Learning about new practices is easy; actually changing the way people work is much harder.

Who Should Read This Book

Anyone involved with defining or understanding the requirements for a software product will find useful information here. The primary audience is those individuals who serve as requirements analysts on a development project, be they full-time requirements specialists or others who occasionally fill the analyst role. A second audience includes the designers, programmers, testers, and other team members who must understand and satisfy user expectations. Marketers and product managers who are charged with specifying the features and attributes that will make a product a commercial success will find these practices valuable. Project managers who must deliver products on schedule will learn how to manage the project's requirements activities and deal with requirements changes. A third audience is customers who want to define a product that meets their functional and quality needs. This book will help customers understand the importance of the requirements process and their role in it.

Looking Ahead

The book is organized into four parts. Part I, "Software Requirements: What, Why, and Who," begins by presenting some definitions and describing several characteristics of excellent requirements. If you're on the technical side of the house, I hope you'll share Chapter 2, on the customer-development partnership, with your key customers. Chapter 3 presents several dozen industry "good practices" for requirements development and management, as well as an overall process for requirements development. The role of the requirements analyst is the subject of Chapter 4.

Part II, "Software Requirements Development," begins with techniques for defining the project's business requirements. Other chapters in Part II address how to find appropriate customer representatives, elicit requirements from them, and document use cases, business rules, functional requirements, and quality attributes. Chapter 11 describes several analysis models that represent the requirements from different perspectives, while Chapter 13 addresses the use of software prototypes to reduce risk. Other chapters in Part II present ways to prioritize and validate requirements. Part II concludes by describing requirements development challenges for some specific project situations and exploring how requirements affect other aspects of project work.

The principles and practices of requirements management are the subject of Part III, with emphasis on techniques for dealing with changing requirements. Chapter 20 describes how requirements traceability connects individual requirements both to their origins and to downstream development deliverables. Part III concludes with a description of commercial tools that can enhance the way you manage your project's requirements.

The final part of the book, "Implementing Requirements Engineering," helps you move from concepts to practice. Chapter 22 helps you incorporate new requirements engineering techniques into your group's development process. Common requirements-related project risks are described in Chapter 23. The current requirements practice self-assessment in Appendix A can help you select areas that are ripe for improvement. Other appendixes present a requirements troubleshooting guide and samples of several requirements documents.

Case Studies

To illustrate the methods described in this book, I've provided examples from several case studies based on actual projects, particularly a medium-sized information system called the Chemical Tracking System. (Don't worry—you don't need to know anything about chemistry to understand this project.) Sample dialogs between project participants from the case study projects are sprinkled throughout the book. No matter what kind of software your group builds, I think you'll find these dialogs pertinent.

From Principles to Practice

It's difficult to muster the energy needed to overcome obstacles to change and to put new knowledge into action. It's tempting to remain in your comfort zone of familiar—if not always effective—practices. To assist you in the journey to improved requirements, each chapter ends with some "Next Steps," actions you can take to begin applying the contents of that chapter. I've provided annotated templates for requirements documents, inspection checklists, a requirements prioritization spreadsheet, a change-control process, and many other process assets on my Web site, *http://www.processimpact.com*. Use these materials to jump-start your application of these techniques. Start with small requirements improvements, but start today.

Some project participants will be reluctant to try new requirements techniques. Some people are downright unreasonable, and none of these techniques will work if you're dealing with unreasonable people. Use the material in this book to educate your peers, customers, and managers. Remind them of requirements-related problems encountered on previous projects, and discuss the potential benefits of trying some new approaches.

You don't need to launch a new development project to begin applying improved requirements engineering practices. Chapter 16 discusses ways to apply many of the techniques in this book to maintenance projects. Implementing requirements practices incrementally is a low-risk process improvement approach that will prepare you for using a suite of new techniques on your next major project.

The goal of requirements engineering is to develop requirements that are good enough to allow you to proceed with design and construction at an acceptable level of risk. You need to spend enough time on requirements engineering to minimize the risks of rework, unacceptable products, and blown schedules. This book gives you the tools to get the right people to collaborate on developing the right requirements for the right product.

Acknowledgments

A number of people took the time to review the manuscript and offer countless recommendations for improvement; they have my deep gratitude. Reviewers for the first edition were Steve Adolph, Nikki Bianco, Bill Dagg, Dale Emery, Chris Fahlbusch, Geoff Flamank, Lynda Fleming, Kathy Getz, Jim Hart, Tammy Hoganson, Mike Malec, Deependra Moitra, Mike Rebatzke, Phil Recchio, Kathy Rhode, Johanna Rothman, Joyce Statz, Doris Sturzenberger, Prakash Upadhyayula, and Scott Whitmire. For this second edition, I greatly appreciate the input from Steve Adolph, Ross Collard, Richard Dalton, Chris Fahlbusch, Lynda Fleming, Ellen Gottesdiener, Linda Lewis, Jeff Pink, Erik Simmons, David Standerford, Dennis Stephenson, Scott Whitmire, Rebecca Wirfs-Brock, and Trish Zwirnbaum.

For the first edition, thanks go to many people at Microsoft Press, including acquisitions editor Ben Ryan, managing editor John Pierce, project editor Mary Kalbach Barnard, copy editor Michelle Goodman, artist Rob Nance, and compositor Paula Gorelick. For this second edition, I thank acquisitions editor Danielle Bird, managing editor Thomas Pohlmann, project editor Devon Musgrave, copy editor Sandi Resnick, artist Michael Kloepfer, and compositor Gina Cassill. The contributions and feedback from hundreds of participants in my requirements seminars over the past several years have also been most helpful. Please share your own experiences with me at *kwiegers@acm.org*.

My deepest appreciation goes to Chris Zambito, the funniest, most patient, and most supportive wife any author could ever hope to have.

I

Software Requirements: What, Why, and Who

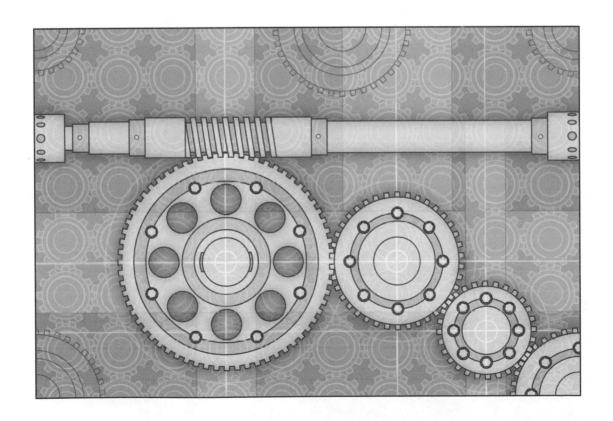

1

The Essential Software Requirement

"Hello, Phil? This is Maria in Human Resources. We're having a problem with the employee system you programmed for us. An employee just changed her name to Sparkle Starlight, and we can't get the system to accept the name change. Can you help?"

"She married some guy named Starlight?"

"No, she didn't get married, just changed her name," Maria replied. "That's the problem. It looks like we can change a name only if someone's marital status changes."

"Well, yeah, I never thought someone might just change her name. I don't remember you telling me about this possibility when we talked about the system. That's why you can get to the Change Name dialog box only from the Change Marital Status dialog box," Phil said.

"I assumed you knew that people could legally change their name anytime they like," responded Maria. "We have to straighten this out by Friday or Sparkle won't be able to cash her paycheck. Can you fix the bug by then?"

"It's not a bug!" Phil retorted. "I never knew you needed this capability. I'm busy on the new performance evaluation system. I think I have some other change requests for the employee system here, too." [sound of rustling paper] "Yeah, here's another one. I can probably fix it by the end of the month, but not within a week. Sorry about that. Next time, tell me these things earlier and please write them down."

"What am I supposed to tell Sparkle?" demanded Maria. "She's really going to be ticked if she can't cash her check."

"Hey, Maria, it's not my fault," Phil protested. "If you'd told me in the first place that you had to be able to change someone's name at any time, this wouldn't have happened. You can't blame me for not reading your mind."

Angry and resigned, Maria snapped, "Yeah, well, this is the kind of thing that makes me hate computer systems. Call me as soon as you get it fixed, will you?"

If you've ever been on the customer side of a conversation like this, you know how frustrating it is to use a software product[1] that doesn't let you perform an essential task. You'd also rather not be at the mercy of a developer who *might* get to your critical change request eventually. Developers know how frustrating it is to learn of functionality that the user expects only after they've implemented the system. It's also annoying to have your current project interrupted by a request to modify a system that does precisely what you were told it should do in the first place.

Many software problems arise from shortcomings in the ways that people gather, document, agree on, and modify the product's requirements. As with Phil and Maria, the problem areas might include informal information gathering, implied functionality, erroneous or uncommunicated assumptions, inadequately defined requirements, and a casual change process.

Most people wouldn't ask a construction contractor to build a custom $300,000 house without extensively discussing their needs and desires and refining the details progressively. Homebuyers understand that making changes carries a price tag; they don't like it, but they understand it. However, people blithely gloss over the corresponding issues when it comes to software development. Errors made during the requirements stage account for 40 to 60 percent of all defects found in a software project (Davis 1993; Leffingwell 1997). The two most frequently reported problems in a large survey of the European software industry concerned specifying and managing customer requirements (ESPITI 1995). Nonetheless, many organizations still practice ineffective methods for these essential project activities. The typical outcome is an expectation gap, a difference between what developers think they are supposed to build and what customers really need.

Nowhere more than in the requirements process do the interests of all the stakeholders in a software or system project intersect. These stakeholders include

- Customers who fund a project or acquire a product to satisfy their organization's business objectives.

- Users who interact directly or indirectly with the product (a subclass of customers).

---

1. I use the terms *product*, *system*, and *application* interchangeably in this book. The concepts and practices I discuss apply to any kind of software or software-containing item that you build.

- Requirements analysts who write the requirements and communicate them to the development community.

- Developers who design, implement, and maintain the product.

- Testers who determine whether the product behaves as intended.

- Documentation writers who produce user manuals, training materials, and help systems.

- Project managers who plan the project and guide the development team to a successful delivery.

- Legal staff who ensure that the product complies with all pertinent laws and regulations.

- Manufacturing people who must build the products that contain software.

- Sales, marketing, field support, help desk, and other people who will have to work with the product and its customers.

Handled well, this intersection can lead to exciting products, delighted customers, and fulfilled developers. Handled poorly, it's the source of misunderstanding, frustration, and friction that undermine the product's quality and business value. Because requirements are the foundation for both the software development and the project management activities, all stakeholders must be committed to following an effective requirements process.

But developing and managing requirements is hard! There are no simple shortcuts or magic solutions. However, so many organizations struggle with the same problems that we can look for techniques in common that apply to many different situations. This book describes dozens of such techniques. They're presented as though you were building a brand-new system, but most of the techniques also apply to maintenance projects and to selecting commercial off-the-shelf package solutions. (See Chapter 16, "Special Requirements Development Challenges.") Nor do these requirements engineering techniques apply only to projects that follow a sequential waterfall development life cycle. Even project teams that build products incrementally need to understand what goes into each increment.

This chapter will help you to

- Understand some key terms used in software requirements engineering.

- Distinguish requirements development from requirements management.

- Be alert to some requirements-related problems that can arise.

- Learn several characteristics of excellent requirements.

Taking Your Requirements Pulse

For a quick check of the current requirements engineering practices in your organization, ask yourself how many of the following conditions apply to your most recent project. If you check more than three or four boxes, this book is for you.

❏   The project's vision and scope are never clearly defined.

❏   Customers are too busy to spend time working with analysts or developers on the requirements.

❏   User surrogates, such as product managers, development managers, user managers, or marketers, claim to speak for the users, but they don't accurately represent user needs.

❏   Requirements exist in the heads of "the experts" in your organization and are never written down.

❏   Customers claim that all requirements are critical, so they don't prioritize them.

❏   Developers encounter ambiguities and missing information when coding, so they have to guess.

❏   Communications between developers and customers focus on user interface displays and not on what the users need to do with the software.

❏   Your customers sign off on the requirements and then change them continuously.

❏   The project scope increases when you accept requirements changes, but the schedule slips because no additional resources are provided and no functionality is removed.

❏   Requested requirements changes get lost, and you and your customers don't know the status of all change requests.

❏   Customers request certain functionality and developers build it, but no one ever uses it.

❏   The specification is satisfied, but the customer is not.

Software Requirements Defined

One problem with the software industry is the lack of common definitions for terms we use to describe aspects of our work. Different observers might describe the same statement as being a user requirement, software requirement, functional requirement, system requirement, technical requirement, business requirement, or product requirement. A customer's definition of *requirements* might sound like a high-level product concept to the developer. The developer's notion of requirements might sound like detailed user interface design to the user. This diversity of definitions leads to confusing and frustrating communication problems.

A key concept is that the requirements must be documented. I was on a project once that had experienced a rotating cast of developers. The primary customer was sick to tears of having each new requirements analyst come along and say, "We have to talk about your requirements." The customer's reaction was, "I already gave your predecessors the requirements. Now build me a system!" In reality, no one had ever documented the requirements, so every new analyst had to start from scratch. To proclaim that you have the requirements is delusional if all you really have is a pile of e-mail and voice-mail messages, sticky notes, meeting minutes, and vaguely recollected hallway conversations.

Some Interpretations of Requirement

Consultant Brian Lawrence suggests that a *requirement* is "anything that drives design choices" (Lawrence 1997). Many kinds of information fit in this category. The *IEEE Standard Glossary of Software Engineering Terminology* (1990) defines a requirement as

1. A condition or capability needed by a user to solve a problem or achieve an objective.

2. A condition or capability that must be met or possessed by a system or system component to satisfy a contract, standard, specification, or other formally imposed document.

3. A documented representation of a condition or capability as in 1 or 2.

This definition encompasses both the user's view of the requirements (the external behavior of the system) and the developer's view (some under-the-hood characteristics). The term *user* should be generalized to *stakeholder* because not all stakeholders are users. I think of a requirement as a property that a product must have to provide value to a stakeholder. The following definition acknowledges the diversity of requirements types (Sommerville and Sawyer 1997):

> *Requirements are...a specification of what should be implemented. They are descriptions of how the system should behave, or of a system property or attribute. They may be a constraint on the development process of the system.*

Clearly, there's no universal definition of what a requirement is. To facilitate communication, we need to agree on a consistent set of adjectives to modify the overloaded term *requirement*, and we need to appreciate the value of recording these requirements in a shareable form.

Trap   Don't assume that all your project stakeholders share a common notion of what requirements are. Establish definitions up front so that you're all talking about the same things.

Levels of Requirements

This section presents definitions that I will use for some terms commonly encountered in the requirements engineering domain. Software requirements include three distinct levels—business requirements, user requirements, and functional requirements. In addition, every system has an assortment of nonfunctional requirements. The model in Figure 1-1 illustrates a way to think about these diverse types of requirements. As with all models, it is not all-inclusive, but it provides a helpful organizing scheme. The ovals represent types of requirements information and the rectangles indicate containers (documents, diagrams, or databases) in which to store that information.

More Info   Chapter 7, "Hearing the Voice of the Customer," contains many examples of these different types of requirements.

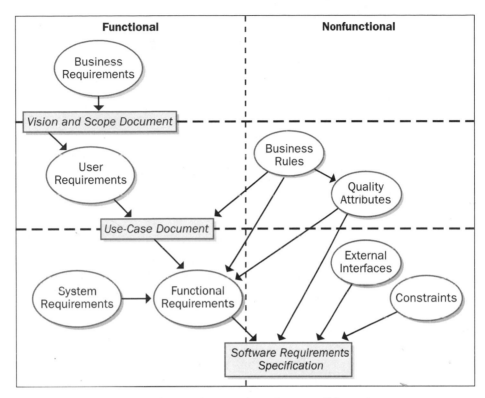

Figure 1-1   Relationship of several types of requirements information.

Business requirements represent high-level objectives of the organization or customer who requests the system. Business requirements typically come from the funding sponsor for a project, the acquiring customer, the manager of the actual users, the marketing department, or a product visionary. Business requirements describe why the organization is implementing the system—the objectives the organization hopes to achieve. I like to record the business requirements in a *vision and scope document*, sometimes called a *project charter* or a *market requirements document*. Creating such a document is the subject of Chapter 5, "Establishing the Product Vision and Project Scope." Defining the project scope is the first step in controlling the common problem of scope creep.

User requirements describe user goals or tasks that the users must be able to perform with the product. Valuable ways to represent user requirements include use cases, scenario descriptions, and event-response tables. User requirements therefore describe what the user will be able to do with the system. An example of a use case is "Make a Reservation" using an airline, a rental car, or a hotel Web site.

> **More Info** Chapter 8, "Understanding User Requirements," addresses user requirements.

Functional requirements specify the software functionality that the developers must build into the product to enable users to accomplish their tasks, thereby satisfying the business requirements. Sometimes called *behavioral requirements*, these are the traditional "shall" statements: "The system shall e-mail a reservation confirmation to the user." As Chapter 10 ("Documenting the Requirements") illustrates, functional requirements describe what the developer needs to implement.

The term *system requirements* describes the top-level requirements for a product that contains multiple subsystems—that is, a *system* (IEEE 1998c). A system can be all software or it can include both software and hardware subsystems. People are a part of a system, too, so certain system functions might be allocated to human beings.

My team once wrote software to control some laboratory apparatus that automated the tedious addition of precise quantities of chemicals to an array of beakers. The requirements for the overall system led us to derive software functional requirements to send signals to the hardware to move the chemical-dispensing nozzles, read positioning sensors, and turn pumps on and off.

Business rules include corporate policies, government regulations, industry standards, accounting practices, and computational algorithms. As you'll see in Chapter 9, "Playing By the Rules," business rules are not themselves software requirements because they exist outside the boundaries of any specific software system. However, they often restrict who can perform certain use cases or they dictate that the system must contain functionality to comply with the pertinent rules. Sometimes business rules are the origin of specific quality attributes that are implemented in functionality. Therefore, you can trace the genesis of certain functional requirements back to a particular business rule.

Functional requirements are documented in a *software requirements specification* (SRS), which describes as fully as necessary the expected behavior of the software system. I'll refer to the SRS as a document, although it can be a database or spreadsheet that contains the requirements, information stored in a commercial requirements management tool—see Chapter 21, "Tools for Requirements Management"—or perhaps even a stack of index cards for a small project. The SRS is used in development, testing, quality assurance, project management, and related project functions.

In addition to the functional requirements, the SRS contains nonfunctional requirements. These include performance goals and descriptions of quality attributes. *Quality attributes* augment the description of the product's functionality by describing the product's characteristics in various dimensions that are important either to users or to developers. These characteristics include usability, portability, integrity, efficiency, and robustness. Other nonfunctional requirements describe external interfaces between the system and the outside world, and design and implementation constraints. *Constraints* impose restrictions on the choices available to the developer for design and construction of the product.

People often talk about product features. A *feature* is a set of logically related functional requirements that provides a capability to the user and enables the satisfaction of a business objective. In the commercial software arena, a feature is a group of requirements recognizable to a stakeholder that aids in making a purchase decision—a bullet item in the product description. A customer's list of desired product features is not equivalent to a description of the user's task-related needs. Web browser favorites or bookmarks, spell check, macro recording, automobile power windows, online update of tax code changes, telephone speed-dialing, and automatic virus signature updating are examples of product features. A feature can encompass multiple use cases, and each use case requires that multiple functional requirements be implemented to allow the user to perform the task.

To get a better grasp on some of the different kinds of requirements I've been discussing, consider a word processing program. A business requirement might read, "The product will allow users to correct spelling errors in a document efficiently." The product's box cover announces that a spell checker is included as a feature that satisfies this business requirement. Corresponding user requirements might include tasks—use cases—such as "Find spelling errors" and "Add word to global dictionary." The spell checker has many individual functional requirements, which deal with operations such as finding and highlighting a misspelled word, displaying a dialog box with suggested replacements, and globally replacing misspelled words with corrected words. The quality attribute called *usability* would specify just what is meant by the word "efficiently" in the business requirement.

Managers or marketing define the business requirements for software that will help their company operate more efficiently (for information systems) or compete successfully in the marketplace (for commercial products). All user requirements must align with the business requirements. The user requirements permit the analyst to derive the bits of functionality that will let the users perform their tasks with the product. Developers use the functional and nonfunctional requirements to design solutions that implement the necessary functionality and achieve the specified quality and performance objectives, within the limits that the constraints impose.

Although the model in Figure 1-1 shows a top-down flow of requirements, you should expect cycles and iteration between the business, user, and functional requirements. Whenever someone proposes a new feature, use case, or functional requirement, the analyst must ask, "Is this in scope?" If the answer is "yes," the requirement belongs in the specification. If the answer is "no," it does not. If the answer is "no, but it ought to be," the business requirements owner or the funding sponsor must decide whether to increase the project scope to accommodate the new requirement. This is a business decision that has implications for the project's schedule and budget.

What Requirements Are Not

Requirements specifications do not include design or implementation details (other than known constraints), project planning information, or testing information (Leffingwell and Widrig 2000). Separate such items from the requirements so that the requirements activities can focus on understanding what the team intends to build. Projects typically have other kinds of requirements, including development environment requirements, schedule or budget limitations, the need for a tutorial to help new users get up to speed, or requirements for releasing a product and moving it into the support environment. These are *project* requirements but not *product* requirements; they don't fall within the scope of this book.

Requirements Development and Management

Confusion about requirements terminology extends even to what to call the whole discipline. Some authors call the entire domain *requirements engineering* (Sommerville and Kotonya 1998); others refer to it as *requirements management* (Leffingwell and Widrig 2000). I find it useful to split the domain of software requirements engineering into *requirements development* (addressed in Part II of this book) and *requirements management* (addressed in Part III), as shown in Figure 1-2.

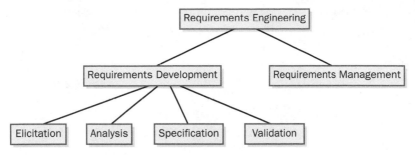

Figure 1-2   Subcomponents of the requirements engineering domain.

Requirements Development

We can further subdivide requirements development into *elicitation, analysis, specification,* and *validation* (Abran and Moore 2001). These subdisciplines encompass all the activities involved with gathering, evaluating, and documenting the requirements for a software or software-containing product, including the following:

- Identifying the product's expected user classes

- Eliciting needs from individuals who represent each user class

- Understanding user tasks and goals and the business objectives with which those tasks align

- Analyzing the information received from users to distinguish their task goals from functional requirements, nonfunctional requirements, business rules, suggested solutions, and extraneous information

- Allocating portions of the top-level requirements to software components defined in the system architecture

- Understanding the relative importance of quality attributes

- Negotiating implementation priorities

- Translating the collected user needs into written requirements specifications and models

- Reviewing the documented requirements to ensure a common understanding of the users' stated requirements and to correct any problems before the development group accepts them

Iteration is a key to requirements development success. Plan for multiple cycles of exploring requirements, refining high-level requirements into details, and confirming correctness with users. This takes time and it can be frustrating, but it's an intrinsic aspect of dealing with the fuzzy uncertainty of defining a new software product.

Requirements Management

Requirements management entails "establishing and maintaining an agreement with the customer on the requirements for the software project" (Paulk et al. 1995). That agreement is embodied in the written requirements specifications and the models. Customer acceptance is only half the equation needed for requirements approval. The developers also must accept the specifications and agree to build them into a product. Requirements management activities include the following:

- Defining the requirements baseline (a snapshot in time representing the currently agreed-upon body of requirements for a specific release)

- Reviewing proposed requirements changes and evaluating the likely impact of each change before approving it

- Incorporating approved requirements changes into the project in a controlled way

- Keeping project plans current with the requirements

- Negotiating new commitments based on the estimated impact of requirements changes

- Tracing individual requirements to their corresponding designs, source code, and test cases

- Tracking requirements status and change activity throughout the project

Figure 1-3 provides another view of the distinction between requirements development and requirements management. This book describes several dozen specific practices for performing requirements elicitation, analysis, specification, validation, and management.

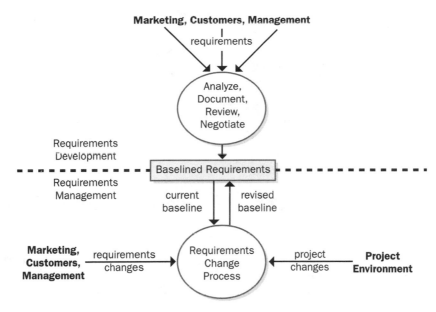

Figure 1-3   The boundary between requirements development and requirements management.

Every Project Has Requirements

Frederick Brooks eloquently stated the critical role of requirements to a software project in his classic 1987 essay, "No Silver Bullet: Essence and Accidents of Software Engineering":

> *The hardest single part of building a software system is deciding precisely what to build. No other part of the conceptual work is as difficult as establishing the detailed technical requirements, including all the interfaces to people, to machines, and to other software systems. No other part of the work so cripples the resulting system if done wrong. No other part is more difficult to rectify later.*

Every software application or software-containing system has users who rely on it to enhance their lives. The time spent understanding user needs is a high-leverage investment in project success. If developers don't have written requirements that the customers agree to, how can they satisfy those customers? Even the requirements for software that isn't intended for commercial use must be well understood. Examples include software libraries, components, and tools created for internal use by a development group.

Often, it's impossible to fully specify the requirements before commencing construction. In those cases, take an iterative and incremental approach to implement one portion of the requirements at a time, obtaining customer feedback before moving on to the next cycle. This isn't an excuse to write code before contemplating requirements for that next increment, though. Iterating on code is more expensive than iterating on concepts.

People sometimes balk at spending the time that it takes to write software requirements, but writing the requirements isn't the hard part. The hard part is *discovering* the requirements. Writing requirements is primarily a matter of clarifying, elaborating, and transcribing. A solid understanding of a product's requirements ensures that your team works on the right problem and devises the best solution to that problem. Requirements let you prioritize the work and estimate the effort and resources needed for the project. Without knowing what the requirements are, you can't tell when the project is done, determine whether it has met its goals, or make trade-off decisions when scope reduction is necessary.

No Assumed Requirements

I recently encountered a development group that used a homegrown software engineering tool that included a source code editor. Unfortunately, no one had specified that the tool should permit users to print the code, although the users undoubtedly assumed that it would. Developers had to hand-transcribe the source statements to hold a code review.

If you don't write down even the implicit and assumed requirements, don't be surprised if the software doesn't meet user expectations. Periodically ask, "What are we assuming?" to try to surface those hidden thoughts. If you come across an assumption during requirements discussions, write it down and confirm its accuracy. If you're developing a replacement system, review the previous system features to determine whether they're required in the replacement rather than assuming that they are or are not.

When Bad Requirements Happen to Nice People

The major consequence of requirements problems is rework—doing over something that you thought was already done. Rework can consume 30 to 50 percent of your total development cost (Boehm and Papaccio 1988), and requirements errors account for 70 to 85 percent of the rework cost (Leffingwell 1997). As illustrated in Figure 1-4, it costs far more to correct a defect that's found late in the project than to fix it shortly after its creation (Grady 1999). Preventing requirements errors and catching them early therefore has a huge lever aging effect on reducing rework. Imagine how different your life would be if you could cut the rework effort in half! You could build products faster, build more and better products in the same amount of time, and perhaps even go home occasionally.

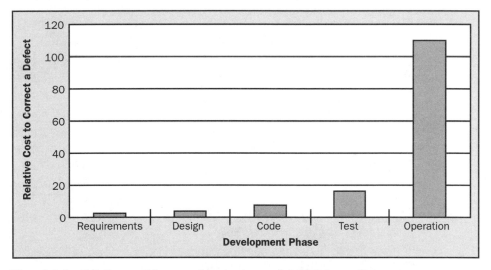

Figure 1-4   Relative cost to correct a requirement defect depending on when it is discovered.

Shortcomings in requirements practices pose many risks to project success, where *success* means delivering a product that satisfies the user's functional and quality expectations at agreed-on cost and schedule. Chapter 23, "Software Requirements and Risk Management," describes how to manage such risks to prevent them from derailing your project. Some of the most common requirements risks are described in the following sections.

Insufficient User Involvement

Customers often don't understand why it is so essential to work hard on gathering requirements and assuring their quality. Developers might not emphasize user involvement, either because working with users isn't as much fun as writing code or because they think they already know what the users need. In some cases, it's difficult to gain access to people who will actually use the product, and user surrogates don't always understand what users really need. Insufficient user involvement leads to late-breaking requirements that delay project completion. There's no substitute for having the development team work directly with actual users throughout the project, as described in Chapter 6.

Creeping User Requirements

As requirements evolve and grow during development, projects often exceed their planned schedules and budgets. Such plans aren't always based on realistic understandings of the size and complexity of the requirements; constant requirements modifications make the problem worse. The problem lies partly in the users' frequent requests for changes in the requirements and partly in the way that developers respond to these requests.

To manage scope creep, begin with a clear statement of the project's business objectives, strategic vision, scope, limitations, success criteria, and expected product usage. Evaluate all proposed new features or requirements changes against this reference framework. An effective change process that includes impact analysis will help the stakeholders make informed business decisions about which changes to accept and the associated costs in time, resources, or feature trade-offs. Change is often critical to success, but change always has a price.

As changes propagate through the product being developed, its architecture can slowly crumble. Code patches make programs harder to understand and maintain. Added code can cause modules to violate the solid design principles of strong cohesion and loose coupling (McConnell 1993). To minimize this type of quality degradation, flow requirements changes through the architecture and design rather than implementing them directly into code.

Ambiguous Requirements

Ambiguity is the great bugaboo of requirements specifications (Lawrence 1996). One symptom of ambiguity is that a reader can interpret a requirement statement in several ways. Another sign is that multiple readers of a requirement arrive at different understandings of what it means. Chapter 10 lists many words and phrases that contribute to ambiguity by placing the burden of interpretation on the reader. Ambiguity also results from imprecise and insufficiently detailed requirements that force developers to fill in the blanks.

Ambiguity leads to different expectations on the part of various stakeholders. Some of them are then surprised with whatever is delivered. Ambiguous requirements result in wasted time when developers implement a solution for the wrong problem. Testers who expect the product to behave differently from what the developers intended waste time resolving the differences.

One way to ferret out ambiguity is to have people who represent different perspectives formally inspect the requirements. (See Chapter 15, "Validating the Requirements," for more on this subject.) Simply passing around the requirements document for comments isn't sufficient to reveal ambiguities. If different reviewers interpret a requirement in different ways but it makes sense to each of them, the ambiguity won't surface until late in the project, when correcting it can be expensive. Writing test cases against the requirements and building prototypes are other ways to discover ambiguities. Gause and Weinberg (1989) describe additional ambiguity-detection methods.

Gold Plating

Gold plating takes place when a developer adds functionality that wasn't in the requirements specification but that the developer believes "the users are just going to love." Often users don't care about this excess functionality, and the time spent implementing it is wasted. Rather than simply inserting new features, developers and analysts should present the customers with creative ideas and alternatives for their consideration. Developers should strive for leanness and simplicity, not for going beyond what the customer requests without customer approval.

Customers sometimes request features or elaborate user interfaces that look cool but add little value to the product. Everything you build costs time and money, so you need to maximize the delivered value. To reduce the threat of gold plating, trace each bit of functionality back to its origin so that you know why it's included. The use-case approach for eliciting requirements helps to focus requirements elicitation on the functionality that lets users perform their business tasks.

Minimal Specification

Sometimes marketing staff or managers are tempted to create a limited specification, perhaps just a product concept sketched on a napkin. They expect the developers to flesh out the spec while the project progresses. This might work for a tightly integrated team that's building a small system, on exploratory or research projects, or when the requirements truly are flexible (McConnell 1996). In most cases, though, it frustrates the developers (who might be operating under incorrect assumptions and with limited direction) and disappoints the customers (who don't get the product they envisioned).

Overlooked User Classes

Most products have several groups of users who might use different subsets of features, have different frequencies of use, or have varying experience levels. If you don't identify the important user classes for your product early on, some user needs won't be met. After identifying all user classes, make sure that each has a voice, as discussed in Chapter 6, "Finding the Voice of the Customer."

Inaccurate Planning

"Here's my idea for a new product; when will you be done?" Don't answer this question until you know more about the problem being discussed. Vague, poorly understood requirements lead to overly optimistic estimates, which come back to haunt us when the inevitable overruns occur. An estimator's off-the-cuff guess sounds a lot like a commitment to the listener. The top contributors to poor software cost estimation are frequent requirements changes, missing requirements, insufficient communication with users, poor specification of requirements, and insufficient requirements analysis (Davis 1995). When you present an estimate, provide either a range (best case, most likely, worst case) or a confidence level ("I'm 90 percent sure I can have that done within three months").

Benefits from a High-Quality Requirements Process

Organizations that implement effective requirements engineering processes can reap multiple benefits. A great reward comes from reducing unnecessary rework during the late development stages and throughout the lengthy maintenance period. The high leveraging effect of quality requirements isn't obvious, and many people mistakenly believe that time spent discussing requirements simply delays delivery by the same duration. A holistic cost-of-quality perspective reveals the value of emphasizing early-stage quality practices (Wiegers 1996a).

Sound requirements processes emphasize a collaborative approach to product development that involves multiple stakeholders in a partnership throughout the project. Collecting requirements enables the development team to better understand its user community or market, a critical success factor for any project. It's far cheaper to reach this understanding before you build the product than after your customers receive it.

Engaging users in the requirements-gathering process generates enthusiasm for the product and builds customer loyalty. By emphasizing user tasks instead of superficially attractive features, the team can avoid writing code that won't ever be used. Customer involvement reduces the expectation gap between what the user needs and what the developer delivers. You're going to get the customer feedback eventually. Try to get it early rather than late, perhaps with the help of prototypes that stimulate user feedback. Requirements development takes time, but it takes less time than correcting a lot of problems in beta testing or after release.

There are additional benefits, too. Explicitly allocating selected system requirements to various software, hardware, and human subsystems emphasizes a systems approach to product engineering. An effective change-control process will minimize the adverse impact of requirements changes. Documented, unambiguous requirements greatly facilitate system testing, which in turn increases your chances of delivering high-quality products that satisfy all stakeholders.

No one can promise a specific return on investment from an improved requirements process. You can go through an analytical thought process to imagine how better requirements could help you, though. First, consider the cost of investing in a better process. This includes the cost of assessing your current practices, developing new procedures and document templates, training the team, buying books and tools, and perhaps using outside consultants. Your greatest investment is the time your teams spend gathering, documenting, reviewing, and managing their requirements. Next, think about the possible benefits you might enjoy and how much time or money they could save you. It's impossible to quantify all the following benefits, but they are real:

- Fewer requirements defects

- Reduced development rework

- Fewer unnecessary features

- Lower enhancement costs

- Faster development

- Fewer miscommunications

- Reduced scope creep

- Reduced project chaos
- More accurate system-testing estimates
- Higher customer and team member satisfaction

Characteristics of Excellent Requirements

How can you distinguish good requirements specifications from those with problems? Several characteristics that individual requirement statements should exhibit are discussed in this section, followed by desirable characteristics of the SRS as a whole (Davis 1993; IEEE 1998b). The best way to tell whether your requirements have these desired attributes is to have several project stakeholders carefully review the SRS. Different stakeholders will spot different kinds of problems. For example, analysts and developers can't accurately judge completeness or correctness, whereas users can't assess technical feasibility.

Requirement Statement Characteristics

In an ideal world, every individual user, business, and functional requirement would exhibit the qualities described in the following sections.

Complete

Each requirement must fully describe the functionality to be delivered. It must contain all the information necessary for the developer to design and implement that bit of functionality. If you know you're lacking certain information, use *TBD* (to be determined) as a standard flag to highlight these gaps. Resolve all TBDs in each portion of the requirements before you proceed with construction of that portion.

Correct

Each requirement must accurately describe the functionality to be built. The reference for correctness is the source of the requirement, such as an actual user or a high-level system requirement. A software requirement that conflicts with its parent system requirement is not correct. Only user representatives can determine the correctness of user requirements, which is why users or their close surrogates must review the requirements.

Feasible

It must be possible to implement each requirement within the known capabilities and limitations of the system and its operating environment. To avoid specifying unattainable requirements, have a developer work with marketing or the requirements analyst throughout the elicitation process. The developer can provide a reality check on what can and cannot be done technically and what can be done only at excessive cost. Incremental development approaches and proof-of-concept prototypes are ways to evaluate requirement feasibility.

Necessary
Each requirement should document a capability that the customers really need or one that's required for conformance to an external system requirement or a standard. Every requirement should originate from a source that has the authority to specify requirements. Trace each requirement back to specific voice-of-the-customer input, such as a use case, a business rule, or some other origin.

Prioritized
Assign an implementation priority to each functional requirement, feature, or use case to indicate how essential it is to a particular product release. If all the requirements are considered equally important, it's hard for the project manager to respond to budget cuts, schedule overruns, personnel losses, or new requirements added during development.

> **More Info**   Chapter 14, "Setting Requirement Priorities," discusses prioritization in further detail.

Unambiguous
All readers of a requirement statement should arrive at a single, consistent interpretation of it, but natural language is highly prone to ambiguity. Write requirements in simple, concise, straightforward language appropriate to the user domain. "Comprehensible" is a requirement quality goal related to "unambiguous": readers must be able to understand what each requirement is saying. Define all specialized terms and terms that might confuse readers in a glossary.

Verifiable
See whether you can devise a few tests or use other verification approaches, such as inspection or demonstration, to determine whether the product properly implements each requirement. If a requirement isn't verifiable, determining whether it was correctly implemented becomes a matter of opinion, not

objective analysis. Requirements that are incomplete, inconsistent, infeasible, or ambiguous are also unverifiable (Drabick 1999).

Requirements Specification Characteristics

It's not enough to have excellent individual requirement statements. Sets of requirements that are collected into a specification ought to exhibit the characteristics described in the following sections.

Complete

No requirements or necessary information should be absent. Missing requirements are hard to spot because they aren't there! Chapter 7 suggests some ways to find missing requirements. Focusing on user tasks, rather than on system functions, can help you to prevent incompleteness.

Consistent

Consistent requirements don't conflict with other requirements of the same type or with higher-level business, system, or user requirements. Disagreements between requirements must be resolved before development can proceed. You might not know which single requirement (if any) is correct until you do some research. Recording the originator of each requirement lets you know who to talk to if you discover conflicts.

Modifiable

You must be able to revise the SRS when necessary and to maintain a history of changes made to each requirement. This dictates that each requirement be uniquely labeled and expressed separately from other requirements so that you can refer to it unambiguously. Each requirement should appear only once in the SRS. It's easy to generate inconsistencies by changing only one instance of a duplicated requirement. Consider cross-referencing subsequent instances back to the original statement instead of duplicating the requirement. A table of contents and an index will make the SRS easier to modify. Storing requirements in a database or a commercial requirements management tool makes them into reusable objects.

Traceable

A traceable requirement can be linked backward to its origin and forward to the design elements and source code that implement it and to the test cases that verify the implementation as correct. Traceable requirements are uniquely labeled with persistent identifiers. They are written in a structured, fine-grained way as opposed to crafting long narrative paragraphs. Avoid lumping multiple requirements together into a single statement; the different requirements might trace to different design and code elements.

More Info   Chapter 10 discusses writing high-quality functional requirements, and Chapter 20, "Links in the Requirements Chain," addresses requirements tracing.

You'll never create an SRS in which *all* requirements demonstrate *all* these ideal attributes. However, if you keep these characteristics in mind while you write and review the requirements, you will produce better requirements documents and you will build better products.

Next Steps

- Write down requirements-related problems that you have encountered on your current or previous project. Identify each as a requirements development or requirements management problem. Identify the impact that each problem had on the project and its root causes.

- Facilitate a discussion with your team members and other stakeholders regarding requirements-related problems from your current or previous projects, the problems' impacts, and their root causes. Explain that the participants have to confront these difficult issues if they ever hope to master them. Are they ready to try?

- Arrange a one-day training class on software requirements for your entire project team. Include key customers, marketing staff, and managers, using whatever it takes to get them into the room. Training is an effective team-building activity. It gives project participants a common vocabulary and a shared understanding of effective techniques and behaviors so that they all can begin addressing their mutual challenges.

2

Requirements from the Customer's Perspective

Gerhard, a senior manager at Contoso Pharmaceuticals, was meeting with Cynthia, the new manager of Contoso's information systems (IS) development group. "We need to build a chemical-tracking information system for Contoso," Gerhard began. "The system should let us keep track of all the chemical containers we already have in the stockroom and in individual laboratories. That way, maybe the chemists can get what they need from someone down the hall instead of buying a new container from a vendor. This should save us a lot of money. Also, the Health and Safety Department needs to generate some reports on chemical usage for the government. Can your group build this system in time for the first compliance audit five months from now?"

"I see why this project is important, Gerhard," said Cynthia. "But before I can commit to a schedule, we'll need to collect some requirements for your system."

Gerhard was confused. "What do you mean? I just told you the requirements."

"Actually, you described a concept and some business objectives for the project," Cynthia explained. "Those high-level business requirements don't give me enough detail to know what software to build or how long it might take. I'd like to have a requirements analyst work with some of the users to understand their needs for the system. Then we can figure out what functionality will meet both your business objectives and the users' needs. You might not even need a new software system to meet your goal of saving money."

Gerhard hadn't encountered this reaction before from an IS person. "The chemists are busy people," he protested. "They don't have time to nail down every detail before you can start programming. Can't your people figure out what to build?"

Cynthia tried to explain her rationale for collecting requirements from the people who would use the new system. "If we just make our best guess at what the users need, we can't do a good job. We're software developers, not chemists. We don't really know what the chemists need to do with the chemical-tracking system. I've learned that if we don't take the time to understand the problem before we start writing code, nobody is happy with the results."

"We don't have time for all that," Gerhard insisted. "I gave you my requirements. Now just build the system, please. Keep me posted on your progress."

Conversations like this take place regularly in the software world. Customers who request a new information system often don't understand the importance of obtaining input from actual users of the proposed system in addition to other internal and external stakeholders. Marketing specialists with a great new product concept believe that they adequately represent the interests of prospective buyers. However, there's no substitute for gathering requirements directly from the people who will actually use the product. Some contemporary "agile" software development methodologies such as Extreme Programming recommend that a full-time, on-site customer work closely with the development team. As one book about Extreme Programming pointed out, "The project is *steered* to success by the customer and programmers working in concert" (Jeffries, Anderson, and Hendrickson 2001).

Part of the requirements problem results from confusion over the different levels of requirements: business, user, and functional. Gerhard stated some business requirements, benefits that he hopes Contoso will enjoy with the help of the new chemical-tracking system. However, Gerhard can't describe the user requirements because he is not an intended user of the system. Users, in turn, can describe the tasks they must be able to perform with the system, but they can't identify all the functional requirements that developers must implement to let them accomplish those tasks.

This chapter addresses the customer-development relationship that is so critical to software project success. I propose a Requirements Bill of Rights for Software Customers and a corresponding Requirements Bill of Responsibilities for Software Customers. These lists underscore the importance of customer—specifically user—involvement in requirements development.

Fear of Rejection

I recently heard a sad story when I visited a corporate information systems department. The developers had recently built a new system for use within the company. They had obtained negligible user input from the beginning. The day the developers proudly unveiled their new system, the users rejected it as completely unacceptable. This came as a shock because the developers had worked hard to satisfy what they perceived to be the users' needs. So what did they do? They fixed it. You always fix the system when you get the requirements wrong, and it always costs much more than if you had engaged user representatives from the outset.

The time the developers had to spend fixing the flawed information system wasn't planned, of course, so the next project that the team was scheduled to work on had to wait. This is a lose-lose-lose situation. The developers were embarrassed and frustrated, the customers were unhappy because their new system wasn't available for use when they expected it, and the company wasted a lot of money. Extensive and ongoing customer engagement from the start could have prevented this unfortunate, but not uncommon, project outcome.

Who Is the Customer?

In the broadest sense, a *customer* is an individual or organization who derives either direct or indirect benefit from a product. Software customers include those project stakeholders who request, pay for, select, specify, use, or receive the output generated by a software product. As we saw in Chapter 1, other project stakeholders include requirements analysts, developers, testers, documentation writers, project managers, support staff, legal staff, and marketing staff.

Gerhard, the manager we met earlier, represents the kind of customer who is paying for or sponsoring a software project. Customers at Gerhard's senior management level are responsible for defining the business requirements. They provide the high-level concept for the product and the business rationale for launching it. As discussed in Chapter 5, "Establishing the Product Vision and Product Scope," *business requirements* describe the business objectives that the customer, company, or other stakeholders want to achieve. Business requirements establish a guiding framework for the rest of the project. All other product features and requirements ought to align with satisfying the business requirements. However, business requirements don't provide sufficient detail to tell developers what to build.

The next level of requirements—user requirements—should come from people who will actually use the product, directly or indirectly. These users (often called *end users*) therefore constitute another kind of customer. Users can describe the tasks they need to perform with the product and the quality characteristics they expect the product to exhibit.

Customers who provide the business requirements sometimes purport to speak for the users, but they are usually too far removed from the actual work to provide accurate user requirements. For information systems, contract development, or custom application development, business requirements should come from the person with the money, whereas user requirements should come from people who will press the keys to use the product. The various stakeholders will need to check for alignment between the user and business requirements.

Unfortunately, both kinds of customers might not believe that they have the time to work with the requirements analysts who gather, analyze, and document the requirements. Sometimes customers expect the analysts or developers to figure out what users need without a lot of discussion. If only it were that easy. The days of sliding some vague requirements and a series of pizzas under the door to the programming department are long past.

The situation is somewhat different for commercial (shrink-wrapped) software development, in which the customer and the user often are the same person. Customer surrogates, such as the marketing department or product management, typically attempt to determine what customers would find appealing. Even for commercial software, though, you should engage end users in the process of developing user requirements, as Chapter 7 ("Hearing the Voice of the Customer") describes. If you don't do this, be prepared to read magazine reviews that describe shortcomings in your product that adequate user input could have helped you avoid.

Not surprisingly, conflicts can arise between business requirements and user requirements. Business requirements sometimes reflect organizational strategies or budgetary constraints that aren't visible to users. Users who are upset about having a new information system forced on them by management might not want to work with the software developers, viewing them as the harbingers of an undesired future. Clear communication about project objectives and constraints might defuse these tensions. Perhaps not everyone will be happy with the realities, but at least they will have an opportunity to understand and buy into them. The analyst should work with the key user representatives and management sponsors to reconcile any conflicts.

The Customer-Development Partnership

Excellent software products are the result of a well-executed design based on excellent requirements. High-quality requirements result from effective communication and collaboration between developers and customers—a partnership. Too often, the relationship between development and customers becomes adversarial. Managers who override user-supplied requirements to suit their own agenda also can generate friction. No one benefits in these situations.

A collaborative effort can work only when all parties involved know what they need to be successful and when they understand and respect what their collaborators need to be successful. As project pressures rise, it's easy to forget that all stakeholders share a common objective: to build a successful software product that provides adequate business value and rewards to all stakeholders.

The Requirements Bill of Rights for Software Customers—see Table 2-1—lists 10 expectations that customers can legitimately hold regarding their interactions with analysts and developers during the project's requirements engineering activities. Each of these rights implies a corresponding responsibility on the part of the software developers or analysts. Conversely, the Requirements Bill of Responsibilities for Software Customers—see Table 2-2—lists 10 responsibilities that the customer has to the analyst and developer during the requirements process. You might prefer to view these as a developer's bill of rights.

These rights and responsibilities apply directly to customers when the software is being developed for internal corporate use, under contract, or for a known set of major customers. For mass-market product development, the rights and responsibilities are more applicable to customer surrogates such as the marketing department.

Table 2-1   Requirements Bill of Rights for Software Customers

You have the right to

1. Expect analysts to speak your language.

2. Expect analysts to learn about your business and your objectives for the system.

3. Expect analysts to structure the information you present during requirements elicitation into a written software requirements specification.

4. Have analysts explain all work products created from the requirements process.

5. Expect analysts and developers to treat you with respect and to maintain a collaborative and professional attitude throughout your interactions.

6. Have analysts and developers provide ideas and alternatives both for your requirements and for implementation of the product.

7. Describe characteristics of the product that will make it easy and enjoyable to use.

8. Be given opportunities to adjust your requirements to permit reuse of existing software components.

9. Receive good-faith estimates of the costs, impacts, and trade-offs when you request a change in the requirements.

10. Receive a system that meets your functional and quality needs, to the extent that those needs have been communicated to the developers and agreed upon.

Table 2-2   Requirements Bill of Responsibilities for Software Customers

You have the responsibility to

1. Educate analysts and developers about your business and define business jargon.

2. Spend the time that it takes to provide requirements, clarify them, and iteratively flesh them out.

3. Be specific and precise when providing input about the system's requirements.

4. Make timely decisions about requirements when requested to do so.

5. Respect a developer's assessment of the cost and feasibility of requirements.

6. In collaboration with the developers, set priorities for functional requirements, system features, or use cases.

7. Review requirements documents and evaluate prototypes.

8. Communicate changes to the requirements as soon as you know about them.

9. Follow the development organization's process for requesting requirements changes.

10. Respect the processes the analysts use for requirements engineering.

As part of project planning, the customer and development participants should review these two lists and reach a meeting of the minds. Busy customers might prefer not to become involved in requirements engineering (that is, they shy away from Responsibility #2). However, we know that lack of customer involvement greatly increases the risk of building the wrong product. Make sure the key participants in requirements development understand and accept their responsibilities. If you encounter some sticking points, negotiate to reach a clear understanding regarding your responsibilities to each other. This understanding can reduce friction later, when one party expects something that the other is not willing or able to provide.

> **Trap**   Don't assume that the project stakeholders instinctively know how to collaborate on requirements development. Take the time to discuss how you can work together most effectively.

Requirements Bill of Rights for Software Customers

Right #1: To Expect Analysts to Speak Your Language
Requirements discussions should center on your business needs and tasks, using your business vocabulary. Consider conveying business terminology to the analysts through a glossary. You shouldn't have to wade through computer jargon when talking with analysts.

Right #2: To Have Analysts Learn About Your Business and Objectives
By interacting with you to elicit requirements, the analysts can better understand your business tasks and how the product fits into your world. This will help developers create a system that satisfies your expectations. Consider inviting developers and analysts to observe what you and your colleagues do on the job. If the system being built is replacing an existing application, the developers should use the current system as you use it. This will help them see how the current application fits into your workflow and where it can be improved.

Right #3: To Expect Analysts to Write a Software Requirements Specification
The analyst will sort through all the information that you and other customers provide to distinguish use cases from business requirements, business rules, functional requirements, quality goals, solution ideas, and other items. The ultimate

deliverable from this analysis is a software requirements specification (SRS), which is the agreement between developers and customers on the functions, qualities, and constraints of the product to be built. The SRS should be organized and written in a way that you find easy to understand. Your review of these specifications and other requirements representations helps to ensure that they accurately and completely represent your needs.

Right #4: To Receive Explanations of Requirements Work Products

The analyst might represent the requirements using various diagrams that complement the textual SRS. Chapter 11, "A Picture Is Worth 1024 Words," describes several such analysis models. These alternative views of the requirements are valuable because sometimes graphics are a clearer medium for expressing some aspects of system behavior, such as workflow. Although these diagrams might be unfamiliar, they aren't difficult to understand. Ask the analyst to explain the purpose of each diagram (and any other requirements development work products), what the notations mean, and how to examine the diagram for errors.

Right #5: To Expect Analysts and Developers to Treat You with Respect

Requirements discussions can be frustrating if customers and developers don't understand each other. Working together can open the eyes of both groups to the problems each group faces. Customers who participate in the requirements development process have the right to expect analysts and developers to treat them with respect and to appreciate the time they are investing in project success. Similarly, customers should demonstrate respect for the development team members as they all collaborate toward their mutual objective of a successful project.

Right #6: To Hear Ideas and Alternatives for Requirements and Their Implementation

Analysts should know about ways that your existing systems don't fit well with your business processes to make sure the new system doesn't automate ineffective or obsolete processes. Analysts who thoroughly understand the business domain can sometimes suggest improvements in your business processes. A creative analyst also adds value by proposing ways that new software can provide capabilities that customers haven't even envisioned.

Right #7: To Describe Characteristics That Make the Product Easy to Use

You can expect analysts to ask you about characteristics of the software that go beyond the user's functional needs. These characteristics—quality attributes—

make the software easier or more pleasant to use, which lets users accomplish their tasks more efficiently. Users sometimes request that the product be *user-friendly* or *robust* or *efficient*, but such terms are too subjective to help the developers. Instead, the analysts should inquire about the specific characteristics that mean user-friendly, robust, or efficient to you. See Chapter 12, "Beyond Functionality: Software Quality Attributes," for further discussion.

Right #8: To Be Given Opportunities to Adjust Requirements to Permit Reuse

Requirements are often flexible. The analyst might know of existing software components that come close to addressing some need you described. In such a case, the analyst should give you the option of modifying your requirements so that the developers can reuse some existing software. Adjusting your requirements when sensible reuse opportunities are available saves time and money. Some requirements flexibility is essential if you want to incorporate commercial off-the-shelf (COTS) components into your product, because they will rarely have precisely the characteristics you want.

Right #9: To Receive Good-Faith Estimates of the Costs of Changes

People make different choices when they know that one alternative is more expensive than another. Estimates of the impact and cost of a proposed change in the requirements are necessary to make good business decisions about which requested changes to approve. You have the right to expect developers to present realistic estimates of impact, cost, and trade-offs. Developers must not inflate the estimated cost of a change just because they don't want to implement it.

Right #10: To Receive a System That Meets Your Functional and Quality Needs

Everyone desires this project outcome, but it can happen only if you clearly communicate all the information that will let developers build the right product and if developers clearly communicate options and constraints. Be sure to state all your assumptions or expectations; otherwise, the developers probably can't address them to your satisfaction.

Requirements Bill of Responsibilities for Software Customers

Responsibility #1: To Educate Analysts and Developers About Your Business

The development team depends on you to educate them about your business concepts and terminology. The intent is not to transform analysts into domain experts, but to help them understand your problems and objectives. Don't expect analysts to grasp the nuances and implicit aspects of your business. Analysts aren't likely to be aware of knowledge that you and your peers take for granted. Unstated assumptions about such knowledge can lead to problems later on.

Responsibility #2: To Spend the Time to Provide and Clarify Requirements

Customers are busy people and those who are involved in developing requirements are often among the busiest. Nonetheless, you have a responsibility to invest time in workshops, brainstorming sessions, interviews, and other requirements-elicitation activities. Sometimes the analyst might think she understands a point you made, only to realize later that she needs further clarification. Please be patient with this iterative approach to developing and refining the requirements; it's the nature of complex human communication and a key to software success. Be tolerant of what might appear to you to be dumb questions; a good analyst asks questions that get you talking.

Responsibility #3: To Be Specific and Precise About Requirements

It is tempting to leave the requirements vague and fuzzy because pinning down details is tedious and time consuming. At some point during development, though, someone must resolve the ambiguities and imprecisions. As the customer, you are the best person to make those decisions. Otherwise, you're relying on the developers to guess correctly.

It's fine to temporarily include *to be determined* (TBD) markers in the SRS to indicate that additional research, analysis, or information is needed. Sometimes, though, TBD is used because a specific requirement is difficult to resolve and no one wants to tackle it. Try to clarify the intent of each requirement so that the analyst can express it accurately in the SRS. If you can't be precise, agree to a process to generate the necessary precision. This often involves some prototyping, in which you work with the developers in an incremental and iterative approach to requirements definition.

Responsibility #4: To Make Timely Decisions

Just as a contractor does when he's building your custom home, the analyst will ask you to make many choices and decisions. These decisions include resolving inconsistent requests received from multiple customers, choosing between conflicting quality attributes, and evaluating the accuracy of information. Customers who are authorized to make such decisions must do so promptly when asked. The developers often can't proceed with confidence until you render your decision, so time spent waiting for an answer can delay progress.

Responsibility #5: To Respect a Developer's Assessment of Cost and Feasibility

All software functions have a cost. Developers are in the best position to estimate those costs, although many developers are not skilled estimators. Some features that you want included might not be technically feasible or might be surprisingly expensive to implement. Certain requirements might demand unattainable performance in the operating environment or require access to data that is simply not available to the system. The developer can be the bearer of bad news about feasibility or cost, and you should respect that judgment.

Sometimes you can rewrite requirements in a way that makes them attainable or cheaper. For example, asking for an action to take place "instantaneously" isn't feasible, but a more specific timing requirement ("within 50 milliseconds") might be achievable.

Responsibility #6: To Set Requirement Priorities

Few projects have the time and resources to implement every bit of desirable functionality. Determining which capabilities are essential, which are useful, and which the customers can live without is an important part of requirements analysis. You have a lead role in setting those priorities because developers can't determine how important every requirement is to the customers. Developers will provide information about the cost and risk of each requirement to help determine final priorities. When you establish priorities, you help the developers deliver the maximum value at the lowest cost and at the right time.

Respect the development team's judgment as to how much of the requested functionality they can complete within the available time and resource constraints. No one likes to hear that something he or she wants can't be completed within the project bounds, but that's just a reality. The project's decision makers will have to elect whether to reduce project scope based on priorities, extend the schedule, provide additional funds or people, or compromise on quality.

Responsibility #7: To Review Requirements Documents and Evaluate Prototypes

As you'll see in Chapter 15, "Validating the Requirements," requirements reviews are among the most valuable software quality activities. Having customers participate in reviews is the only way to evaluate whether the requirements demonstrate the desired characteristics of being complete, correct, and necessary. A review also provides an opportunity for customer representatives to give the analysts feedback about how well their work is meeting the project's needs. If the representatives aren't confident that the documented requirements are accurate, they should tell the people responsible as early as possible and provide suggestions for improvement.

It's hard to develop a good mental picture of how the software will work by reading a requirements specification. To better understand your needs and explore the best ways to satisfy them, developers sometimes build prototypes of the intended product. Your feedback on these preliminary, partial, or exploratory implementations provides valuable information to the developers. Recognize that a prototype is *not* a working product, and don't pressure the developers to deliver a prototype and pretend it is a fully functioning system.

Responsibility #8: To Promptly Communicate Changes to the Requirements

Continually changing requirements pose a serious risk to the development team's ability to deliver a high-quality product on schedule. Change is inevitable, but the later in the development cycle a change is introduced, the greater its impact. Changes can cause expensive rework, and schedules can slip if new functionality is demanded after construction is well under way. Notify the analyst with whom you are working as soon as you become aware that you need to change the requirements.

Responsibility #9: To Follow the Development Organization's Change Process

To minimize the negative impact of change, follow the project's defined change control process. This ensures that requested changes are not lost, the impact of each requested change is analyzed, and all proposed changes are considered in a consistent way. As a result, the business stakeholders can make sound business decisions to incorporate appropriate changes.

Responsibility #10: To Respect the Requirements Engineering Processes the Analysts Use

Gathering and validating requirements are among the greatest challenges in software development. There is a rationale behind the approaches that the analysts use. Although you might become frustrated with the requirements activities, the time spent understanding requirements is an excellent investment. The process will be less painful if you understand and respect the techniques the analysts use for requirements development. Feel free to ask analysts to explain why they're requesting certain information or asking you to participate in some requirements-related activity.

What About Sign-Off?

Reaching agreement on the requirements for the product to be built is at the core of the customer-developer partnership. Many organizations use the concept of signing off (why not "signing on"?) on the requirements document as the mark of customer approval of those requirements. All participants in the requirements approval process should know exactly what sign-off means or problems could ensue. One such problem is the customer representative who regards signing off on the requirements as a meaningless ritual: "I was presented with a piece of paper that had my name typed on it below a line, so I signed on the line because otherwise the developers wouldn't start coding." This attitude can lead to future conflicts when that customer wants to change the requirements or when he's surprised by what is delivered: "Sure, I signed off on the requirements, but I didn't have time to read them all. I trusted you guys—you let me down!"

Equally problematic is the development manager who views sign-off as a way to freeze the requirements. Whenever a change request is presented, he can point to the SRS and protest, "But you signed off on these requirements, so that's what we're building. If you wanted something else, you should have said so."

Both of these attitudes ignore the reality that it's impossible to know all the requirements early in the project and that requirements will undoubtedly change over time. Approving the requirements is an appropriate action that brings closure to the requirements development process. However, the participants have to agree on precisely what they're saying with their signatures.

> **Trap**   Don't use sign-off as a weapon. Use it as a project milestone, with a clear, shared understanding of the activities that lead to sign-off and its implications for future changes.

More important than the sign-off ritual is the concept of establishing a *baseline* of the requirements agreement, a snapshot of it at a point in time. The subtext of a signature on a requirements specification sign-off page should therefore read something like this: "I agree that this document represents our best understanding of the requirements for this project today and that the system described will satisfy our needs. I agree to make future changes in this baseline through the project's defined change process. I realize that approved changes might require us to renegotiate the cost, resource, and schedule commitments for this project." After the analyst defines the baseline, he places the requirements under change control. This allows the team to modify the project's scope when necessary in a controlled way that includes analyzing the impact of each proposed change on the schedule and on other project success factors.

A shared understanding along this line helps reduce the friction that can arise as requirements oversights are revealed or marketplace and business demands evolve in the course of the project. If customers are afraid that they won't be able to make changes after they approve the SRS, they might delay the approval, which contributes to the dreaded trap of analysis paralysis. A meaningful baselining process gives all the major stakeholders confidence in the following ways:

- Customer management is confident that the project scope won't explode out of control, because customers manage the scope change decisions.

- User representatives have confidence that development will work with them to deliver the right system, even if the representatives didn't think of every requirement before construction began.

- Development management has confidence because the development team has a business partner who will keep the project focused on achieving its objectives and will work with development to balance schedule, cost, functionality, and quality.

- Requirements analysts are confident because they know that they can manage changes to the project in a way that will keep chaos to a minimum.

Sealing the initial requirements development activities with such an explicit agreement helps you forge a collaborative customer-development partnership on the way to project success.

Next Steps

- Identify the customers who are responsible for providing the business and user requirements on your project. Which items from the Bill of Rights and the Bill of Responsibilities (on page 32) do these customers understand, accept, and practice? Which do they not?

- Discuss the Bill of Rights with your key customers to learn whether they feel they aren't receiving any of their rights. Discuss the Bill of Responsibilities to reach agreement as to which responsibilities they accept. Modify the Bill of Rights and the Bill of Responsibilities as appropriate so that all parties agree on how they will work together.

- If you're a customer participating in a software development project and you don't feel that your requirements rights are being adequately respected, discuss the Bill of Rights with the software project manager or the requirements analyst. Offer to do your part to satisfy the Bill of Responsibilities as you strive to build a more collaborative working relationship.

- Write a definition of what sign-off really means for your requirements documents approval.

3

Good Practices for Requirements Engineering

Ten or fifteen years ago, I was a fan of software development methodologies—packaged sets of models and techniques that purport to provide holistic solutions to our project challenges. Today, though, I prefer to identify and apply industry best practices. Rather than devising or purchasing a whole-cloth solution, the best-practice approach stocks your software tool kit with a variety of techniques you can apply to diverse problems. Even if you do adopt a commercial methodology, adapt it to best suit your needs and augment its components with other effective practices from your tool kit.

The notion of best practices is debatable: who decides what is "best" and on what basis? One approach is to convene a body of industry experts or researchers to analyze projects from many different organizations (Brown 1996; Brown 1999; Dutta, Lee, and Van Wassenhove 1999). These experts look for practices whose effective performance is associated with successful projects and which are performed poorly or not at all on failed projects. Through these means, the experts reach consensus on the activities that consistently yield superior results. Such activities are dubbed *best practices*. This implies that they represent highly effective ways for software professionals to increase the chance of success on certain kinds of projects and in certain situations.

Table 3-1 lists nearly 50 practices, grouped into seven categories, that can help most development teams do a better job on their requirements activities. Several of the practices contribute to more than one category, but each practice appears only once in the table. These practices aren't suitable for every situation, so use good judgment, common sense, and experience instead of ritualistically following a script. Note that not all of these items have been endorsed as industry best practices, which is why I've titled this chapter "Good Practices for Requirements Engineering," not "Best Practices." I doubt whether all of these practices will ever be systematically evaluated for this purpose. Nonetheless, many other practitioners and I have found these techniques to be effective (Sommerville and Sawyer 1997; Hofmann and Lehner 2001). Each practice is described briefly in this chapter, and references are provided to other chapters in this book or to other sources where you can learn more about the technique. The last section of this chapter suggests a requirements development process—a sequence of activities—that is suitable for most software projects.

Table 3-1   Requirements Engineering Good Practices

Knowledge	Requirements Management	Project Management
• Train requirements analysts	• Define change-control process	• Select appropriate life cycle
• Educate user reps and managers about requirements	• Establish change control board	• Base plans on requirements
• Train developers in application domain	• Perform change impact analysis	• Renegotiate commitments
• Create a glossary	• Baseline and control versions of requirements	• Manage requirements risks
	• Maintain change history	• Track requirements effort
	• Track requirements status	• Review past lessons learned
	• Measure requirements volatility	
	• Use a requirements management tool	
	• Create requirements traceability matrix	

Table 3-1   Requirements Engineering Good Practices

Requirements Development			
Elicitation	*Analysis*	*Specification*	*Validation*
• Define requirements development process	• Draw context diagram	• Adopt SRS template	• Inspect requirements documents
• Define vision and scope	• Create prototypes	• Identify sources of requirements	• Test the requirements
• Identify user classes	• Analyze feasibility	• Uniquely label each requirement	• Define acceptance criteria
• Select product champions	• Prioritize requirements	• Record business rules	
• Establish focus groups	• Model the requirements	• Specify quality attributes	
• Identify use cases	• Create a data dictionary		
• Identify system events and responses	• Allocate requirements to subsystems		
• Hold facilitated elicitation workshops	• Apply Quality Function Deployment		
• Observe users performing their jobs			
• Examine problem reports			
• Reuse requirements			

Knowledge

Few software developers receive formal training in requirements engineering. However, many developers perform the role of requirements analyst at some point in their careers, working with customers to gather, analyze, and document requirements. It isn't reasonable to expect all developers to be instinctively competent at the communication-intensive tasks of requirements engineering. Training can increase the proficiency and comfort level of those who serve as analysts, but it can't compensate for missing interpersonal skills or a lack of interest.

Because the requirements process is essential, all project stakeholders should understand the concepts and practices of requirements engineering. Bringing together the various stakeholders for a one-day overview on software requirements can be an effective team-building activity. All parties will better appreciate the challenges their counterparts face and what the participants require from each other for the whole team to succeed. Similarly, developers should receive grounding in the concepts and terminology of the application domain. You can find further details on these topics in the following chapters:

- Chapter 4—Train requirements analysts.

- Chapter 10—Create a project glossary.

Train requirements analysts.   All team members who will function as analysts should receive basic training in requirements engineering. Requirements analyst specialists need several days of training in these activities. The skilled requirements analyst is patient and well organized, has effective interpersonal and communication skills, understands the application domain, and has an extensive tool kit of requirements-engineering techniques.

Educate user representatives and managers about software requirements.   Users who will participate in software development should receive one or two days of education about requirements engineering. Development managers and customer managers will also find this information useful. The training will help them understand the value of emphasizing requirements, the activities and deliverables involved, and the risks of neglecting requirements processes. Some users who have attended my requirements seminars have said that they came away with more sympathy for the software developers.

Train developers in application domain concepts.   To help developers achieve a basic understanding of the application domain, arrange a seminar on the customer's business activities, terminology, and objectives for the product being created. This can reduce confusion, miscommunication, and rework down the road. You might also match each developer with a "user buddy" for the life of the project to translate jargon and explain business concepts. The product champion could play this role.

Create a project glossary.   A glossary that defines specialized terms from the application domain will reduce misunderstandings. Include synonyms, terms that can have multiple meanings, and terms that have both domain-specific and everyday meanings. Words that can be both nouns and verbs—such as "process" and "order"—can be particularly confusing.

Requirements Elicitation

Chapter 1 discussed the three levels of requirements: business, user, and functional. These come from different sources at different times during the project, have different audiences and purposes, and need to be documented in different ways. The business requirements expressed in the project scope must not exclude any essential user requirements, and you should be able to trace all functional requirements back to specific user requirements. You also need to elicit nonfunctional requirements, such as quality and performance expectations, from appropriate sources. You can find additional information about these topics in the following chapters:

■   Chapter 3—Define a requirements development process.

■   Chapter 5—Write a vision and scope document.

■   Chapter 6—Identify user classes and their characteristics; select a product champion for each user class; observe users performing their jobs.

■   Chapter 7—Hold facilitated elicitation workshops.

■   Chapter 8—Work with user representatives to identify use cases; identify system events and responses.

■   Chapter 22—Define a requirements development process.

Define a requirements development process.   Document the steps your organization follows to elicit, analyze, specify, and validate requirements. Providing guidance on how to perform the key steps will help analysts do a consistently good job. It will also make it easier to plan each project's requirements development tasks, schedule, and required resources.

Write a vision and scope document.   The vision and scope document contains the product's business requirements. The vision statement gives all stakeholders a common understanding of the product's objectives. The scope defines the boundary between what's in and what's out for a specific release. Together, the vision and scope provide a reference against which to evaluate proposed requirements. The product vision should remain relatively stable from release to release, but each release needs its own project scope statement.

Identify user classes and their characteristics.   To avoid overlooking the needs of any user community, identify the various groups of users for your product. They might differ in frequency of use, features used, privilege levels, or skill levels. Describe aspects of their job tasks, attitudes, location, or personal characteristics that might influence product design.

Select a product champion for each user class.   Identify at least one person who can accurately serve as the voice of the customer for each user class. The product champion presents the needs of the user class and makes decisions on its behalf. This is easiest for internal information systems development, where your users are fellow employees. For commercial development, build on your current relationships with major customers or beta test sites to locate appropriate product champions. Product champions must have ongoing participation in the project and the authority to make decisions at the user-requirements level.

Establish focus groups of typical users.   Convene groups of representative users of your previous product releases or of similar products. Collect their input on both functionality and quality characteristics for the product under development. Focus groups are particularly valuable for commercial product development, for which you might have a large and diverse customer base. Unlike product champions, focus groups generally do not have decision-making authority.

Work with user representatives to identify use cases.   Explore with your user representatives the tasks they need to accomplish with the software—their use cases. Discuss the interactions between the users and the system that will allow them to complete each such task. Adopt a standard template for documenting use cases and derive functional requirements from those use cases. A related practice that is often used on government projects is to define a concept of operations (ConOps) document, which describes the new system's characteristics from the user's point of view (IEEE 1998a).

Identify system events and responses.   List the external events that the system can experience and its expected response to each event. Events include signals or data received from external hardware devices and temporal events that trigger a response, such as an external data feed that your system generates at the same time every night. Business events trigger use cases in business applications.

Hold facilitated elicitation workshops.   Facilitated requirements-elicitation workshops that permit collaboration between analysts and customers are a powerful way to explore user needs and to draft requirements documents (Gottesdiener 2002). Specific examples of such workshops include Joint Requirements Planning (JRP) sessions (Martin 1991) and Joint Application Development (JAD) sessions (Wood and Silver 1995).

Observe users performing their jobs.   Watching users perform their business tasks establishes a context for their potential use of a new application (Beyer and Holtzblatt 1998). Simple workflow diagrams—data flow diagrams work well—can depict when the user has what data and how that data is used. Documenting the business process flow will help you identify requirements for a system that's intended to support that process. You might even determine that the customers don't really need a new software application to meet their business objectives (McGraw and Harbison 1997).

Examine problem reports of current systems for requirement ideas.
Problem reports and enhancement requests from customers provide a rich source of ideas for capabilities to include in a later release or in a new product. Help desk and support staff can provide valuable input to the requirements for future development work.

Reuse requirements across projects.   If customers request functionality similar to that already present in an existing product, see whether the requirements (and the customers!) are flexible enough to permit reusing or adapting the existing components. Multiple projects will reuse those requirements that comply with an organization's business rules. These include security requirements that control access to the applications and requirements that conform to government regulations, such as the Americans with Disabilities Act.

Requirements Analysis

Requirements analysis involves refining the requirements to ensure that all stakeholders understand them and scrutinizing them for errors, omissions, and other deficiencies. Analysis includes decomposing high-level requirements into details, building prototypes, evaluating feasibility, and negotiating priorities. The goal is to develop requirements of sufficient quality and detail that managers can construct realistic project estimates and technical staff can proceed with design, construction, and testing.

Often it is helpful to represent some of the requirements in multiple ways—for example, in both textual and graphical forms. These different views will reveal insights and problems that no single view can provide (Davis 1995). Multiple views also help all stakeholders arrive at a common understanding—a shared vision—of what they will have when the product is delivered. Further discussion of requirements analysis practices can be found in the following chapters:

- Chapter 5—Draw a context diagram.

- Chapter 10—Create a data dictionary.

- Chapter 11—Model the requirements.

- Chapter 13—Create user interface and technical prototypes.

- Chapter 14—Prioritize the requirements.

- Chapter 17—Allocate requirements to subsystems.

Draw a context diagram.   The context diagram is a simple analysis model that shows how the new system fits into its environment. It defines the boundaries and interfaces between the system being developed and the entities external to the system, such as users, hardware devices, and other information systems.

Create user interface and technical prototypes.   When developers or users aren't certain about the requirements, construct a prototype—a partial, possible, or preliminary implementation—to make the concepts and possibilities more tangible. Users who evaluate the prototype help the stakeholders achieve a better mutual understanding of the problem being solved.

Analyze requirement feasibility.   Evaluate the feasibility of implementing each requirement at acceptable cost and performance in the intended operating environment. Understand the risks associated with implementing each requirement, including conflicts with other requirements, dependencies on external factors, and technical obstacles.

Prioritize the requirements.   Apply an analytical approach to determine the relative implementation priority of product features, use cases, or individual requirements. Based on priority, determine which release will contain each feature or set of requirements. As you accept requirement changes, allocate each one to a particular future release and incorporate the effort required to make the change into the plan for that release. Evaluate and adjust priorities periodically throughout the project as customer needs, market conditions, and business goals evolve.

Model the requirements.   A graphical analysis model depicts requirements at a high level of abstraction, in contrast to the detail shown in the SRS or the user interface view that a prototype provides. Models can reveal incorrect, inconsistent, missing, and superfluous requirements. Such models include data flow diagrams, entity-relationship diagrams, state-transition diagrams or statecharts, dialog maps, class diagrams, sequence diagrams, interaction diagrams, decision tables, and decision trees.

Create a data dictionary.   Definitions of all the data items and structures associated with the system reside in the data dictionary. This enables everyone working on the project to use consistent data definitions. At the requirements stage, the data dictionary should define data items from the problem domain to facilitate communication between the customers and the development team.

Allocate requirements to subsystems.   The requirements for a complex product that contains multiple subsystems must be apportioned among the various software, hardware, and human subsystems and components (Nelsen 1990). A system engineer or architect typically performs this allocation.

Apply Quality Function Deployment.   Quality Function Deployment (QFD) is a rigorous technique for relating product features and attributes to customer value (Zultner 1993; Pardee 1996). It provides an analytical way to identify those features that will provide the greatest customer satisfaction. QFD addresses three classes of requirements: expected requirements, where the customer might not even state them but will be upset if they are missing; normal requirements; and exciting requirements, which provide high benefit to customers if present but little penalty if not.

Requirements Specification

No matter how you obtain your requirements, document them in some consistent, accessible, and reviewable way. You can record the business requirements in a vision and scope document. The user requirements typically are represented in the form of use cases or as event-response tables. The SRS contains the detailed software functional and nonfunctional requirements. Requirements specification practices are discussed in the following chapters:

- Chapter 9—Record business rules.

- Chapter 10—Adopt an SRS template; uniquely label each requirement.

- Chapter 12—Specify quality attributes.

Adopt an SRS template.   Define a standard template for documenting software requirements in your organization. The template provides a consistent structure for recording the functionality descriptions and other requirements-related information. Rather than inventing a new template, adapt an existing one to fit the nature of your projects. Many organizations begin with the SRS template described in IEEE Standard 830-1998 (IEEE 1998b); Chapter 10 presents an adaptation of that template. If your organization works on different types or sizes of projects, such as large new development efforts as well as small enhancement releases, define an appropriate template for each project type. Templates and processes should both be scalable.

Identify sources of requirements.   To ensure that all stakeholders know why every requirement belongs in the SRS and to facilitate further clarification, trace each requirement back to its origin. This might be a use case or some other customer input, a high-level system requirement, a business rule, or some other external source. Recording the stakeholders who are materially affected by each requirement tells you whom to contact when a change request comes in. Requirement sources can be identified either through traceability links or by defining a requirement attribute for this purpose. See Chapter 18 for more information on requirements attributes.

Uniquely label each requirement.   Define a convention for giving each requirement in the SRS a unique identifying label. The convention must be robust enough to withstand additions, deletions, and changes made in the requirements over time. Labeling the requirements permits requirements traceability and the recording of changes made.

Record business rules.   Business rules include corporate policies, government regulations, and computational algorithms. Document your business rules separately from the SRS because they typically have an existence beyond the scope of a specific project. Some business rules will lead to functional requirements that enforce them, so define traceability links between those requirements and the corresponding rules.

Specify quality attributes.   Go beyond the functionality discussion to explore quality characteristics that will help your product satisfy customer expectations. These characteristics include performance, efficiency, reliability, usability, and many others. Document the quality requirements in the SRS. Customer input on the relative importance of these quality attributes lets the developer make appropriate design decisions.

Requirements Validation

Validation ensures that the requirement statements are correct, demonstrate the desired quality characteristics, and will satisfy customer needs. Requirements that seem fine when you read them in the SRS might turn out to have problems when developers try to work with them. Writing test cases from the requirements often reveals ambiguities and vagueness. You must correct these problems if the requirements are to serve as a reliable foundation for design and for final system verification through system testing or user acceptance testing. Requirements validation is discussed further in Chapter 15.

Inspect requirements documents.   Formal inspection of requirements documents is one of the highest-value software quality practices available. Assemble a small team of inspectors who represent different perspectives (such as analyst, customer, developer, and tester), and carefully examine the SRS, analysis models, and related information for defects. Informal preliminary reviews during requirements development are also valuable. Even though this is not one of the easiest new practices to implement, it's among the most valuable, so begin building requirements inspections into your culture right away.

Test the requirements.   Derive functional test cases from the user requirements to document the expected behavior of the product under specified conditions. Walk through the test cases with customers to ensure that they reflect the desired system behavior. Trace the test cases to the functional requirements to make sure that no requirements have been overlooked and that all have corresponding test cases. Use the test cases to verify the correctness of analysis models and prototypes.

Define acceptance criteria.   Ask users to describe how they will determine whether the product meets their needs and is fit for use. Base acceptance tests on usage scenarios (Hsia, Kung, and Sell 1997).

Requirements Management

Once you have the initial requirements for a body of work in hand, you must cope with the inevitable changes that customers, managers, marketing, the development team, and others request during development. Effective change management demands a process for proposing changes and evaluating their potential cost and impact on the project. A *change control board* (CCB), composed of key stakeholders, decides which proposed changes to incorporate. Tracking the status of each requirement as it moves through development and system testing provides insight into overall project status.

Well-established configuration management practices are a prerequisite for effective requirements management. The same version control tools that you use to control your code base can manage your requirements documents. The techniques involved in requirements management are expanded in the following chapters:

■   Chapter 18—Establish a baseline and control versions of requirements; track the status of each requirement

■   Chapter 19—Define a requirements change-control process; establish a change control board; measure requirements volatility; perform requirements-change impact analysis

■   Chapter 20—Create a requirements traceability matrix

■   Chapter 21—Use a requirements management tool

Define a requirements change-control process.   Establish a process through which requirements changes are proposed, analyzed, and resolved. Manage all proposed changes through this process. Commercial defect-tracking tools can support the change-control process.

Establish a change control board.   Charter a small group of project stakeholders as a CCB to receive proposed requirements changes, evaluate them, decide which ones to accept and which to reject, and set implementation priorities or target releases.

Perform requirements-change impact analysis.   Impact analysis helps the CCB make informed business decisions. Evaluate each proposed requirement change to determine the effect it will have on the project. Use the requirements traceability matrix to identify the other requirements, design elements, source code, and test cases that you might have to modify. Identify the tasks required to implement the change and estimate the effort needed to perform those tasks.

Establish a baseline and control versions of requirements documents.
The baseline consists of the requirements that have been committed to implementation in a specific release. After the requirements have been baselined, changes may be made only through the defined change-control process. Give every version of the requirements specification a unique identifier to avoid confusion between drafts and baselines and between previous and current versions. A more robust solution is to place requirements documents under version control using appropriate configuration management tools.

Maintain a history of requirements changes.   Record the dates that requirements specifications were changed, the changes that were made, who made each change, and why. A version control tool or commercial requirements management tool can automate these tasks.

Track the status of each requirement.   Establish a database with one record for each discrete functional requirement. Store key attributes about each requirement, including its status (such as proposed, approved, implemented, or verified), so that you can monitor the number of requirements in each status category at any time.

Measure requirements volatility.   Record the number of baselined requirements and the number of proposed and approved changes (additions, modifications, deletions) to them per week. Churning requirements might suggest that the problem is not well understood, the project scope is not well defined, the business is changing rapidly, many requirements were missed during elicitation, or politics are running rampant.

Use a requirements management tool.   Commercial requirements management tools let you store various types of requirements in a database. You can define attributes for each requirement, track each requirement's status, and define traceability links between requirements and other software work products. This practice will help you automate the other requirements management tasks described in this section.

Create a requirements traceability matrix.   Set up a table that links each functional requirement to the design and code elements that implement it and the tests that verify it. The requirements traceability matrix can also connect functional requirements to the higher-level requirements from which they were derived and to other related requirements. Populate this matrix during development, not at the end of the project.

Project Management

Software project management approaches are intimately related to a project's requirements processes. Base your project resources, schedules, and commitments on the requirements that are to be implemented. Because changes in requirements will affect those project plans, the plans should anticipate some requirements change and scope growth (Wiegers 2002d). More information about project management approaches to requirements engineering is available in the following chapters:

- Chapter 17—Base project plans on requirements

- Chapter 18—Track the effort spent on requirements engineering

- Chapter 23—Document and manage requirements-related risks

Select an appropriate software development life cycle.   Your organization should define several development life cycles that are appropriate for various types of projects and different degrees of requirements uncertainty (McConnell 1996). Each project manager should select and adapt the life cycle that best suits his project. Include requirements engineering activities in your life cycle definitions. If the requirements or scope are poorly defined early in the project, plan to develop the product in small increments, beginning with the most clearly understood requirements and a robust, modifiable architecture. When possible, implement sets of features so that you can release portions of the product periodically and deliver value to the customer as early as possible (Gilb 1988; Cockburn 2002).

Base project plans on requirements.   Develop plans and schedules for your project iteratively as the scope and detailed requirements become clear. Begin by estimating the effort needed to develop the functional requirements from the initial product vision and project scope. Early cost and schedule estimates based on fuzzy requirements will be highly uncertain, but you can improve the estimates as your understanding of the requirements improves.

Renegotiate project commitments when requirements change.   As you incorporate new requirements into the project, evaluate whether you can still achieve the current schedule and quality commitments with the available resources. If not, communicate the project realities to management and negotiate new, realistically achievable commitments (Humphrey 1997; Fisher, Ury, and Patton 1991; Wiegers 2002b). If your negotiations are unsuccessful, communicate the likely outcomes so that managers and customers aren't blindsided by an unexpected project outcome.

Document and manage requirements-related risks.   Identify and document risks related to requirements as part of the project's risk management activities. Brainstorm approaches to mitigate or prevent these risks, implement the mitigation actions, and track their progress and effectiveness.

Track the effort spent on requirements engineering.   Record the effort your team expends on requirements development and management activities. Use this data to assess whether the planned requirements activities are being performed as intended and to better plan the resources needed for future projects. In addition, monitor the effect that your requirements engineering activities have on the project. This will help you judge the return on your investment in requirements engineering.

Review lessons learned regarding requirements on other projects.   A learning organization conducts project *retrospectives*—also called *postmortems* and *post-project reviews*—to collect lessons learned (Robertson and Robertson 1999; Kerth 2001; Wiegers and Rothman 2001). Studying the lessons learned about requirements issues and practices on previous projects can help project managers and requirements analysts steer a more confident course in the future.

Getting Started with New Practices

Table 3-2 groups the requirements engineering practices described in this chapter by the relative impact they can have on most projects and their relative difficulty of implementation. Although all the practices can be beneficial, you might begin with the "low-hanging fruit," those practices that have a high impact on project success and are relatively easy to implement.

Table 3-2   Implementing Requirements Engineering Good Practices

Impact	Difficulty		
	High	*Medium*	*Low*
High	• Define requirements development process • Base plans on requirements • Renegotiate commitments	• Identify use cases • Specify quality attributes • Prioritize requirements • Adopt SRS template • Define change-control process • Establish CCB • Inspect requirements documents • Allocate requirements to subsystems • Record business rules	• Train developers in application domain • Define vision and scope • Identify user classes • Draw context diagram • Identify sources of requirements • Baseline and control versions of requirements
Medium	• Educate user reps and managers about requirements • Model the requirements • Manage requirements risks • Use a requirements management tool • Create requirements traceability matrix • Hold facilitated elicitation workshops	• Train requirements analysts • Select product champions • Establish focus groups • Create prototypes • Define acceptance criteria • Perform change impact analysis • Select appropriate life cycle	• Analyze feasibility • Create a glossary • Create a data dictionary • Observe users performing their jobs • Identify system events and responses • Uniquely label each requirement • Test the requirements • Track requirements status • Review past lessons learned
Low	• Reuse requirements • Apply Quality Function Deployment • Measure requirements volatility	• Maintain change history • Track requirements effort	• Examine problem reports

Don't try to apply all these techniques on your next project. Instead, think of these good practices as new items for your requirements tool kit. You can begin to use some practices, such as those dealing with change management, no matter where your project is in its development cycle. Elicitation practices will be more useful when you begin the next project or iteration. Still others might not fit your current project, organizational culture, or resource availability. Chapter 22 describes ways to evaluate your current requirements engineering practices. It will also help you devise a road map for implementing selected improvements in your requirements process based on the practices described in this chapter.

A Requirements Development Process

Don't expect to perform the requirements development activities of elicitation, analysis, specification, and validation in a linear, one-pass sequence. In practice, these activities are interleaved, incremental, and iterative, as shown in Figure 3-1. As you work with customers in your analyst role, you'll be asking questions, listening to what the customers say, and watching what they do (elicitation). You'll process this information to understand it, classify it in various categories, and relate the customer needs to possible software requirements (analysis). You'll then structure the customer input and derived requirements as written documents and diagrams (specification). Next, you'll ask your customer representatives to confirm that what you've written is accurate and complete and to correct any errors (validation). This iterative process continues throughout requirements development.

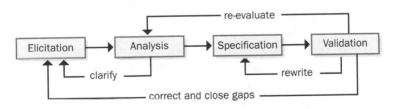

Figure 3-1 Requirements development is an iterative process.

Because of the diversity of software development projects and organizational cultures, there is no single, formulaic approach to requirements development. Figure 3-2 suggests a process framework for requirements development that will work—with sensible adjustments—for many projects. These steps are generally performed approximately in numerical sequence, but the process is not strictly sequential. The first seven steps are typically performed once early in the project (although the team will need to revisit priorities periodically). The remaining steps are performed for each release increment or iteration.

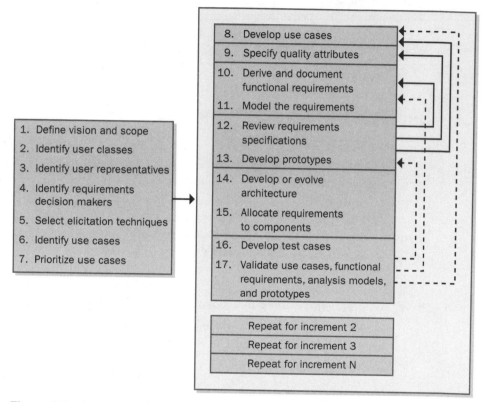

Figure 3-2 A suggested requirements development process, showing quality control feedback cycles and incremental implementation based on use-case priorities.

Select appropriate elicitation techniques (workshops, surveys, interviews, and so on) based on your access to the user representatives, and plan the time and resources that elicitation will consume (step 5 in Figure 3-2). Because many systems are built incrementally, every project team needs to prioritize its use cases or other user requirements (step 7). Prioritizing the use cases lets you decide which ones to plan for each increment so that you can explore the right use cases in detail at the right time. For new systems or major enhancements, you can define or refine the architecture in step 14 and allocate functional requirements to specific subsystems in step 15. Steps 12 and 17 are quality control activities that might lead you to revisit some earlier steps to correct errors, refine analysis models, or detect previously overlooked requirements. Prototypes built in step 13 often lead to refinement and modifications in the requirements that were specified previously. Once you have completed step 17 for any portion of the requirements, you're ready to commence construction of that part of the system. Repeat steps 8 through 17 with the next set of use cases, which might go into a late release.

Next Steps

- Go back to the requirements-related problems you identified from the Next Steps in Chapter 1. Identify good practices from this chapter that might help with each problem you identified. The troubleshooting guide in Appendix C might be helpful. Group the practices into high, medium, and low impact in your organization. Identify any barriers to implementing each practice in your organization or culture. Who can help you break down those barriers?

- Determine how you would assess the benefits from the practices that you think would be most valuable. Would you find fewer requirements defects late in the game, reduce unnecessary rework, better meet project schedules, or enjoy other advantages?

- List all the requirements good practices you identified in the first step. For each practice, indicate your project team's current level of capability: expert, proficient, novice, or unfamiliar. If your team is not at least proficient in any of those practices, ask someone on your project to learn more about the practice and to share what he learns with the rest of the team.

4

The Requirements Analyst

Explicitly or implicitly, someone performs the role of requirements analyst on every software project. Corporate IS organizations identify specialists called *business analysts* to perform this function. Synonyms for *requirements analyst* include *systems analyst, requirements engineer, requirements manager*, and simply *analyst*. In a product-development organization, the job is often the product manager's or marketing staff's responsibility. The analyst is a translator of others' perspectives into a requirements specification and a reflector of information back to other stakeholders. The analyst helps stakeholders find the difference between what they say they want and what they really need. He or she educates, questions, listens, organizes, and learns. It's a tough job.

This chapter looks at the vital functions the requirements analyst performs, the skills and knowledge an effective analyst needs, and how you might develop such people in your organization (Wiegers 2000). You can download a sample job description for a requirements analyst from *http://www.processimpact.com/goodies.shtml*.

The Requirements Analyst Role

The requirements analyst is the individual who has the primary responsibility to gather, analyze, document, and validate the needs of the project stakeholders. The analyst serves as the principal conduit through which requirements flow between the customer community and the software development team, as shown in Figure 4-1. Many other communication pathways also are used, so the analyst isn't solely responsible for information exchange on the project.

The analyst plays a central role in collecting and disseminating product information, whereas the project manager takes the lead in communicating project information.

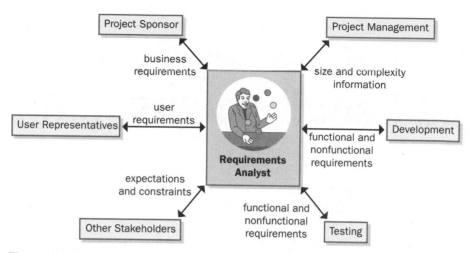

Figure 4-1   The requirements analyst bridges communication between customer and development stakeholders.

Requirements analyst is a project role, not necessarily a job title. One or more dedicated specialists could perform the role, or it could be assigned to team members who also have other job functions. These functions include project manager, product manager, subject matter expert (SME), developer, and even user. Regardless of their other project responsibilities, analysts must have the skills, knowledge, and personality to perform the analyst role well.

> **Trap**   Don't assume that any talented developer or knowledgeable user will automatically be an effective requirements analyst without training, resource materials, and coaching. These roles all demand different skills, knowledge, and personality traits.

A talented analyst can make the difference between a project that succeeds and one that struggles. One of my consulting clients discovered that they could inspect requirements specifications written by experienced analysts twice as fast as those written by novices because they contained fewer defects. In the widely-used Cocomo II model for project estimation, requirements analyst experience and capability have a great influence on a project's effort and cost (Boehm et al. 2000). Using highly experienced analysts can reduce the project's required effort by one third compared to similar projects with inexperienced analysts. Analyst capability has an even greater impact than analyst experience. Projects having the most capable analysts require only half the effort of similar projects that have the least capable analysts.

The Analyst's Tasks

The analyst is a communication middleman, bridging the gap between vague customer notions and the clear specifications that guide the software team's work. The analyst must first understand the users' goals for the new system and then define functional and quality requirements that allow project managers to estimate, developers to design and build, and testers to verify the product. This section describes some of the typical activities that you might perform while you're wearing an analyst's hat.

Define business requirements.   Your work as an analyst begins when you help the business or funding sponsor, product manager, or marketing manager define the project's business requirements. Perhaps the first question to ask is, "Why are we undertaking this project?" Business requirements include a statement of the organization's business objectives and the ultimate vision of what the system will be and do. You might suggest a template for a vision and scope document (shown in Chapter 5) and work with those who hold the vision to help them express it.

Identify project stakeholders and user classes.   The vision and scope document will help you identify the important user classes and other stakeholders for the product. Next, work with the business sponsors to select appropriate representatives for each user class, enlist their participation, and negotiate their responsibilities. User representatives might hesitate to participate in requirements exploration until they know exactly what you expect from them. Write down the contributions that you would like from your customer collaborators and agree on an appropriate level of participation from each one. Chapter 6 lists some activities that you might ask your user representatives to perform.

Elicit requirements.   Requirements for a software product don't just lie around waiting for someone wearing a hat labeled "analyst" to collect them.

A proactive analyst helps users articulate the system capabilities they need to meet their business objectives. See Chapter 7 and Chapter 8 for further discussion. You might employ information-gathering techniques selected from the following list:

- Interviews
- Facilitated requirements workshops
- Document analysis
- Surveys
- Customer site visits
- Business process analysis
- Work flow and task analysis
- Event lists
- Competitive product analysis
- Reverse engineering of existing systems
- Retrospectives performed on the previous project

Users naturally emphasize the system's functional requirements, so steer the discussions to include quality attributes, performance goals, business rules, external interfaces, and constraints. It's appropriate to challenge user assumptions, but don't try to force your own beliefs on the users. Some user requirements might seem absurd, but if the user confirms that they're correct, there's nothing to gain from pushing the point.

Analyze requirements.   Look for derived requirements that are a logical consequence of what the customers requested and for unstated requirements that the customers seem to expect without saying so. Spot the vague, weak words that cause ambiguity. (See Chapter 10 for examples.) Point out conflicting requirements and areas that need more detail. Specify the functional requirements at a level of detail suitable for use by the developers who will implement them. This level of detail will vary from project to project. A Web site being built incrementally by a small, well-synchronized team can get away with limited requirements documentation. In contrast, a complex embedded system that will be outsourced to an offshore supplier needs a precise, detailed SRS.

Write requirements specifications.   Requirements development leads to a shared understanding of a system that will address the customer's problem. The analyst is responsible for writing well-organized specifications that clearly express this shared understanding. Using standard templates for use cases and the SRS accelerates requirements development by reminding the analyst of topics that he needs to discuss with the user representatives. Chapter 8 discusses how to write use cases, Chapter 10 explores writing functional requirements, and Chapter 12 looks at documenting software quality attributes.

Model the requirements.   The analyst should determine when it is helpful to represent requirements using methods other than text. These alternative views include various types of graphical analysis models (discussed in Chapter 11), tables, mathematical equations, storyboards, and prototypes (discussed in Chapter 13). Analysis models depict information at a higher level of abstraction than does detailed text. To maximize communication and clarity, draw analysis models according to the conventions of a standard modeling language.

Lead requirements validation.   The analyst must ensure that requirement statements possess all the desired characteristics that were discussed in Chapter 1 and that a system based on the requirements will satisfy user needs. Analysts are the central participants in peer reviews of requirements documents. They should also review designs, code, and test cases that were derived from the requirements specifications to ensure that the requirements were interpreted correctly.

Facilitate requirements prioritization.   The analyst brokers collaboration and negotiation between the various user classes and the developers to ensure that they make sensible priority decisions. The requirements prioritization spreadsheet tool described in Chapter 14 might be helpful.

Manage requirements.   A requirements analyst is involved throughout the entire software development life cycle, so he should help create, review, and execute the project's requirements management plan. After establishing the requirements baseline, the analyst's focus shifts to managing those requirements and verifying their satisfaction in the product. Storing the requirements in a commercial requirements management tool facilitates this ongoing management. See Chapter 21 for a discussion of requirements management tools.

Requirements management includes tracking the status of individual functional requirements as they progress from inception to verification in the integrated product. With input from various colleagues, the analyst collects traceability information that connects individual requirements to other system elements. The analyst plays a central role in managing changes to the baselined requirements by using a change-control process and tool.

Essential Analyst Skills

It isn't reasonable to expect people to serve as analysts without sufficient training, guidance, and experience. They won't do a good job and they'll find the experience frustrating. Analysts need to know how to use a variety of elicitation techniques and how to represent information in forms other than natural-language text. An effective analyst combines strong communication, facilitation, and interpersonal skills with technical and business domain knowledge and the right personality for the job (Ferdinandi 2002). Patience and a genuine desire to work with people are key success factors. The skills described in the remainder of this section are particularly important.

Listening skills.   To become proficient at two-way communication, learn how to listen effectively. Active listening involves eliminating distractions, maintaining an attentive posture and eye contact, and restating key points to confirm your understanding. You need to grasp what people are saying and also to read between the lines to detect what they might be hesitant to say. Learn how your collaborators prefer to communicate and avoid imposing your personal filter of understanding on what you hear the customers say. Watch for assumptions that underlie either what you hear from others or your own interpretation.

Interviewing and questioning skills.   Most requirements input comes through discussions, so the analyst must be able to talk with diverse individuals and groups about their needs. It can be intimidating to work with senior managers and with highly opinionated or aggressive individuals. You need to ask the right questions to surface essential requirements information. For example, users naturally focus on the system's normal, expected behaviors. However, much code gets written to handle exceptions, so you must also probe for possible error conditions and determine how the system should respond. With experience, you'll become skilled in the art of asking questions that reveal and clarify uncertainties, disagreements, assumptions, and unstated expectations (Gause and Weinberg 1989).

Analytical skills.   An effective analyst can think at multiple levels of abstraction. Sometimes you must drill down from high-level information into details. In other situations, you'll need to generalize from a specific need that one user described to a set of requirements that will satisfy many members of a user class. Critically evaluate the information gathered from multiple sources to reconcile conflicts, separate user "wants" from the underlying true needs, and distinguish solution ideas from requirements.

Facilitation skills.   The ability to facilitate requirements elicitation workshops is a necessary analyst capability (Gottesdiener 2002). A neutral facilitator who has strong questioning, observational, and facilitation skills can help a group build trust and improve the sometimes tense relationship between business and information technology staff. Chapter 7 presents some guidelines for facilitating elicitation workshops.

Observational skills.   An observant analyst will detect comments made in passing that might turn out to be significant. By watching a user perform his job or use a current application, a good observer can detect subtleties that the user might not mention. Strong observational skills sometimes expose new areas for elicitation discussions, revealing additional requirements that no one has mentioned yet.

Writing skills.   The principal deliverable from requirements development is a written specification that communicates information among customers, marketing, managers, and technical staff. The analyst needs a solid command of the language and the ability to express complex ideas clearly.

I know of an organization that appointed as analysts several developers who spoke English as a second language. It's hard enough to write excellent requirements in your native language. It's even more difficult to accomplish in a language in which you might struggle with nuances of expression, ambiguous words, and local idioms. Conversely, analysts should be efficient and critical readers because they have to wade through a lot of material and grasp the essence quickly.

Organizational skills.   Analysts must work with a vast array of jumbled information gathered during elicitation and analysis. Coping with rapidly changing information and structuring all the bits into a coherent whole demands exceptional organizational skills and the patience and tenacity to make sense from ambiguity and disarray.

Modeling skills.   Tools ranging from the venerable flowchart through structured analysis models (data flow diagram, entity-relationship diagram, and the like) to contemporary Unified Modeling Language (UML) notations should be part of every analyst's repertoire. Some will be useful when communicating with users, others when communicating with developers. The analyst will need to educate other stakeholders on the value of using these techniques and how to read them. See Chapter 11 for overviews of several types of analysis models.

Interpersonal skills.   Analysts need the ability to get people with competing interests to work together. An analyst should feel comfortable talking with individuals in diverse job functions and at all levels of the organization. He or she might need to work with distributed virtual teams whose members are separated by geography, time zones, cultures, or native languages. Experienced analysts often mentor their new colleagues, and they educate their customer counterparts about the requirements engineering and software development processes.

Creativity.   The analyst is not merely a scribe who records whatever customers say. The best analysts invent requirements (Robertson 2002). They conceive innovative product capabilities, imagine new markets and business opportunities, and think of ways to surprise and delight their customers. A really valuable analyst finds creative ways to satisfy needs that users didn't even know they had.

Essential Analyst Knowledge

In addition to the specific capabilities and personal characteristics just described, requirements analysts need a breadth of knowledge, much of which is gained through experience. Start with a solid understanding of contemporary requirements engineering techniques and the ability to apply them in the context of various software development life cycles. The effective analyst has a rich tool kit of techniques available and knows when—and when not—to use each one.

Analysts need to thread requirements development and management activities through the entire product life span. An analyst with a sound understanding of project management, risk management, and quality engineering can help prevent requirements issues from torpedoing the project. In a commercial software development setting, the analyst will benefit from knowledge of product management concepts and how enterprise software products are positioned and developed.

Application domain knowledge is a powerful asset for an effective analyst. The business-savvy analyst can minimize miscommunications with users. Analysts who understand the application domain often detect unstated assumptions and implicit requirements. They can suggest ways that users could improve their business processes. Such analysts sometimes propose valuable functionality that no user thought of. Conversely, they do a better job of detecting gold plating than does someone who's unfamiliar with the problem domain.

The Making of an Analyst

Great requirements analysts are grown, not trained. The job includes many "soft skills" that are more people-oriented than technological. There is no standard educational curriculum or job description for a requirements analyst. An organization's analysts will come from diverse backgrounds and they'll likely have gaps in their knowledge and skill sets. All analysts should decide which of the knowledge and skills described in this chapter pertain to their situation and actively seek the information that will let them do a first-rate job. Patricia Ferdinandi (2002) describes skill levels that junior, fully proficient, and lead requirements analysts should exhibit in various categories: practical experience, engineering, project management, techniques and tools, quality, and personality. All new analysts will benefit from mentoring and coaching from those who have more experience, perhaps in the form of an apprenticeship. Let's explore how people with different backgrounds might move into the analyst role.

The Former User

Many corporate IT departments have business analysts who migrated into that role following a career as a user. These individuals have a solid understanding of the business and the work environment, and they easily can gain the trust of their former colleagues. They speak the user's language, and they know the existing systems and business processes.

On the downside, former users who are now in the analyst role often know little about software engineering or how to communicate with technical people. If they aren't familiar with analysis modeling techniques, they will express all information in textual form. Users who become requirements analysts will need to learn more about the technical side of software development so that they can represent information in the most appropriate forms for their multiple audiences.

Some former users believe that their understanding of what is needed is better than that of the current users, so they don't solicit or respect input from those who will use the new system. Recent users can be stuck in the here-and-now of the current ways of working, such that they don't see opportunities to improve business processes with the help of a new information system. It's also easy for a former user to think of requirements strictly from a user interface perspective. Focusing on solution ideas can impose unnecessary design constraints from the outset and often fails to solve the real problem.

From Medical Technologist to Requirements Analyst

The senior manager of a medical devices division in a large company had a problem. "Two years ago, I hired three medical technologists into my division to represent our customers' needs," he said. "They've done a great job, but they are no longer current in medical technology, so they can't speak accurately for what our customers need today. But what's a reasonable career path for them now?"

This manager's former medical technologists might be candidates to become requirements analysts. Although they aren't up on the latest happenings in the hospital laboratory, they can still communicate with other med techs. Spending two years in a product development environment gave them a good appreciation for how it works. They might need some additional training in requirements-writing techniques, but these employees have accumulated a variety of valuable experiences that could make them effective analysts.

The Former Developer

Project managers who lack a dedicated requirements analyst often expect a developer to do the job. Unfortunately, the skills and personality needed for requirements development aren't the same as those needed for software development. The stereotypical "geek" isn't the most socially adroit of human beings. A few developers have little patience with users, considering them a necessary evil to be dealt with quickly so that the developer can hustle back to the real job of cutting code. Of course, many developers recognize the criticality of the requirements process and are willing to work as analysts when necessary. Those who enjoy collaborating with customers to understand the needs that drive software development are good candidates to specialize in requirements analysis.

The developer-turned-analyst might need to learn more about the business domain. Developers can easily lapse into technical thinking and jargon, focusing on the software to be built instead of the users' needs. Developers will benefit from training and mentoring in the soft skills that the best analysts master, such as effective listening, negotiating, and facilitating.

The Subject Matter Expert

Ralph Young (2001) recommends having the requirements analyst be an application domain expert or a subject matter expert, as opposed to being a typical user: "SMEs can determine . . . whether the requirements are reasonable, how they extend the existing system, how the proposed architecture should be designed, and impacts on users, among other areas." Some product development organizations hire expert users of their products who have extensive domain experience into their companies to serve either as analysts or as user representatives.

The requirements analyst who is a domain expert might specify the system's requirements to suit his own preferences, rather than addressing the legitimate needs of the various user classes. SMEs sometimes target a high-end, all-inclusive system, when in fact a less comprehensive solution might meet most users' needs. It often works better to have a requirements analyst from the development team work with the SME, who then serves as a key user representative (product champion). (The product champion is described in Chapter 6.)

Creating a Collaborative Environment

Software projects sometimes experience strained relationships between analysts, developers, users, managers, and marketing. The parties don't always trust each other's motivations or appreciate each other's needs and constraints. In reality, though, the producers and consumers of a software product share common objectives. For corporate information systems development, all parties work for the same company so they all benefit from improvements to the corporate bottom line. For commercial products, happy customers generate revenue for the producer and satisfaction for the developers. The requirements analyst has the major responsibility for forging a collaborative relationship with the user representatives and other project stakeholders. An effective analyst appreciates the challenges that both business and technical stakeholders face and demonstrates respect for his or her collaborators at all times. The analyst steers the project participants toward a requirements agreement that leads to a win/win/win outcome in the following ways:

- Customers are delighted with the product.

- The developing organization is happy with the business outcomes.

- The development team members are proud of the good work they did on a challenging and rewarding project.

Next Steps

- If you are a requirements analyst, compare your own skills and knowledge with those described in this chapter. If you see gaps, select two specific areas for improvement and begin closing those gaps immediately by reading, practicing, finding a mentor, or taking a class.

- Select one new requirements engineering practice from this book to learn more about and try to apply it starting next week—literally! Select two or three additional practices to begin applying within a month. Choose others as long-term improvements, five or six months from now. Identify the situation to which you wish to apply each new practice, the benefits that you hope it will provide, and any help or additional information you might need. Think about whose cooperation you'll need to use the new techniques. Identify any barriers that might impede your ability to use the practice and consider who could help you break down those barriers.

II

Software Requirements Development

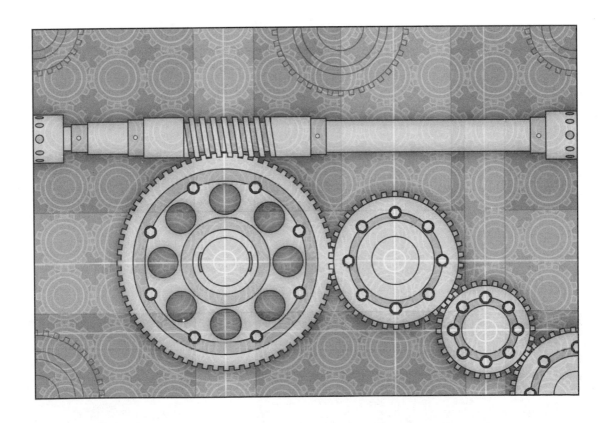

5

Establishing the Product Vision and Project Scope

 When my colleague Karen introduced requirements document inspections in her company, she observed that many of the issues the inspectors raised pertained to project scope. The inspectors often held different understandings of the project's intended scope and objectives. Consequently, they had difficulty agreeing on which functional requirements belonged in the SRS.

As we saw in Chapter 1, "The Essential Software Requirement," the business requirements represent the top level of abstraction in the requirements chain: they define the vision and scope for the software system. The user requirements and software functional requirements must align with the context and objectives that the business requirements establish. Requirements that don't help the project achieve its business objectives shouldn't be included.

A project that lacks a clearly defined and well-communicated direction invites disaster. Project participants can unwittingly work at cross-purposes if they have different objectives and priorities. The stakeholders will never agree on the requirements if they lack a common understanding of the business objectives for the product. A clear vision and scope is especially critical for multisite development projects, where geographical separation inhibits the day-to-day interactions that facilitate teamwork.

One sign that the business requirements are insufficiently defined is that certain features are initially included, then deleted, and then added back in later. Vision and scope issues must be resolved before the detailed functional requirements can be fully specified. A statement of the project's scope and limitations helps greatly with discussions of proposed features and target releases. The vision and scope also provide a reference for making decisions about proposed requirement changes and enhancements. Some companies print the vision and scope highlights on a poster board that's brought to every project meeting so that they can quickly judge whether a proposed change is in or out of scope.

Defining the Vision Through Business Requirements

The *product vision* aligns all stakeholders in a common direction. The vision describes what the product is about and what it eventually could become. The *project scope* identifies what portion of the ultimate long-term product vision the current project will address. The statement of scope draws the boundary between what's in and what's out. That is, the scope also defines the project's limitations. The details of a project's scope are represented by the requirements baseline that the team defines for that project.

The vision applies to the product as a whole. It will change relatively slowly as a product's strategic positioning or an information system's business objectives evolve over time. The scope pertains to a specific project or iteration that will implement the next increment of the product's functionality, as shown in Figure 5-1. Scope is more dynamic than vision because the project manager adjusts the contents of each release within its schedule, budget, resource, and quality constraints. The planner's goal is to manage the scope of a specific development or enhancement project as a defined subset of the grand strategic vision. The scope statement for each project, or for each iteration or enhancement in an evolving product, can appear in that project's SRS, rather than in a separate vision and scope document. Major new projects should have both a complete vision and scope document and an SRS. See Chapter 10, "Documenting the Requirements," for an SRS template.

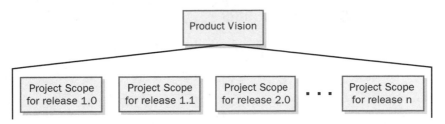

Figure 5-1   The product vision encompasses the scope for each planned release.

For example, a federal government agency is undertaking a massive five-year information system development effort. The agency defined the business objectives and vision for this system early in the process, and they won't change substantially over the next few years. The agency has planned some 15 individual releases of portions of the ultimate system. Each release is created as a separate project with its own scope description. Each scope description must align with the overall product vision and interlock with the scope statements for the other projects to ensure that nothing is inadvertently omitted.

Blue-Sky Requirements

A manager at a product development company that suffered near-catastrophic scope creep once told me ruefully, "We blue-skied the requirements too much." She meant that any idea anyone had was included in the requirements. This company had a solid product vision but didn't manage the scope by planning a series of releases and deferring some suggested features to later (perhaps infinitely later) releases. The team finally released an overinflated product after four years of development. Smart scope management and an evolutionary development approach would have let the team ship a useful product much earlier.

Conflicting Business Requirements

Business requirements collected from multiple sources might conflict. Consider a kiosk containing embedded software, which will be used by a retail store's customers. The kiosk developer's business objectives include the following:

- Generating revenue by leasing or selling the kiosk to the retailer

- Selling consumables through the kiosk to the customer

- Attracting customers to the brand

- Making a wide variety of products available

The retailer's business interests could include the following:

- Maximizing revenue from the available floor space

- Attracting more customers to the store

- Increasing sales volume and profit margins if the kiosk replaces manual operations

The developer might want to establish a high-tech and exciting new direction for customers. The retailer wants a simple turnkey system, and the customer favors convenience and features. The tension among these three parties with their different goals, constraints, and cost factors can lead to inconsistent business requirements. The project sponsor must resolve these conflicts before the analyst can detail the kiosk's system and software requirements. The focus should be on the fundamental objectives for the product that will deliver the maximum business value ("increase sales to new and existing customers"). It's easy to be distracted by superficial product characteristics ("innovative user interface that attracts customers") that don't really state the business objective.

It's also up to the project sponsor (or sponsors) to resolve conflicts among various business stakeholders, rather than expecting the software team to somehow figure these out. As more stakeholders are identified and more constituencies with competing interests climb aboard, the risk of scope creep increases. Uncontrolled scope creep in which stakeholders overstuff the new system in an attempt to satisfy every conceivable interest can cause the project to topple under its own weight, never delivering anything of value. Resolving such issues is often a political and power struggle, which lies outside the scope of this book.

Business Requirements and Use Cases

The business requirements determine both the set of business tasks (use cases) that the application enables (the application *breadth*) and the *depth* or level to which each use case is implemented. If the business requirements help you determine that a particular use case is outside the project's scope, you're making a breadth decision. The depth of support can range from a trivial implementation to full automation with many usability aids. The business requirements will imply which use cases demand robust, comprehensive functional implementation and which require merely superficial implementation, at least initially.

The business requirements influence the implementation priorities for use cases and their associated functional requirements. For example, a business objective to generate maximum revenue from a kiosk implies the early implementation of features that sell more products or services to the customer. Exotic, glitzy features that appeal to only a few technology-hungry customers and don't contribute to the primary business objective shouldn't have high priority.

Business requirements also materially influence the way requirements are implemented. For example, one motivation for building the Chemical Tracking System was to purchase fewer new bottles of a chemical by increasing the use of chemicals that are already in the stockroom or in another laboratory. Interviews and observation should reveal why chemical reuse is not happening now. This information in turn leads to functional requirements and designs that make it easy to track the chemicals in every lab and to help a requester find chemicals in other labs near the requester's location.

Vision and Scope Document

The *vision and scope document* collects the business requirements into a single document that sets the stage for the subsequent development work. Some organizations create a project charter or a business case document that serves a similar purpose. Organizations that build commercial software often create a *market requirements document* (MRD). An MRD might go into more detail than a vision and scope document about the target market segments and the issues that pertain to commercial success.

The owner of the vision and scope document is the project's executive sponsor, funding authority, or someone in a similar role. A requirements analyst can work with the owner to write the vision and scope document. Input on the business requirements should come from individuals who have a clear sense of why they are undertaking the project. These individuals might include the customer or development organization's senior management, a project visionary, a product manager, a subject matter expert, or members of the marketing department.

Figure 5-2 suggests a template for a vision and scope document. Document templates standardize the structure of the documents created by your organization's project teams. As with any template, adapt this one to meet the specific needs of your own projects.

---

1. **Business Requirements**
   1.1   Background
   1.2   Business Opportunity
   1.3   Business Objectives and Success Criteria
   1.4   Customer or Market Needs
   1.5   Business Risks

2. **Vision of the Solution**
   2.1   Vision Statement
   2.2   Major Features
   2.3   Assumptions and Dependencies

3. **Scope and Limitations**
   3.1   Scope of Initial Release
   3.2   Scope of Subsequent Releases
   3.3   Limitations and Exclusions

4. **Business Context**
   4.1   Stakeholder Profiles
   4.2   Project Priorities
   4.3   Operating Environment

Figure 5-2   Template for vision and scope document.

Parts of the vision and scope document might seem repetitive, but they should interlock in a sensible way. Consider the following example:

Business Opportunity   Exploit the poor security record of a competing product.

Business Objective   Capture a market share of 80 percent by being recognized as the most secure product in the market through trade journal reviews and consumer surveys.

Customer Need   A more secure product.

Feature   A new, robust security engine.

1. Business Requirements

Projects are launched in the belief that the new product will make the world a better place in some way for someone. The business requirements describe the primary benefits that the new system will provide to its sponsors, buyers, and users. The emphasis will be different for different kinds of products, such as information systems, commercial software packages, and real-time control systems.

1.1 Background

Summarize the rationale and context for the new product. Provide a general description of the history or situation that led to the decision to build this product.

1.2 Business Opportunity

For a commercial product, describe the market opportunity that exists and the market in which the product will be competing. For a corporate information system, describe the business problem that is being solved or the business process being improved, as well as the environment in which the system will be used. Include a comparative evaluation of existing products and potential solutions, indicating why the proposed product is attractive and the advantages it provides. Describe the problems that cannot currently be solved without the product. Show how it aligns with market trends, technology evolution, or corporate strategic directions. Include a brief description of any other technologies, processes, or resources required to provide a complete customer solution.

1.3 Business Objectives and Success Criteria

Summarize the important business benefits the product will provide in a quantitative and measurable way. Table 5-1 presents some examples of both financial and non-financial business objectives (Wiegers 2002c). If such information appears elsewhere, such as in a business case document, refer to the other document rather than duplicate it here. Determine how the stakeholders will define and measure success on this project (Wiegers 2002c). State the factors that have the greatest impact on achieving that success, including factors both within and outside the organization's control. Specify measurable criteria to assess whether the business objectives have been met.

Table 5-1   Examples of Financial and Nonfinancial Business Objectives

Financial	Nonfinancial
■ Capture a market share of X% within Y months.	■ Achieve a customer satisfaction measure of at least X within Y months of release.
■ Increase market share in country X by Y% in Z months.	■ Increase transaction-processing productivity by X% and reduce data error rate to no more than Y%.
■ Reach a sales volume of X units or revenue of $Y within Z months.	■ Achieve a specified time to market that establishes a dominant market presence.
■ Achieve X% profit or return on investment within Y months.	■ Develop a robust platform for a family of related products.
■ Achieve positive cash flow on this product within Y months.	■ Develop specific core technology competencies in the organization.
■ Save $X per year currently spent on a high-maintenance legacy system.	■ Have X positive product reviews appear in trade journals before a specified date.
■ Reduce support costs by X% within Y months.	■ Be rated as the top product for reliability in published product reviews by a specified date.
■ Receive no more than X service calls per unit and Y warranty calls per unit within Z months after shipping.	■ Comply with specific federal and state regulations.
■ Increase gross margin on existing business from X% to Y%.	■ Reduce turnaround time to X hours on Y% of customer support calls.

1.4 Customer or Market Needs

Describe the needs of typical customers or of the target market segment, including needs that current products or information systems do not meet. Present the problems that customers currently encounter that the new product will address and provide examples of how customers would use the product. Define at a high level any known critical interface or performance requirements, but do not include design or implementation details.

1.5 Business Risks

Summarize the major business risks associated with developing—or not developing—this product. Risk categories include marketplace competition, timing issues, user acceptance, implementation issues, and possible negative impacts on the business. Estimate the potential loss from each risk, the likelihood of it occurring, and your ability to control it. Identify any potential mitigation actions. If you already prepared this information for a business case analysis or a similar document, refer to that other source rather than duplicating the information here.

2. Vision of the Solution

This section of the document establishes a strategic vision for the system that will achieve the business objectives. This vision provides the context for making decisions throughout the course of the product's life. It should not include detailed functional requirements or project planning information.

2.1 Vision Statement

Write a concise vision statement that summarizes the long-term purpose and intent of the new product. The vision statement should reflect a balanced view that will satisfy the needs of diverse stakeholders. It can be somewhat idealistic but should be grounded in the realities of existing or anticipated markets, enterprise architectures, corporate strategic directions, and resource limitations. The following keyword template works well for a product vision statement (Moore 1991):

- *For*   [target customer]

- *Who*   [statement of the need or opportunity]

- *The*   [product name]

- *Is*   [a product category]

- *That*   [key benefit, compelling reason to buy or use]

- *Unlike*   [primary competitive alternative, current system, or current business process],

- *Our product*   [statement of primary differentiation and advantages of new product].

Here's a sample vision statement for the Chemical Tracking System project at Contoso Pharmaceuticals that was introduced in Chapter 2, with the keywords shown in boldface:

> *For scientists **who** need to request containers of chemicals, **the** Chemical Tracking System **is** an information system **that** will provide a single point of access to the chemical stockroom and to vendors. The system will store the location of every chemical container within the company, the quantity of material remaining in it, and the complete history of each container's locations and usage. This system will save the company 25 percent on chemical costs in the first year of use by allowing the company to fully exploit chemicals that are*

*already available within the company, dispose of fewer partially used or expired containers, and use a single standard chemical purchasing process. **Unlike** the current manual ordering processes, **our product** will generate all reports required to comply with federal and state government regulations that require the reporting of chemical usage, storage, and disposal.*

2.2 Major Features

Name or number each of the new product's major features or user capabilities in a unique, persistent way, emphasizing those features that distinguish it from previous or competing products. Giving each feature a unique label (as opposed to a bullet) permits tracing it to individual user requirements, functional requirements, and other system elements.

2.3 Assumptions and Dependencies

Record any assumptions that the stakeholders made when conceiving the project and writing this vision and scope document. Often the assumptions that one party holds are not shared by other parties. If you write them down and review them, you can agree on the project's basic underlying assumptions. This avoids possible confusion and aggravation in the future. For instance, the executive sponsor for the Chemical Tracking System assumed that it would replace the existing chemical stockroom inventory system and that it would interface to Contoso's purchasing systems. Also record major dependencies the project has on external factors outside its control. These could include pending industry standards or government regulations, other projects, third-party suppliers, or development partners.

3. Scope and Limitations

When a chemist invents a new reaction that transforms one kind of chemical into another, he writes a paper that includes a "Scope and Limitations" section, which describes what the reaction will and will not do. Similarly, a software project should define its scope and limitations. You need to state both what the system *is* and what it *is not*.

The project scope defines the concept and range of the proposed solution. The limitations itemize certain capabilities that the product will *not* include. The scope and limitations help to establish realistic stakeholder expectations. Sometimes customers request features that are too expensive or that lie outside the intended product scope. Out-of-scope requirements must be rejected unless they are so valuable that the scope should be enlarged to accommodate them, with corresponding changes in budget, schedule, and staff. Keep a record of rejected requirements and why they were rejected because they have a way of reappearing.

> **More Info**   Chapter 18, "Requirements Management Principles and Practices," describes how to use a requirements attribute to keep a record of rejected or deferred requirements.

3.1 Scope of Initial Release

Summarize the major features that are planned for inclusion in the initial release of the product. Describe the quality characteristics that will let the product provide the intended benefits to its various user classes. If your goals are to focus the development effort and to maintain a reasonable project schedule, avoid the temptation to include in release 1.0 every feature that any potential customer might conceivably want someday. Bloatware and slipped schedules are common outcomes of such insidious scope creep. Focus on those features that will provide the most value, at the most acceptable cost, to the broadest community, in the earliest time frame.

My colleague Scott's last project team decided that users had to be able to run their package delivery business with the first software release. Version 1 didn't have to be fast, pretty, or easy to use, but it had to be reliable; this focus drove everything the team did. The initial release accomplished the basic objectives of the system. Future releases will include additional features, options, and usability aids.

3.2 Scope of Subsequent Releases

If you envision a staged evolution of the product, indicate which features will be deferred and the desired timing of later releases. Subsequent releases let you implement additional use cases and features and enrich the capabilities of the initial use cases and features (Nejmeh and Thomas 2002). You can also improve system performance, reliability, and other quality characteristics as the product matures. The farther out you look, the fuzzier these future scope statements will be. You can expect to shift functionality from one planned release to another and perhaps to add unanticipated capabilities. Short release cycles help by providing frequent opportunities for learning based on customer feedback.

3.3 Limitations and Exclusions

Defining the boundary between what's in and what's out is a way to manage scope creep and customer expectations. List any product capabilities or characteristics that a stakeholder might anticipate but that are not planned for inclusion in the product or in a specific release.

4. Business Context

This section summarizes some of the project's business issues, including profiles of major stakeholder categories and management's priorities for the project.

4.1 Stakeholder Profiles

Stakeholders are the individuals, groups, or organizations who are actively involved in a project, are affected by its outcome, or are able to influence its outcome (Project Management Institute 2000; Smith 2000). The stakeholder profiles describe different categories of customers and other key stakeholders for this project. You needn't describe every stakeholder group, such as legal staff who must check for compliance with pertinent laws. Focus on different types of customers, target market segments, and the different user classes within those segments. Each stakeholder profile should include the following information:

- The major value or benefit that the stakeholder will receive from the product and how the product will generate high customer satisfaction. Stakeholder value might include

    - ❑   Improved productivity.

    - ❑   Reduced rework.

    - ❑   Cost savings.

    - ❑   Streamlined business processes.

    - ❑   Automation of previously manual tasks.

    - ❑   Ability to perform entirely new tasks.

    - ❑   Compliance with pertinent standards or regulations.

    - ❑   Improved usability compared to current products.

- Their likely attitudes toward the product.

- Major features and characteristics of interest.

- Any known constraints that must be accommodated.

4.2 Project Priorities

To enable effective decision making, the stakeholders must agree on the project's priorities. One way to approach this is to consider the five dimensions of a software project: features (or scope), quality, schedule, cost, and staff (Wiegers 1996a). Each dimension fits in one of the following three categories on any given project:

A *constraint*   A limiting factor within which the project manager must operate

A *driver*   A significant success objective with limited flexibility for adjustment

A *degree of freedom*   A factor that the project manager has some latitude to adjust and balance against the other dimensions

The project manager's goal is to adjust those factors that are degrees of freedom to achieve the project's success drivers within the limits imposed by the constraints. Not all factors can be drivers, and not all can be constraints. The project manager needs some degrees of freedom to be able to respond appropriately when project requirements or realities change. Suppose marketing suddenly demands that you release the product one month earlier than scheduled. How do you respond? Do you

- Defer certain requirements to a later release?

- Shorten the planned system test cycle?

- Pay your staff overtime or hire contractors to accelerate development?

- Shift resources from other projects to help out?

The project priorities dictate the actions you take when such eventualities arise.

4.3 Operating Environment

Describe the environment in which the system will be used and define the vital availability, reliability, performance, and integrity requirements. This information will significantly influence the definition of the system's architecture, which is the first—and often the most important—design step. A system that must support widely distributed users who require access around the clock needs a significantly different architecture from one that's employed by co-located users only during normal working hours. Nonfunctional requirements such as fault tolerance and the ability to service the system while it is running can consume considerable design and implementation effort. Ask the stakeholders questions such as the following:

- Are the users widely distributed geographically or located close to each other? How many time zones are they in?

- When do the users in various locations need to access the system?

- Where is the data generated and used? How far apart are these locations? Does data from multiple locations need to be combined?

- Are specific maximum response times known for accessing data that might be stored remotely?

- Can the users tolerate service interruptions or is continuous access to the system critical for the operation of their businesses?

- What access security controls and data protection requirements are needed?

The Context Diagram

The scope description establishes the boundary and connections between the system we are developing and everything else in the universe. The *context diagram* graphically illustrates this boundary. It identifies *terminators* outside the system that interface to it in some way, as well as data, control, and material *flows* between the terminators and the system. The context diagram is the top level of abstraction in a data flow diagram developed according to the principles of structured analysis (Robertson and Robertson 1994), but it's a useful model for projects that follow any development methodology. You can include the context diagram in the vision and scope document, in or as an appendix to the SRS, or as part of a data flow model for the system.

Figure 5-3 illustrates a portion of the context diagram for the Chemical Tracking System. The entire system is depicted as a single circle; the context diagram deliberately provides no visibility into the system's internal objects, processes, and data. The "system" inside the circle could encompass any combination of software, hardware, and human components. The terminators in the rectangles can represent user classes ("Chemist" or "Buyer"), organizations ("Health and Safety Department"), other systems ("Training Database"), or hardware devices ("Bar Code Reader"). The arrows on the diagram represent the flow of data ("request for chemical") or physical items ("chemical container") between the system and the terminators.

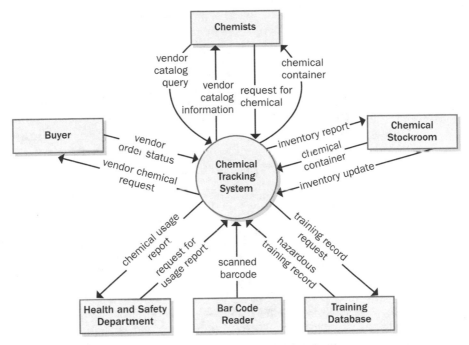

Figure 5-3   Context diagram for the Chemical Tracking System.

You might expect to see chemical vendors shown as a terminator in this diagram. After all, the company will route orders to vendors for fulfillment, the vendors will send chemical containers and invoices to Contoso Pharmaceuticals, and purchasing will send checks to the vendors. However, those processes take place outside the scope of the Chemical Tracking System, as part of the operations of the purchasing and receiving departments. The context diagram makes it clear that this system is not directly involved in placing orders with the vendors, receiving the products, or paying the bills.

The purpose of tools such as the context diagram is to foster clear and accurate communication among the project stakeholders. That clarity is more important than dogmatically adhering to the rules for a "correct" context diagram. I strongly recommend, though, that you adopt the notation illustrated in Figure 5-3 as a standard for drawing context diagrams. Suppose you were to use a triangle for the system instead of a circle and ovals rather than rectangles for terminators. Your colleagues would have difficulty reading a diagram that follows your personal preferences rather than a team standard.

Keeping the Scope in Focus

The business requirements and an understanding of how customers will use the product provide valuable tools for dealing with scope creep. Scope change isn't a bad thing if it helps you steer the project toward satisfying evolving customer needs. The vision and scope document lets you assess whether proposed features and requirements are appropriate for inclusion in the project. Remember, whenever someone requests a new requirement, the analyst needs to ask, "Is this in scope?"

One response might be that the proposed requirement is clearly out of scope. It might be interesting, but it should be addressed in a future release or by another project. Another possibility is that the request obviously lies within the defined project scope. You can incorporate new in-scope requirements in the project if they are of high priority relative to the other requirements that were already committed. Including new requirements often involves making a decision to defer or cancel other planned requirements.

The third possibility is that the proposed new requirement is out of scope but it's such a good idea that the project scope should be modified to accommodate it. That is, there's a feedback loop between the user requirements and the business requirements. This will require that you update the vision and scope document, which should be placed under change control at the time it is baselined. When the project's scope is increased, you will usually have to renegotiate the planned budget, resources, schedule, and perhaps staff. Ideally, the original schedule and resources will accommodate a certain amount of change because of thoughtfully included contingency buffers (Wiegers 2002d). However, unless you originally budgeted for some requirements growth, you'll need to replan after requirements changes are approved.

Scope Management and Timebox Development

 Enrique, a project manager at Lightspeed Financial Systems, had to deliver an Internet-enabled version of Lightspeed's flagship portfolio management software. It would take years to fully supplant the mature application, but Lightspeed needed an Internet presence right away. Enrique selected a timebox development approach, promising to release a new version every 90 days (McConnell 1996). His marketing team carefully prioritized the product's requirements. The SRS for each quarterly release included a committed set of new and enhanced features, as well as a list of lower-priority "stretch" requirements to be implemented as time permitted. Enrique's team didn't incorporate every stretch requirement into each release, but they did ship a new, stable version every three months through this schedule-driven approach to scope management. Schedule and quality are normally constraints on a timeboxed project and scope is a degree of freedom.

A common consequence of scope creep is that completed activities must be reworked to accommodate the changes. Quality often suffers if the allocated resources or time are not increased when new functionality is added. Documented business requirements make it easier to manage legitimate scope growth as the marketplace or business needs change. They also help a harried project manager to justify saying "no"—or at least "not yet"—when influential people try to stuff more features into an overly constrained project.

 Next Steps

- Ask several stakeholders for your project to write a vision statement using the keyword template described in this chapter. See how similar the visions are. Rectify any disconnects and come up with a unified vision statement that all those stakeholders agree to.

- Whether you're near the launch of a new project or in the midst of construction, write a vision and scope document using the template in Figure 5-2 (on page 82) and have the rest of the team review it. This might reveal that your team doesn't share a common understanding of the product vision or project scope. Correct that problem now, rather than let it slide indefinitely; it will be even more difficult to correct if you wait. This activity will also suggest ways to modify the template to best meet the needs of your organization's projects.

6

Finding the Voice of the Customer

If you share my conviction that customer involvement is a critical factor in delivering excellent software, you'll engage customer representatives from the outset of your project. Success in software requirements, and hence in software development, depends on getting the voice of the customer close to the ear of the developer. To find the voice of the customer, take the following steps:

■   Identify the different classes of users for your product.

■   Identify sources of user requirements.

■   Select and work with individuals who represent each user class and other stakeholder groups.

■   Agree on who the requirements decision makers are for your project.

Customer involvement is the only way to avoid an expectation gap, a mismatch between the product that customers expect to receive and the product that developers build. It's not enough simply to ask a few customers what they want and then start coding. If the developers build exactly what customers initially request, they'll probably have to build it again because customers often don't know what they really need.

The features that users present as their "wants" don't necessarily equate to the functionality they need to perform their tasks with the new product. To get a more accurate view of user needs, the requirements analyst must collect user input, analyze and clarify it, and determine just what to build to let users do their jobs. The analyst has the lead responsibility for recording the new system's necessary capabilities and properties and for communicating that information to other stakeholders. This is an iterative process that takes time. If you don't invest the time to achieve this shared understanding—this common vision of the intended product—the certain outcomes are rework, delayed completion, and customer dissatisfaction.

Sources of Requirements

The origins of your software requirements will depend on the nature of your product and your development environment. The need to gather requirements from multiple perspectives and sources exemplifies the communication-intensive nature of requirements engineering. Following are several typical sources of software requirements:

Interviews and discussions with potential users   The most obvious way to find out what potential users of a new software product need is to ask them. This chapter discusses how to find suitable user representatives and Chapter 7 describes techniques for eliciting requirements from them.

Documents that describe current or competing products   Documents can also describe corporate or industry standards that must be followed or regulations and laws with which the product must comply. Descriptions of both present and future business processes also are helpful. Published comparative reviews might point out shortcomings in other products that you could address to gain a competitive advantage.

System requirements specifications   A product that contains both hardware and software has a high-level system requirements specification that describes the overall product. A portion of the system requirements is allocated to each software subsystem (Nelsen 1990). The analyst can derive additional detailed software functional requirements from those allocated system requirements.

Problem reports and enhancement requests for a current system   The help desk and field support personnel are valuable sources of requirements. They learn about the problems that users encounter with the current system and hear ideas from users for improving the system in the next release.

Marketing surveys and user questionnaires   Surveys can collect a large amount of data from a broad spectrum of potential users. Consult with an expert in survey design and administration to ensure that you ask the right questions of the right people (Fowler 1995). A survey tests your understanding of requirements that you have gathered or think that you know, but it's not a good way to stimulate creative thinking. Always beta test a survey before distributing it. It's frustrating to discover too late that a question was phrased ambiguously or to realize that an important question was omitted.

Observing users at work   During a "day in the life" study, an analyst watches users of a current system or potential users of the future system perform their work. Observing a user's workflow in the task environment allows the analyst to validate information collected from previous interviews, to identify new topics for interviews, to see problems with the current system, and to identify ways that the new system can better support the workflow (McGraw and Harbison 1997; Beyer and Holtzblatt 1998). Watching the users at work provides a more accurate and complete understanding than simply asking them to write down the steps they go through. The analyst must abstract and generalize beyond the observed user's activities to ensure that the requirements captured apply to the user class as a whole and not just to that individual. A skillful analyst can also often suggest ideas for improving the user's current business processes.

Scenario analysis of user tasks   By identifying tasks that users need to accomplish with the system, the analyst can derive the necessary functional requirements that will let users perform those tasks. This is the essence of the use-case approach described in Chapter 8. Be sure to include the information consumed and generated by a task and the sources of that information.

Events and responses   List the external events to which the system must react and the appropriate responses. This works particularly well for real-time systems, which must read and process data streams, error codes, control signals, and interrupts from external hardware devices.

User Classes

A product's users differ, among other ways, in the following respects:

- The frequency with which they use the product
- Their application domain experience and computer systems expertise
- The features they use
- The tasks they perform in support of their business processes
- Their access privilege or security levels (such as ordinary user, guest user, or administrator)

You can group users into a number of distinct *user classes* based on these differences. An individual can belong to multiple user classes. For example, an application's administrator might also interact with it as an ordinary user at times. The terminators shown outside your system on a context diagram (as discussed in Chapter 5) are candidates for user classes. A user class is a subset of a product's users, which is a subset of a product's customers, which is a subset of its stakeholders, as shown in Figure 6-1.

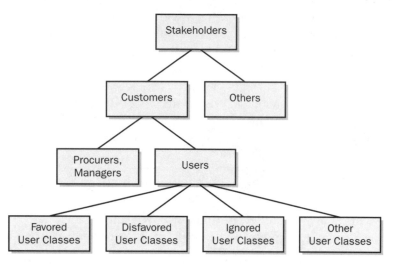

Figure 6-1   A hierarchy of stakeholders, customers, and users.

 It's tempting to separate users into classes based on their geographical location or the kind of company or job that they're in, rather than with regard to how they interact with the system. For example, a company that creates software used in the banking industry initially considered distinguishing users based on whether they worked in a large commercial bank, a small commercial bank, a savings and loan institution, or a credit union. These distinctions really represent potential market segments, not different user classes. The people who accept loan applications at all such financial institutions have similar functional needs for the system, so a more logical user class name might be *application receiver*. This role could be performed by someone with the job title of Loan Officer, Vice-President, Customer Service Agent, or perhaps even Teller, if all those individuals use the system to help someone apply for a loan.

Certain user classes are more important to you than others. Favored user classes receive preferential treatment when you're making priority decisions or resolving conflicts between requirements received from different user classes. Favored user classes include those groups whose acceptance and use of the system will cause it to meet—or fail to meet—its business objectives. This doesn't mean that the stakeholders who are paying for the system (who might not be users at all) or who have the most political clout should necessarily be favored. Disfavored user classes are those groups who aren't supposed to use the product for legal, security, or safety reasons (Gause and Lawrence 1999). You might elect to ignore still other user classes. They get what they get, but you don't specifically build the product to suit them. The remaining user classes are of roughly equal importance in defining the product's requirements.

Each user class will have its own set of requirements for the tasks that members of the class must perform. They might also have different nonfunctional requirements, such as usability, that will drive user interface design choices. Inexperienced or occasional users are concerned with how easy the system is to learn (or relearn) to use. These users like menus, graphical user interfaces, uncluttered screen displays, verbose prompts, wizards, and consistency with other applications they have used. Once users gain sufficient experience with the product, they become more concerned about ease of use and efficiency. They now value keyboard shortcuts, macros, customization options, toolbars, scripting facilities, and perhaps even a command-line interface instead of a graphical user interface.

> **Trap**   Don't overlook indirect or secondary user classes. They might not use your application directly, instead accessing its data or services through other applications or through reports. Your customer once removed is still your customer.

It might sound strange, but user classes need not be human beings. You can consider other applications or hardware components with which your system interacts as additional user classes. A fuel injection system would be a user class for the software embedded in an automobile's engine controller. The fuel injection system can't speak for itself, so the analyst must get the requirements for the fuel-injection control software from the engineer who designed the injection system.

Identify and characterize the different user classes for your product early in the project so that you can elicit requirements from representatives of each important class. A useful technique for this is called "Expand Then Contract" (Gottesdiener 2002). Begin by brainstorming as many user classes as you can think of. Don't be afraid if there are dozens at this stage, because you'll condense and categorize them later. It's important not to overlook a user class because that will come back to bite you later. Next, look for groups with similar needs that you can either combine or treat as a major user class with several subclasses. Try to pare the list down to no more than about 15 distinct user classes.

One company that developed a specialized product for about 65 corporate customers had regarded each company as a distinct user with unique needs. Grouping their customers into just six user classes greatly simplified their requirements challenges for future releases. Remember, you will have other important project stakeholders who won't actually use the product, so the user classes represent just a subset of the people who need to provide input on the requirements.

Document the user classes and their characteristics, responsibilities, and physical locations in the SRS. The project manager of the Chemical Tracking System discussed in earlier chapters identified the user classes and characteristics shown in Table 6-1. Include all pertinent information you have about each user class, such as its relative or absolute size and which classes are favored. This will help the team prioritize change requests and conduct impact assessments later on. Estimates of the volume and type of system transactions help the testers develop a usage profile for the system so that they can plan their verification activities.

Table 6-1   User Classes for the Chemical Tracking System

Chemists (favored)	Approximately 1000 chemists located in six buildings will use the system to request chemicals from vendors and from the chemical stockroom. Each chemist will use the system several times per day, mainly for requesting chemicals and tracking chemical containers into and out of the laboratory. The chemists need to search vendor catalogs for specific chemical structures imported from the tools they currently use for drawing chemical structures.
Buyers	About five buyers in the purchasing department process chemical requests that others submit. They place and track orders with external vendors. They know little about chemistry and need simple query facilities to search vendor catalogs. Buyers will not use the system's container-tracking features. Each buyer will use the system an average of 20 times per day.
Chemical Stockroom Staff	The chemical stockroom staff consists of six technicians and one supervisor who manage an inventory of more than 500,000 chemical containers. They will process requests from chemists to supply containers from three stockrooms, request new chemicals from vendors, and track the movement of all containers into and out of the stockrooms. They are the only users of the inventory-reporting feature. Because of their high transaction volume, the functions that are used only by the chemical stockroom staff must be automated and efficient.
Health and Safety Department Staff (favored)	The Health and Safety Department staff will use the system only to generate predefined quarterly reports that comply with federal and state chemical usage and disposal reporting regulations. The Health and Safety Department manager is likely to request changes in the reports several times per year as government regulations change. These report changes are of the highest priority and implementation will be time critical.

Consider building a catalog of user classes that recur across multiple applications. Defining user classes at the enterprise level lets you reuse those user class descriptions in future projects. The next system you build might serve the needs of some new user classes, but it probably will also be used by user classes from your earlier systems.

To bring the user classes to life, you might create a persona for each one, a description of a representative member of the user class, as follows (Cooper 1999):

> *Fred, 41, has been a chemist at Contoso Pharmaceuticals since he received his Ph.D. 14 years ago. He doesn't have much patience with computers. Fred usually works on two projects at a time in related chemical areas. His lab contains approximately 400 bottles of chemicals and gas cylinders. On an average day, he'll need four new chemicals from the stockroom. Two of these will be commercial chemicals in stock, one will need to be ordered, and one will come from the supply of proprietary Contoso chemical samples. On occasion, Fred will need a hazardous chemical that requires special training for safe handling. When he buys a chemical for the first time, Fred wants the material safety data sheet e-mailed to him automatically. Each year, Fred will generate about 10 new proprietary chemicals to go into the stockroom. Fred wants a report of his chemical usage for the previous month generated automatically and sent to him by e-mail so that he can monitor his chemical exposure.*

As you explore the chemists' requirements, think about Fred as the archetype of this user class and ask, "What would Fred need to do?"

Finding User Representatives

Every kind of project—including corporate information systems, commercial applications, package solutions, integrated systems, embedded systems, Internet applications, and contracted software—needs suitable user representatives to provide the voice of the customer. The user representatives should be involved throughout the development life cycle, not just in an isolated requirements phase at the beginning. Each user class needs to be represented.

It's easiest to gain access to actual users when you're developing applications for deployment within your own company. If you're developing commercial software, you might engage people from your current beta-testing or early-release sites to provide requirements input much earlier in the development process. (See "External Product Champions" later in this chapter). Consider setting up focus groups of current users of your products or your competitors' products.

One company asked a focus group to perform certain tasks with various digital cameras and computers. The results indicated that the company's camera software took too long to perform the most common operation because of a design decision to also accommodate less likely scenarios. The company made a change in their next camera's requirements that helped reduce customer complaints about speed.

Be sure that the focus group represents the kinds of users whose needs should drive your product development. Include both expert and less experienced customers. If your focus group represents only early adopters or blue-sky thinkers, you might end up with many sophisticated and technically difficult requirements that many of your target customers don't find interesting.

Figure 6-2 illustrates some typical communication pathways that connect the voice of the user to the ear of the developer. One study indicated that highly successful projects used more kinds of communication links and more direct links between developers and customers than did less successful projects (Keil and Carmel 1995). The most direct communication occurs when developers can talk to appropriate users themselves, which means that the developer is also performing the analyst role. As in the children's game "Telephone," intervening layers between the user and the developer increase the chance of miscommunication. For instance, requirements that come from the manager of the end users are less likely to accurately reflect the real user needs.

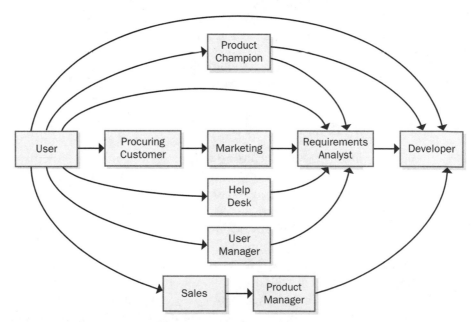

Figure 6-2   Some possible communication pathways between the user and the developer.

Some of these intervening layers add value, though, as when a skilled requirements analyst works with users or other participants to collect, evaluate, refine, and organize their input. Recognize the risks that you assume by using marketing staff, product managers, subject matter experts, or others as surrogates for the actual voice of the customer. Despite the obstacles to, and the cost of, acquiring optimum customer representation, your product and your customers will suffer if you don't talk to the people who can provide the best information.

The Product Champion

 Many years ago I worked in a small software development group that supported the scientific research activities at a major corporation. Each of our projects included a few key members of our user community to provide the requirements. We called these people *product champions* (or *project champions*, although that term more often refers to the management sponsors of a project) (Wiegers 1996a). The product champion approach provides an effective way to structure the customer-development partnership.

> **Trap**   Watch out for user managers or for software developers who think they already understand the needs of the real system users without asking.

Each product champion serves as the primary interface between members of a single user class and the project's requirements analyst. Ideally, the champions will be actual users, not surrogates such as funding sponsors, procuring customers, marketing staff, user managers, or software developers pretending to be users. Product champions collect requirements from other members of the user classes they represent and reconcile inconsistencies. Requirements development is thus a shared responsibility of the analysts and selected customers, although the analyst writes the requirements documents.

The best product champions have a clear vision of the new system and are enthusiastic about it because they see how it will benefit them and their peers. The champions should be effective communicators who are respected by their colleagues. They need a thorough understanding of the application domain and the system's operating environment. Great product champions are in demand for other assignments on their principal job, so you'll have to build a persuasive case for why particular individuals are critical to project success. My team and I found that good product champions made a huge difference in our projects, so we happily offered them public reward and recognition for their contributions.

My software development team enjoyed an additional benefit from the product champion approach. On several projects, we had excellent champions who spoke out on our behalf with their colleagues when the customers wondered why the software wasn't done yet. "Don't worry about it," the champions told their peers and their managers. "I understand and agree with the software group's approach to software engineering. The time we're spending on requirements will help us get the system we really need and will save us time in the long run. Don't worry about it." Such collaboration helps break down the tension that often arises between customers and development teams.

The product champion approach works best if each champion is fully empowered to make binding decisions on behalf of the user class he represents. If a champion's decisions are routinely overruled by managers or by the software group, the champion's time and goodwill are being wasted. However, the champions must remember that they are not the sole customers. Problems arise when the individual filling this critical liaison role doesn't adequately communicate with his peers and presents only his own wishes and ideas.

External Product Champions

When developing commercial software, it can be difficult to find people to serve as product champions from outside your company. If you have a close working relationship with some major corporate customers, they might welcome the opportunity to participate in requirements elicitation. You might give external product champions economic incentives for their participation. Consider offering them discounts on products or paying for the time they spend working with you on requirements. You still face the challenge of how to avoid hearing only the champions' requirements and neglecting the needs of other customers. If you have a diverse customer base, first identify core requirements that are common to all customers. Then define additional requirements that are specific to individual customers, market segments, or user classes.

Commercial product development companies sometimes rely on internal subject matter experts or outside consultants to serve as surrogates for actual users, who might be unknown or difficult to engage. Another alternative is to hire a suitable product champion who has the right background. One company that developed a retail point-of-sale and back-office system for a particular industry hired three store managers to serve as full-time product champions. As another example, my longtime family physician, Art, left his medical practice to become the voice-of-the-physician at a medical software company. Art's new employer believed that it was worth the expense to hire a doctor to help the company build software that other doctors would accept. A third company hired several former employees from one of their major customers. These people provided valuable domain expertise as well as insight into the politics of the customer organization.

Any time the product champion is a former or simulated user, watch out for disconnects between the champion's perceptions and the current needs of real users. Some problem domains change rapidly and some are more stable. The medical field is evolving quickly, whereas many corporate business processes persist in similar form for years. The essential question is whether the product champion, no matter what his background or current job, can accurately represent the needs of real users.

Product Champion Expectations

To help the product champion approach succeed, document what you expect your champions to do. These written expectations can help you build a case for specific individuals to fill this critical role. Table 6-2 identifies some activities that product champions might perform. Not every champion will do all of these; use this table as a starting point to negotiate each champion's responsibilities.

Table 6-2 Possible Product Champion Activities

Category	Activities
Planning	■ Refine the scope and limitations of the product ■ Define interfaces to other systems ■ Evaluate impact of new system on business operations ■ Define a transition path from current applications
Requirements	■ Collect requirements from other users ■ Develop usage scenarios and use cases ■ Resolve conflicts between proposed requirements ■ Define implementation priorities ■ Specify quality and performance requirements ■ Evaluate user interface prototypes
Validation and Verification	■ Inspect requirements documents ■ Define user acceptance criteria ■ Develop test cases from usage scenarios ■ Provide test data sets ■ Perform beta testing

Table 6-2   Possible Product Champion Activities *(continued)*

Category	Activities
User Aids	■ Write portions of user manuals and help text ■ Prepare training materials for tutorials ■ Present product demonstrations to peers
Change Management	■ Evaluate and prioritize defect corrections ■ Evaluate and prioritize enhancement requests ■ Evaluate the impact of proposed requirements changes on users and business processes ■ Participate in making change decisions

Multiple Product Champions

One person can rarely describe the needs for all users of an application. The Chemical Tracking System had four major user classes, so it needed four product champions selected from the internal user community at Contoso Pharmaceuticals. Figure 6-3 illustrates how the project manager set up a team of analysts and product champions to collect the right requirements from the right sources. These champions were not assigned full-time, but each one spent several hours per week working on the project. Three analysts worked with the four product champions to elicit, analyze, and document their requirements. (The same analyst worked with two product champions because the Buyer and the Health and Safety Department user classes were small and had few requirements.) One analyst assembled all the input into a single SRS.

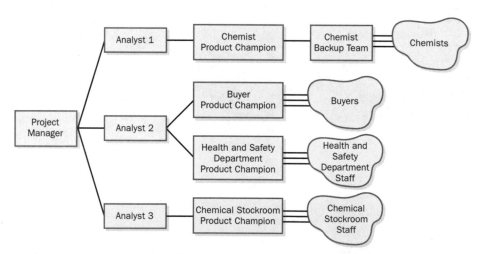

Figure 6-3   Product champion model for the Chemical Tracking System.

One person cannot adequately supply all the diverse requirements for a large user class such as the hundreds of chemists at Contoso. To help him, the product champion for the chemist user class assembled a backup team of five other chemists from other parts of the company. These chemists represented subclasses within the broad "chemist" user class. This hierarchical approach engaged additional users in requirements development while avoiding the expense of massive workshops or dozens of individual interviews. The chemist product champion, Don, always strove for consensus, but he willingly made the necessary decisions when agreement wasn't achieved so that the project could move ahead instead of deadlocking. No backup team was necessary when the user class was small enough or cohesive enough that one individual could adequately represent the group's needs.

The Voiceless User Class

A requirements analyst at Humongous Insurance was delighted that an influential user, Rebecca, agreed to serve as product champion for the new claim processing system. Rebecca had many ideas about the system features and user interface design. Thrilled to have the guidance of an expert, the development team happily complied with her requests. After delivery, though, they were shocked to receive many complaints about how hard the system was to use.

Rebecca was a power user. She specified usability requirements that were great for experts, but the 90 percent of users who *weren't* experts found the system unintuitive and difficult to learn. The requirements analyst failed to recognize that the claim processing system had at least two user classes. The large group of non–power users was disenfranchised in the requirements and user interface design processes, and Humongous paid the price in an expensive redesign. The analyst should have engaged a second product champion to represent the large class of nonexpert users.

Selling the Product Champion Idea

Expect to encounter resistance when you propose the idea of having product champions on your projects. "The users are too busy." "Management wants to make the decisions." "They'll slow us down." "We can't afford it." "I don't know what I'm supposed to do as a product champion." Some users won't want to provide input on a system that they fear will make them change the way they work or might threaten their job with elimination. Managers are sometimes reluctant to delegate authority for requirements to ordinary users.

Separating business requirements from user requirements alleviates these discomforts. As an actual user, the product champion makes decisions at the user requirements level within the constraints that the project's business requirements impose. The management sponsor retains the authority to make decisions that affect the product vision, project scope, schedule, and cost. Documenting and negotiating the product champion's role and responsibilities give candidate champions a comfort level about what they're being asked to do.

If you encounter resistance, point out that insufficient user involvement is well established as a leading cause of software project failure (The Standish Group 1995). Remind the protesters of problems they've experienced on previous projects that trace back to inadequate user involvement. Every organization has horror stories of new systems that didn't satisfy user needs or failed to meet unstated usability or performance expectations. You can't afford to rebuild or discard systems that don't measure up because no one understood the requirements. Product champions mitigate this risk.

Product Champion Traps to Avoid

The product champion model has succeeded in many environments. It works only when the product champion understands and signs up for his responsibilities, has the authority to make decisions at the user requirements level, and has the time to do the job. Watch out for the following potential problems:

- Some managers override the decisions that a qualified and duly authorized product champion makes. Perhaps the manager has a wild new idea at the last minute, wants to change the project direction at a whim, or thinks he knows what the users need. This behavior often results in dissatisfied users, late deliveries as the developers chase the latest management notion, and frustrated product champions who feel that management doesn't trust them.

- A product champion who forgets that he is representing other customers and presents only his own requirements won't do a good job. He might be happy with the outcome, but others likely won't be.

- A product champion who lacks a clear mental image of the new system might defer important decisions to the analyst. If any idea that the analyst has is okay with the champion, the champion isn't much help.

- A senior user might nominate a less experienced user as champion because he doesn't have time to do the job himself. This can lead to backseat driving from the senior user who still wishes to strongly influence the project's direction.

- Beware of users who purport to speak for a user class to which they do not belong. On Contoso's Chemical Tracking System, the product champion for the chemical stockroom staff also insisted on providing what she thought were the needs of the chemist user class. It was difficult to convince her that this wasn't her job, but the analyst didn't let her intimidate him. The project manager lined up a separate product champion for the chemists, and he did a great job of collecting, evaluating, and relaying that community's requirements.

Who Makes the Decisions?

Someone must resolve the conflicting requirements from different user classes, reconcile inconsistencies, and arbitrate the questions of scope that arise. Early in the project, determine who the decision makers will be for requirements issues. If it's not clear who is responsible for making these decisions or if the authorized individuals abdicate their responsibilities, the decisions will fall to the developers by default. This is a poor choice because developers usually don't have the necessary knowledge, experience, and perspective to make the best business decisions.

There's no globally correct answer to the question of who should make decisions about requirements on a software project. Analysts sometimes defer to the loudest voice they hear or to the person highest on the food chain. This is understandable, but it's not the best strategy. Decisions should be made as low in the organization's hierarchy as possible by people who are close to the issues and well informed about them. Every group should select an appropriate *decision rule*—an agreed-upon way to arrive at a decision—prior to encountering their first decision (Gottesdiener 2001). I favor participative or consultative decision making—that is, gathering the ideas and opinions of many stakeholders—over consensus decision making, which is gaining buy-in to the final decision from every affected stakeholder. Reaching a consensus is ideal, but you can't always hold up progress while waiting for every stakeholder to align on every issue.

Following are some requirements conflicts that can arise on projects with suggested ways to handle them. The project leaders need to determine who will decide what to do when such situations arise, who will make the call if agreement is not reached, and to whom significant issues must be escalated for ratifying the decisions made.

- If individual users disagree on requirements, the product champions decide. The essence of the product champion approach is that the champions are empowered and expected to resolve requirements conflicts that arise from those they represent.

- If different user classes or market segments present incompatible needs, go with the needs of the most favored user class or with the market segment that will have the greatest impact on the product's business success.

- Different corporate customers all might demand that the product be designed to satisfy their preferences. Again, use the business objectives for the project to determine which customers most strongly influence the project's success or failure.

- Requirements expressed by user managers sometimes conflict with those from the actual users in their departments. Although the user requirements must align with the business requirements, managers who aren't members of the user class should defer to the product champion who represents their users.

- When the product that the developers think they should build conflicts with what customers say they want, the customer should normally make the decision.

> **Trap**   Don't justify doing whatever any customer demands because "The customer is always right." The customer is *not* always right. The customer always has a point, though, and the software team must understand and respect that point.

- A similar situation arises if marketing or product management presents requirements that conflict with what developers think they should build. As customer surrogates, marketing's input should carry more weight. Nevertheless, I've seen cases where marketing never said no to a customer request, no matter how infeasible or expensive. I've seen other cases in which marketing provided little input and the developers had to define the product and write the requirements themselves.

These negotiations don't always turn out the way the analyst thinks they should. Customers might reject all attempts to consider reasonable alternatives and other points of view. The team needs to decide who will be making decisions on the project's requirements before they confront these types of issues. Otherwise, indecision and the revisiting of previous decisions can cause the project to stall in endless wrangling.

Next Steps

- Relate Figure 6-1 (on page 98) to the way you hear the voice of the customer in your own environment. Do you encounter any problems with your current communication links? Identify the shortest and most appropriate communication paths that you can use to gather user requirements in the future.

- Identify the different user classes for your project. Which ones are favored? Which, if any, are disfavored? Who would make a good product champion for each important user class?

- Use Table 6-2 (on page 105) as a starting point to define the activities you would like your product champions to perform. Negotiate the specific contributions with each candidate product champion and his or her manager.

- Determine who the decision makers are for requirements issues on your project. How well does your current decision-making approach work? Where does it break down? Are the right people making decisions? If not, who should be doing it? Suggest processes that the decision makers should use for reaching agreement on the requirements issues.

7

Hearing the Voice of the Customer

"Good morning, Maria. I'm Phil, the requirements analyst for the new employee information system we're going to build for you. Thanks for agreeing to be the product champion for this project. Your input will really help us a lot. So, can you tell me what you want?"

"Hmmm, what do I want," mused Maria. "I hardly know where to start. It should be a lot faster than the old system. And you know how the old system crashes if some employee has a really long name and we have to call the help desk and ask them to enter the name? The new system should take long names without crashing. Also, a new law says we can't use Social Security numbers for employee IDs anymore, so we'll have to change all the employee IDs when the new system goes in. The new IDs are going to be six-digit numbers. Oh, yes, it'd be great if I could get a report of how many hours of training each employee has had so far this year. And I also need to be able to change someone's name even if their marital status hasn't changed."

Phil dutifully wrote down everything Maria said, but his head was starting to spin. He wasn't sure what to do with all these bits of information, and he had no idea what to tell the developers. "Well," he thought, "if that's what Maria says she wants, I guess we'd better do it."

The heart of requirements engineering is *elicitation*, the process of identifying the needs and constraints of the various stakeholders for a software system. Elicitation focuses on discovering the user requirements, the middle level of the software requirements triad. (As described in Chapter 1, business requirements and functional requirements are the other two levels.) User requirements encompass the tasks that users need to accomplish with the system and the users' expectations of performance, usability, and other quality attributes. This chapter addresses the general principles of effective requirements elicitation.

The analyst needs a structure to organize the array of input obtained from requirements elicitation. Simply asking the users, "What do you want?" generates a mass of random information that leaves the analyst floundering. "What do you need to do?" is a much better question. Chapter 8, "Understanding User Requirements," describes how techniques such as use cases and event-response tables provide helpful organizing structures for user requirements.

The product of requirements development is a common understanding among the project stakeholders of the needs that are being addressed. Once the developers understand the needs, they can explore alternative solutions to address those needs. Elicitation participants should resist the temptation to design the system until they understand the problem. Otherwise, they can expect to do considerable design rework as the requirements become better defined. Emphasizing user tasks rather than user interfaces and focusing on root needs more than on expressed desires help keep the team from being side-tracked by prematurely specifying design details.

Begin by planning the project's requirements elicitation activities. Even a simple plan of action increases the chance of success and sets realistic expectations for the stakeholders. Only by gaining explicit commitment on resources, schedule, and deliverables can you avoid having people pulled off elicitation to fix bugs or do other work. Your plan should address the following items:

- Elicitation objectives (such as validating market data, exploring use cases, or developing a detailed set of functional requirements for the system)

- Elicitation strategies and processes (for example, some combination of surveys, workshops, customer visits, individual interviews, and other techniques, possibly using different approaches for different stakeholder groups)

- Products of elicitation efforts (perhaps a list of use cases, a detailed SRS, an analysis of survey results, or performance and quality attribute specifications)

- Schedule and resource estimates (identify both development and customer participants in the various elicitation activities, along with estimates of the effort and calendar time required)

- Elicitation risks (identify factors that could impede your ability to complete the elicitation activities as intended, estimate the severity of each risk, and decide how you can mitigate or control it)

Requirements Elicitation

Requirements elicitation is perhaps the most difficult, most critical, most error-prone, and most communication-intensive aspect of software development. Elicitation can succeed only through a collaborative partnership between customers and the development team, as described in Chapter 2. The analyst must create an environment conducive to a thorough exploration of the product being specified. To facilitate clear communication, use the vocabulary of the application domain instead of forcing customers to understand computer jargon. Capture significant application domain terms in a glossary, rather than assuming that all participants share the same definitions. Customers should understand that a discussion about possible functionality is not a commitment to include it in the product. Brainstorming and imagining the possibilities is a separate matter from analyzing priorities, feasibility, and the constraining realities. The stakeholders must focus and prioritize the blue-sky wish list to avoid defining an enormous project that never delivers anything useful.

Skill in conducting elicitation discussions comes with experience and builds on training in interviewing, group facilitation, conflict resolution, and similar activities. As an analyst, you must probe beneath the surface of the requirements the customers present to understand their true needs. Simply asking "why" several times can move the discussion from a presented solution to a solid understanding of the problem that needs to be solved. Ask open-ended questions to help you understand the users' current business processes and to see how the new system could improve their performance. Inquire about possible variations in the user tasks that the users might encounter and ways that other users might work with the system. Imagine yourself learning the user's job, or actually do the job under the user's direction. What tasks would you need to perform? What questions would you have? Another approach is to play the role of an apprentice learning from the master user. The user you are interviewing then guides the discussion and describes what he or she views as the important topics for discussion.

Probe around the exceptions. What could prevent the user from successfully completing a task? How should the system respond to various error conditions? Ask questions that begin with "What else could...," "What happens when...," "Would you ever need to...," "Where do you get...," "Why do you (or don't you)...," and "Does anyone ever..." Document the source of each requirement so that you can obtain further clarification if needed and trace development activities back to specific customer origins.

When you're working on a replacement project for a legacy system, ask the users, "What three things annoy you the most about the existing system?"

This question helps get to the bottom of why a system is being replaced. It also surfaces expectations that the users hold for the follow-on system. As with any improvement activity, dissatisfaction with the current situation provides excellent fodder for the new and improved future state.

Try to bring to light any assumptions the customers might hold and to resolve conflicting assumptions. Read between the lines to identify features or characteristics the customers expect to be included without their having explicitly said so. Gause and Weinberg (1989) suggest using *context-free questions*, high-level and open-ended questions that elicit information about global characteristics of both the business problem and the potential solution. The customer's response to questions such as "What kind of precision is required in the product?" or "Can you help me understand why you don't agree with Miguel's reply?" can lead to insights that questions with standard yes/no or A/B/C answers do not.

Rather than simply transcribing what customers say, a creative analyst suggests ideas and alternatives to users during elicitation. Sometimes users don't realize the capabilities that developers can provide and they get excited when you suggest functionality that will make the system especially useful. When users truly can't express what they need, perhaps you can watch them work and suggest ways to automate portions of the job. Analysts can think outside the box that limits the creativity of people who are too close to the problem domain. Look for opportunities to reuse functionality that's already available in another system.

Interviews with individuals or groups of potential users are a traditional source of requirements input for both commercial products and information systems. (For guidance on how to conduct user interviews, see Beyer and Holtzblatt [1998], Wood and Silver [1995], and McGraw and Harbison [1997].) Engaging users in the elicitation process is a way to gain support and buy-in for the project. Try to understand the thought processes that led the users to present the requirements they state. Walk through the processes that users follow to make decisions about their work and extract the underlying logic. Flowcharts and decision trees are useful ways to depict these logical decision paths. Make sure that everyone understands why the system *must* perform certain functions. Proposed requirements sometimes reflect obsolete or ineffective business processes that should not be incorporated into a new system.

After each interview, document the items that the group discussed and ask the interviewees to review the list and make corrections. Early review is essential to successful requirements development because only those people who supplied the requirements can judge whether they were captured accurately. Use further discussions to resolve any inconsistencies and to fill in any blanks.

Elicitation Workshops

Requirements analysts frequently facilitate requirements elicitation workshops. Facilitated, collaborative group workshops are a highly effective technique for linking users and developers (Keil and Carmel 1995). The facilitator plays a critical role in planning the workshop, selecting participants, and guiding the participants to a successful outcome. When a team is getting started with new approaches to requirements elicitation, have an outside facilitator lead the initial workshops. This way the analyst can devote his full attention to the discussion. A scribe assists the facilitator by capturing the points that come up during the discussion.

According to one authority, "Facilitation is the art of leading people through processes toward agreed-upon objectives in a manner that encourages participation, ownership, and productivity from all involved" (Sibbet 1994). A definitive resource on facilitating requirements elicitation workshops is Ellen Gottesdiener's *Requirements by Collaboration* (2002). Gottesdiener describes a wealth of techniques and tools for workshop facilitation. Following are a few tips for conducting effective elicitation sessions.

Establish ground rules.   The participants should agree on some basic operating principles for their workshops (Gottesdiener 2002). Examples include the following:

- Starting and ending meetings on time

- Returning from breaks promptly

- Holding only one conversation at a time

- Expecting everyone to contribute

- Focusing comments and criticisms on issues, not on individuals

Stay in scope.   Use the vision and scope document to confirm whether proposed user requirements lie within the current project scope. Keep each workshop focused on the right level of abstraction for that day's objectives. Groups easily dive into distracting detail during requirements discussions. Those discussions consume time that the group should spend initially on developing a higher-level understanding of user requirements; the details will come later. The facilitator will have to reel in the elicitation participants periodically to keep them on topic.

> **Trap**   Avoid drilling down into excessive requirements detail prematurely. Recording great detail about what people already understand doesn't reduce the risks due to uncertainty in the requirements.

It's easy for users to begin itemizing the precise layout of items in a report or a dialog box before the team even agrees on the pertinent user task. Recording these details as requirements places unnecessary constraints on the subsequent design process. Detailed user interface design comes later, although preliminary screen sketches can be helpful at any point to illustrate how you might implement the requirements. Early feasibility exploration, which requires some amount of design, is a valuable risk-reduction technique.

Use parking lots to capture items for later consideration.   An array of random but important information will surface in an elicitation workshop: quality attributes, business rules, user interface ideas, constraints, and more. Organize this information on flipcharts—parking lots—so that you don't lose it and to demonstrate respect for the participant who brought it up. Don't be distracted into discussing off-track details unless they turn out to be showstopper issues, such as a vital business rule that restricts the way a use case can work.

Timebox discussions.   The facilitator might allocate a fixed period of time to each discussion topic, say, 30 minutes per use case during initial use case explorations. The discussion might need to be completed later, but timeboxing helps avoid the trap of spending far more time than intended on the first topic and neglecting the other planned topics entirely.

Keep the team small and include the right participants.   Small groups can work much faster than larger teams. Elicitation workshops with more than five or six active participants can become mired in side trips down "rat holes," concurrent conversations, and bickering. Consider running multiple workshops in parallel to explore the requirements of different user classes. Workshop participants should include the product champion and other user representatives, perhaps a subject matter expert, a requirements analyst, and a developer. Knowledge, experience, and authority to make decisions are qualifications for participating in elicitation workshops.

Trap   Watch out for off-topic discussions, such as design explorations, during elicitation sessions.

Keep everyone engaged.   Sometimes participants will stop contributing to the discussion. These people might be frustrated because they see that the system is an accident waiting to happen. Perhaps their input isn't being taken seriously because other participants don't find their concerns interesting or don't want to disrupt the work that the group has completed so far. Perhaps the stakeholder who has withdrawn has a submissive personality and is deferring to more aggressive participants or a dominating analyst. The facilitator must read the body language, understand why someone has tuned out of the process, and try to bring the person back. That individual might hold an insightful perspective that could make an important contribution.

Too Many Cooks

Requirements elicitation workshops that involve too many participants can slow to a contentious crawl. My colleague Debbie was frustrated at the sluggish progress of the first use-case workshop she facilitated for a Web development project. The 12 participants held extended discussions of unnecessary details and couldn't agree on how each use case ought to work. The team's progress accelerated nicely when Debbie reduced the number of participants to six who represented the roles of analyst, customer, system architect, developer, and visual designer. The workshop lost some input by using the smaller team but the rate of progress more than compensated for that loss. The workshop participants should exchange information off-line with colleagues who don't attend and then bring the collected input to the workshops.

Classifying Customer Input

Don't expect your customers to present a succinct, complete, and well-organized list of their needs. Analysts must classify the myriad bits of requirements information they hear into various categories so that they can document and use it appropriately. Figure 7-1 illustrates nine such requirement categories.

Figure 7-1   Classifying the voice of the customer.

Information that doesn't fit into one of these buckets might be one of the following:

- A requirement not related to the software development, such as the need to train users on the new system

- A project constraint, such as a cost or schedule restriction (as opposed to the design or implementation constraints described in this chapter)

- An assumption

- A data requirement, which can often be associated with some system functionality (you store data in a computer only so that you can get it out again later)

- Additional information of a historical, context-setting, or descriptive nature

The following discussion suggests some phrases to listen for that will help you in this classification process.

Business requirements.   Anything that describes the financial, marketplace, or other business benefit that either customers or the developing organization wish to gain from the product is a business requirement. Listen for statements about the value that buyers or users of the software will receive, such as these:

■   "Increase market share by X%."

■   "Save $Y per year on electricity now wasted by inefficient units."

■   "Save $Z per year in maintenance costs that are consumed by legacy system W."

Use cases or scenarios.   General statements of user goals or business tasks that users need to perform are use cases; a single specific path through a use case is a usage scenario. Work with the customers to generalize specific scenarios into more abstract use cases. You can often glean use cases by asking users to describe their business workflow. Another way to discover use cases is to ask users to state the goals they have in mind when they sit down to work with the system. A user who says, "I need to <do something>" is probably describing a use case, as in the following examples:

■   "I need to print a mailing label for a package."

■   "I need to manage a queue of chemical samples waiting to be analyzed."

■   "I need to calibrate the pump controller."

Business rules.   When a customer says that only certain user classes can perform an activity under specific conditions, he might be describing a business rule. In the case of the Chemical Tracking System, such a business rule might be, "A chemist may order a chemical on the Level 1 hazard list only if his hazardous-chemical training is current." You might derive some software functional requirements to enforce the rules, such as making the training record database accessible to the Chemical Tracking System. As stated, though, business rules are not functional requirements. Following are some other phrases that suggest the user is describing a business rule:

■   "Must comply with <some law or corporate policy>"

■   "Must conform to <some standard>"

■   "If <some condition is true>, then <something happens>"

■   "Must be calculated according to <some formula>"

> **More Info**   See Chapter 9, "Playing by the Rules," for more examples of business rules.

Functional requirements.   Functional requirements describe the observable behaviors the system will exhibit under certain conditions and the actions the system will let users take. Functional requirements derived from system requirements, user requirements, business rules, and other sources make up the bulk of the SRS. Here are some examples of functional requirements as you might hear them from users:

- "If the pressure exceeds 40.0 psi, the high pressure warning light should come on."

- "The user must be able to sort the project list in forward and reverse alphabetical order."

- "The system sends an e-mail to the Idea Coordinator whenever someone submits a new idea."

These statements illustrate how users typically present functional requirements, but they don't represent good ways to write functional requirements in an SRS. In the first case, we would replace *should* with *shall* to make it clear that illuminating the warning light is essential. The second example is a requirement of the user, not of the system. The requirement of the system is to permit the user to do the sorting.

> **More Info**   Chapter 10, "Documenting the Requirements," contains more guidance for writing good functional requirements.

Quality attributes.   Statements that indicate how well the system performs some behavior or lets the user take some action are quality attributes. Listen for words that describe desirable system characteristics: fast, easy, intuitive, user-friendly, robust, reliable, secure, and efficient. You'll have to work with the users to understand precisely what they mean by these ambiguous and subjective terms and write clear, verifiable quality goals, as described in Chapter 12, "Beyond Functionality: Software Quality Attributes."

External interface requirements.   Requirements in this class describe the connections between your system and the rest of the universe. The SRS should include sections for interfaces to users, hardware, and other software systems. Phrases that indicate that the customer is describing an external interface requirement include the following:

- "Must read signals from <some device>"

- "Must send messages to <some other system>"

- "Must be able to read (or write) files in <some format>"

- "Must control <some piece of hardware>"

- "User interface elements must conform to <some UI style standard>"

Constraints.   Design and implementation constraints legitimately restrict the options available to the developer. Devices with embedded software often must respect physical constraints such as size, weight, and interface connections. Record the rationale behind each constraint so that all project participants know where it came from and respect its validity. Is it truly a restrictive limitation, as when a device must fit into an existing space? Or is it a desirable goal, such as a portable computer that weighs as little as possible?

Unnecessary constraints inhibit creating the best solution. Constraints also reduce your ability to use commercially available components as part of the solution. A constraint that specifies that a particular technology be used poses the risk of making a requirement obsolete or unattainable because of changes in the available technologies. Certain constraints can help achieve quality attribute goals. An example is to improve portability by using only the standard commands of a programming language, not permitting vendor-specific extensions. The following are examples of constraints that a customer might present:

- "Files submitted electronically may not exceed 10 MB in size."

- "The browser must use 128-bit encryption for all secure transactions."

- "The database must use the Framalam 10.2 run-time engine."

Other phrases that indicate the customer is describing a design or implementation constraint include these:

- "Must be written in <a specific programming language>"
- "Can't require more than <some amount of memory>"
- "Must operate identically to (or be consistent with) <some other system>"
- "Must use <a specific user interface control>"

As with functional requirements, the analyst shouldn't simply transcribe the user's statement of a constraint into the SRS. Weak words such as *identically* and *consistent* need to be clarified and the real constraint stated precisely enough for developers to act on the information. Ask why the constraint exists, verify its validity, and record the rationale for including the constraint as a requirement.

Data definitions.   Whenever customers describe the format, data type, allowed values, or default value for a data item or the composition of a complex business data structure, they're presenting a data definition. "The ZIP code consists of five digits, followed by an optional hyphen and an optional four digits that default to 0000" is a data definition. Collect these in a *data dictionary*, a master reference that the team can use throughout the product's development and maintenance.

More Info   See Chapter 10 for more information on data dictionaries.

Data definitions sometimes lead to functional requirements that the user community did not request directly. What happens when a six-digit order number rolls over from 999,999? Developers need to know how the system will handle such data issues. Deferring data-related problems just makes them harder to solve in the future (remember Y2K?).

Solution ideas.   Much of what users present as requirements fits in the category of solution ideas. Someone who describes a specific way to interact with the system to perform some action is presenting a suggested solution. The analyst needs to probe below the surface of a solution idea to get to the real requirement. For instance, functional requirements that deal with passwords are just one of several possible solutions for a security requirement.

Suppose a user says, "Then I select the state where I want to send the package from a drop-down list." The phrase *from a drop-down list* indicates that this is a solution idea. The prudent analyst will ask, "Why from a drop-down list?" If the user replies, "That just seemed like a good way to do it," the real requirement is something like, "The system shall permit the user to specify the state where he wants to send the package." However, maybe the user says, "I suggested a drop-down list because we do the same thing in several other places and I want it to be consistent. Also, it prevents the user from entering invalid data, and I thought we might be able to reuse some code." These are fine reasons to specify a specific solution. Recognize, though, that embedding a solution idea in a requirement imposes a design constraint on that requirement. It limits the requirement to being implemented in only one way. This isn't necessarily wrong or bad; just make sure the constraint is there for a good reason.

Some Cautions About Elicitation

Trying to amalgamate requirements input from dozens of users is difficult without using a structured organizing scheme, such as use cases. Collecting input from too few representatives or hearing the voice only of the loudest, most opinionated customer is also a problem. It can lead to overlooking requirements that are important to certain user classes or to including requirements that don't represent the needs of a majority of the users. The best balance involves a few product champions who have authority to speak for their respective user classes, with each champion backed up by several other representatives from that same user class.

During requirements elicitation, you might find that the project scope is improperly defined, being either too large or too small (Christel and Kang 1992). If the scope is too large, you'll collect more requirements than are needed to deliver adequate business and customer value and the elicitation process will drag on. If the project is scoped too small, customers will present needs that are clearly important yet just as clearly lie beyond the limited scope currently established for the project. The present scope could be too small to yield a satisfactory product. Eliciting user requirements therefore can lead to modifying the product vision or the project scope.

It's often stated that requirements are about *what* the system has to do, whereas *how* the solution will be implemented is the realm of design. Although attractively concise, this is an oversimplification. Requirements elicitation should indeed focus on the *what*, but there's a gray area—not a sharp line—between analysis and design. Hypothetical *hows* help to clarify and refine the understanding of what users need. Analysis models, screen sketches, and prototypes help to make the needs expressed during requirements elicitation more tangible and to reveal errors and omissions. Regard the models and screens generated during requirements development as conceptual suggestions to facilitate effective communication, not as constraints on the options available to the designer. Make it clear to users that these screens and prototypes are illustrative only, not necessarily the final design solution.

The need to do exploratory research sometimes throws a monkey wrench into the works. An idea or a suggestion arises, but extensive research is required to assess whether it should even be considered for possible incorporation into the product. Treat these explorations of feasibility or value as project tasks in their own right, with objectives, goals, and requirements of their own. Prototyping is one way to explore such issues. If your project requires extensive research, use an incremental development approach to explore the requirements in small, low-risk portions.

Finding Missing Requirements

Missing requirements constitute the most common type of requirement defect (Jones 1997). They're hard to spot during reviews because they're invisible! The following techniques will help you detect previously undiscovered requirements.

> **Trap**   Watch out for the dreaded *analysis paralysis*, spending too much time on requirements elicitation in an attempt to avoid missing any requirements. You'll never discover them all up front.

- Decompose high-level requirements into enough detail to reveal exactly what is being requested. A vague, high-level requirement that leaves much to the reader's interpretation will lead to a gap between what the requester has in mind and what the developer builds. Imprecise, fuzzy terms to avoid include *support, enable, permit, process,* and *manage.*

■   Make sure that all user classes have provided input. Make sure that each use case has at least one identified actor.

■   Trace system requirements, use cases, event-response lists, and business rules into their detailed functional requirements to make sure that the analyst derived all the necessary functionality.

■   Check boundary values for missing requirements. Suppose that one requirement states, "If the price of the order is less than $100, the shipping charge is $5.95" and another says, "If the price of the order is more than $100, the shipping charge is 5 percent of the total order price." But what's the shipping charge for an order with a price of exactly $100? It's not specified, so a requirement is missing.

■   Represent requirements information in multiple ways. It's difficult to read a mass of text and notice that something isn't there. An analysis model visually represents requirements at a high level of abstraction—the forest, not the trees. You might study a model and realize that there should be an arrow from one box to another; that missing arrow represents a missing requirement. This kind of error is much easier to spot in a picture than in a long list of textual requirements that all blur together. Analysis models are described in Chapter 11, "A Picture Is Worth 1024 Words."

■   Sets of requirements with complex Boolean logic (ANDs, ORs, and NOTs) often are incomplete. If a combination of logical conditions has no corresponding functional requirement, the developer has to deduce what the system should do or chase down an answer. Represent complex logic using decision tables or decision trees to make sure you've covered all the possible situations, as described in Chapter 11.

A rigorous way to search for missing requirements is to create a CRUD matrix. *CRUD* stands for *Create, Read, Update,* and *Delete.* A CRUD matrix correlates system actions with data entities (individual data items or aggregates of data items) to make sure that you know where and how each data item is created, read, updated, and deleted. Some people add an *L* to the matrix to indicate that the data item appears as a *List* selection (Ferdinandi 2002). Depending on the requirements analysis approaches you are using, you can examine various types of correlations, including the following:

- Data entities and system events (Robertson and Robertson 1999)

- Data entities and user tasks or use cases (Lauesen 2002)

- Object classes and system events (Ferdinandi 2002)

- Object classes and use cases (Armour and Miller 2001)

Figure 7-2 illustrates an entity/use case CRUDL matrix for a portion of the Chemical Tracking System. Each cell indicates how the use case in the leftmost column uses each data entity shown in the other columns. The use case can **C**reate, **R**ead, **U**pdate, **D**elete, or **L**ist the entity. After creating a CRUDL matrix, see whether any of these five letters do not appear in any of the cells in a column. If a business object is updated but never created, where does it come from? Notice that none of the cells under the column labeled Requester (the person who places an order for a chemical) contains a *D*. That is, none of the use cases in Figure 7-2 can delete a Requester from the list of people who have ordered chemicals. There are three possible interpretations:

1. Deleting a Requester is not an expected function of the Chemical Tracking System.

2. We are missing a use case that deletes a Requester.

3. The "Edit Requesters" use case is incorrect. It's supposed to permit the user to delete a Requester, but that functionality is missing from the use case at present.

We don't know which interpretation is correct, but the CRUDL analysis is a powerful way to detect missing requirements.

Entity / Use Case	Order	Chemical	Requester	Vendor Catalog
Place Order	C	R	R	R, L
Change Order	U, D		R	R, L
Manage Chemical Inventory		C, U, D		
Report on Orders	R	R, L	R, L	
Edit Requesters			C, U, L	

Figure 7-2   Sample CRUDL matrix for the Chemical Tracking System.

How Do You Know When You're Done?

No simple signal will indicate when you've completed requirements elicitation. As people muse in the shower each morning and talk with their colleagues, they'll generate ideas for additional requirements. You'll never be completely done, but the following cues suggest that you're reaching the point of diminishing returns on requirements elicitation:

- If the users can't think of any more use cases, perhaps you're done. Users tend to identify use cases in sequence of decreasing importance.

- If users propose new use cases but you've already derived the associated functional requirements from other use cases, perhaps you're done. These "new" use cases might really be alternative courses for other use cases that you've already captured.

- If users repeat issues that they already covered in previous discussions, perhaps you're done.

- If suggested new features, user requirements, or functional requirements are all out of scope, perhaps you're done.

- If proposed new requirements are all low priority, perhaps you're done.

- If the users are proposing capabilities that might be included "sometime in the lifetime of the product" rather than "in the specific product we're talking about right now," perhaps you're done, at least with the requirements for the next release.

Another way to determine whether you're done is to create a checklist of common functional areas to consider for your projects. Examples include error logging, backup and restore, access security, reporting, printing, preview capabilities, and configuring user preferences. Periodically compare this list with the functions you have already specified. If you don't find gaps, perhaps you're done.

Despite your best efforts to discover *all* the requirements, you won't, so expect to make changes as construction proceeds. Remember, your goal is to make the requirements good enough to let construction proceed at an acceptable level of risk.

Next Steps

- Think about missing requirements that were discovered late on your last project. Why were they overlooked during elicitation? How could you have discovered each of these requirements earlier?

- Select a portion of any documented voice-of-the-customer input on your project or a section from the SRS. Classify every item in that requirements fragment into the categories shown in Figure 7-1 (on page 120): business requirements, use cases or scenarios, business rules, functional requirements, quality attributes, external interface requirements, constraints, data definitions, and solution ideas. If you discover items that are classified incorrectly, move them to the correct place in the requirements documentation.

- List the requirements elicitation methods used on your current project. Which ones worked well? Why? Which ones did not work so well? Why not? Identify elicitation techniques that you think would work better and decide how you'd apply them next time. Identify any barriers you might encounter to making those techniques work and brainstorm ways to overcome those barriers.

8

Understanding User Requirements

The Chemical Tracking System project was holding its first requirements elicitation workshop to learn what chemists would need to do with the system. The participants included the requirements analyst, Lori, who was also facilitating; the product champion for the chemists, Tim; two other chemist representatives, Sandy and Peter; and the lead developer, Helen. Lori opened the workshop by thanking the participants for attending and then got right down to business.

"Tim, Sandy, and Peter have identified about 15 use cases that chemists would need to perform using the Chemical Tracking System," she told the group. "In these workshops we'll explore these use cases so that we know what functionality to build into the system. You identified the use case called 'Request a Chemical' as top priority and Tim already wrote a brief description for it, so let's begin there. Tim, how do you imagine requesting a chemical with the system?"

"First," said Tim, "you should know that only people who have been authorized by their lab managers are allowed to request chemicals."

"Okay, that sounds like a business rule," Lori replied. "I'll start a flipchart for business rules because we'll probably find others. It looks like we'll have to verify that the user is on the approved list." She also wrote "user is identified" and "user is authorized to request chemicals" in the "Preconditions" section of the flipchart she had already prepared for the "Request a Chemical" use case. "Are there any other prerequisites before a user can create a request?"

"Before I request a chemical from a vendor, I want to see if it's already available in the stockroom," Sandy said. "The current inventory database should be online when I start to create a request so I don't waste my time."

Lori added that item to the preconditions. Over the next 30 minutes, she guided the group through a discussion of how they envisioned creating a request for a new chemical. She used several flipcharts to collect information about preconditions, postconditions, and the steps in the interaction between the user and the Chemical Tracking System. Lori asked how the use case would be different if the user were requesting a chemical from a vendor rather than from the stockroom. She asked what could go wrong and how the system should handle each error condition. After a half hour, the group had a solid handle on how a user would request a chemical. They moved on to the next use case.

People employ software systems to accomplish useful goals, and the software industry is exhibiting an encouraging trend toward designing software to enhance usability (Constantine and Lockwood 1999; Nielsen 2000). A necessary prerequisite to designing software for use is knowing what the users intend to do with it.

For many years, analysts have employed usage scenarios to elicit user requirements (McGraw and Harbison 1997). A *scenario* is a description of a single instance of usage of the system. Ivar Jacobson and colleagues (1992), Larry Constantine and Lucy Lockwood (1999), Alistair Cockburn (2001), and others have formalized the usage-centered perspective into the use-case approach to requirements elicitation and modeling. Use cases work well for developing the requirements for business applications, Web sites, services that one system provides to another, and systems that let a user control a piece of hardware. Applications such as batch processes, computationally intensive systems, and data warehousing applications might have just a few simple use cases. The complexity of these applications lies in the computations performed or the reports generated, not in the user-system interaction. A requirements technique often used for real-time systems is to list the external events to which the system must react and the corresponding system responses. This chapter describes the application of both use cases and event-response tables to capture user requirements.

Trap   Don't try to force every requirement you encounter to fit into a use case. Use cases can reveal most—but probably not all—of the functional requirements.

The Use-Case Approach

A *use case* describes a sequence of interactions between a system and an external actor. An *actor* is a person, another software system, or a hardware device that interacts with the system to achieve a useful goal (Cockburn 2001). Another name for actor is *user role*, because actors are roles that the members of one or more user classes can perform with respect to the system (Constantine and Lockwood 1999). For example, the Chemical Tracking System's use case called "Request a Chemical" involves an actor named *Requester*. There is no Chemical Tracking System user class named Requester. Both chemists and members of the chemical stockroom staff may request chemicals, so members of either user class may perform the Requester role.

Use cases emerged from the object-oriented development world. However, projects that follow any development approach can use them because the user doesn't care how the software is built. Use cases are at the center of the widely used Unified Software Development Process (Jacobson, Booch, and Rumbaugh 1999).

Use cases shift the perspective of requirements development to discussing what *users* need to accomplish, in contrast to the traditional elicitation approach of asking users what they want the *system* to do. The objective of the use-case approach is to describe all tasks that users will need to perform with the system. The stakeholders ensure that each use case lies within the defined project scope before accepting it into the requirements baseline. In theory, the resulting set of use cases will encompass all the desired system functionality. In practice, you're unlikely to reach complete closure, but use cases will bring you closer than any other elicitation technique I have used.

Use-case diagrams provide a high-level visual representation of the user requirements. Figure 8-1 shows a partial use-case diagram for the Chemical Tracking System, using the UML notation (Booch, Rumbaugh, and Jacobson 1999; Armour and Miller 2001). The box represents the system boundary. Lines from each actor (stick figure) connect to the use cases (ovals) with which the actor interacts. Note the resemblance of this use-case diagram to the context diagram in Figure 5-3 (on page 91). In the use-case diagram, the box separates some top-level internals of the system—the use cases—from the external actors. The context diagram also depicts objects that lie outside the system, but it provides no visibility into the system internals.

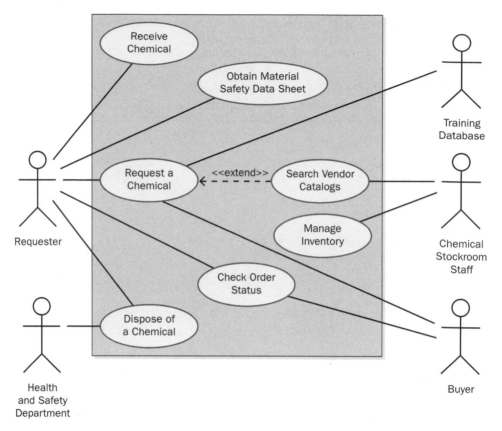

Figure 8-1   Partial use-case diagram for the Chemical Tracking System.

Use Cases and Usage Scenarios

A *use case* is a discrete, stand-alone activity that an actor can perform to achieve some outcome of value. A single use case might encompass a number of similar tasks having a common goal. A use case is therefore a collection of related usage scenarios, and a scenario is a specific instance of a use case. When exploring user requirements, you can start with abstract use cases and develop concrete usage scenarios, or you can generalize from a specific scenario to the broader use case. Later in this chapter we'll see a detailed template for documenting use cases. The essential elements of a use-case description are the following:

■   A unique identifier

■   A name that succinctly states the user task in the form of "verb + object," such as "Place an Order"

■   A short textual description written in natural language

■   A list of preconditions that must be satisfied before the use case can begin

- Postconditions that describe the state of the system after the use case is successfully completed

- A numbered list of steps that shows the sequence of dialog steps or interactions between the actor and the system that leads from the preconditions to the postconditions

One scenario is identified as the *normal course* of events for the use case; it is also called the main course, basic course, normal flow, primary scenario, main success scenario, and happy path. The normal course for the "Request a Chemical" use case is to request a chemical that's available in the chemical stockroom.

Other valid scenarios within the use case are described as *alternative courses* or *secondary scenarios* (Schneider and Winters 1998). Alternative courses also result in successful task completion and satisfy the use case's postconditions. However, they represent variations in the specifics of the task or in the dialog sequence used to accomplish the task. The normal course can branch off into an alternative course at some decision point in the dialog sequence and rejoin the normal course later. Although most use cases can be described in simple prose, a flowchart or a UML activity diagram is a useful way to visually represent the logic flow in a complex use case, as shown in Figure 8-2. Flowcharts and activity diagrams show the decision points and conditions that cause a branch from the main course into an alternative course.

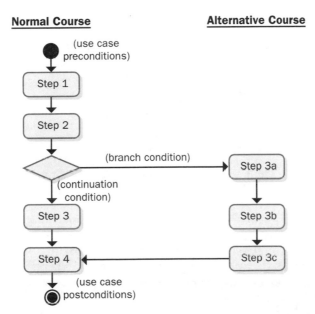

Figure 8-2   UML activity diagram illustrating the dialog flow in the normal and alternative courses of a use case.

An alternative course for the Request a Chemical use case is "Request a Chemical from a Vendor." The actor's ultimate goal—request a chemical—is the same in both situations, so these are two scenarios within the same use case. Some of the steps in an alternative course will be the same as those in the normal course, but certain unique actions are needed to accomplish the alternative path. In this alternative course, the user can search vendor catalogs for a desired chemical. If an alternative course is itself a stand-alone use case, you can *extend* the normal course by inserting that separate use case into the normal flow (Armour and Miller 2001). The use-case diagram in Figure 8-1 illustrates the extends relationship. The "Search Vendor Catalogs" use case extends the "Request a Chemical" use case. In addition, the chemical stockroom staff use the stand-alone "Search Vendor Catalogs" use case by itself.

Sometimes several use cases share a common set of steps. To avoid duplicating these steps in each such use case, define a separate use case that contains the shared functionality and indicate that the other use cases *include* that sub use case. This is analogous to calling a common subroutine in a computer program.

As an example, consider an accounting software package. Two use cases are "Pay Bill" and "Reconcile Credit Card," both of which involve the user writing a check to make the payment. You can create a separate use case called "Write Check" that contains the common steps involved in writing the check. The two transaction use cases both include the "Write Check" use case, as shown in Figure 8-3.

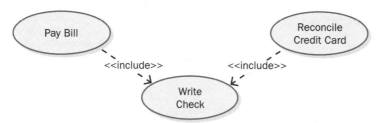

Figure 8-3   An example of the use-case *includes* relationship for an accounting application.

> **Trap**   Don't have protracted debates over when, how, and whether to use the *extends* and *includes* relationships. Factoring common steps into an included use case is the most typical usage.

Conditions that prevent a task from succeeding are called *exceptions*. One exception for the "Request a Chemical" use case is "Chemical is not commercially available." If you don't specify exception handling during elicitation, there are two possible outcomes:

1. The developers will make their best guesses at how to deal with the exceptions.

2. The system will fail when a user hits the error condition because no one thought about it.

It's a safe bet that system crashes aren't on the user's list of requirements.

Exceptions are sometimes regarded as a type of alternative course (Cockburn 2001), but it's useful to separate them. You won't necessarily implement every alternative course that you identify for a use case, and you might defer some to later releases. However, you *must* implement the exceptions that can prevent the scenarios that you do implement from succeeding. Anyone who has done computer programming knows that exceptions often generate the bulk of the coding effort. Many of the defects in a finished product reside in exception handlers (or missing exception handlers!). Specifying exception conditions during requirements elicitation is a way to build robust software products.

In many systems, the user can chain together a sequence of use cases into a "macro" use case that describes a larger task. Some use cases for a commercial Web site might be "Search Catalog," "Add Item to Shopping Cart," and "Pay for Items in Shopping Cart." If you can perform each of these activities independently, they are individual use cases. You might also be able to perform all three tasks in a row as a single large use case called "Buy Product," as shown in Figure 8-4. To make this work, each use case must leave the system in a state that enables the user to commence the next use case immediately. That is, the postconditions of one use case must satisfy the preconditions of the next one in the sequence. Similarly, in a transaction-processing application such as an ATM, each use case must leave the system in a state that permits the next transaction to begin. The preconditions and postconditions of each transaction use case must align.

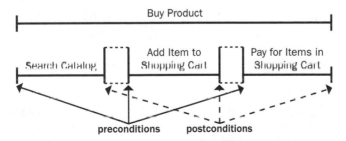

Figure 8-4   Preconditions and postconditions define the boundaries of the individual use cases that can be chained together to perform a larger task.

Identifying Use Cases

You can identify use cases in several ways (Ham 1998; Larman 1998):

- Identify the actors first, and then identify the business processes in which each participates.

- Identify the external events to which the system must respond, and then relate these events to participating actors and specific use cases.

- Express business processes in terms of specific scenarios, generalize the scenarios into use cases, and identify the actors involved in each use case.

- Derive likely use cases from existing functional requirements. If some requirements don't trace to any use case, consider whether you really need them.

The Chemical Tracking System followed the first approach. The analysts facilitated a series of two- to three-hour use-case elicitation workshops, which were held about twice a week. Members of the various user classes participated in separate, parallel workshops. This worked well because only a few use cases were common to multiple user classes. Each workshop included the user class's product champion, other selected user representatives, and a developer. Participating in the elicitation workshops gives developers early insight into the product they will be expected to build. Developers also serve as the voice of reality when infeasible requirements are suggested.

Prior to beginning the workshops, each analyst asked the users to think of tasks they would need to perform with the new system. Each of these tasks became a candidate use case. A few proposed use cases were judged to be out of scope and weren't pursued. As the group explored the use cases in the workshops, they found that some of them were related scenarios that could be consolidated into a single abstract use case. The group also discovered additional use cases beyond those in the initial set.

Some users proposed use cases that were not phrased as a task, such as "Material Safety Data Sheet." A use case's name should indicate the goal the user wants to accomplish, so you need a verb. Does the user want to view, print, order, e-mail, revise, delete, or create a material safety data sheet? Sometimes a suggested use case was just one step the actor would perform as part of the use case, such as "scan bar code." The analyst needs to learn what objective the user has in mind that involves scanning a bar code. The analyst might ask, "When you scan the bar code on the chemical container, what are you trying to accomplish?" Suppose the reply is, "I need to scan the bar code so that I can log the chemical into my laboratory." The real use case, therefore, is something like "Log Chemical

Into Lab." Scanning the bar code label is just one step in the interaction between the actor and the system that logs the chemical into the lab.

Users typically identify their most important use cases first, so the discovery sequence gives some clues as to priority. Another prioritization approach is to write a short description of each candidate use case as it is proposed. Prioritize these candidate use cases and do an initial allocation of use cases to specific product releases. Specify the details for the highest priority use cases first so that the developers can begin implementing them as soon as possible.

Documenting Use Cases

At this stage of the exploration, the participants should be thinking of essential use cases. Constantine and Lockwood (1999) define an *essential use case* as "...a simplified, generalized, abstract, technology-free and implementation-independent description of one task or interaction...that embodies the purpose or intentions underlying the interaction." That is, the focus should be on the goal the user is trying to accomplish and the system's responsibilities in meeting that goal. Essential use cases are at a higher level of abstraction than *concrete use cases*, which discuss specific actions the user takes to interact with the system. To illustrate the difference, consider the following two ways to describe how a user might initiate a use case to request a chemical:

Concrete   Enter the chemical ID number.

Essential   Specify the desired chemical.

The phrasing at the essential level allows many ways to accomplish the user's intention of indicating the chemical to be requested: enter a chemical ID number, import a chemical structure from a file, draw the structure on the screen with the mouse, select a chemical from a list, and others. Proceeding too quickly into specific interaction details begins to constrain the thinking of the use-case workshop participants. The independence from implementation also makes essential use cases more reusable than concrete use cases.

The participants in the Chemical Tracking System workshops began each discussion by identifying the actor who would benefit from the use case and writing a short description of the use case. Then they defined the preconditions and postconditions, which are the boundaries of the use case; all use-case steps take place between these boundaries. Estimating the frequency of use provided an early indicator of concurrent usage and capacity requirements. Next, the analyst asked the participants how they envisioned interacting with the system to perform the task. The resulting sequence of actor actions and system responses became the normal course. Numbering the steps made the sequence clear. Although each participant had a different mental image of the future user interface and specific interaction mechanisms, the group was able to reach a common vision of the essential steps in the actor-system dialog.

Staying in Bounds

While reviewing a use case that contained eight steps, I realized that the postconditions were satisfied after step 5. Steps 6, 7, and 8 therefore were unnecessary, being outside the boundary of the use case. Similarly, a use case's preconditions must be satisfied prior to commencing step 1 of the use case. When you review a use-case description, make sure that its pre- and postconditions properly frame it.

The analyst captured the individual actor actions and system responses on sticky notes, which he placed on a flipchart sheet. Another way to conduct such a workshop is to project a use-case template onto a large screen from a computer and complete the template during the discussion, although this might slow the discussion down.

The elicitation team developed similar dialogs for the alternative courses and exceptions they identified. A user who says, "The default should be…" is describing the normal course of the use case. A phrase such as "The user should also be able to…" suggests an alternative course. Many exception conditions were discovered when the analyst asked questions similar to "What should happen if the database isn't online at that moment?" or "What if the chemical is not commercially available?" The workshop is also a good time to discuss the user's expectations of quality, such as response times, system availability and reliability, user interface design constraints, and security requirements.

After the workshop participants described each use case and no one proposed additional variations, exceptions, or special requirements, they moved on to another use case. They didn't try to cover all the use cases in one marathon workshop or to pin down every detail of every use case they discussed. Instead, they planned to explore the use cases in increments, and then review and refine them into further detail iteratively.

Figure 8-5 shows the sequence of events for developing the use cases. Following the workshop, the analyst wrote a detailed description of each use case like the description in Figure 8-6. There are two ways to represent the actor-system dialog steps, which is the heart of the use case. Figure 8-6 shows the dialog as a numbered list of steps, indicating which entity (the system or a specific actor) performs each step. The same notation is used to describe alternative courses and exceptions, which also show the step in the normal course at which the alternative branches off or where the exception could take place. Another technique is to present the dialog in a two column table, as shown in Figure 8-7 (Wirfs-Brock 1993). The actor actions are shown on the left and the system responses on the right. The numbers indicate the sequence of steps in the dialog. This scheme works well when only a single actor is interacting with the system. To improve the readability, you can write each actor action or system response on a separate line so that the alternating sequence is clear, as shown in Figure 8-8.

Use cases often involve some additional information or requirements that do not fit within any of the template sections. Use the "Special Requirements" section to record pertinent quality attributes, performance requirements, and similar information. Also note any information that might not be visible to the users, such as the need for one system to communicate behind the scenes with another to complete the use case.

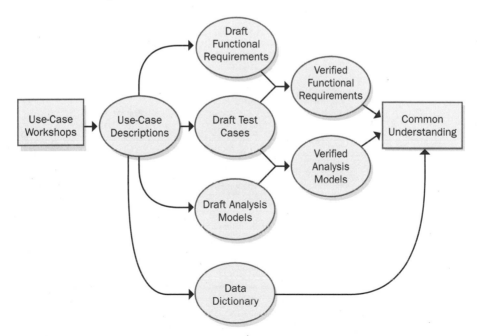

Figure 8-5   Use-case elicitation approach.

Use Case ID	**UC-1**	Use Case Name	**Request a Chemical**
Created By	Tim	Last Updated By	Janice
Date Created	12/4/02	Date Last Updated	12/27/02

Actors	Requester
Description	The Requester specifies the desired chemical to request by entering its name or chemical ID number or by importing its structure from a chemical drawing tool. The system satisfies the request either by offering the Requester a new or used container of the chemical from the chemical stockroom or by letting the Requester create a request to order from an outside vendor.
Preconditons	1. User's identity has been authenticated. 2. User is authorized to request chemicals. 3. Chemical inventory database is online.
Postconditions	1. Request is stored in the Chemical Tracking System. 2. Request was e-mailed to the chemical stockroom or to a Buyer.
Normal Course	**1.0 Request a Chemical from the Chemical Stockroom** 1. Requester specifies the desired chemical. 2. System verifies that the chemical is valid. 3. System lists containers of the desired chemical that are in the chemical stockroom. 4. Requester has the option to View Container History for any container. 5. Requester selects a specific container or asks to place a vendor order (alternative course 1.1). 6. Requester enters other information to complete the request. 7. System stores request and e-mails it to chemical stockroom.
Alternative Courses	**1.1 Request a Chemical from a Vendor (branch after step 5)** 1. Requester searches vendor catalogs for a chemical. 2. System displays a list of vendors with available container sizes, grades, and prices. 3. Requester selects a vendor, container size, grade, and number of containers. 4. Requester enters other information to complete the request. 5. System stores request and e-mails it to Buyer.
Exceptions	**1.0.E.1 Chemical is not valid (at step 2)** 1. System displays message: "That chemical does not exist." 2. System asks Requester whether he wishes to request another chemical or to exit. 3a. Requester asks to request another chemical. 4a. System starts Normal Course over. 3b. Requester asks to exit. 4b. System terminates use case. **1.0.E.2 Chemical is not commercially available (at step 5)** 1. System displays message: "No vendors for that chemical." 2. System asks Requester whether he wishes to request another chemical or to exit. 3a. Requester asks to request another chemical. 4a. System starts Normal Course over. 3b. Requester asks to exit. 4b. System terminates use case.
Includes	**UC-22** View Container History
Priority	High
Frequency of Use	Approximately five times per week by each chemist, 100 times per week by each member of chemical stockroom staff.
Business Rules	**BR-28** Only staff who are authorized by their laboratory managers may request chemicals.
Special Requirements	1. The system must be able to import a chemical structure in the standard encoded form from any of the supported chemical drawing packages.
Assumptions	1. Imported chemical structures are assumed to be valid.
Notes and Issues	1. Tim will find out whether management approval is needed to request a chemical on the Level 1 hazard list. Due date 1/4/03.

Figure 8-6   Partial description of the "Request a Chemical" use case.

Actor Actions	System Responses
1. Specify the desired chemical. 4. If desired, ask to view the history of any container. 5. Select a specific container (done) or ask to place a vendor order (alternative course 1.1).	2. Verify that the chemical requested is valid. 3. Display a list of containers of the desired chemical that are in the chemical stockroom's current inventory.

Figure 8-7   Describing a use-case dialog in a two-column format.

Actor Actions	System Responses
1. Specify the desired chemical.	
	2. Verify that the chemical requested is valid. 3. Display a list of containers of the desired chemical that are in the chemical stockroom's current inventory.
4. If desired, ask to view the history of any container. 5. Select a specific container (done) or ask to place a vendor order (alternative course 1.1).	

Figure 8-8   Alternative layout for describing a use-case dialog in a two-column format.

You don't always need a comprehensive use-case description. Alistair Cockburn (2001) describes *casual* and *fully dressed* use-case templates. Figure 8-6 illustrates a fully dressed use case. A casual use case is simply a textual narrative of the user goal and interactions with the system, perhaps just the "Description" section from Figure 8-6. The user stories that serve as requirements in Extreme Programming are essentially casual use cases typically written on index cards (Jeffries, Anderson, and Hendrickson 2001). Fully dressed use-case descriptions are valuable when

- Your user representatives are not closely engaged with the development team throughout the project.

- The application is complex and has a high risk associated with system failures.

- The use-case descriptions are the lowest level of requirements detail that the developers will receive.

- You intend to develop comprehensive test cases based on the user requirements.

- Collaborating remote teams need a detailed, shared group memory.

> **Trap**   Instead of being dogmatic about how much detail to include in
> a use case, remember your goal: to understand the user's objectives
> with the system well enough to enable developers to proceed at low
> risk of having to do rework.

The process in Figure 8-5 shows that after each workshop, the analysts on the Chemical Tracking System derived software functional requirements from the use-case descriptions. (For more about this, see the next section in this chapter, "Use Cases and Functional Requirements.") They also drew analysis models for some of the complex use cases, such as a state-transition diagram that showed all possible chemical request statuses and the permitted status changes.

> **More Info**   Chapter 11, "A Picture is Worth 1024 Words," illustrates
> several analysis models for the Chemical Tracking System.

A day or two after each workshop the analyst gave the use-case descriptions and functional requirements to the workshop participants, who reviewed them prior to the next workshop. These informal reviews revealed many errors: previously undiscovered alternative courses, new exceptions, incorrect functional requirements, and missing dialog steps. Leave at least one day between successive workshops. The mental relaxation that comes after a day or two away from an intellectually intensive activity allows people to examine their earlier work from a fresh perspective. One analyst who held workshops every day learned that the participants had difficulty finding errors in the documents they reviewed because the information was too fresh in their minds. They mentally recited the workshop discussion that had just taken place and didn't see the errors.

> **Trap**   Don't wait until requirements elicitation is complete to solicit
> review feedback from users, developers, and other stakeholders.

Early in the requirements development process, the Chemical Tracking System's test lead created conceptual test cases, independent of implementation specifics, from the use cases (Collard 1999). These test cases helped the team share a clear understanding of how the system should behave in specific usage scenarios. The test cases let the analysts verify whether they had derived all the functional requirements needed to let users perform each use case. During the final elicitation workshop, the participants walked through the test cases together to be sure they agreed on how the use cases should work. As with any quality control activity, they found additional errors in both the requirements and the test cases.

More Info   Chapter 15, "Validating the Requirements," discusses generating test cases from requirements in more detail.

Use Cases and Functional Requirements

Software developers don't implement business requirements or use cases. They implement functional requirements, specific bits of system behavior that allow users to execute use cases and achieve their goals. Use cases describe system behavior from an actor's point of view, which omits a lot of details. A developer needs many other views to properly design and implement a system.

Some practitioners regard the use cases as being the functional requirements. However, I have seen organizations get into trouble when they simply handed use-case descriptions to developers for implementation. Use cases describe the user's perspective, looking at the externally visible behavior of the system. They don't contain all the information that a developer needs to write the software. For instance, the user of an ATM doesn't care about any back-end processing the ATM must perform, such as communicating with the bank's computer. This detail is invisible to the user, yet the developer needs to know about it. Of course, the use-case descriptions can include this kind of back-end processing detail, but it typically won't come up in discussions with end users. Developers who are presented with even fully dressed use cases often have many questions. To reduce this uncertainty, I recommend that requirements analysts explicitly specify the detailed functional requirements necessary to implement each use case (Arlow 1998).

Many functional requirements fall right out of the dialog steps between the actor and the system. Some are obvious, such as "The system shall assign a unique sequence number to each request." There is no point in duplicating those details in an SRS if they are perfectly clear from reading the use case. Other functional requirements don't appear in the use-case description. The analyst will derive them from an understanding of the use case and the system's operating environment. This translation from the user's view of the requirements to the developer's view is one of the many ways the requirements analyst adds value to the project.

The Chemical Tracking System employed the use cases primarily as a mechanism to reveal the necessary functional requirements. The analysts wrote only casual descriptions of the less complex use cases. They then derived all the functional requirements that, when implemented, would allow the actor to perform the use case, including alternative courses and exception handlers. The analysts documented these functional requirements in the SRS, which was organized by product feature.

You can document the functional requirements associated with a use case in several ways. The approach you choose depends on whether you expect your team to perform the design, construction, and testing from the use-case documents, from the SRS, or from a combination of both. None of these methods is perfect, so select the approach that best fits with how you want to document and manage your project's software requirements.

Use Cases Only

One possibility is to include the functional requirements right in each use-case description. You'll still need a separate supplementary specification to contain the nonfunctional requirements and any functional requirements that are not associated with specific use cases. Several use cases might need the same functional requirement. If five use cases require that the user's identity be authenticated, you don't want to write five different blocks of code for that purpose. Rather than duplicate them, cross-reference functional requirements that appear in multiple use cases. In some instances, the use-case *includes* relationship discussed earlier in this chapter solves this problem.

Use Cases and SRS

Another option is to write fairly simple use-case descriptions and document the functional requirements derived from each use case in an SRS. In this approach, you'll need to establish traceability between the use cases and their associated functional requirements. The best way to manage the traceability is to store all use cases and functional requirements in a requirements management tool.

> **More Info**   See Chapter 21 for more information on requirements management tools.

SRS Only

A third approach is to organize the SRS by use case or by feature and include both the use cases and the functional requirements in the SRS. This is the approach that the Chemical Tracking System team used. This scheme doesn't use separate use-case documents. You'll need to identify duplicated functional requirements or state every functional requirement only once and refer to that initial statement whenever the requirement reappears in another use case.

Benefits of Use Cases

The power of the use-case approach comes from its task-centric and user-centric perspective. The users will have clearer expectations of what the new system will let them do than if you take a function-centric approach. The customer representatives on several Internet development projects found that use cases clarified their notions of what visitors to their Web sites should be able to do. Use cases help analysts and developers understand both the user's business and the application domain. Carefully thinking through the actor-system dialog sequences can reveal ambiguity and vagueness early in the development process, as does generating test cases from the use cases.

It's frustrating and wasteful for developers to write code that never gets used. Overspecifying the requirements up front and trying to include every conceivable function can lead to implementing unnecessary requirements. The use-case approach leads to functional requirements that will allow the user to perform certain known tasks. This helps prevent "orphan functionality," those functions that seem like a good idea during elicitation but which no one uses because they don't relate directly to user tasks.

The use-case approach helps with requirements prioritization. The highest priority functional requirements are those that originated in the top priority use cases. A use case could have high priority for several reasons:

- It describes one of the core business processes that the system enables.

- Many users will use it frequently.

- A favored user class requested it.

- It provides a capability that's required for regulatory compliance.

- Other system functions depend on its presence.

> **Trap**   Don't spend a lot of time detailing use cases that won't be implemented for months or years. They're likely to change before construction begins.

There are technical benefits, too. The use-case perspective reveals some of the important domain objects and their responsibilities to each other. Developers using object-oriented design methods can turn use cases into object models such as class and sequence diagrams. (Remember, though, use cases are by no means restricted to object-oriented development projects.) As the business processes change over time, the tasks that are embodied in specific use cases will change. If you've traced functional requirements, designs, code, and tests back to their parent use cases—the voice of the customer—it will be easier to cascade those business-process changes throughout the entire system.

Use-Case Traps to Avoid

As with any software engineering technique, there are many ways to go astray when applying the use-case approach (Kulak and Guiney 2000; Lilly 2000). Watch out for the following traps:

- **Too many use cases**   If you're caught in a use-case explosion, you might not be writing them at the appropriate level of abstraction. Don't create a separate use case for every possible scenario. Instead, include the normal course, alternative courses, and exceptions as scenarios within a single use case. You'll typically have many more use cases than business requirements and features, but many more functional requirements than use cases.

- **Highly complex use cases**   I once reviewed a use case that had four dense pages of dialog steps, with a lot of embedded logic and branching conditions. It was incomprehensible. You don't have control over the complexity of the business tasks, but you can control how you represent them in use cases. Select one success path through the use case, with one combination of true and false values for the various logical decisions, and call that the normal course. Use alternative courses for the other logic branches that lead to success, and use exceptions to handle the branches that lead to failure. You might have many alternative courses, but each one will be short and easy to understand. To keep them simple, write use cases in terms of the essence of the actor and system behaviors instead of specifying every action in great detail.

- **Including user interface design in the use cases**   Use cases should focus on what the users need to accomplish with the system's help, not on how the screens will look. Emphasize the conceptual interactions between the actors and the system, and defer user interface specifics to the design stage. For example, say "System presents choices" instead of "System displays drop-down list." Don't let the user interface design drive the requirements exploration. Use screen sketches and dialog maps (user interface architecture diagrams, as described in Chapter 11) to help visualize the actor-system interactions, not as firm design specifications.

■ **Including data definitions in the use cases**   I've seen use cases that included definitions of the data items and structures that are manipulated in the use case. This approach makes it difficult for project participants to find the definitions they need because it isn't obvious which use case contains each data definition. It can also lead to duplicate definitions, which get out of synch when one instance is changed and others are not. Instead of sprinkling them throughout the use cases, collect data definitions in a project-wide data dictionary, as discussed in Chapter 10, "Documenting the Requirements."

■ **Use cases that users don't understand**   If users can't relate the use-case description to their business processes or system tasks, there's a problem with the use case. Write use cases from the user's perspective, not the system's point of view, and ask users to review them. Perhaps the complexity of fully dressed use cases is overkill for your situation.

■ **New business processes**   Users will have difficulty coming up with use cases if software is being built to support a process that doesn't yet exist. Rather than requirements elicitation being a matter of modeling the business process, it might be a matter of inventing one. It's risky to expect a new information system to drive the creation of an effective business process. Perform the business process reengineering before fully specifying the new information system.

■ **Excessive use of *includes* and *extends* relationships**   Working with use cases for the first time requires a change in the way that analysts, users, and developers think about requirements. The subtleties of the use-case *includes* and *extends* relationships can be confusing. They are best avoided until you gain a comfort level with the use-case approach.

Event-Response Tables

Another way to organize and document user requirements is to identify the external events to which the system must respond. An *event* is some change or activity that takes place in the user's environment that stimulates a response from the software system (McMenamin and Palmer 1984; Wiley 2000). An *event-response table* (also called an *event table* or an *event list*) lists all such events and the behavior the system is expected to exhibit in reaction to each event. There are several types of system events, as shown in Figure 8-9 and described here:

■   An action by a human user that stimulates a dialog with the software, as when the user initiates a use case (sometimes called a *business event*). The event-response sequences correspond to the dialog steps in a use case. Unlike use cases, the event-response table does not describe the user's goal in using the system or state why this event-response sequence provides value to the user.

■   A control signal, data reading, or interrupt received from an external hardware device, such as when a switch closes, a voltage changes, or the user moves the mouse.

■   A time-triggered event, as when the computer's clock reaches a specified time (say, to launch an automatic data export operation at midnight) or when a preset duration has passed since a previous event (as in a system that logs the temperature read by a sensor every 10 seconds).

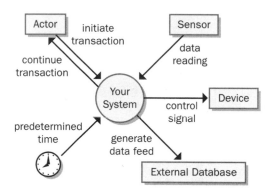

Figure 8-9   Examples of system events and responses.

Event-response tables are particularly appropriate for real-time control systems. Table 8-1 contains a sample event-response table that partially describes the behavior of an automobile's windshield wipers. Note that the expected response depends not only on the event but also on the state the system is in at the time the event takes place. For instance, events 4 and 5.1 in Table 8-1 result in slightly different behaviors depending on whether the wipers were on at the time the user set the wiper control to the intermittent setting. A response might simply alter some internal system information (events 4 and 7.1 in the table) or it could result in an externally visible result (most other events).

The event-response table records information at the user-requirements level. If the table defines and labels every possible combination of event, state, and response (including exception conditions), the table can also serve as part of the functional requirements for that portion of the system. However, the analyst must supply additional functional and nonfunctional requirements in the SRS. For example, how many cycles per minute does the wiper perform on the slow and fast wipe settings? Do the intermittent wipes operate at the slow or fast speed? Is the intermittent setting continuously variable or does it have discrete settings? What are the minimum and maximum delay times between intermittent wipes? If you stop requirements specification at the user-requirements level, the developer has to track down this sort of information himself. Remember, the goal is to specify the requirements precisely enough that a developer knows what to build.

Notice that the events listed in Table 8-1 are written at the *essential level* (describing the essence of the event), not at the *implementation level* (describing the specifics of the implementation). Table 8-1 shows nothing about what the windshield wiper controls look like or how the user manipulates them. The designer could implement these requirements with anything from the traditional stalk-mounted wiper controls in current automobiles to a system that uses voice recognition of spoken commands: "wipers on," "wipers off," "wipers fast," "wipe once," and so on. Writing user requirements at the essential level avoids imposing unnecessary design constraints. However, record any known design constraints to guide the designer's thinking.

Table 8-1   Event-Response Table for an Automobile Windshield-Wiper System

ID	Event	System State	System Response
1.1	set wiper control to low speed	wiper off	set wiper motor to low speed
1.2	set wiper control to low speed	wiper on high speed	set wiper motor to low speed
1.3	set wiper control to low speed	wiper on intermittent	set wiper motor to low speed
2.1	set wiper control to high speed	wiper off	set wiper motor to high speed
2.2	set wiper control to high speed	wiper on low speed	set wiper motor to high speed
2.3	set wiper control to high speed	wiper on intermittent	set wiper motor to high speed
3.1	set wiper control set to off	wiper on high speed	1. complete current wipe cycle 2. turn wiper motor off
3.2	set wiper control set to off	wiper on low speed	1. complete current wipe cycle 2. turn wiper motor off
3.3	set wiper control set to off	wiper on intermittent	1. complete current wipe cycle 2. turn wiper motor off

Table 8-1   Event-Response Table for an Automobile Windshield-Wiper System

ID	Event	System State	System Response
4	set wiper control to intermittent	wiper off	1. read wipe time interval setting 2. initialize wipe timer
5.1	set wiper control to intermittent	wiper on high speed	1. read wipe time interval setting 2. complete current wipe cycle 3. initialize wipe timer
5.2	set wiper control to intermittent	wiper on low speed	1. read wipe time interval setting 2. complete current wipe cycle 3. initialize wipe timer
6	wipe time interval has passed since completing last cycle	wiper on intermittent	perform one low-speed wipe cycle
7.1	change intermittent wiper interval	wiper on intermittent	1. read wipe time interval setting 2. initialize wipe timer
7.2	change intermittent wiper interval	wiper off	no response
7.3	change intermittent wiper interval	wiper on high speed	no response
7.4	change intermittent wiper interval	wiper on low speed	no response
8	immediate wipe signal received	wiper off	perform one low-speed wipe cycle

 Next Steps

■   Write several use cases for your current project using the template in Figure 8-6 (on page 142). Include any alternative courses and exceptions. Identify the functional requirements that will allow the user to successfully complete each use case. Check whether your current SRS already includes all these functional requirements.

■   List the external events that could stimulate your system to behave in specific ways. Create an event-response table that shows the state the system is in when each event is received and how the system is to respond.

9

Playing by the Rules

"Hi, Tim, this is Jackie. I'm having a problem requesting a chemical with the Chemical Tracking System. My manager suggested that I ask you about it. He said you were the product champion who provided many of the requirements for this system."

"Yes, that's correct," Tim replied. "What's the problem?"

"I need to get some more phosgene for those dyes that I make for my research project," said Jackie, "but the Chemical Tracking System won't accept my request. It says I haven't taken a training class in handling hazardous chemicals in more than a year. What's that all about? I've been using phosgene and even nastier chemicals for years with no problem. Why can't I get some more?"

"You're probably aware that Contoso Pharmaceuticals requires an annual refresher class in the safe handling of hazardous chemicals," Tim pointed out. "This is a corporate policy; the Chemical Tracking System just enforces it. I know the stockroom guys used to give you whatever you wanted, but we can't do that anymore for liability insurance reasons. Sorry about the inconvenience, but we have to comply with the rule. You'll have to take the refresher training before the system will let you request more phosgene."

Every business organization operates according to an extensive set of corporate policies, laws, and industry standards. Industries such as banking, aviation, and medical device manufacture must comply with volumes of government regulations. Such controlling principles are collectively known as *business rules*. Software applications often enforce these business rules. In other cases, business rules aren't enforced in software but are controlled through human enforcement of policies and procedures.

Most business rules originate outside the context of any specific software application. Rules such as the corporate policy requiring annual training in handling hazardous chemicals apply even if all chemical purchasing and dispensing is done manually. Standard accounting practices applied even in the days of green eyeshades and fountain pens. However, business rules are a major source of software functional requirements because they dictate capabilities that the system must possess to conform to the rules. Even high-level business requirements can be driven by business rules, such as the Chemical Tracking System's need to generate reports to comply with federal and state regulations regarding chemical storage and disposal.

Not all companies treat their essential business rules as the valuable asset they are. If this information is not properly documented and managed, it exists only in the heads of individuals. Various individuals can have conflicting understandings of the rules, which can lead to different software applications enforcing a common business rule inconsistently. If you know where and how each application implements its pertinent business rules, it's much easier to change the applications when a rule changes.

> **Trap**   Undocumented business rules known only to experts result in a knowledge vacuum when those experts retire or change jobs.

In a large enterprise, only a subset of the collected business rules will pertain to any one software application. Building a collection of rules helps each requirements analyst identify potential sources of requirements that might not otherwise come up in discussions with users. Having a master repository of business rules makes it easier for all applications that are affected by the rules to implement them in a consistent fashion.

The Rules of the Business

According to the Business Rules Group (1993), "A business rule is a statement that defines or constrains some aspect of the business. It is intended to assert business structure or to control or influence the behavior of the business." Whole methodologies have been developed based on the discovery and documentation of business rules and their implementation in automated business rules systems (Ross 1997; von Halle 2002). Unless you're building a system that is heavily business-rule driven, you don't need an elaborate methodology. Simply identify and document the rules that pertain to your system and link them to specific functional requirements.

Many different *taxonomies* (classification schemes) have been proposed for organizing business rules (Ross 2001; Morgan 2002; von Halle 2002). The simple scheme shown in Figure 9-1, with five types of business rules, will work for most situations. A sixth category is *terms*, defined words, phrases, and abbreviations that are important to the business. A glossary is a convenient place to define terms. Recording the business rules in a consistent way so that they add value to your software development efforts is more important than having heated arguments about how to classify each one. Let's look at the different kinds of business rules you might encounter.

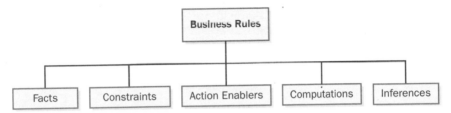

Figure 9-1   A simple business rule taxonomy.

Facts

Facts are simply statements that are true about the business. Often facts describe associations or relationships between important business terms. Facts are also called *invariants*—immutable truths about data entities and their attributes. Other business rules might refer to certain facts, but facts themselves don't usually translate directly into software functional requirements. Facts about data entities that are important to the system might appear in data models that the analyst or database designer creates. (See Chapter 11, "A Picture Is Worth 1024 Words," for more information about data modeling.) Examples of facts are:

- Every chemical container has a unique bar code identifier.

- Every order must have a shipping charge.

- Each line item in an order represents a specific combination of chemical, grade, container size, and number of containers.

- Nonrefundable tickets incur a fee when the purchaser changes the itinerary.

- Sales tax is not computed on shipping charges.

Constraints

Constraints restrict the actions that the system or its users may perform. Some words and phrases that suggest someone is describing a constraint business rule are *must, must not, may not,* and *only.* Examples of constraints are:

- A borrower who is less than 18 years old must have a parent or a legal guardian as cosigner on the loan.

- A library patron may place up to 10 items on hold.

- A user may request a chemical on the Level 1 hazard list only if he has had hazardous-chemical training within the past 12 months.

- All software applications must comply with government regulations for usage by visually impaired persons.

- Correspondence may not display more than four digits of the policy-holder's Social Security number.

- Commercial airline flight crews must receive at least eight hours of continuous rest in every 24-hour period.

So Many Constraints

Software projects have many kinds of constraints. Project managers must work within schedule, staff, and budget limitations. These project-level constraints belong in the software project management plan. Product-level design and implementation constraints that restrict the choices available to the developer belong in the SRS or the design specification. Many business rules impose constraints on the way the business operates. Whenever these constraints are reflected in the software functional requirements, indicate the pertinent rule as the rationale for each such derived requirement.

Your organization likely has security policies that control access to information systems. Such policies typically state that passwords will be used and present rules regarding frequency of required password changes, whether or not previous passwords may be reused, and the like. These are all constraints about application access that could be considered business rules. Tracing each such rule into the specific code that implements it makes it easier to update systems to comply with changes in the rules, such as changing the required frequency of password changes from 90 days to 30 days.

Overruled

I recently redeemed some of my frequent-flyer miles on Fly-By-Night Airlines to buy a ticket for my wife, Chris. When I attempted to finalize the purchase, FlyByNight.com told me that it had encountered an error and couldn't issue the ticket. It told me to call 800-FLY-NITE immediately. The reservation agent I spoke with told me that the airline couldn't issue a mileage award ticket through the mail or e-mail because Chris and I have different last names. I had to go to the airport ticket counter and show identification to have the ticket issued.

This incident resulted from this constraining business rule: "If the passenger has a different last name from the mileage redeemer, then the redeemer must pick up the ticket in person." The reason for this business rule is probably fraud prevention. The software driving the Fly-By-Night Web site enforces the rule, but in a way that resulted in inconvenience for the customer and in usability shortcomings. Rather than simply telling me about the rule regarding different last names and what I needed to do, the system displayed an alarming error message. It wasted my time and the Fly-By-Night reservation agent's time with an unnecessary phone call. Poorly thought-out business rule implementations can have an adverse effect on your customer and hence on your business.

Action Enablers

A rule that triggers some activity under specific conditions is an *action enabler*. A person could perform the activity in a manual process. Alternatively, the rule might lead to specifying some software functionality that makes an application exhibit the correct behavior when the specified conditions are true. The conditions that lead to the action could be complex combinations of true and false values for multiple individual conditions. A decision table such as that shown in Chapter 11 provides a concise way to document action-enabling business rules that involve extensive logic. A statement in the form "If <some condition is true or some event takes place>, then <something happens>" is a clue that someone is describing an action enabler. Following are some examples of action-enabling business rules:

- If the chemical stockroom has containers of a requested chemical in stock, then offer existing containers to the requester.

- If the expiration date for a chemical container has been reached, then notify the person who currently possesses that container.

- On the last day of a calendar quarter, generate the mandated OSHA and EPA reports on chemical handling and disposal for that quarter.

- If the customer ordered a book by an author who has written multiple books, then offer the author's other books to the customer before accepting the order.

Inferences

Sometimes called *inferred knowledge*, an *inference* is a rule that establishes some new knowledge based on the truth of certain conditions. An inference creates a new fact from other facts or from computations. Inferences are often written in the "if/then" pattern also found in action-enabling business rules, but the "then" clause of an inference implies a fact or a piece of information, not an action to be taken. Some examples of inferences are:

- If a payment is not received within 30 calendar days of the date it is due, then the account is delinquent.

- If the vendor cannot ship an ordered item within five days of receiving the order, then the item is back-ordered.

- A container of a chemical that can form explosive decomposition products is considered expired one year after its manufacture date.

- Chemicals with an LD_{50} toxicity lower than 5 mg/kg in mice are considered hazardous.

Computations

Computers compute, so one class of business rules defines *computations* that are performed using specific mathematical formulas or algorithms. Many computations follow rules that are external to the enterprise, such as income tax withholding formulas. Whereas action-enabling business rules lead to specific software functional requirements to enforce them, computational rules can normally serve as software requirements as they are stated. Following are some examples of computational business rules in text form; alternatively, you could represent these in some symbolic form, such as a mathematical expression. Presenting such rules in the form of a table, as Table 9-1 does, is clearer than writing a long list of complex natural language rule statements.

- The unit price is reduced by 10% for orders of 6 to 10 units, by 20% for orders of 11 to 20 units, and by 35% for orders of more than 20 units.

- The domestic ground shipping charge for an order that weighs more than 2 pounds is $4.75 plus 12 cents per ounce or fraction thereof.

- The commission for securities trades completed on line is $12 per trade of 1 through 5000 shares. The commission for trades conducted through an account officer is $45 per trade of 1 through 5000 shares. Commissions on trades of greater than 5000 shares are one-half of these commissions.

- The total price for an order is computed as the sum of the price of the items ordered, less any volume discounts, plus state and county sales tax for the location to which the order is being shipped, plus the shipping charge, plus an optional insurance charge.

Table 9-1   Using a Table to Represent Computational Business Rules

ID	Number of Units Purchased	Percent Discount
DISC-1	1 through 5	0
DISC-2	6 through 10	10
DISC-3	11 through 20	20
DISC-4	more than 20	35

A single computation could include many elements. The total price computation in the final example in the preceding list includes volume discount, sales tax, shipping charge, and insurance charge computations. That rule is complicated and hard to understand. To correct this shortcoming, write your business rules at the atomic level, rather than combining many details into a single rule. A complex rule can point back to the individual rules upon which it relies. This keeps your rules short and simple. It also facilitates reusing the rules and combining them in various ways. To write inferred knowledge and action-enabling business rules in an atomic way, don't have "or" logic on the left-hand side of an "if/then" construct and avoid "and" logic on the right hand side (von Halle 2002). Atomic business rules that could affect the total price computation in the last example in the preceding list include the discount rules in Table 9-1 and the following:

- If the delivery address is in a state that has a sales tax, then the state sales tax is computed on the total discounted price of the items ordered.

- If the delivery address is in a county that has a sales tax, then the county sales tax is computed on the total discounted price of the items ordered.

- The insurance charge is 1 percent of the total discounted price of the items ordered.

- Sales tax is not computed on shipping charges.

- Sales tax is not computed on insurance charges.

These business rules are called *atomic* because they can't be decomposed further. You will likely end up with many atomic business rules, and your computations and functional requirements will depend on various groupings of them.

Documenting Business Rules

Because business rules can influence multiple applications, organizations should manage their business rules as enterprise-level—not project-level—assets. A simple business rules catalog will suffice initially. Large organizations or those whose business operations and information systems are heavily business-rule driven should establish a database of business rules. Commercial rule-management tools become valuable if your rules catalog outgrows a word processor or spreadsheet solution or if you want to automate aspects of implementing the rules in your applications. The Business Rules Group maintains a list of business-rule management products at *http://www.businessrules-group.org/brglink.htm*. As you identify new rules while working on an application, add them to your catalog rather than embedding them in the documentation for that specific application or—worse—only in its code. Rules related to safety, security, finance, or regulatory compliance pose the highest risk if they are not managed and enforced appropriately.

> **Trap**   Don't make your business rules catalog more complex than necessary. Use the simplest form of documenting business rules that ensures that your development teams will use them effectively.

As you gain experience with identifying and documenting business rules, you can apply structured templates for defining rules of different types (Ross 1997; von Halle 2002). These templates describe patterns of keywords and clauses that structure the rules in a consistent fashion. They also facilitate storing the rules in a database, a commercial business-rule management tool, or a rule engine. To begin, though, try the simple format illustrated in Table 9-2 (Kulak and Guiney 2000).

As shown in this table, giving each business rule a unique identifier lets you trace functional requirements back to a specific rule. The "Type of Rule" column identifies the rule as being a fact, a constraint, an action enabler, an inference, or a computation. The "Static or Dynamic" column indicates how likely the rule is to change over time. Sources of business rules include corporate and management policies, subject matter experts and other individuals, documents such as government regulations, and existing software code or database definitions.

Table 9-2 **Sample Business Rules Catalog**

ID	Rule Definition	Type of Rule	Static or Dynamic	Source
ORDER-15	A user may request a chemical on the Level 1 hazard list only if he has had hazardous-chemical training within the past 12 months.	Constraint	Static	Corporate policy
DISC-13	An order discount is calculated based on the size of the current order, as defined in Table 9-1.	Computation	Dynamic	Corporate policy

Business Rules and Requirements

Simply asking users "What are your business rules?" doesn't get you very far, just as asking "What do you want?" doesn't help much when eliciting user requirements. Depending on the application, sometimes you invent business rules as you go along and sometimes you discover them during requirements discussions. Often the project stakeholders already know about business rules that will influence the application, and the development team must work within the boundaries that the rules define. Barbara von Halle (2002) describes a comprehensive process for discovering business rules.

During user requirements elicitation workshops, the analyst can ask questions to probe around the rationale for the requirements and constraints that users present. These discussions frequently surface business rules as the underlying rationale. The analyst can harvest business rules during elicitation workshops that also define other requirements artifacts and models (Gottesdiener 2002). Figure 9-2 shows several potential origins of rules (and, in some cases, of use cases and functional requirements). The figure also suggests the types of questions the analyst can ask when workshop participants are discussing various issues and objects. The analyst should document the business rules that come out of these elicitation discussions and ask the right people to confirm their correctness and to supply any missing information.

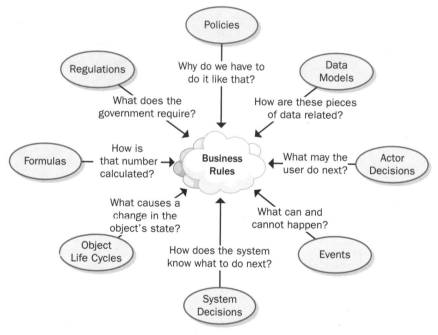

Figure 9-2 Discovering business rules by asking questions from different perspectives.

After identifying and documenting business rules, determine which ones must be implemented in the software. Some rules will lead to use cases and hence to functional requirements that enforce the rule. Consider the following three rules:

- **Rule #1 (action enabler)** "If the expiration date for a chemical container has been reached, then notify the person who currently possesses that container."

- **Rule #2 (inference)** "A container of a chemical that can form explosive decomposition products is considered expired one year after its manufacture date."

- **Rule #3 (fact)**   "Ethers can spontaneously form explosive peroxides."

These rules serve as the origin for a use case called "Notify Chemical Owner of Expiration." One functional requirement for that use case is "The system shall e-mail a notification to the current owner of a chemical container on the date the container expires."

You can define the links between a functional requirement and its parent business rules in the following two ways:

- Use a requirement attribute called "Origin" and indicate the rules as the origin of the functional requirement. (See Chapter 18, "Requirements Management Principles and Practices.")

- Define traceability links between a functional requirement and the pertinent business rules in the requirements traceability matrix. (See Chapter 20, "Links in the Requirements Chain.")

Data referential integrity rules frequently are implemented in the form of database triggers or stored procedures. Such rules describe the data updates, insertions, and deletions that the system must perform because of relationships between data entities (von Halle 2002). For example, the system must delete all undelivered line items in an order if the customer cancels the order.

Sometimes business rules and their corresponding functional requirements look much alike. However, the rules are external statements of policy that must be enforced in software, thereby driving system functionality. Every analyst must decide which existing rules pertain to his application, which ones must be enforced in the software, and how to enforce them.

Recall the constraint rule from the Chemical Tracking System requiring that training records be current before a user can request a hazardous chemical. The analyst would derive different functional requirements to comply with this rule, depending on whether the training records database is available on line. If it is, the system can simply look up the user's training record and decide whether to accept or reject the request. If the records aren't available on-line, the system might store the chemical request temporarily and send e-mail to the training coordinator, who in turn could either approve or reject the request. The rule is the same in either situation, but the software functional requirements— the actions to take when the business rule is encountered during execution— vary depending on the system's environment.

To prevent redundancy, don't duplicate rules from your business rules catalog in the SRS. Instead, the SRS should refer back to specific rules as the source of, say, algorithms for income tax withholding. This approach provides several advantages:

■ It obviates the need to change both the business rule and the corresponding functional requirements if the rule changes.

■ It keeps the SRS current with rule changes because the SRS simply refers to the master copy of the rule.

■ It facilitates reusing the same rule in several places in the SRS and across multiple projects without risking an inconsistency, because the rules are not buried in the documentation for any single application.

A developer reading the SRS will need to follow the cross-reference link to access the rule details. This is the trade-off that results when you elect not to duplicate information. There's another risk of keeping the rules separate from the functional requirements: Rules that make sense in isolation might not be so sensible when viewed in an operational context with other requirements. As with so many aspects of requirements engineering, there is no simple, perfect solution to managing business rules that works in all situations.

Organizations that do a masterful job of managing their business rules often don't publicly share their experiences. They view their use of business rules to guide their software portfolio management as providing a competitive advantage over organizations that deal with their rules more casually. Once you begin actively looking for, recording, and applying business rules, the rationale behind your application development choices will become clearer to all stakeholders.

 Next Steps

■ List all the business rules you can think of that pertain to the project you are currently working on. Begin populating a business rule catalog, classifying the rules according to the scheme shown in Figure 9-1 (on page 155), and noting the origin of each rule.

■ Identify the rationale behind each of your functional requirements to discover other business rules.

■ Set up a traceability matrix to indicate which functional requirements or database elements implement each of the business rules that you identified.

10

Documenting the Requirements

The result of requirements development is a documented agreement between customers and developers about the product to be built. As we saw in earlier chapters, the vision and scope document contains the business requirements, and the user requirements often are captured in the form of use cases. The product's detailed functional and nonfunctional requirements reside in a software requirements specification (SRS). Unless you write all these requirements in an organized and readable fashion and have key project stakeholders review them, people will not be sure what they're agreeing to.

We can represent software requirements in several ways:

- Documents that use well-structured and carefully written natural language

- Graphical models that illustrate transformational processes, system states and changes between them, data relationships, logic flows, or object classes and their relationships

- Formal specifications that define requirements using mathematically precise formal logic languages

Formal specifications provide the greatest rigor and precision, but few software developers—and fewer customers—are familiar with them, so they can't review the specifications for correctness. See Davis (1993) for references to further discussions of formal specification methods. Despite its shortcomings, structured natural language, augmented with graphical models, remains the most practical way for most software projects to document their requirements.

Even the finest requirements specification can never replace interpersonal discussions throughout the project. It's impossible to discover every fragment of information that feeds into software development up front. Keep the communication lines open between the development team, customer representatives, testers, and other stakeholders so that they can quickly address the myriad issues that will arise.

This chapter addresses the purpose, structure, and contents of the SRS. It presents guidelines for writing functional requirements, along with examples of flawed requirements and suggestions for improving them. As an alternative to traditional word-processing documents, the requirements can be stored in a database, such as a commercial requirements management tool. These tools make it much easier to manage, use, and communicate the requirements, but they're only as good as the quality of the information they hold. Chapter 21 discusses requirements management tools.g

The Software Requirements Specification

The software requirements specification is sometimes called a *functional specification,* a *product specification*, a *requirements document*, or a *system specification*, although organizations do not use these terms in the same way. The SRS precisely states the functions and capabilities that a software system must provide and the constraints that it must respect. The SRS is the basis for all subsequent project planning, design, and coding, as well as the foundation for system testing and user documentation. It should describe as completely as necessary the system's behaviors under various conditions. It should not contain design, construction, testing, or project management details other than known design and implementation constraints.

Several audiences rely on the SRS:

- Customers, the marketing department, and sales staff need to know what product they can expect to be delivered.

- Project managers base their estimates of schedule, effort, and resources on the product description.

- The SRS tells the software development team what to build.

- The testing group uses the SRS to develop test plans, cases, and procedures.

- The SRS tells maintenance and support staff what each part of the product is supposed to do.

- Documentation writers base user manuals and help screens on the SRS and the user interface design.

- Training personnel use the SRS and user documentation to develop educational materials.

- Legal staff ensure that the requirements comply with applicable laws and regulations.

- Subcontractors base their work on, and can be legally held to, the SRS.

As the ultimate repository for the product requirements, the SRS must be comprehensive. Developers and customers should make no assumptions. If any desired capability or quality doesn't appear somewhere in the requirements agreement, no one should expect it to appear in the product.

You don't have to write the SRS for the entire product before beginning development, but you do need to capture the requirements for each increment before building that increment. Incremental development is appropriate when the stakeholders cannot identify all the requirements at the outset and if it's imperative to get some functionality into the users' hands quickly. However, every project should baseline an agreement for each set of requirements before the team implements them. *Baselining* is the process of transitioning an SRS under development into one that has been reviewed and approved. Working from the same set of requirements minimizes miscommunication and unnecessary rework.

Organize and write the SRS so that the diverse stakeholders can understand it. Chapter 1, "The Essential Software Requirement," presented several characteristics of high-quality requirements statements and specifications. Keep the following requirements readability suggestions in mind:

- Label sections, subsections, and individual requirements consistently.

- Leave text ragged on the right margin, rather than fully justified.

- Use white space liberally.

- Use visual emphasis (such as bold, underline, italics, and different fonts) consistently and judiciously.

- Create a table of contents and perhaps an index to help readers find the information they need.

- Number all figures and tables, give them captions, and refer to them by number.

- Use your word processor's cross-reference facility rather than hard-coded page or section numbers to refer to other locations within a document.

- Use hyperlinks to let the reader jump to related sections in the SRS or in other documents.

- Use an appropriate template to organize all the necessary information.

Labeling Requirements

To satisfy the quality criteria of traceability and modifiability, every functional requirement must be uniquely and persistently identified. This allows you to refer to specific requirements in a change request, modification history, cross-reference, or requirements traceability matrix. It also facilitates reusing the requirements in multiple projects. Bullet lists aren't adequate for these purposes. Let's look at the advantages and shortcomings of several requirements-labeling methods. Select whichever technique makes the most sense for your situation.

Sequence Number

The simplest approach gives every requirement a unique sequence number, such as UR-9 or SRS-43. Commercial requirements management tools assign such an identifier when a user adds a new requirement to the tool's database. (The tools also support hierarchical numbering.) The prefix indicates the requirement type, such as *UR* for *user requirement*. A number is not reused if a requirement is deleted. This simple numbering approach doesn't provide any logical or hierarchical grouping of related requirements, and the labels give no clues as to what each requirement is about.

Hierarchical Numbering

In the most commonly used convention, if the functional requirements appear in section 3.2 of your SRS, they will all have labels that begin with 3.2 (for example, 3.2.4.3). More digits indicate a more detailed, lower-level requirement. This method is simple and compact. Your word processor can assign the numbers automatically. However, the labels can grow to many digits in even a medium-sized SRS. In addition, numeric labels tell you nothing about the purpose of each requirement. More seriously, this scheme does not generate persistent labels. If you insert a new requirement, the numbers of all following requirements in that section will be incremented. Delete or move a requirement, and the numbers following it in that section will be decremented. These changes disrupt any references to those requirements elsewhere in the system.

> **Trap**   An analyst once told me, "We don't let people insert requirements—it messes up the numbering." Don't let ineffective practices hamper your ability to work effectively and sensibly.

An improvement over hierarchical numbering is to number the major sections of the requirements hierarchically and then identify individual functional requirements in each section with a short text code followed by a sequence number. For example, the SRS might contain "Section 3.5—Editor Functions," and the requirements in that section could be labeled ED-1, ED-2, and so forth. This approach provides some hierarchy and organization while keeping the labels short, somewhat meaningful, and less positionally dependent.

Hierarchical Textual Tags

Consultant Tom Gilb suggests a text-based hierarchical tagging scheme for labeling individual requirements (Gilb 1988). Consider this requirement: "The system shall ask the user to confirm any request to print more than 10 copies." This requirement might be tagged Print.ConfirmCopies. This indicates that it is part of the print function and relates to the number of copies to print. Hierarchical textual tags are structured, meaningful, and unaffected by adding, deleting, or moving other requirements. Their drawback is that they are bulkier than the numeric labels, but that's a small price to pay for stable labels.

Dealing with Incompleteness

Sometimes you know that you lack a piece of information about a specific requirement. You might need to consult with a customer, check an external interface description, or build a prototype before you can resolve this uncertainty. Use the notation *TBD* (to be determined) to flag these knowledge gaps.

Resolve all TBDs before implementing a set of requirements. Any uncertainties that remain increase the risk of a developer or a tester making errors and having to perform rework. When the developer encounters a TBD, he might not go back to the requirement's originator to resolve it. The developer might make his best guess, which won't always be correct. If you must proceed with construction while TBDs remain, either defer implementing the unresolved requirements or design those portions of the product to be easily modifiable when the open issues are resolved.

> **Trap**   TBDs won't resolve themselves. Record who is responsible for resolving each issue, how, and by when. Number the TBDs to help track them to closure.

User Interfaces and the SRS

Incorporating user interface designs in the SRS has both drawbacks and benefits. On the minus side, screen images and user interface architectures describe solutions (designs), not requirements. Delaying baselining of the SRS until the user interface design is complete can try the patience of people who are already concerned about spending too much time on requirements. Including UI design in the requirements can result in the visual design driving the requirements, which leads to functional gaps.

Screen layouts don't replace user and functional requirements. Don't expect developers to deduce the underlying functionality and data relationships from screen shots. One Internet development company got in trouble repeatedly because the team went directly from signing a contract with a customer into an eight-hour visual design workshop. They never sufficiently understood what the user would be able to do at the Web site, so they spent a lot of time fixing it after delivery.

On the plus side, exploring possible user interfaces (such as with a working prototype) makes the requirements tangible to both users and developers. User interface displays can assist with project planning and estimation. Counting graphical user interface (GUI) elements or the number of function points[1] associated with each screen yields a size estimate, which leads to an estimate of implementation effort.

A sensible balance is to include conceptual images—sketches—of selected displays in the SRS without demanding that the implementation precisely follow those models. This enhances communication without handicapping the developers with unnecessary constraints. For example, a preliminary sketch of a complex dialog box will illustrate the intent behind a portion of the requirements, but a skilled visual designer might turn it into a tabbed dialog box to improve usability.

---

1. *Function points* are a measure of the quantity of user-visible functionality of an application, independent of how it is constructed. You can estimate the function points from an understanding of the user requirements, based on the counts of internal logical files, external interface files, and external inputs, outputs, and queries (IFPUG 2002).

A Software Requirements Specification Template

Every software development organization should adopt one or more standard SRS templates for its projects. Various SRS templates are available (Davis 1993; Robertson and Robertson 1999; Leffingwell and Widrig 2000). Many people use templates derived from the one described in IEEE Standard 830-1998, "IEEE Recommended Practice for Software Requirements Specifications" (IEEE 1998b). This template is suitable for many kinds of projects, but it has some limitations and confusing elements If your organization tackles various kinds or sizes of projects, such as new, large system development as well as minor enhancements to legacy systems, adopt an SRS template for each major project class.

Figure 10-1 illustrates an SRS template that was adapted from the IEEE 830 standard; the standard gives many examples of additional specific product requirements to include. Appendix D of this book contains a sample SRS that generally follows this template. Modify the template to fit the needs and nature of your projects. If a section of your template doesn't apply to a particular project, leave the section heading in place but indicate that it isn't applicable. This will keep the reader from wondering whether something important was omitted inadvertently. If your projects consistently omit the same sections, it's time to tune up the template. Include a table of contents and a revision history that lists the changes that were made to the SRS, including the date of the change, who made the change, and the reason. Sometimes a bit of information could logically be recorded in several template sections. It's more important to capture information thoroughly and consistently than to have religious arguments over where each item belongs.

There is a bit of overlap between this SRS template and the vision and scope document template in Figure 5-2 on page 82 (for example, the project scope, product features, and operating environment sections). This is because for some projects you will choose to create only a single requirements document. If you do use both templates, adjust them to eliminate redundancy between the two, combining sections as appropriate. It might be appropriate to use the corresponding section in the SRS to detail some preliminary or high-level information that appeared in the vision and scope document. If you find yourself using cut-and-paste from one project document to another, the documents contain unnecessary duplication.

The rest of this section describes the information to include in each section of the SRS. You can incorporate material by reference to other existing project documents (such as a vision and scope document or an interface specification) instead of duplicating information in the SRS.

1. **Introduction**
   1.1 Purpose
   1.2 Document Conventions
   1.3 Intended Audience and Reading Suggestions
   1.4 Project Scope
   1.5 References
2. **Overall Description**
   2.1 Product Perspective
   2.2 Product Features
   2.3 User Classes and Characteristics
   2.4 Operating Environment
   2.5 Design and Implementation Constraints
   2.6 User Documentation
   2.7 Assumptions and Dependencies
3. **System Features**
   3.x System Feature X
       3.x.1 Description and Priority
       3.x.2 Stimulus/Response Sequences
       3.x.3 Functional Requirements
4. **External Interface Requirements**
   4.1 User Interfaces
   4.2 Hardware Interfaces
   4.3 Software Interfaces
   4.4 Communications Interfaces
5. **Other Nonfunctional Requirements**
   5.1 Performance Requirements
   5.2 Safety Requirements
   5.3 Security Requirements
   5.4 Software Quality Attributes
6. **Other Requirements**
Appendix A: Glossary
Appendix B: Analysis Models
Appendix C: Issues List

Figure 10-1 Template for software requirements specification.

1. Introduction

The introduction presents an overview to help the reader understand how the SRS is organized and how to use it.

1.1 Purpose

Identify the product or application whose requirements are specified in this document, including the revision or release number. If this SRS pertains to only part of an entire system, identify that portion or subsystem.

1.2 Document Conventions

Describe any standards or typographical conventions, including text styles, highlighting, or significant notations. For instance, state whether the priority shown for a high-level requirement is inherited by all its detailed requirements or whether every functional requirement statement is to have its own priority rating.

1.3 Intended Audience and Reading Suggestions

List the different readers to whom the SRS is directed. Describe what the rest of the SRS contains and how it is organized. Suggest a sequence for reading the document that is most appropriate for each type of reader.

1.4 Project Scope

Provide a short description of the software being specified and its purpose. Relate the software to user or corporate goals and to business objectives and strategies. If a separate vision and scope document is available, refer to it rather than duplicating its contents here. An SRS that specifies an incremental release of an evolving product should contain its own scope statement as a subset of the long-term strategic product vision.

1.5 References

List any documents or other resources to which this SRS refers, including hyperlinks to them if possible. These might include user interface style guides, contracts, standards, system requirements specifications, use-case documents, interface specifications, concept-of-operations documents, or the SRS for a related product. Provide enough information so that the reader can access each reference, including its title, author, version number, date, and source or location (such as network folder or URL).

2. Overall Description

This section presents a high-level overview of the product and the environment in which it will be used, the anticipated product users, and known constraints, assumptions, and dependencies.

2.1 Product Perspective

Describe the product's context and origin. Is it the next member of a growing product family, the next version of a mature system, a replacement for an existing application, or an entirely new product? If this SRS defines a component of a larger system, state how this software relates to the overall system and identify major interfaces between the two.

2.2 Product Features

List the major features the product contains or the significant functions that it performs. Details will be provided in Section 3 of the SRS, so you need only a high-level summary here. A picture of the major groups of requirements and how they are related, such as a top-level data flow diagram, a use-case diagram, or a class diagram, might be helpful.

2.3 User Classes and Characteristics

Identify the various user classes that you anticipate will use this product and describe their pertinent characteristics. (See Chapter 6, "Finding the Voice of the Customer.") Some requirements might pertain only to certain user classes. Identify the favored user classes. User classes represent a subset of the stakeholders described in the vision and scope document.

2.4 Operating Environment

Describe the environment in which the software will operate, including the hardware platform, the operating systems and versions, and the geographical locations of users, servers, and databases. List any other software components or applications with which the system must peacefully coexist. The vision and scope document might contain some of this information at a high level.

2.5 Design and Implementation Constraints

Describe any factors that will restrict the options available to the developers and the rationale for each constraint. Constraints might include the following:

- Specific technologies, tools, programming languages, and databases that must be used or avoided.

- Restrictions because of the product's operating environment, such as the types and versions of Web browsers that will be used.

- Required development conventions or standards. (For instance, if the customer's organization will be maintaining the software, the organization might specify design notations and coding standards that a subcontractor must follow.)

- Backward compatibility with earlier products.

- Limitations imposed by business rules (which are documented elsewhere, as discussed in Chapter 9).

- Hardware limitations such as timing requirements, memory or processor restrictions, size, weight, materials, or cost.

- Existing user interface conventions to be followed when enhancing an existing product.

- Standard data interchange formats such as XML.

2.6 User Documentation

List the user documentation components that will be delivered along with the executable software. These could include user manuals, online help, and tutorials. Identify any required documentation delivery formats, standards, or tools.

2.7 Assumptions and Dependencies

An *assumption* is a statement that is believed to be true in the absence of proof or definitive knowledge. Problems can arise if assumptions are incorrect, are not shared, or change, so certain assumptions will translate into project risks. One SRS reader might assume that the product will conform to a particular user interface convention, whereas another assumes something different. A developer might assume that a certain set of functions will be custom-written for this application, but the analyst assumes that they will be reused from a previous project, and the project manager expects to procure a commercial function library.

Identify any *dependencies* the project has on external factors outside its control, such as the release date of the next version of an operating system or the issuing of an industry standard. If you expect to integrate into the system some components that another project is developing, you depend upon that project to supply the correctly operating components on schedule. If these dependencies are already documented elsewhere, such as in the project plan, refer to those other documents here.

3. System Features

The template in Figure 10-1 is organized by system feature, which is just one possible way to arrange the functional requirements. Other organizational options include by use case, mode of operation, user class, stimulus, response, object class, or functional hierarchy (IEEE 1998b). Combinations of these elements are also possible, such as use cases within user classes. There is no single right choice; you should select an organizational approach that makes it easy for readers to understand the product's intended capabilities. I'll describe the feature scheme as an example.

3.x System Feature X

State the name of the feature in just a few words, such as "3.1 Spell Check." Repeat subsections 3.x.1 through 3.x.3 for each system feature.

3.x.1 Description and Priority

Provide a short description of the feature and indicate whether it is of high, medium, or low priority. (See Chapter 14, "Setting Requirement Priorities.") Priorities are dynamic, changing over the course of the project. If you're using a requirements management tool, define a requirement attribute for priority. Requirements attributes are discussed in Chapter 18 and requirements management tools in Chapter 21.

3.x.2 Stimulus/Response Sequences

List the sequences of input stimuli (user actions, signals from external devices, or other triggers) and system responses that define the behaviors for this feature. These stimuli correspond to the initial dialog steps of use cases or to external system events.

3.x.3 Functional Requirements

Itemize the detailed functional requirements associated with this feature. These are the software capabilities that must be present for the user to carry out the feature's services or to perform a use case. Describe how the product should respond to anticipated error conditions and to invalid inputs and actions. Uniquely label each functional requirement.

4. External Interface Requirements

According to Richard Thayer (2002), "External interface requirements specify hardware, software, or database elements with which a system or component must interface...." This section provides information to ensure that the system will communicate properly with external components. If different portions of the product have different external interfaces, incorporate an instance of this section within the detailed requirements for each such portion.

Reaching agreement on external and internal system interfaces has been identified as a software industry best practice (Brown 1996). Place detailed descriptions of the data and control components of the interfaces in the data dictionary. A complex system with multiple subcomponents should use a separate interface specification or system architecture specification (Hooks and Farry 2001). The interface documentation could incorporate material from other documents by reference. For instance, it could point to a separate application programming interface (API) specification or to a hardware device manual that lists the error codes that the device could send to the software.

Interface Wars

Two software teams collaborated to build the A. Datum Corporation's flagship product. The knowledge base team built a complex inference engine in C++ and the applications team implemented the user interface in Microsoft Visual Basic. The two subsystems communicated through an API. Unfortunately, the knowledge base team periodically modified the API, with the consequence that the system would not build and execute correctly. The applications team needed several hours to diagnose each problem they discovered and determine the root cause as being an API change. These changes were not agreed upon, were not communicated to all stakeholders, and were not coordinated with corresponding modifications in the Visual Basic code. The interfaces glue your system components—including the users—together, so document the interface details and synchronize necessary modifications through your project's change-control process.

4.1 User Interfaces

Describe the logical characteristics of each user interface that the system needs. Some possible items to include are

- References to GUI standards or product family style guides that are to be followed.

- Standards for fonts, icons, button labels, images, color schemes, field tabbing sequences, commonly used controls, and the like.

- Screen layout or resolution constraints.

- Standard buttons, functions, or navigation links that will appear on every screen, such as a help button.

- Shortcut keys.

- Message display conventions.

- Layout standards to facilitate software localization.

- Accommodations for visually impaired users.

Document the user interface design details, such as specific dialog box layouts, in a separate user interface specification, not in the SRS. Including screen mock-ups in the SRS to communicate another view of the requirements is helpful, but make it clear that the mock-ups are not the committed screen designs. If the SRS is specifying an enhancement to an existing system, it sometimes makes sense to include screen displays exactly as they are to be implemented. The developers are already constrained by the current reality of the existing system, so it's possible to know up front just what the modified, and perhaps the new, screens should look like.

4.2 Hardware Interfaces

Describe the characteristics of each interface between the software and hardware components of the system. This description might include the supported device types, the data and control interactions between the software and the hardware, and the communication protocols to be used.

4.3 Software Interfaces

Describe the connections between this product and other software components (identified by name and version), including databases, operating systems, tools, libraries, and integrated commercial components. State the purpose of the messages, data, and control items exchanged between the software components. Describe the services needed by external software components and the nature of the intercomponent communications. Identify data that will be shared across software components. If the data-sharing mechanism must be implemented in a specific way, such as a global data area, specify this as a constraint.

4.4 Communications Interfaces

State the requirements for any communication functions the product will use, including e-mail, Web browser, network communications protocols, and electronic forms. Define any pertinent message formatting. Specify communication security or encryption issues, data transfer rates, and synchronization mechanisms.

5. Other Nonfunctional Requirements

This section specifies nonfunctional requirements other than external interface requirements, which appear in section 4, and constraints, recorded in section 2.5.

5.1 Performance Requirements

State specific performance requirements for various system operations. Explain their rationale to guide the developers in making appropriate design choices. For instance, stringent database response time demands might lead the designers to mirror the database in multiple geographical locations or to denormalize relational database tables for faster query responses. Specify the number of transactions per second to be supported, response times, computational accuracy, and timing relationships for real-time systems. You could also specify memory and disk space requirements, concurrent user loads, or the maximum number of rows stored in database tables. If different functional requirements or features have different performance requirements, it's appropriate to specify those performance goals right with the corresponding functional requirements, rather than collecting them all in this one section.

Quantify the performance requirements as specifically as possible—for example, "95 percent of catalog database queries shall be completed within 3 seconds on a single-user 1.1-GHz Intel Pentium 4 PC running Microsoft Windows XP with at least 60 percent of the system resources free." An excellent method for precisely specifying performance requirements is Tom Gilb's Planguage, described in Chapter 12, "Beyond Functionality: Software Quality Attributes."

5.2 Safety Requirements

Safety and security are examples of quality attributes, which are more fully addressed in section 5.4. I've called these two attributes out in separate sections of the SRS template because if they are important at all, they are usually critical. In this section, specify those requirements that are concerned with possible loss, damage, or harm that could result from the use of the product (Leveson 1995). Define any safeguards or actions that must be taken, as well as potentially dangerous actions that must be prevented. Identify any safety certifications, policies, or regulations to which the product must conform. Examples of safety requirements are

- **SA-1**   The system shall terminate any operation within 1 second if the measured tank pressure exceeds 95 percent of the specified maximum pressure.

- **SA-2**   The radiation beam shield shall remain open only through continuous computer control. The shield shall automatically fall into place if computer control is lost for any reason.

5.3 Security Requirements

Specify any requirements regarding security, integrity, or privacy issues that affect access to the product, use of the product, and protection of data that the product uses or creates. Security requirements normally originate in business rules, so identify any security or privacy policies or regulations to which the product must conform. Alternatively, you could address these requirements through the quality attribute called *integrity*. Following are sample security requirements:

- **SE-1**   Every user must change his initially assigned login password immediately after his first successful login. The initial password may never be reused.

- **SE-2**   A door unlock that results from a successful security badge read shall keep the door unlocked for 8.0 seconds.

5.4 Software Quality Attributes

State any additional product quality characteristics that will be important to either customers or developers. (See Chapter 12.) These characteristics should be specific, quantitative, and verifiable. Indicate the relative priorities of various attributes, such as ease of use over ease of learning, or portability over efficiency. A rich specification notation such as Planguage clarifies the needed levels of each quality much better than can simple descriptive statements.

6. Other Requirements

Define any other requirements that are not covered elsewhere in the SRS. Examples include internationalization requirements (currency, date formatting, language, international regulations, and cultural and political issues) and legal requirements. You could also add sections on operations, administration, and maintenance to cover requirements for product installation, configuration, startup and shutdown, recovery and fault tolerance, and logging and monitoring operations. Add any new sections to the template that are pertinent to your project. Omit this section if all your requirements are accommodated in other sections.

Appendix A: Glossary

Define any specialized terms that a reader needs to know to properly interpret the SRS, including acronyms and abbreviations. Spell out each acronym and provide its definition. Consider building an enterprise-level glossary that spans multiple projects. Each SRS would then define only those terms that are specific to an individual project.

Appendix B: Analysis Models

This optional section includes or points to pertinent analysis models such as data flow diagrams, class diagrams, state-transition diagrams, or entity-relationship diagrams. (See Chapter 11, "A Picture Is Worth 1024 Words.")

Appendix C: Issues List

This is a dynamic list of the open requirements issues that remain to be resolved. Issues could include items flagged as TBD, pending decisions, information that is needed, conflicts awaiting resolution, and the like. This doesn't necessarily have to be part of the SRS, but some organizations always attach a TBD list to the SRS. Actively manage these issues to closure so that they don't impede the timely baselining of a high-quality SRS.

Guidelines for Writing Requirements

There is no formulaic way to write excellent requirements; the best teacher is experience. The problems you have encountered in the past will teach you much. Excellent requirements documents follow effective technical-writing style guidelines and employ user terminology rather than computer jargon. Kovitz (1999) presents many recommendations and examples for writing good requirements. Keep the following suggestions in mind:

- Write complete sentences that have proper grammar, spelling, and punctuation. Keep sentences and paragraphs short and direct.

- Use the active voice. (For example, "The system shall do something," not "Something shall happen.")

- Use terms consistently and as defined in the glossary. Watch out for synonyms and near-synonyms. The SRS is not a place to creatively vary your language in an attempt to keep the reader's interest.

- Decompose a vague top-level requirement into sufficient detail to clarify it and remove ambiguity.

- State requirements in a consistent fashion, such as "The system shall" or "The user shall," followed by an action verb, followed by the observable result. Specify the trigger condition or action that causes the system to perform the specified behavior. For example, "If the requested chemical is found in the chemical stockroom, the system shall display a list of all containers of the chemical that are currently in the stockroom." You may use "must" as a synonym for "shall," but avoid "should," "may," "might," and similar words that don't clarify whether the function is required.

- When stating a requirement in the form "The user shall...," identify the specific actor whenever possible (for example, "The Buyer shall...").

- Use lists, figures, graphs, and tables to present information visually. Readers glaze over when confronting a dense mass of turgid text.

- Emphasize the most important bits of information. Techniques for emphasis include graphics, sequence (the first item is emphasized), repetition, use of white space, and use of visual contrast such as shading (Kovitz 1999).

- Ambiguous language leads to unverifiable requirements, so avoid using vague and subjective terms. Table 10-1 lists several such terms, along with some suggestions for how to remove the ambiguity.

> **Trap**   Requirements quality is in the eye of the beholder. The analyst might believe that a requirement he has written is crystal clear, free from ambiguities and other problems. However, if a reader has questions about it, the requirement needs additional work.

Table 10-1   Ambiguous Terms to Avoid in Requirements Specifications

Ambiguous Terms	Ways to Improve Them
acceptable, adequate	Define what constitutes acceptability and how the system can judge this.
as much as practicable	Don't leave it up to the developers to determine what's practicable. Make it a TBD and set a date to find out.
at least, at a minimum, not more than, not to exceed	Specify the minimum and maximum acceptable values.
between	Define whether the end points are included in the range.
depends on	Describe the nature of the dependency. Does another system provide input to this system, must other software be installed before your software can run, or does your system rely on another one to perform some calculations or services?
efficient	Define how efficiently the system uses resources, how quickly it performs specific operations, or how easy it is for people to use.

Table 10-1   Ambiguous Terms to Avoid in Requirements Specifications

Ambiguous Terms	Ways to Improve Them
fast, rapid	Specify the minimum acceptable speed at which the system performs some action.
flexible	Describe the ways in which the system must change in response to changing conditions or business needs.
improved, better, faster, superior	Quantify how much better or faster constitutes adequate improvement in a specific functional area.
including, including but not limited to, and so on, etc., such as	The list of items should include all possibilities. Otherwise, it can't be used for design or testing.
maximize, minimize, optimize	State the maximum and minimum acceptable values of some parameter.
normally, ideally	Also describe the system's behavior under abnormal or non-ideal conditions.
optionally	Clarify whether this means a system choice, a user choice, or a developer choice.
reasonable, when necessary, where appropriate	Explain how to make this judgment.
robust	Define how the system is to handle exceptions and respond to unexpected operating conditions.
seamless, transparent, graceful	Translate the user's expectations into specific observable product characteristics.
several	State how many, or provide the minimum and maximum bounds of a range.
shouldn't	Try to state requirements as positives, describing what the system will do.
state-of-the-art	Define what this means.
sufficient	Specify how much of something constitutes sufficiency.
support, enable	Define exactly what functions the system will perform that constitute supporting some capability.
user-friendly, simple, easy	Describe system characteristics that will achieve the customer's usage needs and usability expectations.

Write requirements specifically enough so that if the requirement is satisfied, the customer's need will be met, but avoid unnecessarily constraining the design. Provide enough detail to reduce the risk of misunderstanding to an acceptable level, based on the development team's knowledge and experience. If a developer can think of several ways to satisfy a requirement and all are acceptable, the specificity and detail are about right. Precisely stated requirements increase the chance of people receiving what they expect; less specific requirements give the developer more latitude for interpretation. If a developer who reviews the SRS isn't clear on the customer's intent, include additional information to reduce the risk of having to fix the product later.

Requirements authors often struggle to find the right level of granularity. A helpful guideline is to write individually testable requirements. If you can think of a small number of related test cases to verify that a requirement was correctly implemented, it's probably at an appropriate level of detail. If the tests you envision are numerous and diverse, perhaps several requirements are lumped together that ought to be separated. Testable requirements have been proposed as a metric for software product size (Wilson 1995).

Write requirements at a consistent level of detail. I've seen requirement statements in the same SRS that varied widely in their scope. For instance, "The keystroke combination Ctrl+S shall be interpreted as File Save" and "The keystroke combination Ctrl+P shall be interpreted as File Print" were split out as separate requirements. However, "The product shall respond to editing directives entered by voice" describes an entire subsystem (or a product!), not a single functional requirement.

Avoid long narrative paragraphs that contain multiple requirements. Words such as "and," "or," and "also" in a requirement suggest that several requirements might have been combined. This doesn't mean you can't use "and" in a requirement; just check to see whether the conjunction is joining two parts of a single requirement or two separate requirements. Never use "and/or" in a requirement; it leaves the interpretation up to the reader. Words such as "unless" and "except" also indicate multiple requirements: "The buyer's credit card on file shall be charged for payment, unless the credit card has expired." Split this into two requirements for the two conditions of the credit card: expired and nonexpired.

Avoid stating requirements redundantly. Writing the same requirement in multiple places makes the document easier to read but harder to maintain. The multiple instances of the requirement all have to be modified at the same time, lest an inconsistency creep in. Cross-reference related items in the SRS to help keep them synchronized when making changes. Storing individual requirements just once in a requirements management tool or a database solves the redundancy problem and facilitates reuse of common requirements across multiple projects.

Think about the most effective way to represent each requirement. I once reviewed an SRS that contained a set of requirements that fit the following pattern: "The Text Editor shall be able to parse <format> documents that define <jurisdiction> laws." There were three possible values for <format> and four possible values for <jurisdiction>, for a total of 12 similar requirements. The SRS had 12 requirements all right, but one was missing and another was duplicated. The only way to find that error was to build a table of all the possible combinations and look for them. This error is prevented if the SRS represents requirements that follow such a pattern in a table, as illustrated in Table 10-2. The higher-level requirement could be stated as "ED-13. The Text Editor shall be able to parse documents in several formats that define laws in the jurisdictions shown in Table 10-2." If any of the combinations don't have a corresponding functional requirement, put *N/A* (not applicable) in that table cell.

Table 10-2   Sample Tabular Format for Listing Requirement Numbers That Fit a Pattern

Jurisdiction	Tagged Format	Untagged Format	ASCII Format
Federal	ED-13.1	ED-13.2	ED-13.3
State	ED-13.4	ED-13.5	ED-13.6
Territorial	ED-13.7	ED-13.8	ED-13.9
International	ED-13.10	ED-13.11	ED-13.12

Sample Requirements, Before and After

Chapter 1 identified several characteristics of high-quality requirement statements: complete, correct, feasible, necessary, prioritized, unambiguous, and verifiable. Because requirements that don't exhibit these characteristics will cause confusion, wasted effort, and rework down the road, strive to correct any problems early. Following are several functional requirements, adapted from real projects, that are less than ideal. Examine each statement for the preceding quality characteristics to see whether you can spot the problems. Verifiability is a good starting point. If you can't devise tests to tell whether the requirement was correctly implemented, it's probably ambiguous or lacks necessary information.

I've presented some observations about what's wrong with these requirements and offered a suggested improvement to each one. Additional review passes would improve them further, but at some point you need to write software. More examples of rewriting poor requirements are available from Hooks and Farry (2001), Florence (2002), and Alexander and Stevens (2002).

Trap   Watch out for analysis paralysis. You can't spend forever trying to perfect the requirements. Your goal is to write requirements that are *good enough* to let your team proceed with design and construction at an acceptable level of risk.

Example 1   *"The Background Task Manager shall provide status messages at regular intervals not less than every 60 seconds."*

What are the status messages? Under what conditions and in what fashion are they provided to the user? If displayed, how long do they remain visible? The timing interval is not clear, and the word "every" just muddles the issue. One way to evaluate a requirement is to see whether a ludicrous but legitimate interpretation is all right with the user. If not, the requirement needs more work. In this example, is the interval between status messages supposed to be at least 60 seconds, so providing a new message once per year is okay? Alternatively, if the intent is to have no more than 60 seconds elapse between messages, would one millisecond be too short an interval? These extreme interpretations are consistent with the original requirement, but they certainly aren't what the user had in mind. Because of these problems, this requirement is not verifiable.

Here's one way to rewrite the preceding requirement to address those shortcomings, after we get some more information from the customer:

1. The Background Task Manager (BTM) shall display status messages in a designated area of the user interface.

1.1 The messages shall be updated every 60 plus or minus 10 seconds after background task processing begins.

1.2 The messages shall remain visible continuously.

1.3 Whenever communication with the background task process is possible, the BTM shall display the percent completed of the background task.

1.4. The BTM shall display a "Done" message when the background task is completed.

1.5 The BTM shall display a message if the background task has stalled.

I split this into multiple child requirements because each will demand separate test cases and to make each one individually traceable. If several requirements are grouped together in a paragraph, it's easy to overlook one during construction or testing. The revised requirements don't specify how the status messages will be displayed. That's a design issue; if you specify it here, it becomes a design constraint placed on the developer. Prematurely constrained design options frustrate the programmers and can result in a suboptimal product design.

Example 2   *"The XML Editor shall switch between displaying and hiding non-printing characters instantaneously."*

Computers can't do anything instantaneously, so this requirement isn't feasible. In addition, it's incomplete because it doesn't state the cause of the state switch. Is the software making the change on its own under certain conditions, or does the user initiate the change? What is the scope of the display change within the document: selected text, the entire document, the current page, or something else? What are nonprinting characters: hidden text, control characters, markup tags, or something else? This requirement cannot be verified until these questions are answered. The following might be a better way to write it:

> The user shall be able to toggle between displaying and hiding all XML tags in the document being edited with the activation of a specific triggering mechanism. The display shall change in 0.1 second or less.

Now it's clear that the nonprinting characters are XML markup tags. We know that the user triggers the display change, but the requirement doesn't constrain the design by defining the precise mechanism. We've also added a performance requirement that defines how rapidly the display must change. "Instantaneously" really meant "instantaneously to the human eye," which is achievable with a fast enough computer.

Example 3   *"The XML parser shall produce a markup error report that allows quick resolution of errors when used by XML novices."*

The ambiguous word "quick" refers to an activity that's performed by a person, not by the parser. The lack of definition of what goes into the error report indicates incompleteness, nor do we know when the report is generated. How would you verify this requirement? Find someone who considers herself an XML novice and see whether she can resolve errors quickly enough using the report?

This requirement incorporates the important notion of a specific user class—in this case, the XML novice who needs help from the software to find XML syntax errors. The analyst should find a suitable representative of that user class to identify the information that the parser's markup error report should contain. Let's try this instead:

> 1. After the XML Parser has completely parsed a file, it shall produce an error report that contains the line number and text of any XML errors found in the parsed file and a description of each error found.
>
> 2. If no parsing errors are found, the parser shall not produce an error report.

Now we know when the error report is generated and what goes in it, but we've left it up to the designer to decide what the report should look like. We've also specified an exception condition that the original requirement didn't address: if there aren't any errors, don't generate a report.

Example 4   *"Charge numbers should be validated on line against the master corporate charge number list, if possible."*

What does "if possible" mean? If it's technically feasible? If the master charge number list can be accessed at run time? If you aren't sure whether a requested capability can be delivered, use TBD to indicate that the issue is unresolved. After investigation, either the TBD goes away or the requirement goes away. This requirement doesn't specify what happens when the validation passes or fails. Avoid imprecise words such as "should." Some requirements authors attempt to convey subtle distinctions by using words such as "shall," "should," and "may" to indicate importance. I prefer to stick with "shall" or "must" as a clear statement of the requirement's intent and to specify the priorities explicitly. Here's a revised version of this requirement:

> At the time the requester enters a charge number, the system shall validate the charge number against the master corporate charge number list. If the charge number is not found on the list, the system shall display an error message and shall not accept the order.

A related requirement would address the exception condition of the master corporate charge number list not being available at the time the validation was attempted.

Example 5 *"The editor shall not offer search and replace options that could have disastrous results."*

The notion of "disastrous results" is open to interpretation. An unintended global change could be disastrous if the user doesn't detect the error or has no way to correct it. Be judicious in the use of inverse requirements, which describe things that the system will *not* do. The underlying concern in this example seems to pertain to protecting the file contents from inadvertent damage or loss. Perhaps the real requirements are

1. The editor shall require the user to confirm global text changes, deletions, and insertions that could result in data loss.

2. The application shall provide a multilevel undo capability limited only by the system resources available to the application.

Example 6 *"The device tester shall allow the user to easily connect additional components, including a pulse generator, a voltmeter, a capacitance meter, and custom probe cards."*

This requirement is for a product containing embedded software that's used to test several kinds of measurement devices. The word *easily* implies a usability requirement, but it is neither measurable nor verifiable. "Including" doesn't make it clear whether this is the complete list of external devices that must be connected to the tester or whether there are many others that we don't know about. Consider the following alternative requirements, which contain some deliberate design constraints:

1. The tester shall incorporate a USB port to allow the user to connect any measurement device that has a USB connection.

2. The USB port shall be installed on the front panel to permit a trained operator to connect a measurement device in 15 seconds or less.

The Data Dictionary

 Long ago I led a project on which the three programmers sometimes inadvertently used different variable names, lengths, and validation criteria for the same data item. This caused confusion about the real definition, corrupted data, and maintenance headaches. We suffered from the lack of a *data dictionary*—a shared repository that defines the meaning, data type, length, format, necessary precision, and allowed range or list of values for all data elements or attributes used in the application.

The information in the data dictionary binds together the various requirements representations. Integration problems are reduced if all developers respect the data dictionary definitions. Begin collecting data definitions as you encounter them during requirements elicitation. The data dictionary complements the project glossary, which defines individual terms. You might want to merge the glossary entries into the data dictionary, although I prefer to keep them separate. The data dictionary can be managed as an appendix to the SRS or as a separate document or file.

Compared with sprinkling data definitions throughout the functional requirements, a separate data dictionary makes it easy to find the information you need, and it avoids redundancy and inconsistencies. Some commercial analysis and design tools include a data dictionary component. If you set up the data dictionary manually, consider using a hypertext approach. Clicking on a data item that is part of a data structure definition would take you to the definition of that individual data item, thereby making it easy to traverse the hierarchical tree of definitions.

Items in the data dictionary are represented using a simple notation (DeMarco 1979; Robertson and Robertson 1994). The item being defined is shown on the left side of an equal sign, with its definition on the right. This notation defines primitive data elements, the composition of multiple data elements into structures, optional data items, iteration (repeats) of a data item, and a list of values for a data item. The following examples are from the Chemical Tracking System (of course!).

Primitive data elements   A primitive data element is one for which no further decomposition is possible or necessary. The definition identifies the primitive's data type, size, range of allowed values, and other pertinent attributes. Primitives typically are defined with a comment, which is any text delimited by asterisks:

> Request ID = * a 6-digit system-generated sequential integer, beginning with 1, that uniquely identifies each request *

Composition   A data structure or record contains multiple data items. If an element in the data structure is optional, enclose it in parentheses:

Requested Chemical = Chemical ID
                        + Number of Containers
                        + Grade
                        + Amount
                        + Amount Units
                        + (Vendor)

This structure identifies all the information associated with a request for a specific chemical. *Vendor* is optional because the person placing the request might not care which vendor supplies the chemical. Each data item that appears in a structure must itself be defined in the data dictionary. Structures can incorporate other structures.

Iteration   If multiple instances of an item can appear in a data structure, enclose that item in curly braces. Show the allowed number of possible repeats in the form *minimum:maximum* in front of the opening brace:

Request = Request ID
            + Request Date
            + Charge Number
            + 1:10{Requested Chemical}

This example shows that a chemical request must contain at least one chemical but may not contain more than 10 chemicals. Each request has the additional attributes of an identifier, the date the request was created, and a charge number to be used for payment.

Selection   A data element that can take on a limited number of discrete values is called an *enumerated primitive*. Show the possible values in a list contained within square brackets, with vertical bars separating the list items:

Quantity Units = ["grams" | "kilograms" | "milligrams" | "each"]
                    * 9-character text string indicating the units associated
                        with the quantity of chemical requested *

This entry shows that there are just four allowed values for the text string *Quantity Units*. The comment inside the asterisks provides the textual definition of the data element.

The time you invest in creating a data dictionary will be more than repaid by the time you save avoiding mistakes that result when project participants have different understandings of key data. If you keep the data dictionary current, it will remain a valuable tool throughout the system's maintenance life and when developing related systems.

Next Steps

- Examine a page of functional requirements from your project's SRS to see whether each statement exhibits the characteristics of excellent requirements. Rewrite any requirements that don't measure up.

- If your organization doesn't already have a standard SRS template, convene a small working group to adopt one. Begin with the template in Figure 10-1 (on page 172) and adapt it to best meet the needs of your organization's projects and products. Agree on a convention for labeling individual requirements.

- Convene three to six project stakeholders to inspect the SRS for your project (Wiegers 2002a). Make sure each requirement demonstrates the desirable characteristics discussed in Chapter 1. Look for conflicts between different requirements in the specification, for missing requirements, and for missing sections of the SRS. Ensure that the defects you find are corrected in the SRS and in any downstream work products based on those requirements.

- Take a complex data object from one of your applications and define it using the data dictionary notation presented in this chapter.

11

A Picture Is Worth 1024 Words

The Chemical Tracking System project team was holding its first SRS review. The participants were Dave (project manager), Lori (requirements analyst), Helen (lead developer), Ramesh (test lead), Tim (product champion for the chemists), and Roxanne (product champion for the chemical stockroom staff). Tim began by saying, "I read the whole SRS. Most of the requirements seemed okay to me, but I had a hard time following parts of it. I'm not sure whether we identified all the steps in the chemical request process."

"It was hard for me to think of all the test cases I'll need to cover the status changes for a request," Ramesh added. "I found a bunch of requirements sprinkled throughout the SRS about the status changes, but I couldn't tell whether any were missing. A couple of requirements seemed to conflict."

Roxanne had a similar problem. "I got confused when I read about the way I would actually request a chemical," she said. "The individual functional requirements made sense, but I had trouble visualizing the sequence of steps I would go through."

After the reviewers raised several other concerns, Lori concluded, "It looks like this SRS doesn't tell us everything we need to know about the system. I'll draw some pictures to help us visualize the requirements and see whether that clarifies these problem areas. Thanks for the feedback."

According to requirements authority Alan Davis, no single view of the requirements provides a complete understanding (Davis 1995). You need a combination of textual and visual requirements representations to paint a full picture of the intended system. Requirements views include functional requirements lists and tables, graphical analysis models, user interface prototypes, test cases, decision trees, and decision tables. Ideally, different people will create various requirements representations. The analyst might write the functional requirements and draw some models, whereas the user interface designer builds a prototype and the test lead writes test cases. Comparing the representations created by different people through diverse thought processes reveals inconsistencies, ambiguities, assumptions, and omissions that are difficult to spot from any single view.

Diagrams communicate certain types of information more efficiently than text can. Pictures help bridge language and vocabulary barriers between different team members. The analyst will need to explain to other stakeholders the purpose of the models and the notations used. This chapter introduces several requirements modeling techniques, with illustrations and pointers to other sources for further details.

Modeling the Requirements

When I began drawing analysis models many years ago, I hoped to find one technique that could pull everything together into a holistic depiction of a system's requirements. Eventually I concluded that there is no such all-encompassing diagram. An early goal of structured systems analysis was to replace entirely the classical functional specification with graphical diagrams and notations more formal than narrative text (DeMarco 1979). However, experience has shown that analysis models should augment—rather than replace—a natural language requirements specification (Davis 1995).

Visual requirements models include data flow diagrams (DFD), entity-relationship diagrams (ERD), state-transition diagrams (STD) or statecharts, dialog maps, use-case diagrams (discussed in Chapter 8), class diagrams, and activity diagrams (also in Chapter 8). The notations presented here provide a common, industry-standard language for project participants to use. Of course, you may also use ad hoc diagrams to augment your verbal and written project communications, but readers might not interpret them the same way. Unconventional modeling approaches sometimes are valuable, however. One project team used a project-scheduling tool to model the timing requirements for an embedded software product, working at the millisecond time scale rather than in days and weeks.

These models are useful for elaborating and exploring the requirements, as well as for designing software solutions. Whether you are using them for analysis or for design depends on the timing and the intent of the modeling. Used for requirements analysis, these diagrams let you model the problem domain or create conceptual representations of the new system. They depict the logical aspects of the problem domain's data components, transactions and transformations, real-world objects, and changes in system state. You can base the models on the textual requirements to represent them from different perspectives, or you can derive the detailed functional requirements from high-level models that are based on user input. During design, models represent specifically how you intend to implement the system: the actual database you plan to create, the object classes you'll instantiate, and the code modules you'll develop.

> **Trap**   Don't assume that developers can simply translate analysis models into code without going through a design process. Because both types of diagrams use the same notations, clearly label each one as an analysis model (the concepts) or a design model (what you intend to build).

The analysis modeling techniques described in this chapter are supported by a variety of commercial computer-aided software engineering, or CASE, tools. CASE tools provide several benefits over ordinary drawing tools. First, they make it easy to improve the diagrams through iteration. You'll never get a model right the first time you draw it, so iteration is a key to success in system modeling (Wiegers 1996a). CASE tools also know the rules for each modeling method they support. They can identify syntax errors and inconsistencies that people who review the diagrams might not see. Many tools link multiple diagrams together and to their shared data definitions in a data dictionary. CASE tools can help you keep the models consistent with each other and with the functional requirements in the SRS.

Rarely does a team need to create a complete set of analysis models for an entire system. Focus your modeling on the most complex and riskiest portions of the system and on those portions most subject to ambiguity or uncertainty. Safety-, security-, and mission-critical system elements are good candidates for modeling because the impact of defects in those areas is so severe.

From Voice of the Customer to Analysis Models

By listening carefully to how customers present their requirements, the analyst can pick out keywords that translate into specific model elements. Table 11-1 suggests possible mappings of significant nouns and verbs from the customer's input into model components, which are described later in this chapter. As you craft customer input into written requirements and models, you should be able to link every model component to a specific user requirement.

Table 11-1   Relating the Customer's Voice to Analysis Model Components

Type of Word	Examples	Analysis Model Components
Noun	■ People, organizations, software systems, data items, or objects that exist	■ Terminators or data stores (DFD) ■ Actors (use-case diagram) ■ Entities or their attributes (ERD) ■ Classes or their attributes (class diagram)
Verb	■ Actions, things a user can do, or events that can take place	■ Processes (DFD) ■ Use cases (use-case diagram) ■ Relationships (ERD) ■ Transitions (STD) ■ Activities (activity diagram)

Throughout this book, I've used the Chemical Tracking System as a case study. Building on this example, consider the following paragraph of user needs supplied by the product champion who represented the Chemist user class. Significant unique nouns are highlighted in **bold** and verbs are in *italics*; look for these keywords in the analysis models shown later in this chapter. For the sake of illustration, some of the models show information that goes beyond that contained in the following paragraph, whereas other models depict just part of the information presented here:

"A **chemist** or a member of the **chemical stockroom staff** can *place* a **request** for one or more **chemicals**. The request can be *fulfilled* either by *delivering* a **container** of the chemical that is already in the **chemical stockroom's inventory** or by *placing* an **order** for a new container of the chemical with an outside **vendor**. The **person** placing the request must be able to *search* **vendor catalogs** on line for specific chemicals while *preparing* his or her request. The system needs to *track* the **status** of every chemical request from the time it is prepared until the request is either fulfilled or *canceled*. It also needs to track the **history** of every chemical container from the time it is *received* at the **company** until it is fully *consumed* or *disposed* of."

Data Flow Diagram

The *data flow diagram* is the basic tool of structured analysis (DeMarco 1979; Robertson and Robertson 1994). A DFD identifies the transformational processes of a system, the collections (stores) of data or material that the system manipulates, and the flows of data or material between processes, stores, and the outside world. Data flow modeling takes a functional decomposition approach to systems analysis, breaking complex problems into progressive levels of detail. This works well for transaction-processing systems and other function-intensive applications. Through the addition of control flow elements, the DFD technique has been extended to permit modeling of real-time systems (Hatley, Hruschka, and Pirbhai 2000).

The DFD provides a way to represent the steps involved in a business process or the operations of a proposed software system. I've often used this tool when interviewing customers, scribbling a DFD on a whiteboard while we discuss how the user's business operates. Data flow diagrams can represent systems over a wide range of abstraction. High-level DFDs provide a holistic, bird's-eye view of the data and processing components in a multistep activity, which complements the precise, detailed view embodied in the SRS. A DFD illustrates how the functional requirements in the SRS combine to let the user perform specific tasks, such as requesting a chemical.

> **Trap**   Don't assume that customers already know how to read analysis models, but don't conclude that they're unable to understand them, either. Explain the purpose and notations of each model to your product champions and ask them to review the diagrams.

The context diagram in Figure 5-3 (on page 91) is the highest level of abstraction of the DFD. The context diagram represents the entire system as a single black-box process, depicted as a circle (a *bubble*). It also shows the *terminators,* or external entities, that connect to the system and the data or material flows between the system and the terminators. Flows on the context diagram often represent complex data structures, which are defined in the data dictionary.

You can elaborate the context diagram into the level 0 DFD, which partitions the system into its major processes. Figure 11-1 shows the level 0 DFD for the Chemical Tracking System (somewhat simplified). The single process bubble that represented the entire Chemical Tracking System on the context diagram has been subdivided into seven major processes (the bubbles). As with the context diagram, the terminators are shown in rectangles. All data flows (arrows) from the context diagram also appear on the level 0 DFD. In addition, the level 0 diagram contains several *data stores*, depicted as a pair of parallel horizontal lines, which are internal to the system and therefore do not appear on the context diagram. A flow from a bubble to a store indicates that data is being placed into the store, a flow out of the store shows a read operation, and a bidirectional arrow between a store and a bubble indicates an update operation.

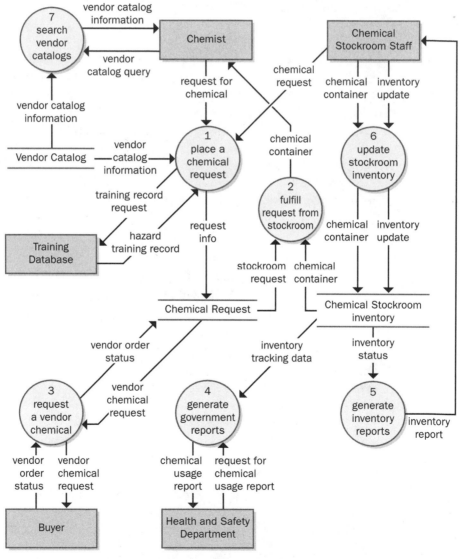

Figure 11-1   Level 0 data flow diagram for the Chemical Tracking System.

Each process that appears as a separate bubble on the level 0 diagram can be further expanded into a separate DFD to reveal more detail about its functioning. The analyst continues this progressive refinement until the lowest-level diagrams contain only primitive process operations that can be clearly represented in narrative text, pseudocode, a flowchart, or an activity diagram. The functional requirements in the SRS will define precisely what happens within each primitive process. Every level of the DFD must be balanced and consistent with the level above it so that all the input and output flows on the child diagram match up with flows on its parent. Complex data flows on the high-level diagrams can be split into their constituent elements, as defined in the data dictionary, on the lower-level DFDs.

Figure 11-1 looks complex at first glance. However, if you examine the immediate environment of any one process, you will see the data items that it consumes and produces and their sources and destinations. To see exactly how a process uses the data items, you'll need to either draw a more detailed child DFD or refer to the functional requirements for that part of the system.

Following are several conventions for drawing data flow diagrams. Not everyone adheres to the same conventions (for example, some analysts show terminators only on the context diagram), but I find them helpful. Using the models to enhance communication among the project participants is more important than dogmatic conformance to these principles.

- Place data stores only on the level 0 DFD and lower levels, not on the context diagram.

- Processes communicate through data stores, not by direct flows from one process to another. Similarly, data cannot flow directly from one store to another; it must pass through a process bubble.

- Don't attempt to imply the processing sequence using the DFD.

- Name each process as a concise action: verb plus object (such as Generate Inventory Reports). Use names that are meaningful to the customers and pertinent to the business or problem domain.

- Number the processes uniquely and hierarchically. On the level 0 diagram, number each process with an integer. If you create a child DFD for process 3, number the processes in that child diagram 3.1, 3.2, and so on.

- Don't show more than eight to ten processes on a single diagram or it becomes difficult to draw, change, and understand. If you have more processes, introduce another layer of abstraction by grouping related processes into a higher-level process.

■   Bubbles with flows that are only coming in or only going out are suspect. The processing that a DFD bubble represents normally requires
both input and output flows.

When customer representatives review a DFD, they should make sure that
all the known processes are represented and that processes have no missing or
unnecessary inputs or outputs. DFD reviews often reveal previously unrecog-
nized user classes, business processes, and connections to other systems.

Entity-Relationship Diagram

Just as a data flow diagram illustrates the processes that take place in a system,
a data model depicts the system's data relationships. A commonly used data
model is the *entity-relationship diagram*, or ERD (Wieringa 1996). If your ERD
represents logical groups of information from the problem domain and their
interconnections, you're using the ERD as a requirements analysis tool. An analysis ERD helps you understand and communicate the data components of the
business or system, without implying that the product will necessarily include a
database. In contrast, when you create an ERD during system design, you're
defining the logical or physical structure of the system's database.

Entities are physical items (including people) or aggregations of data items
that are important to the business you're analyzing or to the system you intend
to build (Robertson and Robertson 1994). Entities are named as singular nouns
and are shown in rectangles in an ERD. Figure 11-2 illustrates a portion of the
entity-relationship diagram for the Chemical Tracking System, using one of several common ERD modeling notations. Notice that the entities named Chemical
Request, Vendor Catalog, and Chemical Stockroom Inventory appeared as data
stores in the data flow diagram in Figure 11-1. Other entities represent actors
who interact with the system (Requester), physical items that are part of the
business operations (Chemical Container), and blocks of data that weren't
shown in the level 0 DFD but would appear on a lower-level DFD (Container
History, Chemical).

Each entity is described by several attributes; individual instances of an
entity will have different attribute values. For example, the attributes for each
chemical include a unique chemical identifier, its formal chemical name, and a
graphical representation of its chemical structure. The data dictionary contains
the detailed definitions of those attributes, which guarantees that entities in the
ERD and their corresponding data stores from the DFD are defined identically.

The diamonds in the ERD represent *relationships*, which identify the logical and numeric linkages between pairs of entities. Relationships are named in
a way that describes the nature of the connections. For example, the relation-

ship between the Requester and the Chemical Request is a *placing* relationship. You can read the relationship as either "a Requester places a Chemical Request" or as "a Chemical Request is placed by a Requester." Some conventions would have you label the relationship diamond "is placed by," which makes sense only if you read the diagram from left to right. When you ask customers to review an ERD, ask them to check whether the relationships shown are all correct and appropriate. Also ask them to identify any possible relationships with entities that the model doesn't show.

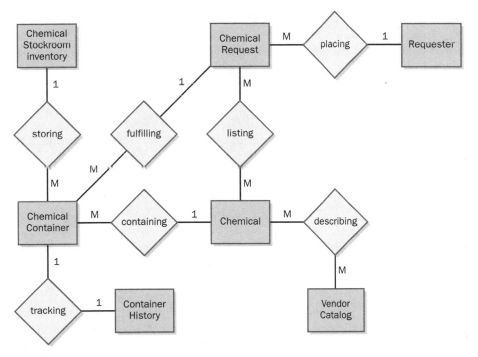

Figure 11-2   Partial entity-relationship diagram for the Chemical Tracking System.

The *cardinality*, or multiplicity, of each relationship is shown with a number or letter on the lines that connect entities and relationships. Different ERD notations use different conventions to represent cardinality; the example in Figure 11-2 illustrates one common approach. Because each Requester can place multiple requests, there's a one-to-many relationship between Requester and Chemical Request. This cardinality is shown with a *1* on the line connecting Requester and the *placing* relationship and an *M* (for many) on the line connecting Chemical Request and the *placing* relationship. Other possible cardinalities are as follows:

■   One-to-one (every Chemical Container is tracked by a single Container History)

- Many-to-many (every Vendor Catalog contains many Chemicals, and some Chemicals appear in multiple Vendor Catalogs)

If you know that a more precise cardinality exists than simply *many*, you can show the specific number or range of numbers instead of the generic *M*.

Modeling Problems, Not Software

I once served as the IT representative on a team that was doing some business process reengineering. Our goal was to reduce by a factor of 10 the time that it took to make a new chemical available for use in a product. The reengineering team included the following representatives of the various functions involved in chemical commercialization:

- The synthetic chemist who first makes the new chemical

- The scale-up chemist who develops a process for making large batches of the chemical

- The analytical chemist who devises techniques for analyzing the chemical's purity

- The patent attorney who applies for patent protection

- The health and safety representative who obtains government approval to use the chemical in consumer products

After we invented a new process that we believed would greatly accelerate the chemical commercialization activity, I interviewed the person on the reengineering team who was responsible for each process step. I asked each owner two questions: "What information do you need to perform this step?" and "What information does this step produce that we should store?" By correlating the answers for all process steps, I found steps that needed data that no one had available. Other steps produced data that no one needed. We fixed all those problems.

Next, I drew a data flow diagram to illustrate the new chemical commercialization process and an entity-relationship diagram to model the data relationships. A data dictionary defined all our data items. These analysis models served as useful communication tools to help the team members arrive at a common understanding of the new process. The models would also be a valuable starting point to scope and specify the requirements for software applications that supported portions of the process.

State-Transition Diagram

All software systems involve a combination of functional behavior, data manipulation, and state changes. Real-time systems and process control applications can exist in one of a limited number of states at any given time. A state change can take place only when well-defined criteria are satisfied, such as receiving a specific input stimulus under certain conditions. An example is a highway intersection that incorporates vehicle sensors, protected turn lanes, and pedestrian crosswalk buttons and signals. Many information systems deal with business objects—sales orders, invoices, inventory items, and the like—with life cycles that involve a series of possible statuses. System elements that involve a set of states and changes between them can be regarded as *finite-state machines* (Booch, Rumbaugh, Jacobson 1999).

Describing a complex finite-state machine in natural language creates a high probability of overlooking a permitted state change or including a disallowed change. Depending on how the SRS is organized, requirements that pertain to the state machine's behavior might be sprinkled throughout it. This makes it difficult to reach an overall understanding of the system's behavior.

The *state-transition diagram* provides a concise, complete, and unambiguous representation of a finite-state machine. A related technique is the *state-chart diagram* included in the Unified Modeling Language (UML), which has a somewhat richer set of notations and which models the states an object goes through during its lifetime (Booch, Rumbaugh, Jacobson 1999). The STD contains three types of elements:

- Possible system states, shown as rectangles.

- Allowed state changes or *transitions*, shown as arrows connecting pairs of rectangles.

- Events or conditions that cause each transition to take place, shown as text labels on each transition arrow. The label might identify both the event and the corresponding system response.

Figure 11-3 illustrates a portion of an STD for a home security system. The STD for a real-time system includes a special state usually called *Idle* (equivalent to *Disarmed* in the figure), to which the system returns whenever it isn't doing other processing. In contrast, the STD for an object that passes through a defined life cycle, such as a chemical request, will have one or more termination states, which represent the final status values that an object can have.

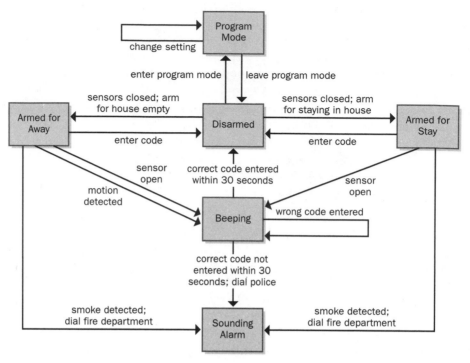

Figure 11-3   Partial state-transition diagram for a home security system.

The STD doesn't show the details of the processing that the system performs; it shows only the possible state changes that result from that processing. An STD helps developers understand the intended behavior of the system. It's a good way to check whether all the required states and transitions have been correctly and completely described in the functional requirements. Testers can derive test cases from the STD that cover all allowed transition paths. Customers can read an STD with just a little coaching about the notation—it's just boxes and arrows.

Recall from Chapter 8 that a primary function of the Chemical Tracking System is to permit actors called Requesters to place requests for chemicals, which can be fulfilled either from the chemical stockroom's inventory or by placing orders to outside vendors. Each request will pass through a series of states between the time it's created and the time it's either fulfilled or canceled (the two termination states). Thus, we can treat the life cycle of a chemical request as a finite-state machine and model it as shown in Figure 11-4.

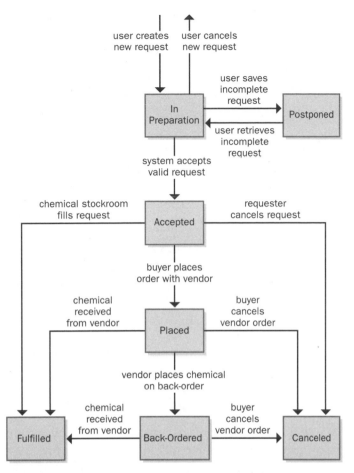

Figure 11-4   State-transition diagram for a chemical request in the
Chemical Tracking System.

This STD shows that an individual request can take on one of the following seven possible states:

■   **In Preparation**   The Requester is creating a new request, having
initiated that function from some other part of the system.

■   **Postponed**   The Requester saved a partial request for future completion without either submitting the request to the system or canceling the request operation.

■   **Accepted**   The user submitted a completed chemical request and
the system accepted it for processing.

■   **Placed**   The request must be satisfied by an outside vendor and a
buyer has placed an order with the vendor.

- **Fulfilled**   The request has been satisfied, either by delivering a chemical container from the chemical stockroom to the Requester or by receiving a chemical from a vendor.

- **Back-Ordered**   The vendor didn't have the chemical available and notified the buyer that it was back-ordered for future delivery.

- **Canceled**   The Requester canceled an accepted request before it was fulfilled or the buyer canceled a vendor order before it was fulfilled or while it was back-ordered.

 When the Chemical Tracking System user representatives reviewed the initial chemical request STD, they identified one state that wasn't needed, saw that another essential state was missing, and pointed out two incorrect transitions. No one had seen those errors when they reviewed the corresponding functional requirements. This underscores the value of representing requirements information at more than one level of abstraction. It's often easier to spot a problem when you step back from the detailed level and see the big picture that an analysis model provides. However, the STD doesn't provide enough detail for a developer to know what software to build. Therefore, the SRS for the Chemical Tracking System included the functional requirements associated with processing a chemical request and its possible state changes.

Dialog Map

A user interface also can be regarded as a finite-state machine. Only one dialog element (such as a menu, workspace, dialog box, line prompt, or touch screen display) is available at any given time for user input. The user can navigate to certain other dialog elements based on the action he takes at the active input location. The number of possible navigation pathways can be large in a complex graphical user interface, but the number is finite and the options usually are known. Therefore, many user interfaces can be modeled with a form of state-transition diagram called a *dialog map* (Wasserman 1985; Wiegers 1996a). Constantine and Lockwood (1999) describe a similar technique called a *navigation map*, which includes a richer set of notations for representing different types of interaction elements and context transitions.

The dialog map represents a user interface design at a high level of abstraction. It shows the dialog elements in the system and the navigation links among them, but it doesn't show the detailed screen designs. A dialog map allows you to explore hypothetical user interface concepts based on your understanding of the requirements. Users and developers can study a dialog map to reach a common vision of how the user might interact with the system to perform a task. Dialog maps are also useful for modeling the visual architecture of a Web site. Navigation links that you build into the Web site appear as transitions on the dialog map.

Dialog maps are related to system storyboards, which also include a short description of each screen's purpose (Leffingwell and Widrig 2000).

Dialog maps capture the essence of the user–system interactions and task flow without bogging the team down in detailed screen layouts. Users can trace through a dialog map to find missing, incorrect, or unnecessary transitions, and hence missing, incorrect, or unnecessary requirements. The abstract, conceptual dialog map formulated during requirements analysis serves as a guide during detailed user interface design.

Just as in ordinary state-transition diagrams, the dialog map shows each dialog element as a state (rectangle) and each allowed navigation option as a transition (arrow). The condition that triggers a user interface navigation is shown as a text label on the transition arrow. There are several types of trigger conditions:

- A user action, such as pressing a function key or clicking a hyperlink or a dialog box button

- A data value, such as an invalid user input that triggers an error message display

- A system condition, such as detecting that a printer is out of paper

- Some combination of these, such as typing a menu option number and pressing the Enter key

Dialog maps look a bit like flowcharts but they serve a different purpose. A flowchart explicitly shows the processing steps and decision points, but not the user interface displays. In contrast, the dialog map does *not* show the processing that takes place along the transition lines that connect one dialog element to another. The branching decisions (usually user choices) are hidden behind the display screens shown as rectangles on the dialog map, and the conditions that lead to displaying one screen or another appear in the labels on the transitions. You can think of the dialog map as a sort of negative image of—or a complement to—a flowchart.

To simplify the dialog map, omit global functions such as pressing the F1 key to bring up a help display from every dialog element. The SRS section on user interfaces should specify that this functionality will be available, but showing lots of help-screen boxes on the dialog map clutters the model while adding little value. Similarly, when modeling a Web site, you needn't include standard navigation links that will appear on every page in the site. You can also omit the transitions that reverse the flow of a Web page navigation sequence because the Web browser's Back button handles that navigation.

A dialog map is an excellent way to represent the interactions between an actor and the system that a use case describes. The dialog map can depict alternative courses as branches off the normal course flow. I found that sketching dialog map fragments on a whiteboard was helpful during use-case elicitation workshops in which a team explored the sequence of actor actions and system responses that would lead to task completion.

Chapter 8 presented a use case for the Chemical Tracking System called "Request a Chemical." The normal course for this use case involved requesting a chemical container from the chemical stockroom's inventory. An alternative course was to request the chemical from a vendor. The user placing the request wanted the option to view the history of the available stockroom containers of that chemical before selecting one. Figure 11-5 shows a dialog map for this fairly complex use case.

This diagram might look complicated at first, but if you trace through it one line and one box at a time, it's not difficult to understand. The user initiates this use case by asking to place a request for a chemical from some menu in the Chemical Tracking System. In the dialog map, this action brings the user to the box called Current Request List, along the arrow in the upper-left part of the dialog map. That box represents the main workspace for this use case, a list of the chemicals in the user's current request. The arrows leaving that box on the dialog map show all the navigation options—and hence functionality—available to the user in that context:

■   Cancel the entire request.

■   Submit the request if it contains at least one chemical.

■   Add a new chemical to the request list.

■   Delete a chemical from the list.

The last operation, deleting a chemical, doesn't involve another dialog element; it simply refreshes the current request list display after the user makes the change.

As you trace through this dialog map, you'll see elements that reflect the rest of the "Request a Chemical" use case:

■   One flow path for requesting a chemical from a vendor

■   Another path for fulfillment from the chemical stockroom

■   An optional path to view the history of a container in the chemical stockroom

■   An error message display to handle entry of an invalid chemical identifier or other error conditions that could arise

Some of the transitions on the dialog map allow the user to back out of operations. Users get annoyed if they are forced to complete a task even though they change their minds partway through it. The dialog map lets you enhance usability by designing in those back-out and cancel options at strategic points.

A user who reviews this dialog map might spot a missing requirement. For example, a cautious user might want to confirm the operation that leads to canceling an entire request to avoid inadvertently losing data. It costs less to add this new function at the analysis stage than to build it into a completed product. Because the dialog map represents just the conceptual view of the possible elements involved in the interaction between the user and the system, don't try to pin down all the user interface design details at the requirements stage. Instead, use these models to help the project stakeholders reach a common understanding of the system's intended functionality.

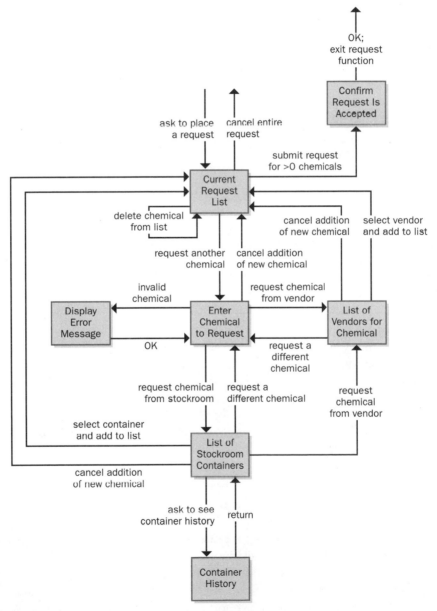

Figure 11-5   Dialog map for the "Request a Chemical" use case from the Chemical Tracking System.

Class Diagrams

Object-oriented software development has superseded structured analysis and design on many projects, spawning object-oriented analysis and design. *Objects* typically correspond to real-world items in the business or problem domain. They represent individual instances derived from a generic template called a *class*. Class descriptions encompass both attributes (data) and the operations that can be performed on the attributes. A *class diagram* is a graphical way to depict the classes identified during object-oriented analysis and the relationships among them.

Products developed using object-oriented methods don't demand unique requirements development approaches. This is because requirements development focuses on what the users need to do with the system and the functionality it must contain, not with how it will be constructed. Users don't care about objects or classes. However, if you know that you're going to build the system using object-oriented techniques, it can be helpful to begin identifying domain classes and their attributes and behaviors during requirements analysis. This facilitates the transition from analysis to design, as the designer maps the problem-domain objects into the system's objects and further details each class's attributes and operations.

The standard object-oriented modeling language is the Unified Modeling Language (Booch, Rumbaugh, and Jacobson 1999). At the level of abstraction that's appropriate for requirements analysis, you can use the UML notation to draw class diagrams, as illustrated in Figure 11-6 for a portion of—you guessed it—the Chemical Tracking System. A designer can elaborate these conceptual class diagrams, which are free from implementation specifics, into more detailed class diagrams for object-oriented design and implementation. Interactions among the classes and the messages they exchange can be shown using sequence diagrams and collaboration diagrams, which are not addressed further in this book; see Booch, Rumbaugh, and Jacobson (1999) and Lauesen (2002).

Figure 11-6 contains four classes, each shown in a large box: Requester, Vendor Catalog, Chemical Request, and Request Line Item. There are some similarities between the information in this class diagram and that shown in the other analysis models presented in this chapter (no surprise there—all the diagrams are representing the same problem). The Requester appeared in the entity-relationship diagram in Figure 11-2, where it represented an actor role that could be played by a member of either the Chemist or Chemical Stockroom Staff user class. The data flow diagram in Figure 11-1 also showed that both of these user classes could place requests for chemicals. Don't confuse a *user class* with an *object class*; despite the similarity in names, there's no intentional connection.

The *attributes* associated with the Requester class are shown in the middle portion of its class box: name, employeeNumber, department, and roomNumber (this capitalization convention is commonly used with UML diagrams).

Those are the properties or data items associated with each object that is a member of the Requester class. Similar attributes will appear in the definitions of the stores on a data flow diagram and in the data dictionary.

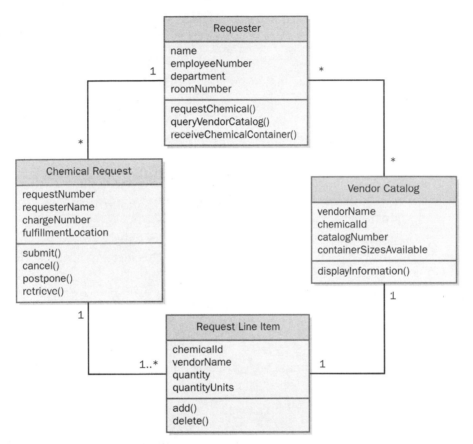

Figure 11-6   Class diagram for part of the Chemical Tracking System.

The *operations* are services that an object in the Requester class can perform. Operations are shown in the bottom portion of the class box and typically are followed by empty parentheses. In a class diagram that represents a design, these operations will correspond to the class's functions or methods, and the function arguments often appear in the parentheses. The analysis class model simply has to show that a Requester can request chemicals, query vendor catalogs, and receive chemical containers. The operations shown in the class diagram correspond roughly to the processes that appear in bubbles on low-level data flow diagrams.

The lines that connect the class boxes in Figure 11-6 represent associations between the classes. The numbers on the lines show the multiplicity of the association, just as the numbers on lines in the entity-relationship diagram show the multiplicity relationships between entities. In Figure 11-6, an asterisk indicates a one-to-many association between a Requester and a Chemical Request: one requester can place many requests, but each request belongs to just one requester.

Decision Tables and Decision Trees

A software system is often governed by complex logic, with various combinations of conditions leading to different system behaviors. For example, if the driver presses the accelerate button on a car's cruise control system and the car is currently cruising, the system increases the car's speed, but if the car isn't cruising, the input is ignored. The SRS needs functional requirements that describe what the system should do under all possible combinations of conditions. However, it's easy to overlook a condition, which results in a missing requirement. These gaps are hard to spot by manually reviewing a textual specification.

Decision tables and decision trees are two alternative techniques for representing what the system should do when complex logic and decisions come into play (Davis 1993). The *decision table* lists the various values for all the factors that influence the behavior and indicates the expected system action in response to each combination of factors. The factors can be shown either as statements with possible conditions of true and false or as questions with possible answers of yes and no. Of course, you can also use decision tables with factors that can have more than two possible values.

> **Trap**   Don't create both a decision table and a decision tree to show the same information; either one will suffice.

Table 11-2 shows a decision table with the logic that governs whether the Chemical Tracking System should accept or reject a request for a new chemical. Four factors influence this decision:

- Whether the user who is creating the request is authorized to do so

- Whether the chemical is available either in the chemical stockroom or from a vendor

- Whether the chemical is on the list of hazardous chemicals that require special training in safe handling

- Whether the user who is creating the request has been trained in handling this type of hazardous chemical

Each of these four factors has two possible conditions, true or false. In principle, this gives rise to 2^4, or 16, possible true/false combinations, for a potential of 16 distinct functional requirements. In practice, though, many of the combinations lead to the same system response. If the user isn't authorized to request chemicals, then the system won't accept the request, so the other conditions are irrelevant (shown as a dash in a cell in the decision table). The table shows that only five distinct functional requirements arise from the various logic combinations.

Table 11-2   Sample Decision Table for the Chemical Tracking System

	Requirement Number				
Condition	**1**	**2**	**3**	**4**	**5**
User is authorized	F	T	T	T	T
Chemical is available	—	F	T	T	T
Chemical is hazardous	—	—	F	T	T
Requester is trained	—	—	—	F	T
Action					
Accept request			X		X
Reject request	X	X		X	

Figure 11-7 shows a decision tree that represents this same logic. The five boxes indicate the five possible outcomes of either accepting or rejecting the chemical request. Both decision tables and decision trees are useful ways to document requirements (or business rules) to avoid overlooking any combinations of conditions. Even a complex decision table or tree is easier to read than a mass of repetitious textual requirements.

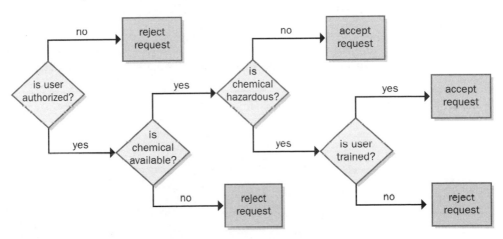

Figure 11-7   Sample decision tree for the Chemical Tracking System.

A Final Reminder

Each of the modeling techniques described in this chapter has its advantages and its limitations. They overlap in the views they provide, so you won't need to create every kind of diagram for your project. For instance, if you create an ERD and a data dictionary, you might not want to create a class diagram (or vice versa). Keep in mind that you draw analysis models to provide a level of understanding and communication that goes beyond what a textual SRS or any other single view of the requirements can provide. Avoid getting caught up in the dogmatic mindsets and religious wars that sometimes take place in the world of software development methods and models. Instead, use what you need to best explain your system's requirements.

 Next Steps

- Practice using the modeling techniques described in this chapter by documenting the design of an existing system. For example, draw a dialog map for an automated teller machine or for a Web site that you use.

- Identify a portion of your SRS that has proven difficult for readers to understand or in which defects have been found. Choose an analysis model described in this chapter that's appropriate for representing that portion of the requirements. Draw the model and assess whether it would have been helpful had you created it earlier.

- The next time you need to document some requirements, select a modeling technique that complements the textual description. Sketch the model on paper or a whiteboard once or twice to make sure you're on the right track, and then use a commercial CASE tool that supports the model notation you're using.

12

Beyond Functionality: Software Quality Attributes

"Hi, Phil, this is Maria again. I have a question about the new employee system you programmed. As you know, this system runs on our mainframe, and every department has to pay for its disk storage and CPU processing charges every month. It looks like the new system's files are using about twice as much disk space as the old system did. Even worse, the CPU charges are nearly three times what they used to be for a session. Can you tell me what's going on, please?"

"Sure, Maria," said Phil. "Remember that you wanted this system to store much more data about each employee than the old system did, so naturally the database is much larger. Therefore, you're paying more for disk space usage each month. Also, you and the other product champions requested that the new system be much easier to use than the old one, so we designed that nice graphical user interface. However, the GUI consumes a lot more computer horsepower than the old system's simple character-mode display. So that's why your per-session processing charges are so much higher. The new system's a lot easier to use, isn't it?"

"Well, yes, it is," Maria replied, "but I didn't realize it would be so expensive to run. I could get in trouble for this. My manager's getting nervous. At this rate, he'll burn through his whole year's computing budget by April. Can you fix the system so that it costs less to run?"

Phil was frustrated. "There's really nothing to fix. The new employee system is just what you said you needed. I assumed you'd realize that if you store more data or do more work with the computer, it costs more. Maybe we should have talked about this earlier because we can't do much about it now. Sorry."

Users naturally focus on specifying their functional, or behavioral, requirements—the things the software will let them do—but there's more to software success than just delivering the right functionality. Users also have expectations about *how well* the product will work. Characteristics that fall into this category include how easy it is to use, how quickly it runs, how often it fails, and how it handles unexpected conditions. Such characteristics, collectively known as *software quality attributes* or *quality factors*, are part of the system's nonfunctional (also called nonbehavioral) requirements.

Quality attributes are difficult to define, yet often they distinguish a product that merely does what it's supposed to from one that delights its customers. As Robert Charette (1990) pointed out, "In real systems, meeting the nonfunctional requirements often is more important than meeting the functional requirements in the determination of a system's perceived success or failure." Excellent software products reflect an optimum balance of competing quality characteristics. If you don't explore the customers' quality expectations during requirements elicitation, you're just lucky if the product satisfies them. Disappointed users and frustrated developers are the more typical outcome.

From a technical perspective, quality attributes drive significant architectural and design decisions, such as partitioning system functions onto various computers to achieve performance or integrity objectives. It's far more difficult and costly to rearchitect a completed system to achieve essential quality goals than to design for them at the outset.

Customers generally don't present their quality expectations explicitly, although the information they provide during elicitation supplies some clues about what they have in mind. The trick is to pin down just what the users are thinking when they say the software must be user-friendly, fast, reliable, or robust. Quality, in its many dimensions, must be defined both by the customers and by those who will build, test, and maintain the software. Questions that explore the customers' implicit expectations can lead to quality goal statements and design criteria that help the developers create a fully satisfactory product.

Quality Attributes

Several dozen product characteristics can be called quality attributes (Charette 1990), although most projects need to carefully consider only a handful of them. If developers know which of these characteristics are most crucial to project success, they can select architecture, design, and programming approaches to achieve the specified quality goals (Glass 1992; DeGrace and Stahl 1993). Quality attributes have been classified according to various schemes (Boehm, Brown, and Lipow 1976; Cavano and McCall 1978; IEEE 1992; DeGrace and Stahl 1993).

One way to classify attributes distinguishes those characteristics that are discernible at run time from those that aren't (Bass, Clements, and Kazman 1998). Another approach is to separate the visible characteristics that are primarily important to the users from under-the-hood qualities that are primarily significant to technical staff. The latter indirectly contribute to customer satisfaction by making the product easier to change, correct, verify, and migrate to new platforms.

Table 12-1 lists several quality attributes in both categories that every project should consider. Some attributes are critical to embedded systems (efficiency and reliability), whereas others might be especially pertinent to Internet and mainframe applications (availability, integrity, and maintainability) or to desktop systems (interoperability and usability). Embedded systems often have additional significant quality attributes, including safety (which was discussed in Chapter 10), installability, and serviceability. Scalability is another attribute that's important to Internet applications.

Table 12-1 **Software Quality Attributes**

Important Primarily to Users	Important Primarily to Developers
Availability	Maintainability
Efficiency	Portability
Flexibility	Reusability
Integrity	Testability
Interoperability	
Reliability	
Robustness	
Usability	

In an ideal universe, every system would exhibit the maximum possible value for all its attributes. The system would be available at all times, would never fail, would supply instantaneous results that are always correct, and would be intuitively obvious to use. Because nirvana is unattainable, you have to learn which attributes from Table 12-1 are most important to your project's success. Then define the user and developer goals in terms of these essential attributes so that designers can make appropriate choices.

Different parts of the product need different combinations of quality attributes. Efficiency might be critical for certain components, while usability is paramount for others. Differentiate quality characteristics that apply to the entire product from those that are specific to certain components, certain user classes, or particular usage situations. Document any global quality goals in section 5.4 of the SRS template presented in Chapter 10, and associate specific goals with individual features, use cases, or functional requirements.

Defining Quality Attributes

Most users won't know how to answer questions such as "What are your interoperability requirements?" or "How reliable does the software have to be?" On the Chemical Tracking System, the analysts developed several prompting questions based on each attribute that they thought might be significant. For example, to explore integrity they asked, "How important is it to prevent users from viewing orders they didn't place?" or "Should everyone be able to search the stockroom inventory?" They asked the user representatives to rank each attribute on a scale of 1 (don't give it another thought) to 5 (critically important). The responses helped the analysts to determine which attributes were most important. Different user classes sometimes had different quality preferences, so the favored user classes got the nod whenever conflicts arose.

The analysts then worked with users to craft specific, measurable, and verifiable requirements for each attribute (Robertson and Robertson 1997). If the quality goals are not verifiable, you can't tell whether you've achieved them. Where appropriate, indicate the scale or units of measure for each attribute and the target, minimum, and maximum values. The notation called Planguage, which is described later in this chapter, helps with this specification. If you can't quantify all the important quality attributes, at least define their priorities and customer preferences. *The IEEE Standard for a Software Quality Metrics Methodology* presents an approach for defining software quality requirements in the context of an overall quality metrics framework (IEEE 1992).

> **Trap**   Don't neglect stakeholders such as maintenance programmers when exploring quality attributes.

Consider asking users what would constitute *unacceptable* performance, usability, integrity, or reliability. That is, specify system properties that would violate the user's quality expectations, such as allowing an unauthorized user to delete files (Voas 1999). By defining unacceptable characteristics—a kind of inverse requirement—you can devise tests that attempt to force the system to demonstrate those characteristics. If you can't force them, you've probably achieved your attribute goals. This approach is particularly valuable for safety-critical applications, in which a system that violates reliability or performance tolerances poses a risk to life or limb.

The remainder of this section briefly describes each of the quality attributes in Table 12-1 and presents some sample quality attributes (a bit simplified) from various projects. Soren Lauesen (2002) provides many excellent examples of quality requirements.

Attributes Important to Users

Users rightfully consider the quality attributes described in the following sections important.

Availability   Availability is a measure of the planned *up time* during which the system is actually available for use and fully operational. More formally, availability equals the mean time to failure (MTTF) for the system divided by the sum of the MTTF and the mean time to repair the system after a failure is encountered. Scheduled maintenance periods also affect availability. Some authors view availability as encompassing reliability, maintainability, and integrity (Gilb 1988).

Certain tasks are more time-critical than others are, and users become frustrated—even irate—when they need to get essential work done and the system isn't available. Ask users what percentage of up time is really needed and whether there are any times for which availability is imperative to meet business or safety objectives. Availability requirements become more complex and more important for Web sites or global applications with worldwide users. An availability requirement might read like this:

> *AV-1. The system shall be at least 99.5 percent available*
> *on weekdays between 6:00 a.m. and midnight local time,*
> *and at least 99.95 percent available on weekdays between*
> *4:00 p.m. and 6:00 p.m. local time.*

As with many of the examples presented here, this requirement is somewhat simplified. It doesn't define the level of performance that constitutes being *available*. Is the system considered available if only one person can use it on the network in a degraded mode? Write quality requirements to make them measurable and to establish a precise agreement on expectations between the requirements analyst, the development team, and the customers.

The Cost of Quality

Beware of specifying 100 percent of a quality attribute such as reliability or availability because it will be impossible to achieve and expensive to strive for. One company had an availability requirement for its shop floor manufacturing systems of 100 percent, 24 hours a day, 365 days a year. To try to achieve such stringent availability, the company installed two independent computer systems so that software upgrades could be installed on the machine that wasn't running at the moment. This was an expensive solution to the availability requirement, but it was cheaper than *not* manufacturing their highly profitable product.

Efficiency   Efficiency is a measure of how well the system utilizes processor capacity, disk space, memory, or communication bandwidth (Davis 1993). Efficiency is related to performance, another class of nonfunctional requirement, which is discussed later in this chapter. If a system consumes too much of the available resources, users will encounter degraded performance, a visible indication of inefficiency. Poor performance is an irritant to the user who is waiting for a database query to display results. But performance problems can also represent serious risks to safety, such as when a real-time process control system is overloaded. Consider minimum hardware configurations when defining efficiency, capacity, and performance goals. To allow engineering margins for unanticipated conditions and future growth, you might specify something like the following:

> *EF-1. At least 25 percent of the processor capacity and RAM available to the application shall be unused at the planned peak load conditions.*

Typical users won't state efficiency requirements in such technical terms. They'll think primarily in terms of response times or disk space consumption. The analyst must ask the questions that will surface user expectations regarding issues such as acceptable performance degradation, demand spikes, and anticipated growth.

I Haven't Got All Day

A major corporation once designed an elaborate graphical store metaphor for its e-business component. The customer could enter the Web site's store, browse various services, and buy a variety of products. The graphics were stunning, the metaphor was sound, and the performance was appalling. The user interface worked fine for the developers working over a high-speed Internet connection to local servers. Unfortunately, the standard 14.4 or 28.8 KBps modem connection that customers used back then resulted in a painfully slow download of the huge image files. Beta testers invariably lost interest before the main page was fully displayed. In their enthusiasm about the graphical metaphor, the development team hadn't considered operating environment constraints, efficiency, or performance requirements. The whole approach was abandoned after it was completed, an expensive lesson in the importance of discussing software quality attributes early in the project.

Flexibility   Also known as *extensibility, augmentability, extendability,* and *expandability,* flexibility measures how easy it is to add new capabilities to the product. If developers anticipate making many enhancements, they can choose design approaches that maximize the software's flexibility. This attribute is essential for products that are developed in an incremental or iterative fashion through a series of successive releases or by evolutionary prototyping. A project I worked on set the following flexibility goal:

> *FL-1. A maintenance programmer who has at least six months of experience supporting this product shall be able to make a new hardcopy output device available to the product, including code modifications and testing, with no more than one hour of labor.*

The project isn't a failure if it takes a programmer 75 minutes to install a new printer, so the requirement has some latitude. If we hadn't specified this requirement, though, the developers might have made design choices that made installing a new device to the system very time-consuming. Write quality requirements in a way that makes them measurable.

Integrity   Integrity—which encompasses security, as discussed in Chapter 10—deals with blocking unauthorized access to system functions, preventing information loss, ensuring that the software is protected from virus infection, and protecting the privacy and safety of data entered into the system. Integrity is a major issue with Internet software. Users of e-commerce systems want their credit card information to be secure. Web surfers don't want personal information or a record of the sites they visit to be used inappropriately, and providers want to protect against denial-of-service or hacking attacks. Integrity requirements have no tolerance for error. State integrity requirements in unambiguous terms: user identity verification, user privilege levels, access restrictions, or the precise data that must be protected. A sample integrity requirement is the following:

> IN-1. Only users who have Auditor access privileges shall
> be able to view customer transaction histories.

As with many integrity requirements, this one is also a constraining business rule. It's a good idea to know the rationale for your quality attribute requirements and to trace them back to specific origins, such as a management policy. Avoid stating integrity requirements in the form of design constraints. Password requirements for access control are a good example. The real requirement is to restrict access to the system to authorized users; passwords are merely one way (albeit the most commonly used way) to accomplish that objective. Depending on which user authentication technique is chosen, this underlying integrity requirement will lead to specific functional requirements that implement the system's authentication functions.

Interoperability   Interoperability indicates how easily the system can exchange data or scrvices with other systems. To assess interoperability, you need to know which other applications the users will employ in conjunction with your product and what data they expect to exchange. Users of the Chemical Tracking System were accustomed to drawing chemical structures with several commercial tools, so they presented the following interoperability requirement:

> IO-1. The Chemical Tracking System shall be able to
> import any valid chemical structure from the ChemiDraw
> (version 2.3 or earlier) and Chem-Struct (version 5 or
> earlier) tools.

You could also state this requirement as an external interface requirement and define the standard file formats that the Chemical Tracking System can import. Alternatively, you could define several functional requirements dealing with the import operation. Sometimes, though, thinking about the system from the perspective of quality attributes reveals previously unstated, implicit requirements. The customers hadn't stated this need when discussing external interfaces or system functionality. As soon as the analyst asked about other systems to which the Chemical Tracking System had to connect, though, the product champion immediately mentioned the two chemical structure drawing packages.

Reliability   The probability of the software executing without failure for a specific period of time is known as reliability (Musa, Iannino, and Okumoto 1987). Robustness is sometimes considered an aspect of reliability. Ways to measure software reliability include the percentage of operations that are completed correctly and the average length of time the system runs before failing. Establish quantitative reliability requirements based on how severe the impact would be if a failure occurred and whether the cost of maximizing reliability is justifiable. Systems that require high reliability should also be designed for high testability to make it easier to find defects that could compromise reliability.

My team once wrote some software to control laboratory equipment that performed daylong experiments using scarce, expensive chemicals. The users required the software component that actually ran the experiments to be highly reliable. Other system functions, such as logging temperature data periodically, were less critical. A reliability requirement for this system was

> *RE-1. No more than five experimental runs out of 1000*
> *can be lost because of software failures.*

Robustness   A customer once told a company that builds measurement devices that its next product should be "built like a tank." The developing company therefore adopted, slightly tongue-in-cheek, the new quality attribute of "tankness." Tankness is a colloquial way of saying *robustness*, which is sometimes called *fault tolerance*. Robustness is the degree to which a system continues to function properly when confronted with invalid inputs, defects in connected software or hardware components, or unexpected operating conditions. Robust software recovers gracefully from problem situations and is forgiving of user mistakes. When eliciting robustness requirements, ask users about error conditions the system might encounter and how the system should react. One example of a robustness requirement is

> *RO-1. If the editor fails before the user saves the file, the*
> *editor shall be able to recover all changes made in the file*
> *being edited up to one minute prior to the failure the next*
> *time the same user starts the program.*

Several years ago I led a project to develop a reusable software component called the Graphics Engine, which interpreted data files that defined graphical plots and rendered the plots on a designated output device (Wiegers 1996b). Several applications that needed to generate plots invoked the Graphics Engine. Because the developers had no control over the data that these applications fed into the Graphics Engine, robustness was an essential quality. One of our robustness requirements was

> *RO-2. All plot description parameters shall have default values specified, which the Graphics Engine shall use if a parameter's input data is missing or invalid.*

With this requirement, the program wouldn't crash if, for example, an application requested a color that the plotter being used couldn't generate. The Graphics Engine would use the default color of black and continue executing. This would still constitute a product failure because the end user didn't get the desired color. But designing for robustness reduced the severity of the failure from a program crash to generating an incorrect color, an example of fault tolerance.

Usability Also referred to as *ease of use* and *human engineering*, usability addresses the myriad factors that constitute what users often describe as *user-friendliness*. Analysts and developers shouldn't talk about friendly software but about software that's designed for effective and unobtrusive usage. Several books have been published recently on designing usable software systems; for examples see Constantine and Lockwood (1999) and Nielsen (2000). Usability measures the effort required to prepare input for, operate, and interpret the output of the product.

The Chemical Tracking System requirements analysts asked their user representatives questions such as "How important is it that you be able to request chemicals quickly and simply?" and "How long should it take you to complete a chemical request?" These are simple starting points toward defining the many characteristics that will make the software easy to use. Discussions about usability can lead to measurable goals (Lauesen 2002) such as this one:

> *US-1. A trained user shall be able to submit a complete request for a chemical selected from a vendor catalog in an average of four and a maximum of six minutes.*

Inquire whether the new system must conform to any user interface standards or conventions, or whether its user interface needs to be consistent with those of other frequently used systems. You might state such a usability requirement in the following way:

> *US-2. All functions on the File menu shall have shortcut keys defined that use the Control key pressed simultaneously with one other key. Menu commands that also appear on the Microsoft Word XP File menu shall use the same shortcut keys that Word uses.*

Usability also encompasses how easy it is for new or infrequent users to learn to use the product. Ease-of-learning goals can be quantified and measured:

> *US-3. A chemist who has never used the Chemical Tracking System before shall be able to place a request for a chemical correctly with no more than 30 minutes of orientation.*

Attributes Important to Developers

The following sections describe quality attributes that are particularly important to software developers and maintainers.

Maintainability   Maintainability indicates how easy it is to correct a defect or modify the software. Maintainability depends on how easily the software can be understood, changed, and tested. It is closely related to flexibility and testability. High maintainability is critical for products that will undergo frequent revision and for products that are being built quickly (and are perhaps cutting corners on quality). You can measure maintainability in terms of the average time required to fix a problem and the percentage of fixes that are made correctly. The Chemical Tracking System included the following maintainability requirement:

> *MA-1. A maintenance programmer shall be able to modify existing reports to conform to revised chemical-reporting regulations from the federal government with 20 labor hours or less of development effort.*

On the Graphics Engine project, we knew we would be doing frequent software surgery to satisfy evolving user needs. We specified design criteria such as the following to guide developers in writing the code to enhance the program's maintainability:

> *MA-2. Function calls shall not be nested more than two levels deep.*

> *MA-3. Each software module shall have a ratio of nonblank comments to source code statements of at least 0.5.*

State such design goals carefully to discourage developers from taking silly actions that conform to the letter, but not the intent, of the goal. Work with maintenance programmers to understand what properties of the code would make it easy for them to modify it or correct defects.

Hardware devices with embedded software often have maintainability requirements. Some of these lead to software design choices, whereas others influence the hardware design. An example of the latter is the following requirement:

> *MA-4. The printer design shall permit a certified repair technician to replace the printhead cable in no more than 10 minutes, the ribbon sensor in no more than 5 minutes, and the ribbon motor in no more than 5 minutes.*

Portability   The effort required to migrate a piece of software from one operating environment to another is a measure of portability. Some practitioners include the ability to internationalize and localize a product under the heading of portability. The design approaches that make software portable are similar to those that make it reusable (Glass 1992). Portability is typically either immaterial or critical to project success. Portability goals should identify those portions of the product that must be movable to other environments and describe those target environments. Developers can then select design and coding approaches that will enhance the product's portability appropriately.

For example, some compilers define an *integer* as being 16 bits long and others define it as 32 bits. To satisfy a portability requirement, a programmer might symbolically define a data type called *WORD* as a 16-bit unsigned integer and use the WORD data type instead of the compiler's default integer data type. This ensures that all compilers will treat data items of type WORD in the same way, which helps to make the system work predictably in different operating environments.

Reusability   A long-sought goal of software development, reusability indicates the relative effort involved to convert a software component for use in other applications. Developing reusable software costs considerably more than creating a component that you intend to use in just one application. Reusable software must be modular, well documented, independent of a specific application and operating environment, and somewhat generic in capability. Reusability goals are difficult to quantify. Specify which elements of the new system need to be constructed in a manner that facilitates their reuse, or stipulate the libraries of reusable components that should be created as a spin-off from the project, such as:

> *RU-1. The chemical structure input functions shall be designed to be reusable at the object code level in other applications that use the international standard chemical structure representations.*

Testability   Also known as *verifiability*, testability refers to the ease with which software components or the integrated product can be tested to look for defects. Designing for testability is critical if the product has complex algorithms and logic, or if it contains subtle functionality interrelationships. Testability is also important if the product will be modified often because it will undergo frequent regression testing to determine whether the changes damaged any existing functionality.

Because my team and I knew that we'd have to test the Graphics Engine many times while it was repeatedly enhanced, we included the following design guideline in the SRS to enhance testability:

> *TE-1. The maximum cyclomatic complexity of a module*
> *shall not exceed 20.*

Cyclomatic complexity is a measure of the number of logic branches in a source code module (McCabe 1982). Adding more branches and loops to a module makes it harder to test, to understand, and to maintain. The project wasn't going to be a failure if some module had a cyclomatic complexity of 24, but documenting such design guidelines helped the developers achieve a desired quality objective. Had we not stated that design guideline (presented here in the form of a quality requirement), the developers might not have considered cyclomatic complexity when writing their programs. This could have resulted in a program with complex code that was nearly impossible to test thoroughly, difficult to extend, and a nightmare to debug.

Performance Requirements

Performance requirements define how well or how rapidly the system must perform specific functions. Performance requirements encompass speed (database response times, for instance), throughput (transactions per second), capacity (concurrent usage loads), and timing (hard real-time demands). Stringent performance requirements seriously affect software design strategies and hardware choices, so define performance goals that are appropriate for the operating environment. All users want their applications to run instantly, but the real performance requirements will be different for the spell-check feature of a word processing program and a radar guidance system for a missile. Performance requirements should also address how the system's performance will degrade in an overloaded situation, such as when a 911 emergency telephone system is flooded with calls. Following are some simple performance requirement examples:

> *PE-1. The temperature control cycle must execute*
> *completely in 80 milliseconds.*

PE-2. The interpreter shall parse at least 5000 error-free statements per minute.

PE-3. Every Web page shall download in 15 seconds or less over a 50 KBps modem connection.

PE-4. Authorization of an ATM withdrawal request shall not take more than 10 seconds.

> **Trap**   Don't forget to consider how you'll evaluate a product to see whether it satisfies its quality attributes. Unverifiable quality requirements are no better than unverifiable functional requirements.

Defining Nonfunctional Requirements By Using Planguage

Some of the quality attribute examples presented in this chapter are incomplete or nonspecific, a limitation of the attempt to state them in a concise sentence or two. You can't evaluate a product to judge whether it satisfies imprecisely worded quality requirements. In addition, simplistic quality and performance goals can be unrealistic. Specifying a maximum response time of two seconds for a database query might be fine for a simple lookup in a local database but impossible for a six-way join of relational tables residing on geographically separated servers.

To address the problem of ambiguous and incomplete nonfunctional requirements, consultant Tom Gilb (1988; 1997) has developed *Planguage*, a planning language with a rich set of keywords that permits precise statements of quality attributes and other project goals (Simmons 2001). Following is an example of how to express a performance requirement using just a few of the many Planguage keywords. This example is a Planguage version of a performance requirement from Chapter 10: "95 percent of catalog database queries shall be completed within 3 seconds on a single-user 1.1-GHz Intel Pentium 4 PC running Microsoft Windows XP with at least 60 percent of the system resources free."

TAG   Performance.QueryResponseTime

AMBITION   Fast response time to database queries on the base user platform.

SCALE   Seconds of elapsed time between pressing the Enter key or clicking OK to submit a query and the beginning of the display of query results.

METER   Stopwatch testing performed on 250 test queries that represent a defined usage operational profile.

MUST   No more than 10 seconds for 98 percent of queries. <-- Field Support Manager

PLAN   No more than three seconds for category one queries, eight seconds for all queries.

WISH   No more than two seconds for all queries.

base user platform DEFINED   1.1-GHz Intel Pentium 4 processor, 128 MB RAM, Microsoft Windows XP, QueryGen 3.3 running, single user, at least 60 percent of system resources free, no other applications running.

Each requirement receives a unique *tag,* or label. The *ambition* states the purpose or objective of the system that leads to this requirement. *Scale* defines the units of measurement and *meter* describes precisely how to make the measurements. All stakeholders need to have the same understanding of how to measure the performance. Suppose that a user interprets the measurement to be from the time that she presses the Enter key until the complete set of query results appears, rather than until the beginning of the result display, as stated in the example. The developer might claim that the requirement is satisfied while this user insists that it is not. Unambiguous quality requirements and measurements prevent these sorts of arguments.

You can specify several target values for the quantity being measured. The *must* criterion is the minimum acceptable achievement level. The requirement isn't satisfied unless every *must* condition is completely satisfied, so the *must* condition should be justifiable in business terms. An alternative way to state the *must* requirement is to define the *fail* (another Planguage keyword) condition: "More than 10 seconds on more than 2 percent of all queries." The *plan* value is the nominal target, and the *wish* value represents the ideal outcome. Also, show the origin of performance goals; for instance, the preceding *must* criterion shows that it came from the Field Support Manager. Any specialized terms in the Planguage statement are *defined* to make them perfectly clear to the reader.

Planguage includes many additional keywords to permit great flexibility and precision in requirements specification. See *http://www.gilb.com* for the most recent information on the still-evolving Planguage vocabulary and syntax. Planguage provides a powerful ability to specify unambiguous quality attribute and performance requirements. Specifying multiple levels of achievement yields a far richer statement of a quality requirement than a simple black-and-white, yes-or-no construct can.

Attribute Trade-Offs

Certain attribute combinations have inescapable trade-offs. Users and developers must decide which attributes are more important than others, and they must respect those priorities consistently when they make decisions. Figure 12-1 illustrates some typical interrelationships among the quality attributes from Table 12-1, although you might encounter exceptions to these (Charette 1990; IEEE 1992; Glass 1992). A plus sign in a cell indicates that increasing the attribute in the corresponding row has a positive effect on the attribute in the column. For example, design approaches that increase a software component's portability also make the software more flexible, easier to connect to other software components, easier to reuse, and easier to test.

	Availability	Efficiency	Flexibility	Integrity	Interoperability	Maintainability	Portability	Reliability	Reusability	Robustness	Testability	Usability
Availability							+		+			
Efficiency			−	−	−	−	−			−	−	−
Flexibility		−		−	+	+	+			+		
Integrity		−			−			−			−	−
Interoperability		−	+	−			+					
Maintainability	+	−	+				+		+			
Portability		−	+	−	+				+	+		−
Reliability	+	−	+			+			+	+	+	
Reusability		−	+	−	+	+	+	−			+	
Robustness	+	−				+						+
Testability	+	−	+			+		+				+
Usability		−								+	−	

Figure 12-1 Positive and negative relationships among selected quality attributes.

A minus sign in a cell means that increasing the attribute in that row adversely affects the attribute in the column. A blank cell indicates that the attribute in the row has little impact on the attribute in the column. Efficiency has a negative impact on most other attributes. If you write the tightest, fastest code you can, using coding tricks and relying on execution side effects, it's likely to be hard to maintain and enhance; in addition, it won't be easy to port to other platforms. Similarly, systems that optimize ease of use or that are designed to be flexible, reusable, and interoperable with other software or hardware components often incur a performance penalty. Using the general-purpose Graphics Engine component described earlier in the chapter to generate plots resulted in degraded performance compared with the old applications that incorporated custom graphics code. You have to balance the possible performance reductions against the anticipated benefits of your proposed solution to ensure that you're making sensible trade-offs.

The matrix in Figure 12-1 isn't symmetrical because the effect that increasing attribute A has on attribute B isn't necessarily the same as the effect that increasing B will have on A. For example, Figure 12-1 shows that designing the system to increase efficiency doesn't necessarily have any effect on integrity. However, increasing integrity likely will hurt efficiency because the system must go through more layers of user authentications, encryption, virus scanning, and data checkpointing.

To reach the optimum balance of product characteristics, you must identify, specify, and prioritize the pertinent quality attributes during requirements elicitation. As you define the important quality attributes for your project, use Figure 12-1 to avoid making commitments to conflicting goals. Following are some examples:

- Don't expect to maximize usability if the software must run on multiple platforms (portability).

- It's hard to completely test the integrity requirements of highly secure systems. Reused generic components or interconnections with other applications could compromise security mechanisms.

- Highly robust code will be less efficient because of the data validations and error checking that it performs.

As usual, overconstraining system expectations or defining conflicting requirements makes it impossible for the developers to fully satisfy the requirements.

Implementing Nonfunctional Requirements

The designers and programmers will have to determine the best way to satisfy each quality attribute and performance requirement. Although quality attributes are nonfunctional requirements, they can lead to derived functional requirements, design guidelines, or other types of technical information that will produce the desired quality characteristics. Table 12-2 indicates the likely categories of technical information that different types of quality attributes will generate. For example, a medical device with stringent availability requirements might include a backup battery power supply (architecture) and a functional requirement to visibly or audibly indicate that the product is operating on battery power. This translation from user-centric or developer-centric quality requirements into corresponding technical information is part of the requirements and high-level design process.

Table 12-2   Translating Quality Attributes into Technical Specifications

Quality Attribute Types	Likely Technical Information Category
Integrity, interoperability, robustness, usability, safety	Functional requirement
Availability, efficiency, flexibility, performance, reliability	System architecture
Interoperability, usability	Design constraint
Flexibility, maintainability, portability, reliability, reusability, testability, usability	Design guideline
Portability	Implementation constraint

Next Steps

■ Identify several quality attributes from Table 12-1 (on page 217) that might be important to users on your current project. Formulate a few questions about each attribute that will help your users articulate their expectations. Based on the user responses, write one or two specific goals for each important attribute.

■ Rewrite several of the quality attribute examples in this chapter by using Planguage, making assumptions when necessary for the sake of illustration. Can you state those quality requirements with more precision and less ambiguity using Planguage?

■ Write one of your own quality attribute requirements using Planguage. Ask customer, development, and testing representatives to judge whether the Planguage version is more informative than the original version.

■ Examine your users' quality expectations for the system for possible conflicts and resolve them. The favored user classes should have the most influence on making the necessary trade-off choices.

■ Trace your quality attribute requirements into the functional requirements, design and implementation constraints, or architectural and design choices that implement them.

13

Risk Reduction Through Prototyping

"Sharon, today I'd like to talk with you about the requirements that the buyers in the Purchasing Department have for the new Chemical Tracking System," began Lori, the requirements analyst. "Can you tell me what you want the system to do?"

"Wow, I'm not sure how to do this," replied Sharon with a puzzled expression. "I don't know how to describe what I need, but I'll know it when I see it."

IKIWISI—"I'll know it when I see it"—is a phrase that chills the blood of requirements analysts. It conjures an image of the development team having to make their best guess at the right software to build, only to have users tell them, "Nope, that's not right; try again." To be sure, envisioning a future software system and articulating its requirements is hard to do. Many people have difficulty describing their needs without having something tangible in front of them to contemplate, and critiquing is much easier than creating.

Software prototyping makes the requirements more real, brings use cases to life, and closes gaps in your understanding of the requirements. Prototyping puts a mock-up or an initial slice of a new system in front of users to stimulate their thinking and catalyze the requirements dialog. Early feedback on prototypes helps the stakeholders arrive at a shared understanding of the system's requirements, which reduces the risk of customer dissatisfaction.

Even if you apply the requirements development practices described in earlier chapters, portions of your requirements might still be uncertain or unclear to customers, developers, or both. If you don't correct these problems, an expectation gap between the user's vision of the product and the developer's understanding of what to build is guaranteed. It's hard to visualize exactly how software will behave by reading textual requirements or studying analysis models. Users are more willing to try out a prototype (which is fun) than to read an SRS (which is tedious). When you hear *IKIWISI* from your users, think about what you can provide that would help them articulate their needs (Boehm 2000). However, if no stakeholder really has an idea of what the developers should build, your project is doomed.

Prototype has multiple meanings, and participants in a prototyping activity can have significantly different expectations. A prototype airplane actually flies—it's the first instance of the real airplane. In contrast, a software prototype is only a portion or a model of a real system—it might not do anything useful at all. Software prototypes can be working models or static designs; highly detailed screens or quick sketches; visual displays or slices of actual functionality; simulations; or emulations (Constantine and Lockwood 1999; Stevens et al. 1998). This chapter describes different kinds of prototypes, how to use them during requirements development, and ways to make prototyping an effective part of your software engineering process (Wood and Kang 1992).

Prototyping: What and Why

A software prototype is a partial or possible implementation of a proposed new product. Prototypes serve three major purposes:

- **Clarify and complete the requirements.**   Used as a requirements tool, the prototype is a preliminary implementation of a part of the system that's not well understood. User evaluation of the prototype points out problems with the requirements, which you can correct at low cost before you construct the actual product.

- **Explore design alternatives.**   Used as a design tool, a prototype lets stakeholders explore different user interaction techniques, optimize system usability, and evaluate potential technical approaches. Prototypes can demonstrate requirements feasibility through working designs.

- **Grow into the ultimate product.**   Used as a construction tool, a prototype is a functional implementation of an initial subset of the product, which can be elaborated into the complete product through a sequence of small-scale development cycles.

The primary reason for creating a prototype is to resolve uncertainties early in the development process. Use these uncertainties to decide which parts of the system to prototype and what you hope to learn from the prototype evaluations. A prototype is useful for revealing and resolving ambiguity and incompleteness in the requirements. Users, managers, and other nontechnical stakeholders find that prototypes give them something concrete to contemplate while the product is being specified and designed. Prototypes, especially visual ones, are easier to understand than the technical jargon that developers sometimes use.

Horizontal Prototypes

When people say "software prototype," they are usually thinking about a *horizontal prototype* of a possible user interface. A horizontal prototype is also called a *behavioral prototype* or a *mock-up*. It is called *horizontal* because it doesn't dive into all the layers of an architecture or into system details but rather primarily depicts a portion of the user interface. This type of prototype lets you explore some specific behaviors of the intended system, with the goal of refining the requirements. The prototype helps users judge whether a system based on the prototype will let them get the job done.

Like a movie set, the horizontal prototype implies functionality without actually implementing it. It displays the facades of user interface screens and permits some navigation between them, but it contains little or no real functionality. Think of the typical Western movie: the cowboy walks into the saloon and then walks out of the livery stable, yet he doesn't have a drink and he doesn't see a horse because there's nothing behind the false fronts of the buildings.

Horizontal prototypes can demonstrate the functional options the user will have available, the look and feel of the user interface (colors, layout, graphics, controls), and the information architecture (navigation structure). The navigations might work, but at some points the user might see only a message that describes what would really be displayed. The information that appears in response to a database query could be faked or constant, and report contents are hardcoded. Try to use actual data in sample reports, charts, and tables to enhance the validity of the prototype as a model of the real system.

The horizontal prototype doesn't perform any useful work, although it looks as if it should. The simulation is often good enough to let the users judge whether any functionality is missing, wrong, or unnecessary. Some prototypes represent the developer's concept of how a specific use case might be implemented. The user's prototype evaluation can point out alternative courses for the use case, missing interaction steps, or additional exception conditions.

When working with a horizontal prototype, the user should focus on broad requirements and workflow issues without becoming distracted by the precise appearance of screen elements (Constantine 1998). Don't worry at this stage about exactly where the screen elements will be positioned, fonts, colors, graphics, or controls. The time to explore the specifics of user interface design is after you've clarified the requirements and determined the general structure of the interface.

Vertical Prototypes

A *vertical prototype*, also known as a *structural prototype* or *proof of concept*, implements a slice of application functionality from the user interface through the technical services layers. A vertical prototype works like the real system is supposed to work because it touches on all levels of the system implementation. Develop a vertical prototype when you're uncertain whether a proposed architectural approach is feasible and sound, or when you want to optimize algorithms, evaluate a proposed database schema, or test critical timing requirements. To make the results meaningful, vertical prototypes are constructed using production tools in a production-like operating environment. Vertical prototypes are used to explore critical interface and timing requirements and to reduce risk during design.

I once worked with a team that wanted to implement an unusual client/ server architecture as part of a transitional strategy from a mainframe-centric world to an application environment based on networked UNIX servers and workstations (Thompson and Wiegers 1995). A vertical prototype that implemented just a bit of the user interface client (on a mainframe) and the corresponding server functionality (on a UNIX workstation) allowed us to evaluate the communication components, performance, and reliability of our proposed architecture. The experiment was a success, as was the implementation based on that architecture.

Throwaway Prototypes

Before constructing a prototype, make an explicit and well-communicated decision as to whether the prototype will be discarded after evaluation or become part of the delivered product. Build a *throwaway prototype* (or *exploratory prototype*) to answer questions, resolve uncertainties, and improve requirements quality (Davis 1993). Because you'll discard the prototype after it has served its purpose,[1] build it as quickly and cheaply as you can. The more effort you invest in the prototype, the more reluctant the project participants are to discard it.

When developers build a throwaway prototype, they ignore much of what they know about solid software construction techniques. A throwaway prototype emphasizes quick implementation and modification over robustness, reliability, performance, and long-term maintainability. For this reason, don't allow low-quality code from a throwaway prototype to migrate into a production system. Otherwise, the users and the maintainers will suffer the consequences for the life of the product.

The throwaway prototype is most appropriate when the team faces uncertainty, ambiguity, incompleteness, or vagueness in the requirements. Resolving these issues reduces the risk of proceeding with construction. A prototype that helps users and developers visualize how the requirements might be implemented can reveal gaps in the requirements. It also lets users judge whether the requirements will enable the necessary business processes.

> **Trap**   Don't make a throwaway prototype more elaborate than is necessary to meet the prototyping objectives. Resist the temptation—or the pressure from users—to keep adding more capabilities to the prototype.

Figure 13-1 shows a sequence of development activities that move from use cases to detailed user interface design with the help of a throwaway prototype. Each use-case description includes a sequence of actor actions and system responses, which you can model using a dialog map to depict a possible user interface architecture. A throwaway prototype elaborates the dialog elements into specific screens, menus, and dialog boxes. When users evaluate the prototype, their feedback might lead to changes in the use-case descriptions (if, say, an alternative course is discovered) or to changes in the dialog map. Once the requirements are refined and the screens sketched out, each user interface element can be optimized for usability. This progressive refinement approach is cheaper than leaping directly from use-case descriptions to a complete user interface implementation and then discovering major problems with the requirements that necessitate extensive rework.

---

1. You don't actually have to throw the prototype away if you see merit in keeping it for possible future reuse. However, it won't be incorporated into the deliverable product. For this reason, you might prefer to call it a *nonreleasable prototype*.

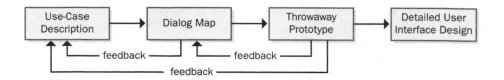

Figure 13-1   Activity sequence from use cases to user interface design using a throwaway prototype.

Evolutionary Prototypes

In contrast to a throwaway prototype, an *evolutionary prototype* provides a solid architectural foundation for building the product incrementally as the requirements become clear over time. Evolutionary prototyping is a component of the spiral software development life cycle model (Boehm 1988) and of some object-oriented software development processes (Kruchten 1996). In contrast to the quick-and-dirty nature of throwaway prototyping, an evolutionary prototype must be built with robust, production-quality code from the outset. Therefore, an evolutionary prototype takes longer to create than a throwaway prototype that simulates the same system capabilities. An evolutionary prototype must be designed for easy growth and frequent enhancement, so developers must emphasize software architecture and solid design principles. There's no room for shortcuts in the quality of an evolutionary prototype.

Think of the first increment of an evolutionary prototype as a pilot release that implements a well-understood and stable portion of the requirements. Lessons learned from user acceptance testing and initial usage lead to modifications in the next iteration. The full product is the culmination of a series of evolutionary prototypes. Such prototypes quickly get useful functionality into the hands of the users. Evolutionary prototypes work well for applications that you know will grow over time, such as projects that gradually integrate various information systems.

Evolutionary prototyping is well suited for Internet development projects. On one such project that I led, my team created a series of four prototypes, based on requirements that we developed from a use-case analysis. Several users evaluated each prototype, and we revised each one based on their responses to questions we posed. The revisions following the fourth prototype evaluation resulted in our production Web site.

Figure 13-2 illustrates several ways to combine the various types of proto-typing. For example, you can use the knowledge gained from a series of throw-away prototypes to refine the requirements, which you might then implement incrementally through an evolutionary prototyping sequence. An alternative path through Figure 13-2 uses a throwaway horizontal prototype to clarify the requirements prior to finalizing the user interface design, while a concurrent vertical prototyping effort validates the architecture, application components, and core algorithms. What you *cannot* do successfully is turn the intentional low quality of a throwaway prototype into the maintainable robustness that a production system demands. In addition, working prototypes that appear to get the job done for a handful of concurrent users likely won't scale up to handle thousands of users without major architectural changes. Table 13-1 summarizes some typical applications of throwaway, evolutionary, horizontal, and vertical prototypes.

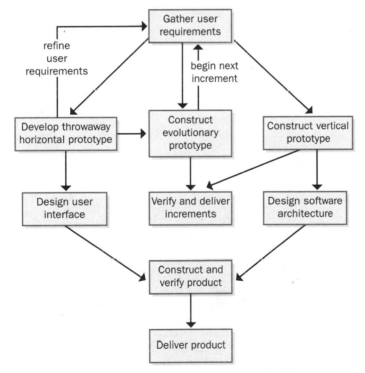

Figure 13-2   Several possible ways to incorporate prototyping into the software development process.

Table 13-1   Typical Applications of Software Prototypes

	Throwaway	Evolutionary
Horizontal	■ Clarify and refine use cases and functional requirements. ■ Identify missing functionality. ■ Explore user interface approaches.	■ Implement core use cases. ■ Implement additional use cases based on priority. ■ Implement and refine Web sites. ■ Adapt system to rapidly changing business needs.
Vertical	■ Demonstrate technical feasibility.	■ Implement and grow core client/server functionality and communication layers. ■ Implement and optimize core algorithms. ■ Test and tune performance.

Paper and Electronic Prototypes

You don't always need an executable prototype to resolve requirements uncertainties. A *paper prototype* (sometimes called a *lo-fi prototype*) is a cheap, fast, and low-tech way to explore what a portion of an implemented system might look like (Rettig 1994; Hohmann 1997). Paper prototypes help you test whether users and developers hold a shared understanding of the requirements. They let you take a tentative and low-risk step into a possible solution space prior to developing production code. A similar technique is called a *storyboard* (Leffingwell and Widrig 2000). Storyboards often illustrate the proposed user interface without engaging the user in interacting with it.

Paper prototypes involve tools no more sophisticated than paper, index cards, sticky notes, and clear plastic sheets. The designer sketches ideas of what the screens might look like without worrying about exactly where the controls appear and what they look like. Users willingly provide feedback that can lead to profound changes on a piece of paper. Sometimes, though, they're less eager to critique a lovely computer-based prototype in which it appears the developer has invested a lot of work. Developers, too, might resist making substantial changes in a carefully crafted electronic prototype.

With lo-fi prototyping, a person plays the role of the computer while a user walks through an evaluation scenario. The user initiates actions by saying aloud what she would like to do at a specific screen: "I'm going to select Print Preview from the File menu." The person simulating the computer then displays the page or index card that represents the display that would appear when the user takes that action. The user can judge whether that is indeed the expected response and whether the item displayed contains the correct elements. If it's wrong, you simply take a fresh piece of paper or a blank index card and draw it again.

Off to See the Wizard

A development team that designed photocopiers once lamented to me that their last copier had a usability problem. A common copying activity required five discrete steps, which the users found clumsy. "I wish we'd prototyped that activity before we designed the copier," one developer said wistfully.

How do you prototype a product as complex as a photocopier? First, buy a big-screen television. Write *COPIER* on the side of the box that it came in. Have someone sit inside the box, and ask a user to stand outside the box and simulate doing copier activities. The person inside the box responds in the way he expects the copier to respond, and the user representative observes whether that response is what he has in mind. A simple, fun prototype like this—sometimes called a "Wizard of Oz prototype"—often gets the early user feedback that effectively guides the development team's design decisions. Plus you get to keep the big-screen television.

No matter how efficient your prototyping tools are, sketching displays on paper is faster. Paper prototyping facilitates rapid iteration, and iteration is a key success factor in requirements development. Paper prototyping is an excellent technique for refining the requirements prior to designing detailed user interfaces, constructing an evolutionary prototype, or undertaking traditional design and construction activities. It also helps the development team manage customer expectations.

If you decide to build an electronic throwaway prototype, several appropriate tools are available (Andriole 1996). These include the following:

- Programming languages such as Microsoft Visual Basic, IBM VisualAge Smalltalk, and Inprise Delphi
- Scripting languages such as Perl, Python, and Rexx

- Commercial prototyping tool kits, screen painters, and graphical user interface builders

- Drawing tools such as Microsoft Visio and Microsoft PowerPoint

Web-based approaches using HTML (Hypertext Markup Language) pages, which can be modified quickly, are useful for creating prototypes that are intended to clarify requirements. They aren't as useful for exploring detailed interface designs quickly. Suitable tools will let you easily implement and modify user interface components, regardless of how inefficient the code behind the interface is. Of course, if you're building an evolutionary prototype, you must use the production development tools from the outset.

Prototype Evaluation

To improve the evaluation of horizontal prototypes, create scripts that guide the users through a series of steps and ask specific questions to elicit the information you need. This supplements a general invitation to "tell me what you think of this prototype." Derive the evaluation scripts from the use cases or functions that the prototype addresses. The script asks evaluators to perform specific tasks and steers them through the parts of the prototype that have the most uncertainty. At the end of each task, and possibly at intermediate points, the script presents specific task-related questions. In addition, you might ask the following general questions:

- Does the prototype implement the functionality in the way you expected?

- Is any functionality missing?

- Can you think of any error conditions that the prototype doesn't address?

- Are any unnecessary functions present?

- How logical and complete does the navigation seem to you?

- Were any tasks overly complex?

Make sure the right people evaluate the prototype from the appropriate perspectives. Include both experienced and inexperienced user class representatives. When you present the prototype to the evaluators, stress that it addresses only a portion of the functionality; the rest will be implemented when the actual system is developed.

> **Trap**   Watch out for users who put production data into a prototype they're evaluating because the prototype seems to really work. They'll be unhappy if their data disappears when the prototype goes away.

You'll learn more by watching users work with the prototype than by just asking them to tell you what they think of it. Formal usability testing is powerful, but simple observation also is illuminating. Watch where the user's fingers try to go instinctively. Spot places where the prototype conflicts with the behavior of other applications that the evaluators use or where there are no clues concerning the user's next action. Look for the furrowed brow that indicates a puzzled user who can't tell what to do next, how to navigate to a desired destination, or how to take a side trip to another part of the application to look something up.

Ask evaluators to share their thoughts aloud as they work with the prototype so that you understand what they're thinking and can detect any requirements that the prototype handles poorly. Create a nonjudgmental environment in which the evaluators feel free to express their thoughts, ideas, and concerns. Avoid coaching users on the "right" way to perform some function with the prototype.

Document what you learn from the prototype evaluation. For a horizontal prototype, use the information to refine the requirements in the SRS. If the prototype evaluation led to some user interface design decisions or to the selection of specific interaction techniques, record those conclusions and how you arrived at them. Decisions that are missing the attendant thought processes tend to be revisited over and over, a waste of time. For a vertical prototype, document the evaluations you performed and their results, culminating in the decisions you made about the technical approaches explored. Look for any conflicts between the SRS and the prototype.

The Risks of Prototyping

Although prototyping reduces the risk of software project failure, it introduces its own risks. The biggest risk is that a stakeholder will see a running prototype and conclude that the product is nearly completed. "Wow, it looks like you're almost done!" says the enthusiastic prototype evaluator. "It looks great. Can you just finish this up and give it to me?"

In a word: NO! A throwaway prototype is never intended for production use, no matter how much it looks like the real thing. It is merely a model, a simulation, or an experiment. Unless there's a compelling business motivation to achieve a marketplace presence immediately (and management accepts the resulting high maintenance burden), resist the pressure to deliver a throwaway prototype. Delivering this prototype will actually delay the project's completion because the design and code intentionally were created without regard to quality or durability.

> **Trap**   Watch out for stakeholders who think that a prototype is just an early version of the production software. Expectation management is a key to successful prototyping. Everyone who sees the prototype must understand its purpose and its limitations.

Don't let the fear of premature delivery pressure dissuade you from creating prototypes. Make it clear to those who see the prototype that you will not release it as production software. One way to control this risk is to use paper, rather than electronic, prototypes. No one who evaluates a paper prototype will think the product is nearly done. Another option is to use prototyping tools that are different from those used for actual development. This will help you resist pressure to "just finish up" the prototype and ship it. Leaving the prototype looking a bit rough and unpolished also mitigates this risk.

Another risk of prototyping is that users become fixated on the *how* aspects of the system, focusing on how the user interface will look and how it will operate. When working with real-looking prototypes, it's easy for users to forget that they should be primarily concerned with the *what* issues at the requirements stage. Limit the prototype to the displays, functions, and navigation options that will let you clear up uncertainty in the requirements.

A third risk is that users will infer the expected performance of the final product from the prototype's performance. You won't be evaluating a horizontal prototype in the intended production environment. You might have built it using tools that differ in efficiency from the production development tools, such as interpreted scripts versus compiled code. A vertical prototype might not use tuned algorithms, or it might lack security layers that will compromise the ultimate performance. If evaluators see the prototype respond instantaneously to a simulated database query using hard-coded query results, they might expect the same fabulous performance in the production software with an enormous distributed database. Consider building in time delays to more realistically simulate the expected behavior of the final product (and perhaps to make the prototype look even less ready for immediate delivery).

Finally, beware of prototyping activities that consume so much effort that the development team runs out of time and is forced to deliver the prototype as the product or to rush through a haphazard product implementation. Treat a prototype as an experiment. You're testing the hypothesis that the requirements are sufficiently defined and the key human-computer interface and architectural issues are resolved so that design and construction can proceed. Do just enough prototyping to test the hypothesis, answer the questions, and refine your understanding of the requirements.

Prototyping Success Factors

Software prototyping provides a powerful set of techniques that can shorten development schedules, increase customer satisfaction, and produce higher-quality products. To make prototyping an effective part of your requirements process, follow these guidelines:

- Include prototyping tasks in your project plan. Schedule time and resources to develop, evaluate, and modify the prototypes.

- State the purpose of each prototype before you build it.

- Plan to develop multiple prototypes. You'll rarely get them right on the first try (which is the whole point of prototyping!).

- Create throwaway prototypes as quickly and cheaply as possible. Invest the minimum effort in developing prototypes that will answer questions or resolve requirements uncertainties. Don't try to perfect a throwaway prototype.

- Don't include extensive input data validations, defensive coding techniques, error-handling code, or code documentation in a throwaway prototype.

- Don't prototype requirements that you already understand, except to explore design alternatives.

- Use plausible data in prototype screen displays and reports. Evaluators can be distracted by unrealistic data and fail to focus on the prototype as a model of how the real system might look and behave.

■   Don't expect a prototype to fully replace an SRS. A lot of behind-the-scenes functionality is only implied by the prototype and should be documented in an SRS to make it complete, specific, and traceable. The visible part of an application is the proverbial tip of the iceberg. Screen images don't give the details of data field definitions and validation criteria, relationships between fields (such as UI controls that appear only if the user makes certain selections in other controls), exception handling, business rules, and other essential bits of information.

 ## Next Steps

■   Identify a portion of your project, such as a use case, that reflects confusion about requirements. Sketch out a portion of a possible user interface that represents your understanding of the requirements and how they might be implemented—a paper prototype. Have some users walk through your prototype to simulate performing a usage scenario. Identify places where the initial requirements were incomplete or incorrect. Modify the prototype accordingly and walk through it again to confirm that the shortcomings are corrected.

■   Summarize this chapter for your prototype evaluators to help them understand the rationale behind the prototyping activities and to help them have realistic expectations for the outcome.

14

Setting Requirement Priorities

After most of the user requirements for the Chemical Tracking System were documented, the project manager, Dave, and the requirements analyst, Lori, met with two of the product champions. Tim represented the chemist community and Roxanne spoke for the chemical stockroom staff.

"As you know," Dave began, "the product champions provided many requirements for the Chemical Tracking System. Unfortunately, we can't include all the functionality you requested in the first release. Since most of the requirements came from the chemists and the chemical stockroom, I'd like to talk with you about prioritizing your requirements."

Tim was puzzled. "Why do you need the requirements prioritized? They're all important, or we wouldn't have given them to you."

Dave explained, "I know they're all important, but we can't fit everything in and still deliver a high-quality product on schedule. We want to make sure we address the most urgent requirements in the first release, which is due at the end of next quarter. We're asking you to help us distinguish the requirements that must be included initially from those that can wait."

"I know the reports that the Health and Safety Department needs to generate for the government have to be available by the end of the quarter or the company will get in trouble," Roxanne pointed out. "We can use our current inventory system for a few more months if we have to. But the barcode labeling and scanning features are essential, more important than searchable vendor catalogs for the chemists."

> Tim protested. *"I promised the catalog search function to the chemists as a way for this system to save them time. The catalog search has to be included from the beginning,"* he insisted.
>
> Lori, the analyst, said, *"While I was discussing use cases with the chemists, it seemed that some would be performed very often and others just occasionally or only by a few people. Could we look at your complete set of use cases and figure out which ones you don't need immediately? I'd also like to defer some of the bells and whistles from the top-priority use cases if we can."*
>
> Tim and Roxanne weren't thrilled that they'd have to wait for some of the system's functionality to be delivered later. However, they realized that it was unreasonable to expect miracles. If the product couldn't contain every requirement in release 1.0, it would be better if everyone could agree on the set to implement first.

Every software project with resource limitations needs to define the relative priorities of the requested product capabilities. Prioritization helps the project manager resolve conflicts, plan for staged deliveries, and make the necessary trade-offs. This chapter discusses the importance of prioritizing requirements, suggests a simple priority classification scheme, and describes a more rigorous prioritization analysis based on value, cost, and risk.

Why Prioritize Requirements?

When customer expectations are high and timelines are short, you need to make sure the product delivers the most valuable functionality as early as possible. Prioritization is a way to deal with competing demands for limited resources. Establishing the relative priority of each capability lets you plan construction to provide the highest value at the lowest cost. Prioritization is critical for timeboxed or incremental development with tight, immovable release schedules. In the Extreme Programming methodology, customers select which *user stories* they'd like implemented in each two- to three-week incremental release, and the developers estimate how many of these stories they can fit into each increment.

A project manager must balance the desired project scope against the constraints of schedule, budget, staff, and quality goals. One way to accomplish this is to drop—or to defer to a later release—low-priority requirements when new, more vital requirements are accepted or when other project conditions change. If the customers don't distinguish their requirements by importance and urgency, project managers must make these decisions on their own. Not surprisingly, customers might not agree with a project manager's priorities;

therefore, customers must indicate which requirements are needed initially and which can wait. Establish priorities early in the project, when you have more options available for achieving a successful project outcome, and revisit them periodically.

It's difficult enough to get any one customer to decide which of his requirements are top priority. Achieving consensus among multiple customers with diverse expectations is even harder. People naturally have their own interests at heart and aren't eager to compromise their needs for someone else's benefit. However, contributing to requirements prioritization is one of the customer's responsibilities in the customer-development partnership, as was discussed in Chapter 2, "Requirements from the Customer's Perspective." More than simply defining the sequence of requirements implementation, discussing priorities helps to clarify the customers' expectations.

Customers and developers both should provide input to requirements prioritization. Customers place a high priority on those functions that provide the greatest business or usability benefit. However, once a developer points out the cost, difficulty, technical risk, or trade-offs associated with a specific requirement, the customers might conclude that it isn't as essential as they initially believed. The developer might also decide to implement certain lower priority functions early on because of their impact on the system's architecture.

Games People Play with Priorities

The knee-jerk response to a request for customers to set priorities is, "I need all these features. Just make it happen somehow." It can be difficult to persuade customers to discuss priorities if they know that low-priority requirements might never be implemented. One developer told me that it wasn't politically acceptable in his company to say that a requirement had low priority. The priority categories they adopted were high, super-high, and incredibly high. Another developer claimed that priorities weren't necessary: if he wrote something in the SRS, he intended to build it. That doesn't address the issue of *when* each piece of functionality gets built, though. Some developers shun prioritization because it conflicts with the "we can do it all" attitude they want to convey.

> **Trap**   Avoid "decibel prioritization," in which the loudest voice heard gets top priority, and "threat prioritization," in which stakeholders holding the most political power always get what they demand.

In reality, some system capabilities are more essential than others. This becomes apparent during the all-too-common "rapid descoping phase" late in the project, when nonessential features are jettisoned to ensure that the critical capabilities ship on schedule. Setting priorities early in the project and reassessing them in response to changing customer preferences, market conditions, and business events let the team spend time wisely on high-value activities. Implementing most of a feature before you conclude that it isn't necessary is wasteful and frustrating.

If left to their own devices, customers will establish perhaps 85 percent of the requirements as high priority, 10 percent as medium, and 5 percent as low. This doesn't give the project manager much flexibility. If nearly all requirements truly are of top priority, your project has a high risk of not being fully successful and you need to plan accordingly. Scrub the requirements to eliminate any that aren't essential and to simplify those that are unnecessarily complicated (McConnell 1996). To encourage customer representatives to identify lower-priority requirements, the analyst can ask questions such as the following:

- Is there some other way to satisfy the need that this requirement addresses?

- What would the consequence be of omitting or deferring this requirement?

- What would the impact be on the project's business objectives if this requirement weren't implemented immediately?

- Why would a user be unhappy if this requirement were deferred to a later release?

 The management steering team on one large commercial project displayed impatience over the analyst's insistence on prioritizing the requirements. The managers pointed out that often they can do without a particular feature but that another feature might need to be beefed up to compensate. If they deferred too many requirements, the resulting product wouldn't achieve the projected revenue. When you evaluate priorities, look at the connections and interrelationships among different requirements and their alignment with the project's business objectives.

A Prioritization Scale

A common prioritization approach groups requirements into three categories. No matter how you label them, if you're using three categories they boil down to high, medium, and low priority. Such prioritization scales are subjective and imprecise. The stakeholders must agree on what each level means in the scale they use.

One way to assess priority is to consider the two dimensions of *importance* and *urgency* (Covey 1989). Every requirement can be considered as being either important or not important and as being either urgent or not urgent. As Table 14-1 shows, these alternatives yield four possible combinations, which we can use to define a priority scale:

- *High priority* requirements are both important (the user needs the capability) and urgent (the user needs it in the next release). Contractual or legal obligations might dictate that the requirement must be included, or there might be compelling business reasons to implement it promptly.

- *Medium priority* requirements are important (the user needs the capability) but not urgent (they can wait for a later release).

- *Low priority* requirements are not important (the user can live without the capability if necessary) and not urgent (the user can wait, perhaps forever).

- Requirements in the fourth quadrant appear to be urgent but they really aren't important. Don't waste your time working on these. They don't add sufficient value to the product.

Table 14-1   Requirements Prioritization Based on Importance and Urgency

	Important	Not Important
Urgent	High Priority	Don't do these!
Not Urgent	Medium Priority	Low Priority

Include the priority of each requirement in the use-case descriptions, the SRS, or the requirements database. Establish a convention so that the reader knows whether the priority assigned to a high-level requirement is inherited by all its subordinate requirements or whether every individual functional requirement is to have its own priority attribute.

Even a medium-sized project can have hundreds of functional requirements, too many to classify analytically and consistently. To keep it manageable, choose an appropriate level of abstraction for the prioritization—features, use cases, or functional requirements. Within a use case, some alternative courses could have a higher priority than others. You might decide to do an initial prioritization at the feature level and then to prioritize the functional requirements within certain features separately. This will help you to distinguish the core functionality from refinements to schedule for later releases. Document even the low-priority requirements. Their priority might change later, and knowing about them now will help the developers to plan for future enhancements.

Prioritization Based on Value, Cost, and Risk

On a small project the stakeholders can agree on requirement priorities informally. Large or contentious projects demand a more structured approach, which removes some of the emotion, politics, and guesswork from the process. Several analytical and mathematical techniques have been proposed to assist with requirements prioritization. These methods involve estimating the relative value and relative cost of each requirement. The highest priority requirements are those that provide the largest fraction of the total product value at the smallest fraction of the total cost (Karlsson and Ryan 1997; Jung 1998). Subjectively estimating the cost and value by pairwise comparisons of all the requirements is impractical for more than a couple dozen requirements.

Another alternative is Quality Function Deployment (QFD), a comprehensive method for relating customer value to proposed product features (Zultner 1993; Cohen 1995). A third approach, borrowed from Total Quality Management (TQM), rates each requirement against several weighted project success criteria and computes a score to rank the priority of the requirements. However, few software organizations seem to be willing to undertake the rigor of QFD or TQM.

Table 14-2 illustrates a spreadsheet model to help you to estimate the relative priorities for a set of use cases, features, or functional requirements. This Microsoft Excel spreadsheet is available for downloading at *http://www.processimpact.com/goodies.shtml*. The example in Table 14-2 lists several features from (what else?) the Chemical Tracking System. This scheme borrows from the QFD concept of basing customer value on both the benefit provided to the customer if a specific product feature is present and the penalty paid if that feature is absent (Pardee 1996). A feature's attractiveness is directly proportional to the value it provides and inversely proportional to its cost and the technical risk associated with implementing it. All other things being equal, those features with the highest risk-adjusted value/cost ratio should have the highest priority. This approach distributes a set of estimated priorities across a continuum, rather than grouping them into just a few discrete levels.

Apply this prioritization scheme to discretionary requirements, those that aren't top priority. You wouldn't include in this analysis items that implement the product's core business functions, items that you view as key product differentiators, or items that are required for compliance with government regulations. Unless there's a chance that those capabilities could shift to lower priority if conditions change, you're going to incorporate them into the product promptly. Once you've identified those features that absolutely must be included for the product to be releasable, use the model in Table 14-2 to scale the relative priorities of the remaining capabilities. The typical participants in the prioritization process include:

- The project manager, who leads the process, arbitrates conflicts, and adjusts input from the other participants if necessary

- Customer representatives, such as product champions or marketing staff, who supply the benefit and penalty ratings

- Development representatives, such as team technical leads, who provide the cost and risk ratings

Table 14-2   Sample Prioritization Matrix for the Chemical Tracking System

Relative Weights	2	1		1		0.5		
Feature	Relative Benefit	Relative Penalty	Total Value	Value %	Relative Cost	Cost %	Relative Risk	Risk %	Priority
1. Print a material safety data sheet.	2	4	8	5.2	1	2.7	1	3.0	1.22
2. Query status of a vendor order.	5	3	13	8.4	2	5.4	1	3.0	1.21
3. Generate a Chemical Stockroom inventory report.	9	7	25	16.1	5	13.5	3	9.1	0.89
4. See history of a specific chemical container.	5	5	15	9.7	3	8.1	2	6.1	0.87

Table 14-2   Sample Prioritization Matrix for the Chemical Tracking System *(continued)*

Relative Weights	2	1			1		0.5		
5. Search vendor catalogs for a specific chemical.	9	8	26	16.8	3	8.1	8	24.2	0.83
6. Maintain a list of hazardous chemicals.	3	9	15	9.7	3	8.1	4	12.1	0.68
7. Modify a pending chemical request.	4	3	11	7.1	3	8.1	2	6.1	0.64
8. Generate an individual laboratory inventory report.	6	2	14	9.0	4	10.8	3	9.1	0.59
9. Check training database for hazardous chemical training record.	3	4	10	6.5	4	10.8	2	6.1	0.47
10. Import chemical structures from structure drawing tools.	7	4	18	11.6	9	24.3	7	21.2	0.33
Totals	**53**	**49**	**155**	**100.0**	**37**	**100.0**	**33**	**100.0**	

Follow these steps to use this prioritization model:

1. List in the spreadsheet all the features, use cases, or requirements that you want to prioritize; in the example, I've used features. All the items must be at the same level of abstraction—don't mix functional requirements with product features. If certain features are logically

linked (for example, you'd implement feature B only if feature A were included), list only the driving feature in the analysis. This model will work with up to several dozen features before it becomes unwieldy. If you have more items than that, group related features together to create a manageable initial list. You can do a second round of analysis at a finer level of detail if necessary.

2.   Have your customer representatives estimate the relative benefit that each feature would provide to the customer or to the business on a scale of 1 to 9. A rating of 1 indicates that no one would find it useful and 9 means it would be extremely valuable. These benefit ratings indicate alignment of the features with the product's business requirements.

3.   Estimate the relative penalty that the customer or business would suffer if the feature were not included. Again, use a scale of 1 to 9. A rating of 1 means that no one will be upset if it's excluded; 9 indicates a serious downside. Requirements that have both a low benefit and a low penalty add cost but little value; they might be instances of gold plating, functions that look appealing but aren't worth the investment. When assigning penalty ratings, consider how unhappy the customers will be if a specific capability isn't included. Ask yourselves questions such as the following:

❏   Would your product suffer in comparison with other products that do contain that capability?

❏   Would there be any legal or contractual consequences?

❏   Would you be violating some government or industry standard?

❏   Would users be unable to perform some necessary or expected functions?

❏   Would it be a lot harder to add that capability later as an enhancement?

❏   Would problems arise because marketing has promised a feature to satisfy some potential customers but the team decided to omit it?

4.   The spreadsheet calculates the total value for each feature as the sum of its benefit and penalty scores. By default, benefit and penalty are weighted equally. As a refinement, you can change the relative weights for these two factors in the top row of the spreadsheet. In

the example in Table 14-2, all benefit ratings are weighted twice as heavily as the corresponding penalty ratings. The spreadsheet sums the feature values and calculates the percentage of the total value contributed by this set of features that comes from each of the features (the Value % column).

5. Have developers estimate the relative cost of implementing each feature, again on a scale of 1 (quick and easy) to 9 (time consuming and expensive). The spreadsheet will calculate the percentage of the total cost that each proposed feature contributes. Developers estimate the cost ratings based on the feature's complexity, the extent of user interface work required, the potential ability to reuse existing code, the amount of testing and documentation that will be needed, and so forth.

6. Similarly, have developers rate the relative degree of technical or other risks associated with each feature on a scale of 1 to 9. Technical risk is the probability of *not* getting the feature right on the first try. A rating of 1 means that you can program it in your sleep. A 9 indicates serious concerns about feasibility, the lack of staff with the necessary expertise, or the use of unproven or unfamiliar tools and technologies. Ill-defined requirements that might need rework will incur a high risk rating. The spreadsheet will calculate the percentage of the total risk that comes from each feature.

   In the standard model, the benefit, penalty, cost, and risk terms are weighted equally, but you may adjust all four weightings. In the spreadsheet in Table 14-2, risk has half the weight of the cost factor, which has the same weight as the penalty term. If you don't want to consider risk at all in the model, set the risk weighting value to zero.

7. Once you've entered all the estimates into the spreadsheet, it will calculate a priority value for each feature using the following formula:

$$\text{priority} = \frac{\text{value \%}}{(\text{cost \%} * \text{cost weight}) + (\text{risk \%} * \text{risk weight})}$$

8. Sort the list of features in descending order by calculated priority. The features at the top of the list have the most favorable balance of value, cost, and risk and thus—all other factors being equal—should have highest priority.

Or, We Could Arm Wrestle

One company that introduced a requirements prioritization procedure based on the spreadsheet described in this chapter found that it helped a project team to break through an impasse. Several stakeholders had different opinions about which features were most important on a large project, and the team was deadlocked. The spreadsheet analysis made the priority assessment more objective and less emotionally charged, enabling the team to reach some appropriate conclusions and move ahead.

Consultant Johanna Rothman (2000) reported that, "I have suggested this spreadsheet to my clients as a tool for decision-making. Although the ones who tried it have never completely filled out the spreadsheet, they found the discussion it stimulated extremely helpful in deciding the relative priorities of the different requirements." That is, use the framework of benefit, penalty, cost, and risk to guide the discussions about priorities. This is more valuable than the formalism of completely working through the spreadsheet analysis and relying exclusively on the calculated priority sequence.

This technique's accuracy is limited by the team's ability to estimate the benefit, penalty, cost, and risk for each item. Therefore, use the calculated priority sequence only as a guideline. Customer and development representatives should review the completed spreadsheet to agree on the ratings and the resulting sorted priority sequence. Calibrate this model for your own use with a set of completed requirements from a previous project. Adjust the weighting factors until the calculated priority sequence correlates well with your after-the-fact evaluation of how important the requirements in your calibration set really were. This will give you some confidence in using the tool as a model of how you make priority decisions on your projects.

> **Trap**   Don't overinterpret small differences in calculated priority numbers. This semiquantitative method is not mathematically rigorous. Look for groups of requirements that have similar priority numbers.

Different stakeholders often have conflicting ideas about the relative importance of a specific requirement or the penalty of omitting it. The prioritization spreadsheet has a variant that accommodates input from several user classes or other stakeholders. In the Multiple Stakeholders worksheet tab in the downloadable spreadsheet, duplicate the Relative Benefit and Relative Penalty columns so that you have a set for each stakeholder who's contributing to the analysis. Then assign a weighting factor to each stakeholder, giving higher weights to favored user classes than to groups who have less influence on the project's decisions. Have each stakeholder representative provide his own benefit and penalty ratings for each feature. The spreadsheet will incorporate the stakeholder weights when it calculates the total value scores.

This model can also help you to make trade-off decisions when you're evaluating proposed requirements changes. See how their priorities align with those of the existing requirements baseline so that you can choose an appropriate implementation sequence.

Keep your prioritization process as simple as possible, but no simpler. Strive to move requirements away from the political arena into a forum in which stakeholders can make honest assessments. This will give you a better chance of building products that deliver the maximum business value.

 ## Next Steps

- Apply the prioritization model described in this chapter to 10 or 15 features or use cases from a recent project. How well do the calculated priorities compare with the priorities you had determined by some different method? How well do they compare with your subjective sense of the proper priorities?

- If there's a disconnect between what the model predicts for priorities and what you think is right, analyze which part of the model isn't giving sensible results. Try using different weighting factors for benefit, penalty, cost, and risk. Adjust the model until it provides results consistent with what you expect.

- Once you've calibrated and adjusted the prioritization model, apply it to a new project. Incorporate the calculated priorities into the decision-making process. See whether this yields results that the stakeholders find more satisfying than those from their previous prioritization approach.

15

Validating the Requirements

Barry, a test lead, was the moderator for an inspection meeting whose participants were carefully examining a software requirements specification for problems. The meeting included representatives from the two major user classes, a developer named Jeremy, and Trish, the analyst who wrote the SRS. Requirement 83 stated, "The system shall provide unattended terminal timeout security of workstations accessing DMV." Jeremy presented his interpretation of this requirement to the rest of the group. "Requirement 83 says that the system will automatically log off the current user of any workstation logged into the DMV system if there hasn't been any activity within a certain period of time."

"Does anyone have any issues with requirement 83?" asked Barry.

Hui-Lee, one of the product champions, spoke first. "How does the system determine that the terminal is unattended? Is it like a screen saver, so if there isn't any mouse or keyboard activity for, say, five minutes, it logs the user off? That could be annoying if the user were just talking to someone for a few minutes."

Trish added, "Actually, the requirement doesn't say anything about logging off the user. I guess I'm not exactly sure what timeout security *means. I assumed it would be a logoff, but maybe the user just has to type his password again."*

Jeremy was confused also. "Does this mean any workstation that can connect to the DMV system, or just workstations that are actively logged into the DMV system at the moment? How long a timeout period are we talking about? Maybe there's a security guideline for this kind of thing."

Barry made sure that the inspection recorder had captured all these concerns accurately. "Okay, it looks like requirement 83 contains several ambiguities and some missing information, such as the timeout period. Trish, can you please check with the department security coordinator to clear this up?"

Most software developers have experienced the frustration of being asked to implement requirements that were ambiguous or incomplete. If they can't get the information they need, the developers have to make their own interpretations, which aren't always correct. Substantial effort is needed to fix requirement errors after work based on those requirements has already been completed. Studies have shown that it can cost approximately 100 times more to correct a customer-reported requirement defect than to correct an error found during requirements development (Boehm 1981; Grady 1999). Another study found that it took an average of 30 minutes to fix an error discovered during the requirements phase. In contrast, 5 to 17 hours were needed to correct a defect identified during system testing (Kelly, Sherif, and Hops 1992). Clearly, any measures you can take to detect errors in the requirements specifications will save you substantial time and money.

On many projects, testing is a late-stage activity. Requirements-related problems linger in the product until they're finally revealed through time-consuming system testing or by the customer. If you start your test planning and test-case development early, you'll detect many errors shortly after they're introduced. This prevents them from doing further damage and reduces your testing and maintenance costs.

Figure 15-1 illustrates the V model of software development, which shows test activities beginning in parallel with the corresponding development activities (Davis 1993). This model indicates that acceptance testing is based on the user requirements, system testing is based on the functional requirements, and integration testing is based on the system's architecture.

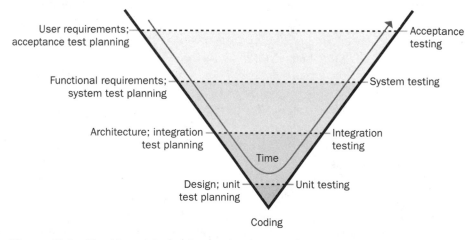

Figure 15-1   The V model of software development incorporates early test planning and test design.

Plan your testing activities and begin developing preliminary test cases during the corresponding development phase. You can't actually run any tests during requirements development because you don't have any software to execute yet. However, conceptual (that is, implementation-independent) test cases based on the requirements will reveal errors, ambiguities, and omissions in your SRS and analysis models long before the team writes any code.

Requirements validation is the fourth component—with elicitation, analysis, and specification—of requirements development (Abran and Moore 2001).[1] Requirements validation activities attempt to ensure that

- The SRS correctly describes the intended system capabilities and characteristics that will satisfy the various stakeholders' needs.

- The software requirements were correctly derived from the system requirements, business rules, or other sources.

- The requirements are complete and of high quality.

- All requirements representations are consistent with each other.

- The requirements provide an adequate basis to proceed with design and construction.

Validation ensures that the requirements exhibit the desirable characteristics of excellent requirement statements (complete, correct, feasible, necessary, prioritized, unambiguous, and verifiable) and of excellent requirements specifications (complete, consistent, modifiable, and traceable). Of course, you can validate only requirements that have been documented, not implicit requirements that exist only in someone's mind.

Validation isn't a single discrete phase that you perform after gathering and documenting all the requirements. Some validation activities, such as incremental reviews of the growing SRS, are threaded throughout the iterative elicitation, analysis, and specification processes. Other activities, such as formal SRS inspection, provide a final quality gate prior to baselining the SRS. Include requirements validation activities as discrete tasks in your project plan.

Project participants sometimes are reluctant to invest time in reviewing and testing an SRS. Intuitively, it seems that inserting time into the schedule to improve requirements quality would delay the planned ship date by that same duration. However, this expectation assumes a zero return on your investment

---

1. Some authors use the term *verification* for this step (Thayer and Dorfman 1997). Verification determines whether the product of a development activity meets the requirements established for it (doing the thing right). *Validation* assesses whether a product actually satisfies the customer needs (doing the right thing). In this book, I've adopted the terminology of the *Software Engineering Body of Knowledge* (Abran and Moore 2001) and refer to the fourth subdomain of requirements development as *validation*.

in requirements validation. In reality, that investment can actually *shorten* the delivery schedule by reducing the rework required and by accelerating system integration and testing (Blackburn, Scudder, and Van Wassenhove 1996). Capers Jones (1994) reports that every dollar spent to prevent defects will reduce your defect repair costs by 3 to 10 dollars. Better requirements lead to higher product quality and customer satisfaction, which reduce the product's lifetime costs for maintenance, enhancement, and customer support. Investing in requirements quality always saves you more money than you spend.

Various techniques can help you to evaluate the correctness and quality of your requirements (Wallace and Ippolito 1997). One approach is to quantify each requirement so that you can think of a way to measure how well a proposed solution satisfies it. Suzanne and James Robertson use the term *fit criteria* to describe such quantifications (Robertson and Robertson 1999). This chapter addresses the validation techniques of formal and informal requirements reviews, developing test cases from requirements, and having customers define their acceptance criteria for the product.

Reviewing Requirements

Any time someone other than the author of a software work product examines the product for problems, a *peer review* is taking place. Reviewing requirements documents is a powerful technique for identifying ambiguous or unverifiable requirements, requirements that aren't defined clearly enough for design to begin, and other problems.

Different kinds of peer reviews go by a variety of names (Wiegers 2002a). Informal reviews are useful for educating other people about the product and collecting unstructured feedback. However, they are not systematic, thorough, or performed in a consistent way. Informal review approaches include:

- A *peer deskcheck*, in which you ask one colleague to look over your work product

- A *passaround*, in which you invite several colleagues to examine a deliverable concurrently

- A *walkthrough*, during which the author describes a deliverable and solicits comments on it

In contrast to the ad hoc nature of informal reviews, formal peer reviews follow a well-defined process. A formal review produces a report that identifies the material, the reviewers, and the review team's judgment as to whether the product is acceptable. The principal deliverable is a summary of the defects found and the issues raised. The members of a formal review team share responsibility for the quality of the review, although authors are ultimately responsible for the quality of the products they create (Freedman and Weinberg 1990).

The best-established type of formal peer review is called an *inspection* (Gilb and Graham 1993; Radice 2002). Inspection of requirements documents is arguably the highest-leverage software quality technique available. Several companies have avoided as much as 10 hours of labor for every hour they invested in inspecting requirements documents and other software deliverables (Grady and Van Slack 1994). A 1000 percent return on investment is not to be sneezed at.

If you're serious about maximizing the quality of your software, your team will inspect every requirements document it creates. Detailed inspection of large requirements documents is tedious and time consuming. Nonetheless, the people I know who have adopted requirements inspections agree that every minute they spent was worthwhile. If you don't have time to inspect everything, use risk analysis to differentiate those requirements that demand inspection from less critical material for which an informal review will suffice. Begin holding SRS inspections when the requirements are perhaps only 10 percent complete. Detecting major defects early and spotting systemic problems in the way the requirements are being written is a powerful way to prevent—not just find—defects.

The Closer You Look, the More You See

On the Chemical Tracking System, the user representatives informally reviewed their latest contribution to the growing SRS after each elicitation workshop. These quick reviews uncovered many errors. After elicitation was complete, one analyst combined the input from all user classes into a single SRS of about 50 pages plus several appendices. Two analysts, one developer, three product champions, the project manager, and one tester then inspected this full SRS in three two-hour inspection meetings held over the course of a week. The inspectors found 223 additional errors, including dozens of major defects. All the inspectors agreed that the time they spent grinding through the SRS, one requirement at a time, saved the project team countless more hours in the long run.

The Inspection Process

Michael Fagan developed the inspection process at IBM in the mid-1970s (Fagan 1976), and others have extended or modified his methods (Gilb and Graham 1993). Inspection has been recognized as a software industry best practice (Brown 1996). Any software work product can be inspected, including requirements and design documents, source code, test documentation, and project plans.

Inspection is a well-defined multistage process. It involves a small team of trained participants who carefully examine a work product for defects and improvement opportunities. Inspections provide a quality gate through which documents must pass before they are baselined. There's some debate whether the Fagan method is the best form of inspection (Glass 1999), but there's no question that inspections are a powerful quality technique. Many helpful work aids for software peer reviews and inspections are available at *http://www.processimpact.com/goodies.shtml*, including a sample peer review process description, defect checklists, and inspection forms.

Participants

The participants in an inspection should represent four perspectives (Wiegers 2002a):

■ **The author of the work product and perhaps peers of the author** The analyst who wrote the requirements document provides this perspective.

■ **The author of any predecessor work product or specification for the item being inspected** This might be a system engineer or an architect who can ensure that the SRS properly details the system specification. In the absence of a higher-level specification, the inspection must include customer representatives to ensure that the SRS describes their requirements correctly and completely.

■ **People who will do work based on the item being inspected** For an SRS, you might include a developer, a tester, a project manager, and a user documentation writer. These inspectors will detect different kinds of problems. A tester is most likely to catch an unverifiable requirement; a developer can spot requirements that are technically infeasible.

■ **People who are responsible for work products that interface with the item being inspected** These inspectors will look for problems with the external interface requirements. They can also spot ripple effects, in which changing a requirement in the SRS being inspected affects other systems.

Try to limit the team to six or fewer inspectors. This means that some perspectives won't be represented in every inspection. Large teams easily get bogged down in side discussions, problem solving, and debates over whether something is really an error. This reduces the rate at which they cover the material during the inspection and increases the cost of finding each defect.

Inspection Roles

All participants in an inspection, including the author, look for defects and improvement opportunities. Some of the inspection team members perform the following specific roles during the inspection.

Author   The author created or maintains the work product being inspected. The author of an SRS is usually the analyst who gathered customer requirements and wrote the specification. During informal reviews such as walkthroughs, the author often leads the discussion. However, the author takes a more passive role during an inspection. The author may not assume any of the other assigned roles—moderator, reader, or recorder. By not having an active role and by parking his ego at the door, the author can listen to the comments from other inspectors, respond to—but not debate—their questions, and think. The author will often spot errors that other inspectors don't see.

Moderator   The moderator, or *inspection leader*, plans the inspection with the author, coordinates the activities, and facilitates the inspection meeting. The moderator distributes the materials to be inspected to the participants several days before the inspection meeting. Moderator responsibilities include starting the meeting on time, encouraging contributions from all participants, and keeping the meeting focused on finding defects rather than resolving problems. Reporting the inspection results to management or to someone who collects data from multiple inspections is another moderator activity. The moderator follows up on proposed changes with the author to ensure that the defects and issues that came out of the inspection were addressed properly.

Reader   One inspector is assigned the role of reader. During the inspection meeting, the reader paraphrases the SRS one requirement at a time. The other participants then point out potential defects and issues. By stating a requirement in her own words, the reader provides an interpretation that might differ from that held by other inspectors. This is a good way to reveal an ambiguity, a possible defect, or an assumption. It also underscores the value of having someone other than the author serve as the reader.

Recorder   The recorder, or *scribe*, uses standard forms to document the issues raised and the defects found during the inspection meeting. The recorder should review aloud what he wrote to confirm the record's accuracy. The other inspectors should help the recorder capture the essence of each issue in a way that clearly communicates to the author the location and nature of the issue.

Entry Criteria

You're ready to inspect a requirements document when it satisfies specific prerequisites. These *entry criteria* set some clear expectations for authors to follow while preparing for an inspection. They also keep the inspection team from spending time on issues that should be resolved prior to the inspection. The moderator uses the entry criteria as a checklist before deciding to proceed with the inspection. Following are some suggested inspection entry criteria for requirements documents:

❑   The document conforms to the standard template.

❑   The document has been spell-checked.

❑   The author has visually examined the document for any layout errors.

❑   Any predecessor or reference documents that the inspectors will require to examine the document are available.

❑   Line numbers are printed on the document to facilitate referring to specific locations during the inspection meeting.

❑   All open issues are marked as TBD (to be determined).

❑   The moderator didn't find more than three major defects in a ten-minute examination of a representative sample of the document.

Inspection Stages

An inspection is a multistep process, as illustrated in Figure 15-2. The purpose of each inspection process stage is summarized briefly in the rest of this section.

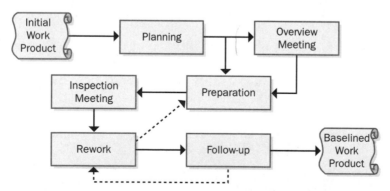

Figure 15-2   Inspection is a multistep process. The dotted lines indicate that portions of the inspection process might be repeated.

Planning   The author and moderator plan the inspection together. They determine who should participate, what materials the inspectors should receive prior to the inspection meeting, and how many inspection meetings will be needed to cover the material. The inspection rate has a large impact on how many defects are found (Gilb and Graham 1993). As Figure 15-3 shows, proceeding through the SRS slowly reveals the most defects. (An alternative interpretation of this frequently reported relationship is that the inspection slows down if you encounter a lot of defects.) Because no team has infinite time available for requirements inspections, select an appropriate rate based on the risk of overlooking major defects. Two to four pages per hour is a practical guideline, although the optimum inspection rate for maximum defect-detection effectiveness is about half that rate (Gilb and Graham 1993). Adjust this rate based on the following factors:

■   The team's previous inspection data

■   The amount of text on each page

■   The specification's complexity

■   The risk of having errors remain undetected

■   How critical the material being inspected is to project success

■   The experience level of the person who wrote the SRS

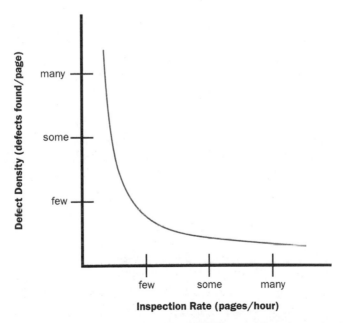

Figure 15-3   The number of defects found depends on the inspection rate.

Overview meeting   During the overview meeting, the author describes the background of the material the team will be inspecting, any assumptions he made, and his specific inspection objectives. You can omit this stage if all inspectors are already familiar with the items being inspected.

Preparation   Prior to the inspection meeting, each inspector examines the product to identify possible defects and issues to be raised, using the checklists of typical defects described later in this chapter or other analysis techniques (Wiegers 2002a). Up to 75 percent of the defects found by an inspection are discovered during preparation (Humphrey 1989), so don't omit this step.

> **More Info**   The techniques for finding missing requirements described in Chapter 7, "Hearing the Voice of the Customer," can be helpful during inspection preparation.

> **Trap**   Don't proceed with an inspection meeting if the participants haven't already examined the work product on their own. Ineffective meetings can lead to the erroneous conclusion that inspections are a waste of time.

Written requirements documents can never replace clarifying discussions between project participants, but serious shortcomings in the specification need to be corrected. Consider asking developers who review the SRS to rate each requirement as to how well they understand it on a scale of 1 to 5 (Pfleeger 2001). A rating of 1 means that the developer doesn't have a clue what the requirement is about. A rating of 5 says that it's perfectly clear, complete, and unambiguous.

Inspection meeting   During the inspection meeting, the reader leads the other inspectors through the SRS, describing one requirement at a time in his or her own words. As inspectors bring up possible defects and other issues, the recorder captures them on a form that becomes the action item list for the requirements author. The purpose of the meeting is to identify as many major defects in the requirements document as possible. The inspection meeting shouldn't last more than about two hours because tired people aren't effective inspectors. If you need more time to cover all the material, schedule another meeting.

At the meeting's conclusion, the team decides whether to accept the requirements document as is, accept it with minor revisions, or indicate that major revision is needed. An outcome of *major revision needed* indicates problems with the requirements development process. Consider holding a retrospective to explore how the process can be improved prior to the next specification activity (Kerth 2001).

Sometimes inspectors report only superficial and cosmetic issues. In addition, inspectors are easily sidetracked into discussing whether an issue really is a defect, debating questions of project scope, and brainstorming solutions to problems. These activities are useful, but they distract attention from the core objective of finding significant defects and improvement opportunities.

Some researchers suggest that inspection meetings are too labor intensive to justify holding them (Votta 1993). I've found that the meetings can reveal additional defects that no inspectors found during their individual preparation. As with all quality activities, make a risk-based decision as to how much energy to devote to improving requirements quality before you proceed with design and construction.

Rework   Nearly every quality control activity reveals some defects. The author should plan to spend some time reworking the requirements following the inspection meeting. Uncorrected requirement defects will be expensive to fix down the road, so this is the time to resolve the ambiguities, eliminate the fuzziness, and lay the foundation for a successful development project. There's little point in holding an inspection if you don't intend to correct the defects it reveals.

Follow-up   In this final inspection step, the moderator or a designated individual works with the author to ensure that all open issues were resolved and that errors were corrected properly. Follow-up brings closure to the inspection process and enables the moderator to determine whether the inspection's exit criteria have been satisfied.

Exit Criteria

Your inspection process should define the exit criteria that must be satisfied before the moderator declares the inspection complete. Here are some possible exit criteria for requirements document inspections:

- ❏   All issues raised during the inspection have been addressed.
- ❏   Any changes made in the document and related work products were made correctly.
- ❏   The revised document has been spell-checked.

❑   All TBDs have been resolved, or each TBD's resolution process, target date, and owner has been documented.

❑   The document has been checked into the project's configuration management system.

Defect Checklists

To help inspectors look for typical kinds of errors in the products they inspect, develop a defect checklist for each type of requirements document your organization creates. Such checklists call the inspectors' attention to historically frequent requirement problems. Figure 15-4 illustrates a use-case inspection checklist, and Figure 15-5 presents a checklist for inspecting an SRS.

No one can remember all the items on a long checklist. Pare the lists to meet your organization's needs, and modify them to reflect the problems that people encounter most often in your own requirements. You might ask certain inspectors to use different subsets of the overall checklist during preparation. One person could check that all internal document cross-references are correct, while another determines whether the requirements can serve as the basis for design and a third evaluates verifiability. Some studies have shown that giving inspectors specific defect-detection responsibilities—providing structured thought processes or scenarios to help them hunt for particular kinds of errors—is more effective than simply handing all inspectors the same checklist (Porter, Votta, and Basili 1995).

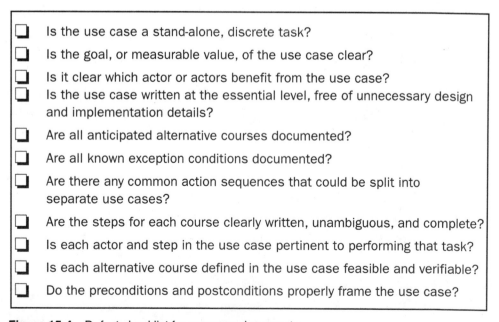

Figure 15-4   Defect checklist for use-case documents.

Organization and Completeness

☐ Are all internal cross-references to other requirements correct?
☐ Are all requirements written at a consistent and appropriate level of detail?
☐ Do the requirements provide an adequate basis for design?
☐ Is the implementation priority of each requirement included?
☐ Are all external hardware, software, and communication interfaces defined?
☐ Are algorithms intrinsic to the functional requirements defined?
☐ Does the SRS include all the known customer or system needs?
☐ Is any necessary information missing from a requirement? If so, is it identified as a TBD?
☐ Is the expected behavior documented for all anticipated error conditions?

Correctness

☐ Do any requirements conflict with or duplicate other requirements?
☐ Is each requirement written in clear, concise, and unambiguous language?
☐ Is each requirement verifiable by testing, demonstration, review, or analysis?
☐ Is each requirement in scope for the project?
☐ Is each requirement free from content and grammatical errors?
☐ Can all the requirements be implemented within known constraints?
☐ Are all specified error messages unique and meaningful?

Quality Attributes

☐ Are all performance objectives properly specified?
☐ Are all security and safety considerations properly specified?
☐ Are other pertinent quality attribute goals explicitly documented and quantified, with the acceptable trade-offs specified?

Traceability

☐ Is each requirement uniquely and correctly identified?
☐ Is each software functional requirement traced to a higher-level requirement (for example, system requirement or use case)?

Special Issues

☐ Are all requirements actually requirements, not design or implementation solutions?
☐ Are the time-critical functions identified and their timing criteria specified?
☐ Have internationalization issues been adequately addressed?

Figure 15-5   Defect checklist for software requirements specifications.

Requirements Review Challenges

Peer reviews are both a technical practice and a social activity. Asking some colleagues to tell you what's wrong with your work is a learned—not instinctive—behavior. It takes time for a software organization to instill peer reviews into its culture. Following are some common challenges that an organization must face when it reviews its requirements documents, with suggestions for how to address each one (Wiegers 1998a; Wiegers 2002a).

Large requirements documents   The prospect of thoroughly inspecting a several-hundred-page SRS is daunting. You might be tempted to skip the inspection entirely and just proceed with construction—not a wise choice. Even given an SRS of moderate size, all inspectors might carefully examine the first part and a few stalwarts will study the middle, but it's unlikely that anyone will look at the last part.

To avoid overwhelming the inspection team, perform incremental reviews throughout requirements development, prior to inspecting the completed document. Identify the high-risk areas that need a careful look, and use informal reviews for less risky material. Ask specific inspectors to start at different locations in the document to make certain that fresh eyes have looked at every page. Consider using several small teams to inspect different portions of the material, although this increases the chance of overlooking inconsistencies. To judge whether you really need to inspect the entire specification, examine a representative sample. The number and types of errors found will help you determine whether investing in a complete inspection is likely to pay off (Gilb and Graham 1993).

Large inspection teams   Many project participants and customers hold a stake in the requirements, so you might have a long list of potential participants for requirements inspections. However, large inspection teams make it hard to schedule meetings, tend to hold side conversations during inspection meetings, and have difficulty reaching agreement on issues.

I once participated in a meeting with 13 other inspectors, which had been set up by someone who didn't understand the importance of keeping the team small. Fourteen people can't agree to leave a burning room, let alone agree on whether a particular requirement is correct. Try the following approaches to deal with a potentially large inspection team:

■   Make sure every participant is there to find defects, not to be educated or to protect a political position.

- Understand which perspective (such as customer, developer, or tester) each inspector represents. Politely decline the participation of people who duplicate a perspective that's already covered. Several people who represent the same community can pool their input and send just one representative to the inspection meeting.

- Establish several small teams to inspect the SRS in parallel and combine their defect lists, removing any duplicates. Research has shown that multiple inspection teams find more defects in a requirements document than does a single large group (Martin and Tsai 1990; Schneider, Martin, and Tsai 1992; Kosman 1997). The results of parallel inspections are primarily additive rather than redundant.

Geographical separation of inspectors   More and more development organizations are building products through the collaboration of geographically dispersed teams. This separation makes reviews more challenging. Videoconferencing can be an effective solution, but teleconferencing doesn't let you read the body language and expressions of other reviewers like you can in a face-to-face meeting.

Document reviews of an electronic file placed in a shared network folder provide an alternative to a traditional inspection meeting (Wiegers 2002a). In this approach, reviewers use word processor features to insert their comments into the text under review. Each comment is labeled with the reviewer's initials, and each reviewer can see what previous reviewers had to say. Web-based collaboration software embedded in tools such as ReviewPro from Software Development Technologies (*http://www.sdtcorp.com*) also can help. If you choose not to hold an inspection meeting, recognize that this can reduce the inspection's effectiveness by perhaps 25 percent (Humphrey 1989), but it also reduces the cost of the inspection.

Testing the Requirements

It's hard to visualize how a system will function under specific circumstances just by reading the SRS. Test cases that are based on the functional requirements or derived from user requirements help make the expected system behaviors tangible to the project participants. The simple act of designing test cases will reveal many problems with the requirements even if you don't execute the tests on an operational system (Beizer 1990). If you begin to develop test cases as soon as portions of the requirements stabilize, you can find problems while it's still possible to correct them inexpensively.

> **Trap**   Watch out for testers who claim that they can't begin their work until the requirements are done and for testers who claim that they don't need requirements to test the software. Testing and requirements have a synergistic relationship because they represent complementary views of the system.

Writing black box (functional) test cases crystallizes your vision of how the system should behave under certain conditions. Vague and ambiguous requirements will jump out at you because you won't be able to describe the expected system response. When analysts, developers, and customers walk through the test cases together, they'll achieve a shared vision of how the product will work.

Making Charlie Happy

I once asked my group's UNIX scripting guru, Charlie, to build a simple e-mail interface extension for a commercial defect-tracking system we were using. I wrote a dozen functional requirements that described how the e-mail interface should work. Charlie was thrilled. He'd written many scripts for people, but he'd never seen written requirements before.

Unfortunately, I waited a couple of weeks before I wrote the test cases for this e-mail function. Sure enough, I had made an error in one of the requirements. I found the mistake because my mental image of how I expected the function to work, represented in about 20 test cases, was inconsistent with one requirement. Chagrined, I corrected the defective requirement before Charlie had completed his implementation, and when he delivered the script, it was defect free. It was a small victory, but small victories add up.

You can begin deriving conceptual test cases from use cases or other user requirements representations very early in the development process (Ambler 1995; Collard 1999; Armour and Miller 2001). You can then use the test cases to evaluate textual requirements, analysis models, and prototypes. The test cases should cover the normal course of the use case, alternative courses, and the exceptions you identified during elicitation and analysis. These conceptual (or abstract) test cases are independent of implementation. For example, consider a use case called "View Order" for the Chemical Tracking System. Some conceptual test cases would be the following:

■ User enters order number to view, order exists, user placed the order. Expected result: show order details.

■ User enters order number to view, order doesn't exist. Expected result: Display message "Sorry, I can't find that order."

■ User enters order number to view, order exists, user didn't place the order. Expected result: Display message "Sorry, that's not your order."

Ideally, an analyst will write the functional requirements and a tester will write the test cases from a common starting point, the user requirements, as shown in Figure 15-6. Ambiguities in the user requirements and differences of interpretation will lead to inconsistencies between the views represented by the functional requirements, models, and test cases. As developers translate the requirements into user interface and technical designs, testers can elaborate the conceptual tests into detailed test procedures for formal system testing (Hsia, Kung, and Sell 1997).

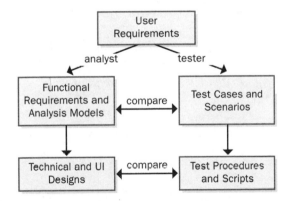

Figure 15-6   Development and testing work products are derived from a common source.

The notion of testing requirements might seem abstract to you at first. Let's see how the Chemical Tracking System team tied together requirements specification, analysis modeling, and early test-case generation. Following are a business requirement, a use case, some functional requirements, part of a dialog map, and a test case, all of which relate to the task of requesting a chemical.

Business requirement   One of the primary business objectives for the Chemical Tracking System was the following:

> *This system will save the company 25 percent on chemical costs in the first year of use by allowing the company to fully exploit chemicals that are already available within the company....*

More Info   This business requirement is from the vision and scope document described in Chapter 5, "Establishing the Product Vision and Project Scope."

Use case   A use case that supports this business requirement is "Request a Chemical." This use case includes a path that permits the user to request a chemical container that's already available in the chemical stockroom. Here's the use-case description:

> *The Requester specifies the desired chemical to request by entering its name or chemical ID number or by importing its structure from a chemical drawing tool. The system satisfies the request either by offering the Requester a new or used container of the chemical from the chemical stockroom or by letting the Requester create a request to order from an outside vendor.*

More Info   This use case appeared in Figure 8-6 (on page 142).

Functional requirement   Here's a bit of functionality associated with this use case:

1.   If the stockroom has containers of the chemical being requested, the system shall display a list of the available containers.

2.   The user shall either select one of the displayed containers or ask to place an order for a new container from a vendor.

Dialog map   Figure 15-7 illustrates a portion of the dialog map for the "Request a Chemical" use case that pertains to this function. The boxes in this dialog map represent user interface displays, and the arrows represent possible navigation paths from one display to another.

More Info   See Chapter 11, "A Picture Is Worth 1024 Words," for more information on dialog maps.

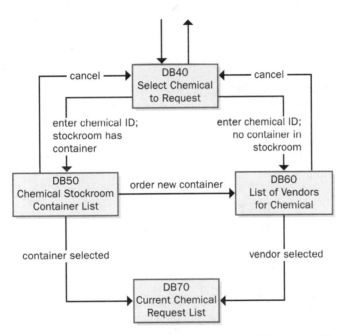

Figure 15-7   Portion of the dialog map for the "Request a Chemical" use case.

Test case   Because this use case has several possible execution paths, you can envision several test cases to address the normal course, alternative courses, and exceptions. The following is just one test case, based on the path that shows the user the available containers in the chemical stockroom. This test case was derived from both the use-case description of this user task and the dialog map in Figure 15-7.

At dialog box DB40, enter a valid chemical ID; the chemical stockroom has two containers of this chemical. Dialog box DB50 appears, showing the two containers. Select the second container. DB50 closes and container 2 is added to the bottom of the Current Chemical Request List in dialog box DB70.

Ramesh, the test lead for the Chemical Tracking System, wrote several test cases like this one, based on his understanding of how the user might interact with the system to request a chemical. Such abstract test cases are independent of implementation details. They don't discuss entering data into fields, clicking buttons, or other specific interaction techniques. As the user interface design activities progressed, Ramesh refined these abstract test cases into specific test procedures.

Now comes the fun part—testing requirements with the test cases. Ramesh first mapped each test case to the functional requirements. He checked to make certain that every test case could be executed by the existing set of requirements. He also made sure that at least one test case covered every functional requirement. Next, Ramesh traced the execution path for every test case on the dialog map with a highlighter pen. The shaded line in Figure 15-8 shows how the preceding sample test case traces onto the dialog map.

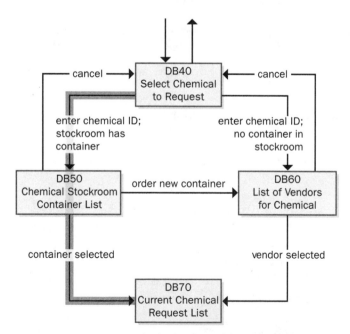

Figure 15-8 Tracing a test case onto the dialog map for the "Request a Chemical" use case.

By tracing the execution path for each test case, you can find incorrect or missing requirements, correct errors in the dialog map, and refine the test cases. Suppose that after "executing" all the test cases in this fashion, the dialog map navigation line labeled "order new container" that goes from DB50 to DB60 in Figure 15-7 hasn't been highlighted. There are two possible interpretations, as follows:

- The navigation from DB50 to DB60 is not a permitted system behavior. The analyst needs to remove that line from the dialog map. If the SRS contains a requirement that specifies the transition, that requirement must also be removed.

- The navigation is a legitimate system behavior, but the test case that demonstrates the behavior is missing.

Similarly, suppose that a test case states that the user can take some action to move directly from dialog box DB40 to DB70. However, the dialog map in Figure 15-7 doesn't contain such a navigation line, so the test case can't be executed with the existing requirements. Again, there are two possible interpretations, and you'll need to determine which of the following is correct:

- The navigation from DB40 to DB70 is not a permitted system behavior, so the test case is wrong.

- The navigation from DB40 to DB70 is a legitimate function, but the dialog map and perhaps the SRS are missing the requirement that allows you to execute the test case.

In these examples, the analyst and the tester combined requirements, analysis models, and test cases to detect missing, erroneous, or unnecessary requirements long before any code was written. Conceptual testing of software requirements is a powerful technique for controlling a project's cost and schedule by finding requirement ambiguities and errors early in the game. Every time I use this technique, I find errors in all the items I'm comparing to each other. As Ross Collard (1999) pointed out,

Use cases and test cases work well together in two ways: If the use cases for a system are complete, accurate, and clear, the process of deriving the test cases is straightforward. And if the use cases are not in good shape, the attempt to derive test cases will help to debug the use cases.

Defining Acceptance Criteria

Software developers might believe that they've built the perfect product, but the customer is the final arbiter. Customers perform acceptance testing to determine whether a system satisfies its *acceptance criteria* (IEEE 1990). If it does, the customer can pay for a product developed under contract or the user can cut over to a new corporate information system. Acceptance criteria—and hence acceptance testing—should evaluate whether the product satisfies its documented requirements and whether it is fit for use in the intended operating environment (Hsia, Kung, and Sell 1997). Having users devise acceptance tests is an effective requirements development strategy. The earlier in the development process that users write acceptance tests, the sooner they can begin to filter out defects in the requirements and in the implemented software.

Acceptance testing should focus on anticipated usage scenarios (Steven 2002; Jeffries, Anderson, and Hendrickson 2001). Key users should consider the most commonly used and most important use cases when deciding how to evaluate the software's acceptability. Acceptance tests focus on the normal courses of the use cases, not on the less common alternative courses or whether the system handles every exception condition properly. Automate acceptance tests whenever possible. This makes it easier to repeat the tests when changes are made and additional functionality is added in future releases. Acceptance tests also ought to address nonfunctional requirements. They should ensure that performance goals are achieved on all platforms, that the system complies with usability standards, and that all committed user requirements are implemented.

> **Trap**   User acceptance testing does not replace comprehensive requirements-based system testing, which covers both normal and exception paths and a wide variety of data combinations.

Having customers develop acceptance criteria thus provides another opportunity to validate the most important requirements. It's a shift in perspective from the requirements-elicitation question of "What do you need to do with the system?" to "How would you judge whether the system satisfies your needs?" If the customer can't express how she would evaluate the system's satisfaction of a particular requirement, that requirement is not stated sufficiently clearly.

Writing requirements isn't enough. You need to make sure that they're the right requirements and that they're good enough to serve as a foundation for design, construction, testing, and project management. Acceptance test planning, informal reviews, SRS inspections, and requirements testing techniques will help you to build higher-quality systems faster and more inexpensively than you ever have before.

Next Steps

- Choose a page of functional requirements at random from your project's SRS. Ask a group of people who represent different stakeholder perspectives to carefully examine that page of requirements for problems, using the defect checklist in Figure 15-5 (on page 270).

- If you found enough errors during the random sample review to make the reviewers nervous about the overall quality of the requirements, persuade the user and development representatives to inspect the entire SRS. For maximum effectiveness, train the team in the inspection process.

- Define conceptual test cases for a use case or for a portion of the SRS that hasn't yet been coded. See whether the user representatives agree that the test cases reflect the intended system behavior. Make sure you've defined all the functional requirements that will permit the test cases to be executed and that there are no superfluous requirements.

- Work with your product champions to define the criteria that they and their colleagues will use to assess whether the system is acceptable to them.

16

Special Requirements Development Challenges

This book has described requirements development as though you were beginning a new software or system development project, sometimes called a *green-field project*. However, many organizations devote most of their effort to maintaining existing legacy systems or building the next release of an established commercial product. Other organizations build few new systems from scratch, instead integrating, customizing, and extending commercial off-the-shelf (COTS) products to meet their needs. Still others outsource their development efforts to contract development companies. This chapter describes appropriate requirements practices for these types of projects, as well as for emergent projects with volatile and uncertain business needs.

Requirements for Maintenance Projects

Maintenance refers to modifications made to software that is currently in operation. Sometimes called *continuing engineering* or *ongoing development*, maintenance often consumes the majority of a software organization's resources. Maintenance programmers typically correct defects, add new features or reports to existing systems, and modify functionality to comply with revised business rules. Few legacy systems have adequate documentation. The original developers who held all the critical information in their heads are often long gone. The approaches described in this chapter can help you to deal with requirements for ongoing maintenance and support projects to improve both product quality and your ability to perform future maintenance (Wiegers 2001).

The Case of the Missing Spec

The requirements specification for the next release of a mature system often says essentially, "The new system should do everything the old system does, except add these new functions and fix those bugs." An analyst once received just such a specification for version 5 of a major product. To find out exactly what the current release did, she looked at the SRS for version 4. Unfortunately, it also said in essence, "Version 4 should do everything that version 3 does, except add these new functions and fix those bugs." She followed the trail back but never found a real requirements specification. Every SRS described the differences that the new version should exhibit compared to the previous version, but nowhere was there a description of the original system. Consequently, everyone had a different understanding of the current system's capabilities. If you're in this situation, document the requirements for the next release more thoroughly so that all the stakeholders understand what the system does.

Begin Capturing Information

In the absence of accurate requirements documentation, maintainers must reverse-engineer an understanding of what the system does from the code. I think of this as "software archaeology." To maximize the benefit from reverse engineering, the archaeology expedition should record what it learns in the form of requirements or design descriptions. Accumulating accurate information about certain portions of the current system positions the team to perform future enhancements more efficiently.

Perhaps your current system is a shapeless mass of history and mystery like the one in Figure 16-1. Imagine that you've been asked to implement some new functionality in region *A* in this figure. Begin by recording the new requirements in a structured, if incomplete, SRS or in a requirements management tool. When you add the new functionality, you'll have to figure out how new screens and features will interface to the existing system. The bridges in Figure 16-1 between region *A* and your current system represent these interfaces. This analysis provides insight into the white portion of the current system, region *B*. That insight is the new knowledge you need to capture.

One useful technique is to draw a dialog map for the new screens you have to add, showing the navigation connections to and from existing display elements. Other modeling techniques such as class and interaction diagrams, data flow diagrams, and entity-relationship diagrams are also useful. A context diagram or use-case diagram depicts the external entities or actors that interact with the system. Another way to begin filling the information void is to create data dictionary entries when you add new data elements to the system and modify existing definitions.

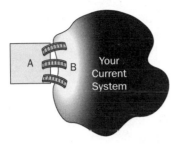

Figure 16-1   Adding enhancement *A* to an ill-documented legacy system provides some visibility into the *B* area.

Building a requirements representation that includes portions of the current system achieves three useful goals:

- It halts the knowledge drain, so future maintainers better understand the changes that were just made.

- It collects some information about the current system that previously was undocumented. When the team performs additional maintenance over time, it can extend these fractional knowledge representations, thereby steadily improving the system documentation. The incremental cost of recording this newly found knowledge is small compared with the costs of someone having to rediscover it later on.

- It provides an indication of functional coverage by the current set of system tests. (Conversely, the test suite will be useful as an initial source of information to recover the software requirements.)

If you have to perform software surgery because of a new or revised government regulation or company policy, begin listing the business rules that affect the system. If you don't do this, vital information will remain distributed among many team members' brains. Information fragmentation contributes to wasted effort as people work from different interpretations of the important business influences on your project.

Many problems show up at interfaces, including software-to-software, software-to-hardware, and software-to-people junctures. When you implement a change, take the time to document what you discovered about the current system's external user, software, hardware, and communication interfaces. Architectural information about how the system's components fit together can help you to add future extensions safely and efficiently. A contractor once had to add a major enhancement to a robot-control system that my team had built.

Our existing design models got him up to speed quickly, so he could efficiently mesh the new capabilities with the existing system architecture. Without this information, the contractor would have had to reverse-engineer the code to understand the architecture and design.

It's not always worth taking the time to generate a complete SRS for an entire production system. Many options lie between the two extremes of continuing forever with no requirements documentation and reconstructing a perfect SRS. Knowing why you'd like to have written requirements available lets you judge whether the cost of rebuilding all or part of the specification is a sound investment. The earlier you are in the product life cycle, the more worthwhile it will be to tune up the requirements.

I worked with one team that was just beginning to develop the requirements for version 2 of a major product with embedded software. They hadn't done a good job on the requirements for version 1, which was currently being implemented. The lead requirements analyst wondered, "Is it worth going back to improve the SRS for version 1?" The company anticipated that this product line would be a major revenue generator for at least 10 years. They also planned to reuse some of the core requirements in several spin-off products. In this case, it made sense to improve the requirements documentation for version 1 because it was the foundation for all subsequent development work in this product family. Had they been working on version 5.3 of a legacy system that they expected to retire within a year, reconstructing an accurate SRS wouldn't be a wise investment.

From Code to Requirements to Tests

A. Datum Corporation needed a comprehensive set of test cases for their flagship product, a complex and mission-critical financial application that was several years old. They decided to reverse-engineer use cases from the existing code and then derive the test cases from those use cases.

First, an analyst reverse-engineered class diagrams from the production software by using a tool that could generate models from source code. Next, the analyst wrote use-case descriptions for the most common user tasks, some of which were highly complex. These use cases addressed all the scenario variations that users performed, as well as many exception conditions. The analysts drew UML sequence diagrams to link the use cases to the system classes (Armour and Miller 2001). The final step was to manually generate a rich set of test cases to cover all the normal and exceptional courses of the use cases. When you create requirements and test artifacts by reverse engineering, you can be confident that they reflect the system as actually built and its known usage modes.

Practice New Requirements Techniques

All software development is based on requirements, perhaps just in the form of a simple change request. Maintenance projects provide an opportunity to try new requirements engineering methods in a small-scale and low-risk way. It's tempting to claim that a small enhancement doesn't warrant writing any requirements. The pressure to get the next release out might make you think that you don't have time for requirements. But enhancement projects let you tackle the learning curve in bite-sized chunks. When the next big project comes along, you'll have some experience and confidence in better requirements practices.

Suppose that marketing or a customer requests that a new feature be added to a mature product. Explore the new feature from the use-case perspective, discussing with the requester the tasks that users will perform with that feature. If you haven't worked with use cases before, try documenting the use case according to a standard template, such as that illustrated in Figure 8-6 (on page 142). Practicing reduces the risk of applying use cases for the first time on a green-field project, when your skill might mean the difference between success and high-profile failure. Some other techniques that you can try on a small scale during maintenance include:

- Creating a data dictionary (Chapter 10)

- Drawing analysis models (Chapter 11)

- Specifying quality attributes and performance goals (Chapter 12)

- Building user interface and technical prototypes (Chapter 13)

- Inspecting requirements specifications (Chapter 15)

- Writing test cases from requirements (Chapter 15)

- Defining customer acceptance criteria (Chapter 15)

Follow the Traceability Chain

Requirements traceability data will help the maintenance programmer determine which components he might have to modify because of a change in a specific requirement. However, a poorly documented legacy system won't have traceability information available. When someone on your team has to modify the existing system, he should create a partial requirements traceability matrix to link the new or changed requirements to the corresponding design elements, code, and test cases. Accumulating traceability links as you perform the development work takes little effort, whereas it's nearly impossible to regenerate the links from a completed system.

> **More Info**   Chapter 20, "Links in the Requirements Chain," describes requirements traceability.

Because of the large ripple effect of many software modifications, you need to make sure that each requirement change is correctly propagated into the downstream work products. Inspections are a good way to check for this consistency. Chapter 15 described the following four perspectives that the inspection participants should represent; these also apply to maintenance work.

- The author of the requirements for the modification or enhancement

- The requesting customer or a marketing representative who can ensure that the new requirements accurately describe the needed change

- Developers, testers, or others who will have to do work based on the new requirements

- People whose work products might be affected by the change

Update the Documentation

Any existing requirements representations must be kept current during maintenance to reflect the capabilities of the modified system. If the updating is burdensome, it will quickly fall by the wayside as busy people rush on to the next change request. Obsolete requirements and design documents aren't helpful for future maintenance. There's a widespread fear in the software industry that writing documentation will consume too much time; the knee-jerk reaction is to neglect all updating of requirements documentation. But what's the cost if you *don't* update the requirements and a future maintainer (perhaps you!) has to regenerate that information? The answer to this question will let you make a thoughtful business decision concerning whether to revise the requirements documentation when you change the software.

Requirements for Package Solutions

Even if you're purchasing a commercial off-the-shelf package as part or all of the solution for a new project, you still need requirements. COTS products typically need to be configured, customized, integrated, and extended to work in the target environment. These activities demand requirements. Requirements also let you evaluate the candidates to identify the most appropriate package for your needs. One evaluation approach includes the following activities (Lawlis et al. 2001):

- Weight your requirements on a scale of 0 to 10 to distinguish their importance.

- Rate each candidate package as to how well it satisfies each requirement. Use a rating of 1 for full satisfaction, 0.5 for partial satisfaction, and 0 for no coverage. You can find the information to make this assessment from product literature, a vendor's response to a request for proposal (an invitation to bid on a project), or direct examination of the product.

- Evaluate each package for the nonfunctional requirements that are important to your users, such as performance and usability, as well as the other quality attributes listed in Chapter 12, "Beyond Functionality: Software Quality Attributes."

- Evaluate product cost, vendor viability, vendor support for the product, external interfaces that will enable extension and integration, and compliance with any technology requirements or constraints for your environment.

This section describes several ways to approach requirements definition when you plan to acquire a commercial package to meet your needs, as shown in Figure 16-2.

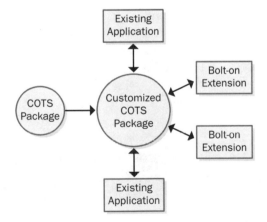

Figure 16-2 COTS packages are customized, integrated into the existing application environment, and extended with bolt-ons.

Develop Use Cases

There's little point in specifying detailed functional requirements or designing a user interface if you're going to buy an existing product. Focus the requirements for COTS acquisition at the user requirements level. Use cases work well for this purpose. Any package you select must let your users accomplish their task objectives, although each package will do so in a different way. The use cases permit a gap analysis, so you can see the places where customization or extension will be needed to meet your needs. Many packages purport to provide canned solutions for some portion of your enterprise information-processing needs. Therefore, specify the reports that the COTS product must generate and determine to what extent the product will let you customize its standard reports. No package solution is likely to accommodate every use case you identify, so prioritize the use cases and reports. Distinguish capabilities that must be available on day one from those that can wait for future extensions and those that your users can live without.

To determine whether—and how well—the package will let the users perform their tasks, derive test cases from the high-priority use cases. Include test cases that explore how the system handles significant exception conditions that might arise. A similar approach is to run the COTS product through a suite of scenarios that represent the expected usage patterns, called an *operational profile* (Musa 1996).

Consider Business Rules

Your requirements exploration should identify pertinent business rules to which the COTS product must conform. Can you configure the package to comply with your corporate policies, industry standards, or government regulations? How easily can you modify the package when these rules change? Does it generate mandated reports in the correct formats? You might also define the data structures required to satisfy your use cases and business rules. Look for major disconnects between your data structures and the package vendor's data model.

Some packages incorporate global business rules, such as income tax withholding computations or printed tax forms. Do you trust that these are implemented correctly? Will the package vendor provide you with new versions when those rules and computations change? If so, how quickly? Will the vendor supply a list of the business rules the package implements? If the product implements any intrinsic business rules that don't apply to you, can you disable or modify them?

Define Quality Requirements

The quality attribute and performance goals discussed in Chapter 12 are another aspect of user requirements that feeds into package solution selection. Explore at least the following attributes:

- **Performance** What maximum response times are acceptable for specific operations? Can the package handle the anticipated load of concurrent users and transaction throughput?

- **Usability** Does the package conform to any established user interface conventions? Is the interface similar to that used in other applications with which the users are familiar? How easily can your customers learn to use the package?

- **Flexibility** How hard will it be for your developers to modify or extend the package to meet your specific needs? Does the package provide appropriate "hooks" (connection and extension points) and application programming interfaces for adding extensions?

- **Interoperability** How easily can you integrate the package with your other enterprise applications? Does it use standard data interchange formats?

- **Integrity** Does the package permit control over which users are allowed to access the system or use specific functions? Does it safeguard data from loss, corruption, or unauthorized access? Can you define various user privilege levels?

COTS packages give the acquiring organization less flexibility over requirements than does custom development. You need to know which requested capabilities aren't negotiable and which you can adjust to fit within the package's constraints. The only way to choose the right package solution is to understand your user and the business activities the package must let them perform.

Requirements for Outsourced Projects

Contracting product development to a separate company demands high-quality written requirements because your direct interactions with the engineering team are likely to be minimal. You'll be sending the supplier a request for proposal, a requirements specification, and some product acceptance criteria, and they'll return the finished product and supporting documentation, as shown in Figure 16-3.

Figure 16-3 Requirements are the cornerstone of an outsourced project.

You won't have the opportunity for the day-to-day clarifications, decision making, and changes that you experience when developers and customers work in close proximity. Poorly defined and managed requirements are a common cause of outsourced project failure (Wiegers 2003). Keep in mind the suggestions in the following sections when you prepare requirements for outsourcing.

Provide the details.   If you distribute a request for proposal, suppliers need to know exactly what you're requesting before they can produce realistic responses and estimates (Porter-Roth 2002).

Avoid ambiguity.   Watch out for the ambiguous terms from Table 10-1 (on page 182) that cause so much confusion. I once read an SRS intended for outsourcing that contained the word *support* in many places. However, a contractor who was going to implement the software wouldn't know what *support* meant in each case. It's the requirements author's responsibility to express the acquirer's intentions clearly.

Arrange touch points with the supplier.   In the absence of real-time, face-to-face communication, you need other mechanisms to stay on top of what the supplier is doing. Peer reviews and prototypes provide insight into how the supplier is interpreting the requirements. Incremental development, in which the supplier delivers small portions of the system periodically, is a risk-management technique. This permits quick course corrections when a misunderstanding sends the supplier's developers in the wrong direction.

> **Trap**   Don't assume that suppliers will interpret ambiguous and incomplete requirements the same way that you do. Some suppliers will interpret the requirements literally and will build precisely what the acquirer specifies. The burden is on the acquirer to communicate all necessary information to the supplier, using frequent conversations to resolve requirements questions.

Define a mutually acceptable change-control process.   Some 45 percent of outsourced projects are at risk from creeping user requirements (Jones 1994). Change always has a price, so using change management to control scope creep is vital in a contract development situation. The contract should specify who will pay for various kinds of changes, such as newly requested functionality or corrections made in the original requirements.

Plan time for multiple cycles and reviews of requirements.   The project schedule for one failed outsourced project included a one-week task named "Hold requirements workshops," followed by tasks to implement several sub-systems. The supplier forgot to include vital intermediate tasks to document, review, and revise the requirements specifications. The iterative and communication-intensive nature of requirements development dictates that you must allow time for these review cycles. The acquirer and the supplier on this project were a continent apart. They experienced slow turnaround on the myriad questions that arose as the SRS cycled back and forth. Failure to resolve requirements issues in a timely way derailed the schedule and eventually helped to send the two parties into litigation.

Define acceptance criteria.   In keeping with Stephen Covey's recommendation to "begin with the end in mind" (Covey 1989), define how you'll assess whether the contracted product is acceptable to you and your customers. How will you judge whether to make the final payment to the supplier?

> **More Info**   Chapter 15 suggested some approaches to defining acceptance criteria.

Requirements for Emergent Projects

When I hear the phrase "gathering requirements," I get a mental image of looking for requirements lying around the office, like flowers that we can pick and place in a basket. If only it were that simple! On some projects, typically those in well-established problem domains, it is indeed possible to specify much of the intended functionality early on. It makes sense to have a concerted requirements development process up front for such projects.

On more exploratory or volatile projects, however, the intended system capabilities become known only over time. Such *emergent* projects are characterized by uncertain requirements and frequent changes. They demand iterative, incremental, and adaptive approaches to both requirements development and software development (Highsmith 2000). Rapidly moving projects with evolving market needs often shy away from established requirements engineering approaches. Instead, they might base development on vague, high-level statements of business objectives. I once spoke to the president of an Internet development company that had encountered many requirements-related problems. One reason was that the development team went directly from signing a contract with a client into a full-day visual design workshop. They didn't take the time to understand how users would be able to obtain value from the Web site, which resulted in considerable rework.

The prevalence of emergent and fast-moving projects has led to the creation of various *agile development* methodologies. These methodologies emphasize rapidly putting useful functionality into the hands of users (Gilb 1988; Beck 2000; Cockburn 2002). The agile methodologies take a lean approach to requirements development and an informal approach to requirements management. Requirements are described in terms of product features or in the form of *user stories*, which are similar to the casual use cases described in Chapter 8, "Understanding User Requirements." Detailed requirements documentation is rejected in favor of continuous interaction with an on-site customer representative, who supplies the requirement details and answers questions.

The agile development philosophy views software change as both inevitable and desirable. The system evolves in response to customer feedback and changing business needs. To cope with change, systems are built in small increments with the expectation that subsequent increments will modify what already exists, enrich the initial features, and add new ones. This approach works well for dealing with a high degree of requirements uncertainty in information systems or Internet projects. It's less well suited to applications whose requirements are well understood and to embedded systems development.

Clearly, development work must be based on some understanding of what users want to accomplish with the software. The requirements for rapidly changing projects are too unstable to justify investing a lot of requirements development effort up front. As Jeff Gainer (1999) points out, though, "The difficulty for the software developers, however, is that iterative development cycles actually encourage requirements change and scope creep." Properly managed, these cycles help the software to meet current business needs, albeit at the expense of reworking previously completed designs, code, and tests.

Stakeholders sometimes claim that the requirements are unknown and unknowable in their desire to dive right into coding, disregarding the potential need for extensive recoding. Resist the temptation to use "Internet time" as an excuse to skimp on sound requirements development. If you really are working on an emergent project, consider using the following approaches to requirements.

Casual User Requirements Specification

Informally documented requirements are appropriate for evolving systems being built by small, co-located teams. The agile methodology called Extreme Programming advocates recording requirements in the form of simple user stories written on index cards (Beck 2000; Jeffries, Anderson, and Hendrickson 2001). Note that even this approach demands that the customers understand their requirements well enough to describe the system behavior in the form of stories.

> **Trap**   Don't expect unwritten requirements communicated telepathically to suffice for project success. Every project should represent its requirements in forms that can be shared among the stakeholders, be updated, and be managed throughout the project. Someone needs to be responsible for this documenting and updating.

On-Site Customer

Frequent conversations between project team members and appropriate customers are the most effective way to resolve many requirements issues. Written documentation, however detailed, is an incomplete substitute for these ongoing communications. A fundamental tenet of Extreme Programming is the presence of a full-time, on-site customer for these discussions. As we saw in Chapter 6, "Finding the Voice of the Customer," though, most projects have multiple user classes, as well as additional stakeholders.

On-Sight Customer

I once wrote programs for a research scientist who sat about 10 feet from my desk. John could provide instantaneous answers to my questions, give feedback on user interface displays, and clarify our informally written requirements. One day John moved to a new office on the same floor of the same building. I perceived an immediate drop in my programming productivity because of the cycle time delay in getting John's input. I spent more time correcting problems because sometimes I proceeded down the wrong path before I could get a course correction. There's no substitute for having the right customers continuously available to the developers both on-site and on-sight. Beware, though, of too-frequent interruptions that make it hard for people to refocus their attention on their work. It can take 15 minutes to reimmerse yourself into the highly productive, focused state of mind called *flow* (DeMarco and Lister 1999).

An on-site customer doesn't guarantee the desired outcome. My colleague Chris helped to establish a development team environment with minimal physical barriers and engaged two product champions. Chris offered this report: "While the close proximity seems to work for the development team, the results with product champions have been mixed. One sat in our midst and still managed to avoid us all. The current champion does a fine job of interacting with the developers and has truly enabled the rapid development of software."

> **Trap**   Don't expect a single individual to resolve all the requirements issues that arise. The product champion approach, with a small number of user representatives, is a more effective solution.

Early and Frequent Prioritization

Incremental development succeeds when customers and developers collaborate on choosing the sequence of implementing features. The development team's goal is to get useful functionality and quality enhancements into the users' hands on a regular basis, so they need to know what capabilities are planned for each increment.

Simple Change Management

Your software development processes should be as simple as they can be to get the job done right, but no simpler. A sluggish change-control process won't work on emergent projects that demand frequent modifications. Streamline your change process so that the minimum number of people can make decisions about requested changes as quickly as possible. This doesn't mean every developer should simply make any changes he likes or that customers request, though; that's a path to chaos, not rapid delivery.

Next Steps

- If you're working on a maintenance, package-solution, outsourced, or emergent project, study the requirements engineering good practices from Chapter 3, "Good Practices for Requirements Engineering," to see which ones would add value to your project and increase its chance of success.

- If you had problems related to requirements on previous projects of the types described in this chapter, perform a project retrospective to diagnose the problems and identify root causes. Would any of the good practices from Chapter 3 or the approaches described in this chapter prevent those same problems from hampering your next project of that type?

17

Beyond Requirements Development

The Chemical Tracking System was coming along nicely. The project sponsor, Gerhard, and the chemical stockroom product champion, Roxanne, had been skeptical of the need to spend much time defining requirements. However, they joined the development team and other product champions at a one-day training class on software requirements. This class stressed the importance of having all project stakeholders reach a shared understanding of their business objectives and the users' needs. The class exposed all the team members to the requirements terminology, concepts, and practices they'd be using. It also motivated them to put some improved requirements techniques into action.

As the project progressed, Gerhard received excellent feedback from the user representatives about how well requirements development had gone. He even sponsored a luncheon for the analysts and product champions to celebrate reaching the significant milestone of baselined requirements for the first system release. At the luncheon, Gerhard thanked the requirements elicitation participants for their contributions and teamwork. Then he said, "Now that the requirements are in good order, I look forward to seeing some code coming out of the development group very soon."

"We aren't quite ready to start writing the production code yet," the project manager explained. "We plan to release the system in stages, so we need to design the system to accommodate the future additions. Our prototypes

provided good ideas about technical approaches and helped us understand the interface characteristics the users prefer. If we spend some time now on design, we can avoid problems as we add functionality to the system over the next several months."

Gerhard was frustrated. It looked like the development team was stalling rather than getting down to the real work of programming. But was he jumping the gun?

Experienced project managers and developers understand the value of translating software requirements into robust designs and rational project plans. These steps are necessary whether the next release represents 1 percent or 100 percent of the final product. This chapter explores some approaches for bridging the gap between requirements development and a successful product release. We'll look at several ways in which requirements influence project plans, designs, code, and tests, as shown in Figure 17-1.

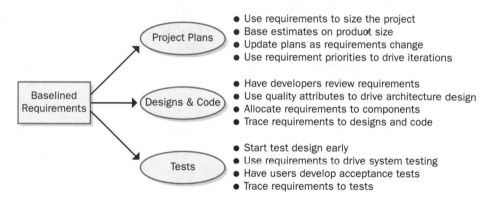

Figure 17-1   Requirements drive project planning, design, coding, and testing activities.

From Requirements to Project Plans

Because the requirements define the project's intended outcomes, you should base project plans, estimates, and schedules on the requirements. Remember, though, that the most important project outcome is a system that meets its business objectives, not necessarily one that implements all the initial requirements according to the original project plan. The requirements and plans represent the team's initial assessment of what it will take to achieve that outcome. But the project's scope might have been off target, or the initial plans might not have been realistic. Also, business needs, business rules, and project constraints all can change. The project's business success will be problematic if you don't update your plans to align with evolving objectives and realities.

Project managers often wonder how much of their schedule and effort they should devote to requirements engineering. Small projects that my teams worked on typically spent 12 to 15 percent of their total effort on requirements engineering (Wiegers 1996a), but the appropriate percentage depends on the size and complexity of the project. Despite the fear that exploring requirements will slow down a project, considerable evidence shows that taking time to understand the requirements actually accelerates development, as the following examples illustrate:

■   A study of 15 projects in the telecommunications and banking industries revealed that the most successful projects spent 28 percent of their resources on requirements engineering (Hofmann and Lehner 2001). Eleven percent of this work went into requirements elicitation, 10 percent into modeling, and 7 percent into validation and verification. The average project devoted 15.7 percent of its effort and 38.6 percent of its schedule to requirements engineering.

■   NASA projects that invested more than 10 percent of their total resources on requirements development had substantially lower cost and schedule overruns than projects that devoted less effort to requirements (Hooks and Farry 2001).

■   In a European study, teams that developed products more quickly devoted more of their schedule and effort to requirements than did slower teams, as shown in Table 17-1 (Blackburn, Scudder, and Van Wassenhove 1996).

Table 17-1   Investing in Requirements Accelerates Development

	Effort Devoted to Requirements	Schedule Devoted to Requirements
Faster Projects	14%	17%
Slower Projects	7%	9%

Not all of the requirements development effort should be allocated to the beginning of the project, as is done in the waterfall, or sequential, life cycle model. Projects that follow an iterative life cycle model will spend time on requirements during every iteration through the development process. Incremental development projects aim to release functionality every few weeks, so they will have frequent but small requirements development efforts. Figure 17-2 illustrates how different life cycle models allocate requirements effort across the product development period.

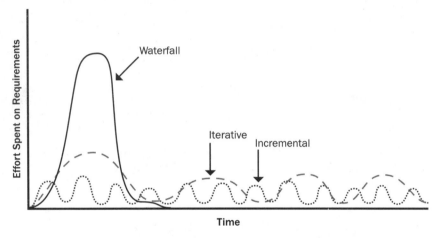

Figure 17-2   The distribution of requirements effort over time varies for projects that follow different development life cycle models.

> **Trap**   Watch out for analysis paralysis. A project with massive up-front effort aimed at perfecting the requirements "once and for all" often delivers little useful functionality in an appropriate time frame. On the other hand, don't avoid requirements development because of the specter of analysis paralysis.

Requirements and Estimation

The first step in project estimating is to assess the size of the software product. You can base size estimates on textual requirements, analysis models, prototypes, or user interface designs. Although there's no perfect measure of software size, the following are some frequently used metrics:

- The number of individually testable requirements (Wilson 1995)

- Function points and feature points (Jones 1996b) or 3-D function points that incorporate data, function, and control (Whitmire 1995)

- The number, type, and complexity of graphical user interface (GUI) elements

- Estimated lines of code needed to implement specific requirements

- A count of object classes or other object-oriented metrics (Whitmire 1997)

All these methods can work for estimating size. Base whatever approach you choose on your experience and on the nature of the software you're developing. Understanding what the development team has successfully achieved on similar projects using similar technologies lets you gauge team productivity. Once you have a size estimate, you can use a commercial estimating tool that suggests feasible combinations of development effort and schedule. These tools let you adjust estimates based on factors such as the skill of the developers, project complexity, and the team's experience in the application domain. Information about some of the available software estimation tools is available at *http://www.laatuk.com/tools/effort estimation tools.html.*

If you don't compare your estimates to the actual project results and improve your estimating ability, your estimates will forever remain guesses. It takes time to accumulate enough data to correlate some measure of software size with development effort. Your objective is to develop equations so that you can reliably judge the size of the completed software from its requirements.

Even the best estimating process will break down if your project must cope with requirements that customers, managers, or lawmakers frequently change. If the changes are so great that the analyst and the development team can't keep up, the project team can become paralyzed, unable to make meaningful progress. In that case, perhaps the project should be deferred until the customer needs are clearer.

Imposed delivery deadlines are a common frustration for project managers. Any time an imposed deadline and a carefully estimated schedule don't agree, negotiation is in order. A project manager who can justify an estimate based on a well-thought-out process and historical data is in a better bargaining position than someone who simply makes his best guess. If the stakeholders can't resolve the schedule conflict, the project's business objectives should dictate whether to reduce scope, add resources, or compromise on quality. These decisions aren't easy, but making them is the only way to maximize the delivered product value.

Got an Hour?

A customer once asked our development team to port a tiny program that he had written for his personal use to our shared computer network so that his colleagues could also use it. "Got an hour?" my manager asked me, giving his top-of-the-head assessment of the project's size. When I spoke with the customer and his colleagues to understand what they needed, the problem turned out to be a bit larger. I spent 100 hours writing the program they were looking for, without any gold plating. A 100-fold expansion factor suggested that my manager's initial estimate of one hour was a trifle hasty and was based on incomplete information. The analyst should explore the requirements, evaluate scope, and judge size *before* anyone makes estimates or commitments.

Uncertain requirements inevitably lead to uncertain estimates of size, effort, and schedule. Because requirements uncertainty is unavoidable early in the project, include contingency buffers in your schedule and budget to accommodate some requirements growth (Wiegers 2002d). Scope growth takes place because business situations change, users and markets shift, and stakeholders reach a better understanding of what the software can or should do. Extensive requirements growth, however, usually indicates that many requirements were missed during elicitation.

Spend some time selecting appropriate size metrics for the kinds of projects your teams work on. Complex, nonlinear relationships exist between product size, effort, development time, productivity, and staff buildup time (Putnam and Myers 1997). Understanding these relationships can keep you from being trapped in the "impossible region," combinations of product size, schedule, and staff where no similar project has ever been completed successfully.

Trap   Don't let your estimates be swayed by what you think someone else wants to hear. Your prediction of the future doesn't change just because someone doesn't like it. Too large a mismatch in predictions indicates the need for negotiation, though.

Requirements and Scheduling

Many projects practice "right-to-left scheduling": a delivery date is cast in concrete and then the product's requirements are defined. In such cases, it often proves impossible for the developers to meet the specified ship date while including all the demanded functionality at the expected quality level. It's more realistic to define the software requirements *before* making detailed plans and commitments. A design-to-schedule strategy can work, however, if the project manager can negotiate what portion of the desired functionality can fit within the schedule constraints. As always, requirements prioritization is a key project success factor.

For complex systems in which software is only a part of the final product, high-level schedules are generally established after developing the product-level (system) requirements and a preliminary architecture. At this point, the key delivery dates can be established and agreed on, based on input from sources including marketing, sales, customer service, and development.

Consider planning and funding the project in stages. An initial requirements exploration stage will provide enough information to let you make realistic plans and estimates for one or more construction stages. Projects that have uncertain requirements benefit from an incremental development life cycle. Incremental development lets the team begin delivering useful software long before the requirements become fully clear. Your prioritization of requirements dictates the functionality to include in each increment.

Software projects frequently fail to meet their goals because the developers and other project participants are poor planners, not because they're poor software engineers. Major planning mistakes include overlooking common tasks, underestimating effort or time, failing to account for project risks, not anticipating rework, and deceiving yourself with unfounded optimism. Effective project planning requires the following elements:

- Estimated product size

- Known productivity of the development team, based on historical performance

- A list of the tasks needed to completely implement and verify a feature or use case

- Reasonably stable requirements

- Experience, which helps the project manager adjust for intangible factors and the unique aspects of each project

Trap   Don't succumb to pressure to make commitments that you know are unachievable. This is a recipe for a lose-lose outcome.

From Requirements to Designs and Code

The boundary between requirements and design is not a sharp line, but keep your specifications free from implementation bias except when you have a compelling reason to intentionally constrain the design. Ideally, the descriptions of what the system is intended to do should not be slanted by design considerations (Jackson 1995). Practically speaking, many projects contain design constraints from prior products, and backward compatibility is a common requirement. Because of this, a requirements specification almost always contains some design information. However, the specification should not contain *inadvertent* design—that is, needless or unintended restrictions on the final design. Include designers or developers in requirements inspections to make sure that the requirements can serve as a solid foundation for design.

A product's requirements, quality attributes, and user characteristics drive its architecture (Bass, Clements, and Kazman 1998). Studying a proposed architecture provides a different perspective that helps to verify the requirements and tune their precision, as does prototyping. Both methods use the following thought process: "If I understand the requirements correctly, this approach I'm reviewing is a good way to satisfy them. And now that I have a preliminary architecture (or a prototype) in hand, does it help me better understand the requirements?"

Architecture is especially critical for systems that include both software and hardware components and for complex software-only systems. An essential requirements analysis step is to allocate the high-level system requirements to the various subsystems and components. A system engineer, an analyst, or an architect decomposes the system requirements into functional requirements for both the software and the hardware subsystems (Leffingwell and Widrig 2000). Traceability information lets the development team track where each requirement is addressed in the design.

Poor allocation decisions can result in the software being expected to perform functions that should have been assigned to hardware components (or the converse), in poor performance, or in the inability to replace one component easily with an improved version. On one project, the hardware engineer blatantly told my group that he expected our software to overcome all limitations of his hardware design! Although software is more malleable than hardware, engineers shouldn't use software's flexibility as a reason to skimp on hardware design. Take a system engineering approach to make optimal decisions about which capabilities each system component will satisfy within its imposed constraints.

Allocation of system capabilities to subsystems and components must be done from the top down (Hooks and Farry 2001). Consider a DVD player, which includes motors to open and close the disk tray and to spin the disk, an optical subsystem to read the data on the disk, image-rendering software, a multifunction remote control, and more, as shown in Figure 17-3. The subsystems interact to control the behaviors that result when, say, the user presses a button on the remote control to open the disk tray while the disk is playing. The system requirements drive the architecture design for such complex products, and the architecture influences the requirements allocation.

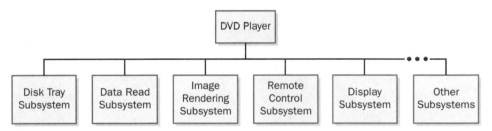

Figure 17-3   Complex products such as DVD players contain multiple software and hardware subsystems.

Software design receives short shrift on some projects, yet the time spent on design is an excellent investment. A variety of software designs will satisfy most products' requirements. These designs will vary in their performance, efficiency, robustness, and the technical methods employed. If you leap directly from requirements into code, you're essentially designing the software on the fly. You come up with *a* design but not necessarily with *an excellent* design, and poorly structured software is the likely result. Refactoring the code can improve the design (Fowler 1999), but an ounce of up-front design is worth a pound of post-release refactoring. Thinking about design alternatives will also help to ensure that developers respect any stated design constraints.

The Incredible Shrinking Design

I once worked on a project that simulated the behavior of a photographic system with eight computational processes. After working hard on requirements analysis, the team was eager to start coding. Instead, we took the time to create a design model—now we were thinking about how we'd build a solution rather than trying to understand the problem. We quickly realized that three of the simulation's steps used identical computational algorithms, three more used another set, and the remaining two shared a third set. The design perspective simplified the problem from eight complex calculations to just three. Had we begun coding immediately after our requirements analysis, we doubtless would have noticed the code repetition at some point, but we saved a lot of time by detecting these simplifications early on. It's more efficient to revise design models than to rewrite code!

As with requirements, excellent designs are the result of iteration. Make multiple passes through the design to refine your initial concepts as you gain information and generate additional ideas. Shortcomings in design lead to products that are difficult to maintain and extend and that don't satisfy the customer's performance, usability, and reliability objectives. The time you spend translating requirements into designs is an excellent investment in building high-quality, robust products.

You needn't develop a complete, detailed design for the entire product before you begin implementation, but you should design each component before you code it. Design planning is of most benefit to particularly difficult projects, projects involving systems with many internal component interfaces and interactions, and projects staffed with inexperienced developers (McConnell 1998). All kinds of projects, however, will benefit from the following actions:

■ Develop a solid architecture of subsystems and components that will hold up during enhancement.

■ Identify the key object classes or functional modules you need to build, defining their interfaces, responsibilities, and collaborations with other units.

- For parallel-processing systems, understand the planned execution threads or allocations of functionality to concurrent processes.

- Define each code unit's intended functionality, following the sound design principles of strong cohesion, loose coupling, and information hiding (McConnell 1993).

- Make sure that your design accommodates all the functional requirements and doesn't contain unnecessary functionality.

- Ensure that the design accommodates exceptional conditions that can arise.

- Ensure that the design will achieve performance, robustness, reliability, and other stated quality goals.

As developers translate requirements into designs and code, they'll encounter points of ambiguity and confusion. Ideally, developers can route these issues back to customers or analysts for resolution. If an issue can't be resolved immediately, any assumptions, guesses, or interpretations that a developer makes should be documented and reviewed with customer representatives. If you encounter many such problems, the requirements weren't sufficiently clear or adequately detailed before the analyst passed them to the developers. Review the remaining requirements with a developer or two and tune them up before continuing with construction. Also, revisit your requirements validation processes to see how the low-quality requirements made it into the developers' hands.

From Requirements to Tests

Testing and requirements engineering have a synergistic relationship. As consultant Dorothy Graham points out, "Good requirements engineering produces better tests; good test analysis produces better requirements" (Graham 2002). The requirements provide the foundation for system testing. The product should be tested against what it was intended to do as recorded in the requirements documentation, not against its design or code. System testing that's based on the code can become a self-fulfilling prophecy. The product might correctly exhibit all the behaviors described in test cases based on the code, but that doesn't mean that it correctly implements the user or functional requirements. Include testers in requirements inspections to make sure the requirements are verifiable and can serve as the basis for system testing.

What to Test?

A seminar attendee once said, "I'm in our testing group. We don't have written requirements, so we have to test what we think the software is supposed to do. Sometimes we're wrong, so we have to ask the developers what the software does and test it again." Testing what the developers built isn't the same as testing what they were *supposed* to build. Requirements are the ultimate reference for system and user acceptance testing. If the system has poorly specified requirements, the testers will discover many implied requirements that developers implemented. Some of these implied requirements will reflect appropriate developer decisions, but others might constitute gold plating or misunderstandings. The analyst should incorporate the legitimate implied requirements and their origins into the SRS to make future regression testing more effective.

The project's testers should determine how they'd verify each requirement. Possible methods include

- Testing (executing the software to look for defects)
- Inspection (examining the code to ensure that it satisfies the requirements)
- Demonstration (showing that the product works as expected)
- Analysis (reasoning through how the system should work under certain circumstances)

The simple act of thinking through how you'll verify each requirement is itself a useful quality practice. Use analytical techniques such as cause-and-effect graphs to derive test cases based on the logic described in a requirement (Myers 1979). This will reveal ambiguities, missing or implied *else* conditions, and other problems. Every functional requirement should trace to at least one test case in your system test suite so that no expected system behavior goes unverified. You can measure testing progress in part by tracking the percentage of the requirements that have passed their tests. Skillful testers will augment requirements-based testing with additional testing based on the product's history, intended usage scenarios, overall quality characteristics, and quirks.

Specification-based testing applies several test design strategies: action-driven, data-driven (including boundary value analysis and equivalence class partitioning), logic-driven, event-driven, and state-driven (Poston 1996). It's possible to generate test cases automatically from formal specifications, but you'll have to develop test cases manually from the more common natural-language requirements specifications.

As development progresses, the team will elaborate the requirements from the high level of abstraction found in use cases, through the detailed software functional requirements, and ultimately down to specifications for individual code modules. Testing authority Boris Beizer (1999) points out that testing against requirements must be performed at every level of software construction, not just the end-user level. Much of the code in an application isn't directly accessed by users but is needed for infrastructure operations. Each module must satisfy its own specification, even if that module's function is invisible to the user. Consequently, testing the system against user requirements is a necessary—but not sufficient—strategy for system testing.

From Requirements to Success

I recently encountered a project in which a contract development team came on board to implement an application for which an earlier team had developed the requirements. The new team took one look at the dozen three-inch binders of requirements, shuddered in horror, and began coding. They didn't refer to the SRS during construction. Instead, they built what they thought they were supposed to, based on an incomplete and inaccurate understanding of the intended system. Not surprisingly, this project encountered a lot of problems. The prospect of trying to understand a huge volume of even excellent requirements is certainly daunting, but ignoring them is a decisive step toward project failure. It's faster to read the requirements, however extensive, before implementation than it is to build the wrong system and then build it again. It's even faster to engage the development team early in the project so that they can participate in the requirements work and perform early prototyping.

A more successful project had a practice of listing all the requirements that were incorporated in a specific release. The project's quality assurance (QA) group evaluated each release by executing the tests for those requirements. A requirement that didn't satisfy its test criteria was counted as an error. The QA group rejected the release if more than a predetermined number of requirements weren't met or if specific high-impact requirements weren't satisfied. This project was successful largely because it used its documented requirements to decide when a release was ready to ship.

The ultimate deliverable from a software development project is a software system that meets the customers' needs and expectations. The requirements are an essential step on the path from business need to satisfied customers. If you don't base your project plans, software designs, and system tests on a foundation of high-quality requirements, you're likely to waste a great deal of effort trying to deliver a solid product. Don't become a slave to your requirements processes, though. There's no point in spending so much time generating unnecessary documents and holding ritualized meetings that no software gets written and the project is canceled. Strive for a sensible balance between rigorous specification and off-the-top-of-the-head coding that will reduce to an acceptable level the risk of building the wrong product.

Next Steps

- Try to trace all the requirements in an implemented portion of your SRS to individual design elements. These might be processes in data flow models, tables in an entity-relationship diagram, object classes or methods, or other design elements. Missing design elements might indicate that developers did their design work mentally on the short path from requirements to code. If your developers don't routinely create designs before cutting code, perhaps they need some training in software design.

- Record the number of lines of code, function points, object classes, or GUI elements that are needed to implement each product feature or use case. Also record your estimates for the effort needed to fully implement and verify each feature or use case, as well as the actual effort required. Look for correlations between size and effort that will help you make more accurate estimates from future requirements specifications.

- Estimate the average percentage of unplanned requirements growth on your last several projects. Can you build contingency buffers into your project schedules to accommodate a similar scope increase on future projects? Use the growth data from previous projects to justify the schedule contingency so that it doesn't look like arbitrary padding to managers, customers, and other stakeholders.

III

Software Requirements Management

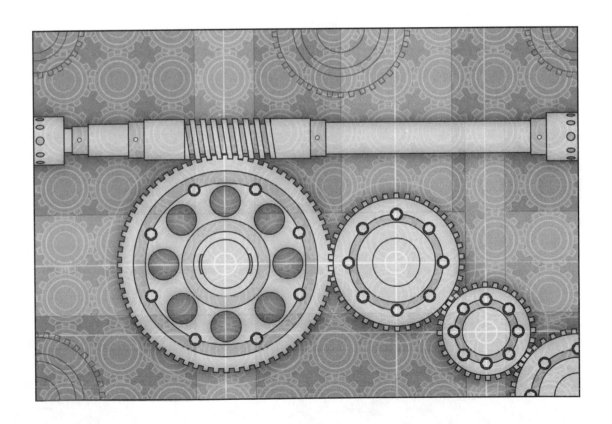

18

Requirements Management Principles and Practices

Chapter 1, "The Essential Software Requirement," divided the discipline of requirements engineering into requirements development and requirements management. Requirements development involves eliciting, analyzing, specifying, and validating a software project's requirements. Typical requirements development deliverables include a vision and scope document, use-case documents, a software requirements specification, a data dictionary, and associated analysis models. Once reviewed and approved, these artifacts define the requirements baseline for the development effort, an agreement between the development group and its customers. The project likely will have additional agreements regarding deliverables, constraints, schedules, budgets, or contractual commitments; those topics lie beyond the scope of this book.

The requirements agreement is the bridge between requirements development and requirements management. Team members must have ready access to the current requirements throughout the project's duration, perhaps through a Web-based gateway to the contents of a requirements management tool. Requirements management includes all activities that maintain the integrity, accuracy, and currency of the requirements agreement as the project progresses. As Figure 18-1 shows, requirements management involves

- Controlling changes to the requirements baseline
- Keeping project plans current with the requirements
- Controlling versions of both individual requirements and requirements documents

- Tracking the status of the requirements in the baseline
- Managing the logical links between individual requirements and other project work products

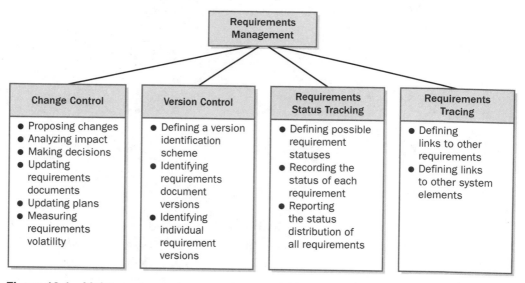

Figure 18-1   Major requirements management activities.

A development team that accepts newly proposed requirements changes might not be able to fulfill its existing schedule and quality commitments. The project manager must negotiate changes to those commitments with affected managers, customers, and other stakeholders. The project can respond to new or changed requirements in various ways:

- Defer lower-priority requirements
- Obtain additional staff
- Mandate overtime work, preferably with pay, for a short time
- Slip the schedule to accommodate the new functionality
- Let quality suffer in the press to ship by the original date (Too often, this is the default reaction.)

No one approach is universally correct because projects differ in their flexibility of features, staff, budget, schedule, and quality (Wiegers 1996a). Base your choice on the priorities that the key stakeholders established during project planning. No matter how you respond to changing requirements, accept the reality of adjusting expectations and commitments when necessary. This is better than imagining that somehow all the new features will be incorporated by the original delivery date without consequences such as budget overruns or team member burnout.

This chapter addresses basic principles of requirements management. The other chapters in Part III describe certain requirements management practices in more detail, including change control (Chapter 19, "Change Happens"), change-impact analysis (also Chapter 19), and requirements tracing (Chapter 20, "Links in the Requirements Chain"). Part III concludes with a discussion of commercial tools that can help a project team manage its requirements (Chapter 21, aptly titled "Tools for Requirements Management").

The Requirements Baseline

The requirements *baseline* is the set of functional and nonfunctional requirements that the development team has committed to implement in a specific release. Defining a baseline gives the project stakeholders a shared understanding of the capabilities and properties they can expect to see in the release. At the time the requirements are baselined—typically following formal review and approval—they are placed under configuration management. Subsequent changes can be made only through the project's defined change-control process. Prior to baselining, the requirements are still evolving, so there's no point in imposing unnecessary process overhead on those modifications. However, begin practicing version control—uniquely identifying different versions of each requirements document—as soon as you create a preliminary draft of a document.

From a practical perspective, the requirements in the baseline must be distinguished from others that have been proposed but not accepted. The baselined SRS document should contain only those requirements that are planned for a specific release. It should be clearly identified as a baseline version to distinguish it from a series of prior draft versions that had not yet been approved. Storing requirements in a requirements management tool facilitates identifying the requirements that belong to a specific baseline and managing changes to that baseline. This chapter describes some ways to manage the requirements in a baseline.

Requirements Management Procedures

Your organization should define the activities that project teams are expected to perform to manage their requirements. Documenting these activities and training practitioners in their effective application enables the members of the organization to perform them consistently and effectively. Consider addressing the following topics:

- Tools, techniques, and conventions for controlling versions of the various requirements documents and of individual requirements

- How the requirements are baselined

- The requirement statuses that you will use and who may change them

- Requirement status-tracking procedures

- The ways that new requirements and changes to existing ones are proposed, processed, negotiated, and communicated to all affected stakeholders

- How to analyze the impact of a proposed change

- How the project's plans and commitments will reflect requirements changes

You can include all this information in a single requirements management process description. Alternatively, you might prefer to write separate change-control, impact-analysis, and status-tracking procedures. These procedures should apply across your organization because they represent common functions that should be performed by every project team.

> **More Info**   Chapter 22, "Improving Your Requirements Processes," describes several useful process assets for requirements management.

Someone must own the requirements management activities, so your process descriptions should also identify the team role that's responsible for performing each task. The project's requirements analyst typically has the lead responsibility for requirements management. The analyst will set up the requirements storage mechanisms (such as a requirements management tool), define requirement attributes, coordinate requirement status and traceability data updates, and generate reports of change activity.

> **Trap**   If no one on the project has responsibility for performing requirements management activities, don't expect them to get done.

Requirements Version Control

"I finally finished implementing the multivendor catalog query feature," Shari reported at the Chemical Tracking System's weekly project status meeting. "Man, that was a lot of work!"

"Oh, the customers canceled that feature two weeks ago," the project manager, Dave, replied. "Didn't you get the revised SRS?"

Shari was confused. "What do you mean, it was canceled? Those requirements are at the top of page 6 of my latest SRS."

Dave said, "Hmmm, they're not in my copy. I've got version 1.5 of the SRS. What version are you looking at?"

"Mine says version 1.5 also," said Shari disgustedly. "These documents should be identical, but obviously they're not. So, is this feature still in the baseline or did I just waste 40 hours of my life?"

If you've ever heard a conversation like this one, you know how frustrating it is when people waste time working from obsolete or inconsistent requirements. Version control is an essential aspect of managing requirements specifications and other project documents. Every version of the requirements documents must be uniquely identified. Every team member must be able to access the current version of the requirements, and changes must be clearly documented and communicated to everyone affected. To minimize confusion, conflicts, and miscommunication, permit only designated individuals to update the requirements and make sure that the version identifier changes whenever a requirement changes.

It's Not a Bug; It's a Feature!

A contract development team received a flood of defect reports from the people testing the latest release of a system they had just delivered to a client. The contract team was perplexed—the system had passed all their own tests. After considerable investigation, it turned out that the client had been testing the new software against an obsolete version of the software requirements specification. What the testers were reporting as bugs truly were features. (Normally, this is just a little joke that software people like to make.) Much of the testing effort was wasted because the testers were looking for the wrong system behaviors. The testers spent considerable time rewriting the tests against the correct version of the SRS and retesting the software, all because of a version control problem.

Each circulated version of the requirements documents should include a revision history that identifies the changes made, the date of each change, the individual who made the change, and the reason for each change. Consider appending a version number to each individual requirement label, which you can increment whenever the requirement is modified, such as Print.Confirm-Copies-1.

The simplest version control mechanism is to manually label each revision of the SRS according to a standard convention. Schemes that try to differentiate document versions based on revision date or the date the document was printed are prone to error and confusion; I don't recommend them. Several of my teams have successfully used a manual convention that labels the first version of any new document "Version 1.0 draft 1." The next draft is "Version 1.0 draft 2." The author increments the draft number with each iteration until the document is approved and baselined. At that time, the label is changed to "Version 1.0 approved." The next version is designated either "Version 1.1 draft 1" for a minor revision or "Version 2.0 draft 1" for a major change. (Of course, "major" and "minor" are subjective or, at least, context-driven). This scheme clearly distinguishes between draft and baselined document versions, but it does require manual discipline.

If you're storing requirements in a word-processing document, you can track changes by using the word processor's revision marks feature. This feature visually highlights changes made in the text with notations such as strikethrough highlighting for deletions, underscores for additions, and vertical revision bars in the margin to show the location of each change. Because these notations visually clutter the document, the word processor lets you view and print either the marked-up document or its final image with the changes applied. When you baseline a document marked up in this way, first archive a marked-up version, then accept all the revisions, and then store the now-clean version as the new baseline file, ready for the next round of changes.

A more sophisticated technique stores the requirements documents in a version control tool, such as those used for controlling source code through check-in and check-out procedures. Many commercial configuration management tools are available for this purpose. I know of one project that stored several hundred use-case documents written in Microsoft Word in such a version control tool. The tool let the team members access all previous versions of every use case, and it logged the history of changes made to each one. The project's requirements analyst and her back-up person had read-write access to the documents stored in the tool; the other team members had read-only access.

The most robust approach to version control is to store the requirements in the database of a commercial requirements management tool, as described in Chapter 21. These tools track the complete history of changes made to every requirement, which is valuable when you need to revert to an earlier version of a requirement. Such a tool allows for comments describing the rationale behind a decision to add, modify, or delete a requirement; these comments are helpful if the requirement becomes a topic for discussion again in the future.

Requirement Attributes

Think of each requirement as an object with properties that distinguish it from other requirements. In addition to its textual description, each functional requirement should have several supporting pieces of information or *attributes* associated with it. These attributes establish a context and background for each requirement that goes well beyond the description of intended functionality. You can store attribute values in a spreadsheet, a database, or, most effectively, a requirements management tool. Such tools provide several system-generated attributes in addition to letting you define others. The tools let you filter, sort, and query the database to view selected subsets of requirements based on their attribute values. For instance, you could list all high-priority requirements that were assigned to Shari for implementation in release 2.3 and that have a status of Approved.

A rich set of attributes is especially important on large, complex projects. Consider specifying attributes such as the following for each requirement:

- Date the requirement was created

- Its current version number

- Author who wrote the requirement

- Person who is responsible for ensuring that the requirement is satisfied

- Owner of the requirement or a list of stakeholders (to make decisions about proposed changes)

- Requirement status

- Origin or source of the requirement

- The rationale behind the requirement

- Subsystem (or subsystems) to which the requirement is allocated

- Product release number to which the requirement is allocated

- Verification method to be used or acceptance test criteria

- Implementation priority

- Stability (an indicator of how likely it is that the requirement will change in the future; unstable requirements might reflect ill-defined or volatile business processes or business rules)

Wherefore This Requirement?

 The product manager at a company that makes electronic measurement devices wanted to keep a record of which requirements were included simply because a competitor's product had the same capability. A good way to make note of such features is with a Rationale attribute, which indicates why a specific requirement is included in the product.

Select the smallest set of attributes that will help you manage your project effectively. For example, you might not need both the name of the person responsible for the requirement and the subsystem to which it is allocated. If any of this attribute information is stored elsewhere—for example, in an overall development-tracking system—don't duplicate it in the requirements database.

Trap   Selecting too many requirements attributes can overwhelm a team such that they never supply all attribute values for all requirements and don't use the attribute information effectively. Start with perhaps three or four key attributes. Add others when you know how they will add value to your project.

Requirements baselines are dynamic. The set of requirements planned for a specific release will change as new requirements are added and existing ones are deleted or deferred to a later release. The team might be juggling separate requirements documents for the current project and for future releases. Managing these moving baselines with a document-based requirements specification is tedious. If deferred or rejected requirements remain in the SRS, readers can be confused about whether those requirements are included in that baseline.

However, you don't want to spend a lot of time dragging requirements from one SRS to another. One way to handle this situation is to store the requirements in a requirements management tool and define a Release Number attribute. Deferring a requirement means changing its planned release, so simply updating the release number shifts the requirement into a different baseline. Rejected requirements are best handled using a requirement status attribute, as described in the next section.

Defining and updating these attribute values is part of the cost of requirements management, but that investment can yield a significant payback. One company periodically generated a requirements report that showed which of the 750 requirements from three related specifications were assigned to each designer. One designer discovered several requirements that she didn't realize were her responsibility. She estimated that she saved one to two months of engineering design rework that would have been required had she not found out about those requirements until later in the project.

Tracking Requirements Status

"How are you coming on that subsystem, Jackie?" asked Dave.

"Pretty good, Dave. I'm about 90 percent done."

Dave was puzzled. "Weren't you 90 percent done a couple of weeks ago?" he asked.

Jackie replied, "I thought I was, but now I'm really 90 percent done."

Software developers are sometimes overly optimistic when they report how much of a task is complete. They often give themselves credit for activities they've started but haven't entirely finished. They might be 90 percent done with the originally identified work, only to encounter additional unanticipated tasks. This tendency to overestimate progress leads to the common situation of software projects or major tasks being reported as 90 percent done for a long time. Tracking the status of each functional requirement throughout development provides a more accurate gauge of project progress. Track status against the expectation of what "complete" means for this product iteration. For example, you might have planned to implement only a part of a use case in the next release, leaving final implementation for a future iteration. In this case, just monitor the status of those functional requirements that were committed for the upcoming release, because that's the set that's supposed to be 100 percent done before shipping the release.

> **Trap**   There's an old joke that the first half of a software project con-
> sumes the first 90 percent of the resources and the second half con-
> sumes the other 90 percent of the resources. Overoptimistic estimation
> and overgenerous status tracking constitute a reliable formula for
> project overruns.

Table 18-1 lists several possible requirement statuses. (For an alternative scheme, see Caputo 1998.) Some practitioners add the statuses Designed (that is, the design elements that address the functional requirement have been created and reviewed) and Delivered (the software containing the requirement is in the hands of the users, as for a beta test). It's valuable to keep a record of rejected requirements and the reasons they were rejected, because dismissed requirements have a way of resurfacing during development. The Rejected status lets you keep a proposed requirement available for possible future reference without cluttering up a specific release's set of committed requirements.

Classifying requirements into several status categories is more meaningful than trying to monitor the percent completion of each requirement or of the complete baseline. Define who is permitted to change a status, and update a requirement's status only when specified transition conditions are satisfied. Certain status changes also lead to updating the requirements traceability data to indicate which design, code, and test elements addressed the requirement, as shown in Table 18-1.

Table 18-1   Suggested Requirement Statuses

Status	Definition
Proposed	The requirement has been requested by an authorized source.
Approved	The requirement has been analyzed, its impact on the project has been estimated, and it has been allocated to the baseline for a specific release. The key stakeholders have agreed to incorporate the requirement, and the software development group has committed to implement it.
Implemented	The code that implements the requirement has been designed, written, and unit tested. The requirement has been traced to the pertinent design and code elements.

Table 18-1   Suggested Requirement Statuses   *(continued)*

Status	Definition
Verified	The correct functioning of the implemented requirement has been confirmed in the integrated product. The requirement has been traced to pertinent test cases. The requirement is now considered complete.
Deleted	An approved requirement has been removed from the baseline. Include an explanation of why and by whom the decision was made to delete it.
Rejected	The requirement was proposed but is not planned for implementation in any upcoming release. Include an explanation of why and by whom the decision was made to reject it.

Figure 18-2 illustrates the tracking of requirements status throughout a hypothetical 10-month project. It shows the percentage of all the system's requirements having each status value at the end of each month. Note that tracking the distribution by percentages doesn't show whether the number of requirements in the baseline is changing over time. The curves illustrate how the project is approaching its goal of complete verification of all approved requirements. A body of work is done when all the allocated requirements have a status of either Verified (implemented as intended) or Deleted (removed from the baseline).

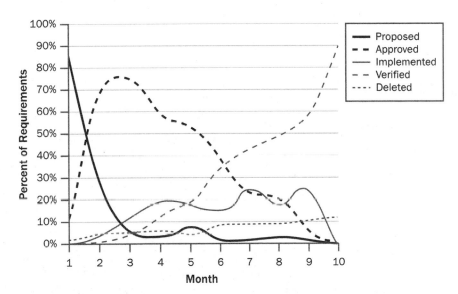

Figure 18-2   Tracking the distribution of requirements status throughout a project's development cycle.

Measuring Requirements Management Effort

As with requirements development, your project plan should include tasks and resources for the requirements management activities described in this chapter. If you track how much effort you spend on requirements management, you can evaluate whether that was too little, about right, or too much and adjust your processes and future planning accordingly.

An organization that has never measured any aspect of its work usually finds it difficult to begin recording how team members spend their time. Measuring actual development and project management effort requires a culture change, and the individual discipline to record daily work activities. Effort tracking isn't as time-consuming as people fear. The team will gain valuable insights from knowing how it has actually devoted its effort to various project tasks (Wiegers 1996a). Note that work effort is not the same as elapsed calendar time. Tasks can be interrupted or they might require interactions with other people that lead to delays. The total effort for a task, in units of labor hours, doesn't necessarily change because of such factors, but the duration increases.

Tracking effort also indicates whether the team is indeed performing the intended actions to manage its requirements. Failing to manage requirements increases the project's risk from uncontrolled changes and from requirements that are inadvertently overlooked during implementation. Count the effort devoted to the following activities as requirements management effort:

- Submitting requirements changes and proposing new requirements

- Evaluating proposed changes, including performing impact analysis

- Change control board activities

- Updating the requirements documents or database

- Communicating requirements changes to affected groups and individuals

- Tracking and reporting requirements status

- Collecting requirements traceability information

Requirements management helps to ensure that the effort you invest in gathering, analyzing, and documenting requirements isn't squandered. For example, failing to keep the requirements set current as changes are made makes it hard for stakeholders to know exactly what they can expect to have delivered in each release. Effective requirements management can reduce the expectation gap by keeping all project stakeholders informed about the current state of the requirements throughout the development process.

Next Steps

- Define a version control scheme to identify your requirements documents. Document the scheme as part of your requirements management process.

- Select the statuses that you want to use to describe the life cycle of your functional requirements. Draw a state-transition diagram to show the conditions that trigger a change from one status to another.

- Define the current status for each functional requirement in your baseline. Keep status current as development progresses.

- Write a description of the processes your organization will follow to manage the requirements on each project. Engage several analysts to draft, review, pilot, and approve the process activities and deliverables. The process steps you define must be practical and realistic, and they must add value to the project.

19

Change Happens

"How's your development work coming, Glenn?" asked Dave, the Chemical Tracking System project manager, during a status meeting.

"I'm not as far along as I'd planned to be," Glenn admitted. "I'm adding a new catalog query function for Sharon, and it's taking a lot longer than I expected."

Dave was puzzled. "I don't remember discussing a new catalog query function at a change control board meeting recently. Did Sharon submit that request through the change process?"

"No, she approached me directly with the suggestion," said Glenn. "I should have asked her to submit it as a formal change request, but it seemed pretty simple so I told her I'd work it in. It turned out not to be simple at all. Every time I think I'm done, I realize I missed a change needed in another file, so I have to fix that, rebuild the component, and test it again. I thought this would take about six hours, but I've spent almost four days on it so far. That's why I'm not done with my other scheduled tasks. I know I'm holding up the next build. Should I finish adding this query function or go back to what I was working on before?"

Most developers have encountered an apparently simple change that turned out to be far more complicated than expected. Developers sometimes don't—or can't—produce realistic estimates of the cost and other ramifications of a proposed software change. And, when developers who want to be accommodating agree to add enhancements that a user requests, requirements changes slip in through the back door instead of being approved by the right stakeholders. Such uncontrolled change is a common source of project chaos, schedule slips, and quality problems, especially on multisite and outsourced development projects. An organization that's serious about managing its software projects must ensure that

- Proposed requirements changes are carefully evaluated before being committed to.

- The appropriate individuals make informed business decisions about requested changes.

- Approved changes are communicated to all affected participants.

- The project incorporates requirements changes in a consistent fashion.

Software change isn't a bad thing. It's virtually impossible to define all of a product's requirements up front, and the world changes as development progresses. An effective software team can nimbly respond to necessary changes so that the product they build provides timely customer value.

But change always has a price. Revising a simple Web page might be quick and easy; making a change in an integrated chip design can cost tens of thousands of dollars. Even a rejected change request consumes the resources needed to submit, evaluate, and decide to reject it. Unless project stakeholders manage changes during development, they won't really know what will be delivered, which ultimately leads to an expectation gap. The closer you get to the release date, the more you should resist changing that release because the consequences of making changes become more severe.

The requirements analyst should incorporate approved changes in the project's requirements documentation. Your philosophy should be that the requirements documentation will accurately describe the delivered product. If you don't keep the SRS current as the product evolves, its value will decrease and the team might function as though it doesn't even have an SRS.

When you need to make a change, start at the highest level of abstraction that the change touches and cascade the impact of the change through related system components. For example, a proposed change might affect a use case and its functional requirements but not any business requirements. A modified high-level system requirement could have an impact on multiple software requirements. Some changes pertain only to system internals, such as the way a communications layer is implemented. These are not user-visible requirements changes but rather design or code changes.

Several problems can arise if a developer implements a requirement change directly in the code without flowing it through the requirements and design descriptions. The description of what the product does, as embodied in the requirements specification, becomes less accurate because the code is the ultimate software reality. The code can become brittle and fragile if changes are made without respecting the program's architecture and design structure. On one project, developers introduced new and modified functionality that the rest of the team didn't discover until system testing. This required unplanned rework of test procedures and user documentation. Consistent change-control practices help prevent such problems and the associated frustration, development rework, and wasted testing time.

Managing Scope Creep

Capers Jones (1994) reports that creeping requirements pose a major risk to

- 80 percent of management information systems projects.
- 70 percent of military software projects.
- 45 percent of outsourced software projects.

Creeping requirements include new functionality and significant modifications that are presented after the project requirements have been baselined. The longer that projects go on, the more growth in scope they experience. The requirements for management information systems typically grow about 1 percent per month (Jones 1996b). The growth rate ranges up to 3.5 percent per month for commercial software, with other kinds of projects in between. The problem is not that requirements change but that late changes have a big impact on work already performed. If every proposed change is approved, it might appear to project sponsors, participants, and customers that the project will never be completed—and indeed, it might not.

Some requirements evolution is legitimate, unavoidable, and even advantageous. Business processes, market opportunities, competing products, and technologies can change during the time it takes to develop a product, and management might determine that redirecting the project in response is necessary. Uncontrolled scope creep, in which the project continuously incorporates new functionality without adjusting resources, schedules, or quality goals, is more insidious. A small modification here, an unexpected enhancement there, and soon the project has no hope of delivering what the customers expect on schedule and with acceptable quality.

The first step in managing scope creep is to document the vision, scope, and limitations of the new system as part of the business requirements, as described in Chapter 5. Evaluate every proposed requirement or feature against the business objectives, product vision, and project scope. Engaging customers in elicitation reduces the number of requirements that are overlooked, only to be added to the team's workload after commitments are made and resources allocated (Jones 1996a). Prototyping is another effective technique for controlling scope creep (Jones 1994). A prototype provides a preview of a possible implementation, which helps developers and users reach a shared understanding of user needs and prospective solutions. Using short development cycles to release a system incrementally provides frequent opportunities for adjustments when requirements are highly uncertain or rapidly changing (Beck 2000).

The most effective technique for controlling scope creep is being able to say no (Weinberg 1995). People don't like to say no, and development teams can receive intense pressure to incorporate every proposed requirement. Philosophies such as "the customer is always right" or "we will achieve total customer satisfaction" are fine in the abstract, but you pay a price for them. Ignoring the price doesn't alter the fact that change is not free. The president of one software tool vendor is accustomed to hearing the development manager say "not now" when he suggests a new feature. "Not now" is more palatable than a simple rejection. It holds the promise of including the feature in a subsequent release. Including every feature that customers, marketing, product management, and developers request leads to missed commitments, slipshod quality, burned-out developers, and bloatware. Customers aren't always right, but they do always have a point, so capture their ideas for possible inclusion in later development cycles.

In an ideal world, you would collect all of a new system's requirements before beginning construction and they'd remain stable throughout the development effort. This is the premise behind the sequential or waterfall software development life cycle model, but it doesn't work well in practice. At some point you must freeze the requirements for a specific release or you'll never get it out the door. However, stifling change prematurely ignores the realities that customers aren't always sure what they need, customer needs change, and developers want to respond to those changes. Every project needs to incorporate the most appropriate changes into the project in a controlled way.

> **Trap**   Freezing the requirements for a new system after performing some initial elicitation activities is unwise and unrealistic. Instead, define a baseline when you think the requirements are well enough defined for design and construction to begin, and then manage the inevitable changes to minimize their adverse impact on the project.

The Change-Control Process

 While performing a software process assessment once, I asked the project team how they incorporated changes in the product's requirements. After an awkward silence, one person said, "Whenever the marketing rep wants to make a change, he asks Bruce or Sandy because they always say 'yes' and the rest of us give marketing a hard time about changes." This didn't strike me as a great change process.

A change control process lets the project's leaders make informed business decisions that will provide the greatest customer and business value while controlling the product's life cycle costs. The process lets you track the status of all proposed changes, and it helps ensure that suggested changes aren't lost or overlooked. Once you've baselined a set of requirements, follow this process for all proposed changes to that baseline.

Customers and other stakeholders often balk at being asked to follow a new process, but a change-control process is not an obstacle to making necessary modifications. It's a funneling and filtering mechanism to ensure that the project incorporates the most appropriate changes. If a proposed change isn't important enough for a stakeholder to take just a couple of minutes to submit it through a standard, simple channel, then it's not worth considering for inclusion. Your change process should be well documented, as simple as possible, and—above all—effective.

> **Trap**   If you ask your stakeholders to follow a new change-control process that's ineffective, cumbersome, or too complicated, people will find ways to bypass the process—and perhaps they should.

Managing requirements changes is similar to the process for collecting and making decisions about defect reports. The same tools can support both activities. Remember, though: a tool is not a substitute for a process. Using a commercial problem-tracking tool to manage proposed modifications to requirements doesn't replace a written process that describes the contents and processing of a change request.

Change-Control Policy

Management should clearly communicate a policy that states its expectations of how project teams will handle proposed requirements changes. Policies are meaningful only if they are realistic, add value, and are enforced. I've found the following change-control policy statements to be helpful:

- All requirements changes shall follow the process. If a change request is not submitted in accordance with this process, it won't be considered.

- No design or implementation work other than feasibility exploration shall be performed on unapproved changes.

- Simply requesting a change doesn't guarantee that it will be made. The project's change control board (CCB) will decide which changes to implement. (We'll discuss change control boards later in this chapter.)

- The contents of the change database shall be visible to all project stakeholders.

- The original text of a change request shall not be modified or deleted.

- Impact analysis shall be performed for every change.

- Every incorporated requirement change shall be traceable to an approved change request.

- The rationale behind every approval or rejection of a change request shall be recorded.

Of course, tiny changes will hardly affect the project and big changes will have a significant impact. In principle, you'll handle all of these through your change-control process. In practice, you might elect to leave certain detailed requirements decisions to the developers' discretion, but no change affecting more than one individual's work should bypass your change-control process. However, your process should include a "fast path" to expedite low-risk, low-investment change requests in a compressed decision cycle.

> **Trap**   Development shouldn't use the change-control process as a barrier to halt any changes. Change is inevitable—deal with it.

Change-Control Process Description

Figure 19-1 illustrates a template for a change-control process description to handle requirements modifications and other project changes. You can download a sample change-control process description from *http://www.processimpact.com/goodies.shtml.* The following discussion pertains primarily to how the process would handle requirements changes. I find it helpful to include the following four components in all procedures and process descriptions:

■ Entry criteria—the conditions that must be satisfied before executing the process or procedure

■ The various tasks involved in the process or procedure, the project role responsible for each task, and other participants in the task

■ Steps to verify that the tasks were completed correctly

■ Exit criteria—the conditions that indicate when the process or procedure is successfully completed

1. Introduction
   1.1 Purpose
   1.2 Scope
   1.3 Definitions
2. Roles and Responsibilities
3. Change-Request Status
4. Entry Criteria
5. Tasks
   5.1 Evaluate Request
   5.2 Make Decision
   5.3 Make Change
   5.4 Notify All Affected Parties
6. Verification
   6.1 Verify Change
   6.2 Install Product
7. Exit Criteria
8. Change-Control Status Reporting
Appendix: Data Items Stored for Each Request

Figure 19-1   Sample template for a change-control process description.

1. Introduction

The introduction describes the purpose of this process and identifies the organizational scope to which it applies. If this process covers changes only in certain work products, identify them here. Also indicate whether any specific kinds of changes are exempted, such as changes in interim or temporary work products created during the course of a project. Define any terms that are necessary for understanding the rest of the document in section 1.3.

2. Roles and Responsibilities

List the project team members—by role, not by name—who participate in the change-control activities and describe their responsibilities. Table 19-1 suggests some pertinent roles; adapt these to each project situation. Different individuals need not fill each role. For example, the CCB Chair might also receive submitted change requests. Several—perhaps all—roles can be filled by the same person on a small project.

Table 19-1 Possible Project Roles in Change-Management Activities

Role	Description and Responsibilities
CCB Chair	Chairperson of the change control board; generally has final decision-making authority if the CCB does not reach agreement; selects the Evaluator and the Modifier for each change request
CCB	The group that decides to approve or reject proposed changes for a specific project
Evaluator	The person whom the CCB Chair asks to analyze the impact of a proposed change; could be a technical person, a customer, a marketing person, or a combination
Modifier	The person responsible for making changes in a work product in response to an approved change request
Originator	Someone who submits a new change request
Request Receiver	The person to whom new change requests are submitted
Verifier	The person who determines whether the change was made correctly

3. Change-Request Status

A change request passes through a defined life cycle, having a different status at each stage in its life. You can represent these status changes by using a state-transition diagram, as illustrated in Figure 19-2. Update a request's status only when the specified criteria are met.

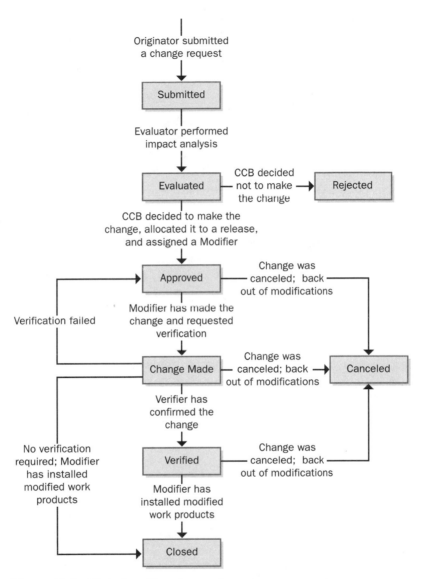

Figure 19-2 State-transition diagram for a change request.

4. Entry Criteria

The basic entry criterion for your change-control process is

☐ A valid change request has been received through an approved channel.

All potential originators should know how to submit a change request, whether it's by completing a paper or Web-based form, sending an e-mail message, or using a change-control tool. Assign a unique identification tag to every change request, and route them all to a single point of contact, the Request Receiver.

5. Tasks

The next step is to evaluate the request for technical feasibility, cost, and alignment with the project's business requirements and resource constraints. The CCB Chair might assign an evaluator to perform an impact analysis, risk analysis, hazard analysis, or other assessments. This analysis ensures that the potential consequences of accepting the change are well understood. The evaluator and the CCB should also consider the business and technical implications of rejecting the change.

The appropriate decision makers, chartered as the CCB, then elect whether to approve or reject the requested change. The CCB gives each approved change a priority level or target implementation date, or it allocates the change to a specific build or release number. The CCB communicates the decision by updating the request's status and notifying all team members who might have to modify work products. Affected work products could include the requirements documentation, design descriptions and models, user interface components, code, test documentation, help screens, and user manuals. The modifier(s) update the affected work products as necessary.

6. Verification

Requirements changes are typically verified through a peer review to ensure that modified specifications, use cases, and models correctly reflect all aspects of the change. Use traceability information to find all the parts of the system that the change touched and that therefore must be verified. Multiple team members might verify the changes made in downstream work products through testing or review. Following verification, the modifier installs the updated work products to make them available to the rest of the team and redefines the baseline to reflect the changes.

7. Exit Criteria

All of the following exit criteria must be satisfied to properly complete an execution of your change-control process:

❑ The status of the request is Rejected, Closed, or Canceled.

❑ All modified work products are installed into the correct locations.

❑ The originator, CCB Chair, project manager, and other relevant project participants have been notified of the change details and the current status of the change request.

❑   The requirements traceability matrix has been updated. (Chapter 20, "Links in the Requirements Chain," will discuss requirements traceability in greater detail.)

8. Change-Control Status Reporting

Identify the charts and reports you'll use to summarize the contents of the change-control database. These charts typically show the number of change requests in each status category as a function of time. Describe the procedures for producing the charts and reports. The project manager uses these reports when tracking the project's status.

Appendix: Data Items Stored for Each Request

Table 19-2 lists some data items to consider storing for each change request. When you define your own list, indicate which items are required and which are optional. Also, indicate whether the value for each item is set automatically by your change-control tool or manually by one of the change-management participants.

Table 19-2   Suggested Change-Request Data Items

Item	Description
Change Origin	Functional area that requested the change; possible groups include marketing, management, customer, software engineering, hardware engineering, and testing
Change-Request ID	Identification tag or sequence number assigned to the request
Change Type	Type of change request, such as a requirement change, a proposed enhancement, or a defect report
Date Submitted	Date the originator submitted the change request
Date Updated	Date the change request was most recently modified
Description	Free-form text description of the change being requested
Implementation Priority	The relative importance of making the change as determined by the CCB: low, medium, or high
Modifier	Name of the person who is primarily responsible for implementing the change
Originator	Name of the person who submitted this change request; consider including the originator's contact information
Originator Priority	The relative importance of making the change from the originator's point of view: low, medium, or high
Planned Release	Product release or build number for which an approved change is scheduled
Project	Name of the project in which a change is being requested

Table 19-2   Suggested Change-Request Data Items *(continued)*

Item	Description
Response	Free-form text of responses made to the change request; multiple responses can be made over time; do not change existing responses when entering a new one
Status	The current status of the change request, selected from the options in Figure 19-2 (on page 335)
Title	One-line summary of the proposed change
Verifier	Name of the person who is responsible for determining whether the change was made correctly

The Change Control Board

The change control board (sometimes known as the *configuration control board*) has been identified as a best practice for software development (McConnell 1996). The CCB is the body of people, be it one individual or a diverse group, who decides which proposed requirement changes and newly suggested features to accept for inclusion in the product. The CCB also decides which reported defects to correct and when to correct them. Many projects already have some de facto group that makes change decisions; establishing a CCB formalizes this group's composition and authority and defines its operating procedures.

A CCB reviews and approves changes to any baselined work product on a project, of which the requirements documents are only one example. Some CCBs are empowered to make decisions and simply inform management about them, whereas others can only make recommendations for management decision. On a small project it makes sense to have only one or two people make the change decisions. Large projects or programs might have several levels of CCBs. Some are responsible for business decisions, such as requirements changes, and some for technical decisions (Sorensen 1999). A higher-level CCB has authority to approve changes that have a greater impact on the project. For instance, a large program that encompasses multiple projects would establish a program-level CCB and an individual CCB for each project. Each project CCB resolves issues and changes that affect only that project. Issues that affect other projects and changes that exceed a specified cost or schedule impact are escalated to the program-level CCB.

To some people, the term "change control board" conjures an image of wasteful bureaucratic overhead. Instead, think of the CCB as providing a valuable structure to help manage even a small project. This structure doesn't have to be time-consuming or cumbersome—just effective. An effective CCB will consider all proposed changes promptly and will make timely decisions based on analysis of the potential impacts and benefits of each proposal. The CCB should be no larger and no more formal than necessary to ensure that the right people make good business decisions about every requested modification.

CCB Composition

The CCB membership should represent all groups who need to participate in making decisions within the scope of that CCB's authority. Consider selecting representatives from the following areas:

- Project or program management

- Product management or requirements analyst

- Development

- Testing or quality assurance

- Marketing or customer representatives

- User documentation

- Technical support or help desk

- Configuration management

Only a subset of these people need to make the decisions, although all must be informed of decisions that affect their work.

The same handful of individuals will fill several of these roles on small projects, and other roles won't need to contemplate every change request. The CCB for a project that has both software and hardware components might also include representatives from hardware engineering, system engineering, manufacturing, or perhaps hardware quality assurance and configuration management. Keep the CCB as small as possible so that the group can respond promptly and efficiently to change requests. As most of us have discovered, large groups have difficulty scheduling meetings and reaching decisions. Make sure that the CCB members understand their responsibilities and take them seriously. To ensure that the CCB has adequate technical and business information, invite other individuals to a CCB meeting when specific proposals are being discussed that relate to those individuals' expertise.

CCB Charter

A charter describes the CCB's purpose, scope of authority, membership, operating procedures, and decision-making process (Sorensen 1999). A template for a CCB charter is available from *http://www.processimpact.com/goodies.shtml*.

The charter should state the frequency of regularly scheduled CCB meetings and the conditions that trigger a special meeting. The scope of the CCB's authority indicates which decisions it can make and which ones it must pass on to a higher-level CCB or a manager.

Making Decisions

As with all decision-making bodies, each CCB needs to select an appropriate decision rule and process (Gottesdiener 2002). The decision-making process description should indicate the following:

- The number of CCB members or the key roles that constitutes a quorum for making decisions

- Whether voting, consensus, consultative decision making, or some other decision rule is used

- Whether the CCB Chair may overrule the CCB's collective decision

- Whether a higher level of CCB or someone else must ratify the decision

The CCB balances the anticipated benefits against the estimated impact of accepting a proposed change. Benefits from improving the product include financial savings, increased revenue, higher customer satisfaction, and competitive advantage. The impact indicates the adverse effects that accepting the proposal could have on the product or project. Possible impacts include increased development and support costs, delayed delivery, degraded product quality, reduced functionality, and user dissatisfaction. If the estimated cost or schedule impact exceeds the established thresholds for this level of CCB, refer the change to management or to a higher-level CCB. Otherwise, use the CCB's decision-making process to approve or reject the proposed change.

Communicating Status

Once the CCB makes its decision, a designated individual updates the request's status in the change database. Some tools automatically generate e-mail messages to communicate the new status to the originator who proposed the change and to others affected by the change. If e-mail is not generated automatically, inform the affected people manually so that they can properly process the change.

Renegotiating Commitments

It's not realistic to assume that stakeholders can stuff more and more functionality into a project that has schedule, staff, budget, and quality constraints and still succeed. Before accepting a significant requirement change, renegotiate commitments with management and customers to accommodate the change (Humphrey 1997). You might negotiate for more time or staff or ask to defer pending requirements of lower priority. If you don't obtain some commitment adjustments, document the threats to success in your project's risk list so that people aren't surprised if the project doesn't fully achieve the desired outcomes.

Change-Control Tools

Automated tools can help your change-control process operate more efficiently (Wiegers 1996a). Many teams use commercial problem- or issue-tracking tools to collect, store, and manage requirements changes. A list of recently submitted change proposals generated from the tool can serve as the agenda for a CCB meeting. Problem-tracking tools can also report the number of requests in each status category at any given time.

Because the available tools, vendors, and features frequently change, I won't provide specific tool recommendations here. Look for the following features in a tool to support your requirements change process:

- Lets you define the data items included in a change request

- Lets you define a state-transition model for the change-request life cycle

- Enforces the state-transition model so that only authorized users can make the permitted status changes

- Records the date of every status change and the identity of the person who made it

- Lets you define who receives automatic e-mail notification when an originator submits a new request or when a request's status is updated

- Produces both standard and custom reports and charts

Some commercial requirements management tools—such tools are discussed in Chapter 21—have a simple change-proposal system built in. These systems can link a proposed change to a specific requirement so that the individual responsible for each requirement is notified by e-mail whenever someone submits a pertinent change request.

Tooling Up a Process

When I worked in a Web development team, one of our first process improvements was to implement a change-control process to manage our huge backlog of change requests (Wiegers 1999b). We began with a process similar to the one described in this chapter. We piloted it for a few weeks by using paper forms while I evaluated several issue-tracking tools. During the pilot process we found several ways to improve the process and discovered several additional data items we needed in the change requests. We selected a highly configurable issue-tracking tool and tailored it to match our process. The team used this process and tool to handle requirements changes in systems under development, defect reports and suggested enhancements in production systems, updates to Web site content, and requests for new development projects. Change control was one of our most successful process improvement initiatives.

Measuring Change Activity

Software measurements provide insights into your projects, products, and processes that are more accurate than subjective impressions or vague recollections of what happened in the past. The measurements you select should be motivated by the questions you or your managers are trying to answer and the goals you're trying to achieve. Measuring change activity is a way to assess the stability of the requirements. It also reveals opportunities for process improvement that might lead to fewer change requests in the future. Consider tracking the following aspects of your requirements change activity (Paulk et al. 1995):

- The number of change requests received, currently open, and closed

- The cumulative number of changes made, including added, deleted, and modified requirements (You can also express this as a percentage of the total number of requirements in the baseline.)

- The number of change requests that originated from each source

- The number of changes proposed and made in each requirement since it was baselined

- The total effort devoted to processing and implementing change requests

■   The number of cycles through the change process that it took to correctly implement each approved change (Sometimes changes are implemented improperly or cause other errors that need to be corrected.)

You don't necessarily need to monitor your requirements change activities to this degree. As with all software metrics, understand your goals and how you'll use the data before you decide what to measure (Wiegers 1999a). Start with simple measurements to begin establishing a measurement culture in your organization and to collect the key data you need to manage your projects effectively. As you gain experience, make your measurements as sophisticated as necessary to help your projects succeed.

Figure 19-3 illustrates a way to track the number of requirements changes your project experiences during development. This chart tracks the rate at which proposals for new requirements changes arrive. You can track the number of approved change requests similarly. Don't count changes made before baselining; you know the requirements are still evolving prior to establishing the baseline. Once you've baselined the requirements, though, all proposed changes should follow your change-control process. You should also begin to track the frequency of change (requirements volatility). This change-frequency chart should trend toward zero as the project approaches its ship date. A sustained high frequency of changes implies a risk of failing to meet your schedule commitments. It probably also indicates that the original baselined requirements were incomplete, suggesting that improving your requirements elicitation practices might be a good idea.

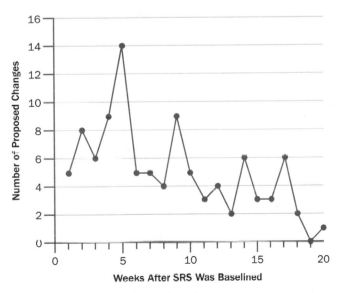

Figure 19-3   Sample chart of requirements change activity.

A project manager who's concerned that frequent changes might prevent the project from finishing on schedule can gain further insight by tracking the requirements change origins. Figure 19-4 shows a way to represent the number of change requests that came from different sources. The project manager could discuss a chart like this with the marketing manager and point out that marketing has requested the most requirements changes. This might lead to a fruitful discussion about what actions the team could take to reduce the number of post-baselining changes received from marketing in the future. Using data as a starting point for such discussions is more constructive than holding a confrontational meeting stimulated by frustration.

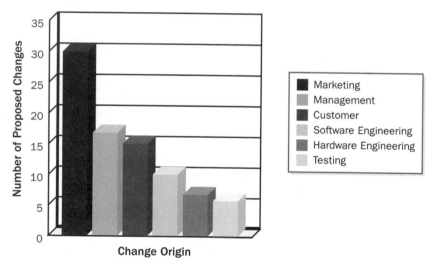

Figure 19-4 Sample chart of requirement change origins.

Change Isn't Free: Impact Analysis

 The need for impact analysis is obvious for major enhancements. However, unexpected complications can lurk below the surface of even minor change requests. A company once had to change the text of one error message in its product. What could be simpler? The product was available in both English and German language versions. There were no problems in English, but in German the new message exceeded the maximum character length allocated for error message displays in both the message box and a database. Coping with this apparently simple change request turned out to be much more work than the developer had anticipated when he promised a quick turnaround.

Trap Because people don't like to say "no," it's easy to accumulate a huge backlog of approved change requests. Before accepting a proposed change, make sure you understand the rationale behind it, its alignment with the product vision, and the business value that the change will provide.

Impact analysis is a key aspect of responsible requirements management (Arnold and Bohner 1996). It provides accurate understanding of the implications of a proposed change, which helps the team make informed business decisions about which proposals to approve. The analysis examines the proposed change to identify components that might have to be created, modified, or discarded and to estimate the effort associated with implementing the change. Before a developer says, "Sure, no problem" in response to a change request, he or she should spend a little time on impact analysis.

Impact Analysis Procedure

The CCB Chair will typically ask a knowledgeable developer to perform the impact analysis for a specific change proposal. Impact analysis has three aspects:

1. Understand the possible implications of making the change. Change often produces a large ripple effect. Stuffing too much functionality into a product can reduce its performance to unacceptable levels, as when a system that runs daily requires more than 24 hours to complete a single execution.

2. Identify all the files, models, and documents that might have to be modified if the team incorporates the requested change.

3. Identify the tasks required to implement the change, and estimate the effort needed to complete those tasks.

> **Trap**   Skipping impact analysis doesn't change the size of the task. It just turns the size into a surprise. Software surprises are rarely good news.

Figure 19-5 presents a checklist of questions designed to help the impact analyst understand the implications of accepting a proposed change. The checklist in Figure 19-6 contains prompting questions to help identify all software elements that the change might affect. Traceability data that links the affected requirement to other downstream deliverables helps greatly with impact analysis. As you gain experience using these checklists, modify them to suit your own projects.

❏ Do any existing requirements in the baseline conflict with the proposed change?
❏ Do any other pending requirements changes conflict with the proposed change?
❏ What are the business or technical consequences of not making the change?
❏ What are possible adverse side effects or other risks of making the proposed change?
❏ Will the proposed change adversely affect performance requirements or other quality attributes?
❏ Is the proposed change feasible within known technical constraints and current staff skills?
❏ Will the proposed change place unacceptable demands on any computer resources required for the development, test, or operating environments?
❏ Must any tools be acquired to implement and test the change?
❏ How will the proposed change affect the sequence, dependencies, effort, or duration of any tasks currently in the project plan?
❏ Will prototyping or other user input be required to verify the proposed change?
❏ How much effort that has already been invested in the project will be lost if this change is accepted?
❏ Will the proposed change cause an increase in product unit cost, such as by increasing third-party product licensing fees?
❏ Will the change affect any marketing, manufacturing, training, or customer support plans?

Figure 19-5   Checklist of possible implications of a proposed change.

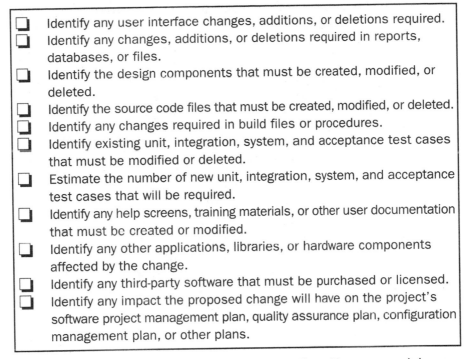

☐ Identify any user interface changes, additions, or deletions required.
☐ Identify any changes, additions, or deletions required in reports, databases, or files.
☐ Identify the design components that must be created, modified, or deleted.
☐ Identify the source code files that must be created, modified, or deleted.
☐ Identify any changes required in build files or procedures.
☐ Identify existing unit, integration, system, and acceptance test cases that must be modified or deleted.
☐ Estimate the number of new unit, integration, system, and acceptance test cases that will be required.
☐ Identify any help screens, training materials, or other user documentation that must be created or modified.
☐ Identify any other applications, libraries, or hardware components affected by the change.
☐ Identify any third-party software that must be purchased or licensed.
☐ Identify any impact the proposed change will have on the project's software project management plan, quality assurance plan, configuration management plan, or other plans.

Figure 19-6   Checklist of possible software elements affected by a proposed change.

Following is a simple procedure for evaluating the impact of a proposed requirement change. Many estimation problems arise because the estimator doesn't think of all the work required to complete an activity. Therefore, this impact analysis approach emphasizes comprehensive task identification. For substantial changes, use a small team—not just one developer—to do the analysis and effort estimation to avoid overlooking important tasks.

1. Work through the checklist in Figure 19-5.

2. Work through the checklist in Figure 19-6, using available traceability information. Some requirements management tools include an impact analysis report that follows traceability links and finds the system elements that depend on the requirements affected by a change proposal.

3. Use the worksheet in Figure 19-7 to estimate the effort required for the anticipated tasks. Most change requests will require only a portion of the tasks on the worksheet, but some will involve additional tasks.

4. Total the effort estimates.

5. Identify the sequence in which the tasks must be performed and how they can be interleaved with currently planned tasks.

6. Determine whether the change is on the project's critical path. If a task on the critical path slips, the project's completion date will slip. Every change consumes resources, but if you can plan a change to avoid affecting tasks that are currently on the critical path, the change won't cause the entire project to slip.

7. Estimate the impact of the proposed change on the project's schedule and cost.

8. Evaluate the change's priority by estimating the relative benefit, penalty, cost, and technical risk compared to other discretionary requirements.

9. Report the impact analysis results to the CCB so that they can use the information to help them decide whether to approve or reject the change request.

> **More Info**   Regarding step 8, Chapter 14 ("Setting Requirement Priorities") describes the rating scales for prioritizing requirements based on benefit, penalty, cost, and risk.

In most cases, this procedure shouldn't take more than a couple of hours to complete. This seems like a lot of time to a busy developer, but it's a small investment in making sure the project wisely invests its limited resources. If you can adequately assess the impact of a change without such a systematic evaluation, go right ahead; just make sure you aren't stepping into quicksand. To improve your ability to estimate the impacts of future changes, compare the actual effort needed to implement each change with the estimated effort. Understand the reasons for any differences, and modify the impact estimation checklists and worksheet accordingly.

Money Down the Drain

Two developers at the A. Datum Corporation estimated that it would take four weeks to add an enhancement to one of their information systems. The customer approved the estimate, and the developers set to work. After two months, the enhancement was only about half done and the customer lost patience: "If I'd known how long this was really going to

Money Down the Drain   *(continued)*

take and how much it was going to cost, I wouldn't have approved it. Let's forget the whole thing." In the rush to gain approval and begin implementation, the developers didn't do enough impact analysis to develop a reliable estimate that would let the customer make an appropriate business decision. Consequently, the A. Datum Corporation wasted several hundred hours of work that could have been avoided by spending a few hours on an up-front impact analysis.

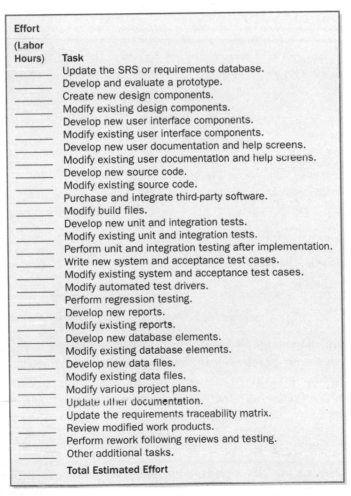

Figure 19-7   Estimating effort for a requirement change.

Impact Analysis Report Template

Figure 19-8 suggests a template for reporting the results from analyzing the potential impact of each requirement change. Using a standard template makes it easier for the CCB members to find the information they need to make good decisions. The people who will implement the change will need the analysis details and the effort planning worksheet, but the CCB needs only the summary of analysis results. As with all templates, try it and then adjust it to meet your project needs.

```
Change Request ID: _____
Title: _____
Description: _____
             _____
             _____

Analyst: _____
Date Prepared: _____
Prioritization Estimates:
    Relative Benefit:     _____  (1–9)
    Relative Penalty:     _____  (1–9)
    Relative Cost:        _____  (1–9)
    Relative Risk:        _____  (1–9)
    Calculated Priority:  _____  (relative to other pending requirements)
Estimated total effort:  _____  labor hours
Estimated lost effort:   _____  labor hours (from discarded work)
Estimated schedule impact: _____  days
Additional cost impact:  _____  dollars
Quality impact: _____

Other requirements affected: _____
Other tasks affected: _____
Integration issues: _____
Life-cycle cost issues: _____
Other components to examine for possible changes: _____
_____
```

Figure 19-8   Impact analysis report template.

Requirements change is a reality for all software projects, but disciplined change-management practices can reduce the disruption that changes can cause. Improved requirements elicitation techniques can reduce the number of requirements changes, and effective requirements management will improve your ability to deliver on project commitments.

> **Note**   Figures 19-5 through 19-8 are available at *http://www.process-impact.com/goodies.shtml*.

Next Steps

- Identify the decision makers on your project, and set them up as a change control board. Have the CCB adopt a charter to make sure everyone understands the board's purpose, composition, and decision-making process.

- Define a state-transition diagram for the life cycle of proposed requirements changes in your project, starting with the diagram in Figure 19-2 (on page 335). Write a process to describe how your team will handle proposed requirements changes. Use the process manually until you're convinced that it's practical and effective.

- Select a commercial problem- or issue-tracking tool that's compatible with your development environment. Tailor it to align with the change-control process you created in the previous step.

- The next time you evaluate a requirement change request, first estimate the effort by using your old method. Then estimate it again using the impact analysis approach described in this chapter. If you implement the change, compare the two estimates to see which agrees more closely with the actual effort. Modify the impact analysis checklists and worksheet based on your experience.

20

Links in the Requirements Chain

"We just found out that the new union contract is changing how overtime pay and shift bonuses are calculated," Justin reported at the weekly team meeting. "They're also changing how the seniority rules affect priority for vacation scheduling, shift preferences, and everything else. We have to update the payroll and staff scheduling systems to handle all these changes right away. How long do you think it will take to get this done, Chris?"

"Man, that's going to be a lot of work," said Chris. "The logic for the seniority rules is sprinkled all through the scheduling system. I can't give you a decent estimate. It's going to take hours just to scan through the code and try to find all the places where those rules show up."

Simple requirement changes often have far-reaching impacts, necessitating that many parts of the product be modified. It's hard to find all the system components that might be affected by a requirement modification. Chapter 19 discussed the importance of performing an impact analysis to make sure the team knows what it's getting into before it commits to making a proposed change. Change impact analysis is easier if you have a road map that shows where each requirement or business rule was implemented in the software.

This chapter addresses the subject of requirements tracing (or traceability). Requirements tracing documents the dependencies and logical links between individual requirements and other system elements. These elements include other requirements of various types, business rules, architecture and other design components, source code modules, test cases, and help files. Traceability information facilitates impact analysis by helping you identify all the work products you might have to modify to implement a proposed requirement change.

Tracing Requirements

Traceability links allow you to follow the life of a requirement both forward and backward, from origin through implementation (Gotel and Finkelstein 1994). Chapter 1, "The Essential Software Requirement," identified traceability as one of the characteristics of excellent requirements specifications. To permit traceability, each requirement must be uniquely and persistently labeled so that you can refer to it unambiguously throughout the project. Write the requirements in a fine-grained fashion, rather than creating large paragraphs containing many individual functional requirements that lead to an explosion of design and code elements.

Figure 20-1 illustrates four types of requirements traceability links (Jarke 1998). Customer needs are traced *forward to requirements*, so you can tell which requirements will be affected if those needs change during or after development. This also gives you confidence that the requirements specification has addressed all stated customer needs. Conversely, you can trace *backward from requirements* to customer needs to identify the origin of each software requirement. If you represented customer needs in the form of use cases, the top half of Figure 20-1 illustrates tracing between use cases and functional requirements.

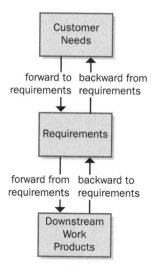

Figure 20-1   Four types of requirements traceability.

The bottom half of Figure 20-1 indicates that, as requirements flow into downstream deliverables during development, you can trace *forward from requirements* by defining links between individual requirements and specific product elements. This type of link assures that you've satisfied every requirement because you know which components address each one. The fourth type of link traces specific product elements *backward to requirements* so that you know why each item was created. Most applications include code that doesn't relate directly to user-specified requirements, but you should know why someone wrote every line of code.

Suppose a tester discovers unexpected functionality with no corresponding written requirement. This code could indicate that a developer implemented a legitimate implied requirement that the analyst can now add to the specification. Alternatively, it might be "orphan" code, an instance of gold plating that doesn't belong in the product. Traceability links can help you sort out these kinds of situations and build a more complete picture of how the pieces of your system fit together. Conversely, test cases that are derived from—and traced back to—individual requirements provide a mechanism for detecting unimplemented requirements because the expected functionality will be missing.

Traceability links help you keep track of parentage, interconnections, and dependencies among individual requirements. This information reveals the propagation of change that can result when a specific requirement is deleted or modified. If you've mapped specific requirements to tasks in your project's work-breakdown structure, those tasks will be affected when a requirement is changed or deleted.

Figure 20-2 illustrates many kinds of direct traceability relationships that can be defined on a project. You don't need to define and manage all these traceability link types. On many projects you can gain 80 percent of the desired traceability benefits for perhaps 20 percent of the potential effort. Perhaps you only need to trace system tests back to functional requirements or use cases. Decide which links are pertinent to your project and can contribute the most to successful development and efficient maintenance. Don't ask team members to spend time recording information unless you have a clear idea of how you expect to use it.

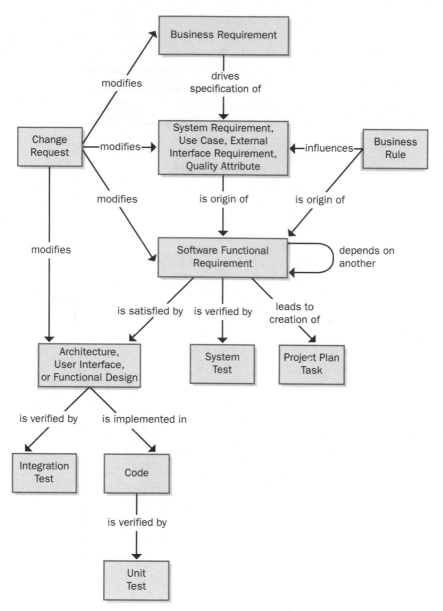

Figure 20-2   Some possible requirements traceability links.

Motivations for Tracing Requirements

 I've had the embarrassing experience of writing a program and then realizing I had inadvertently omitted a requirement. It was in the spec—I simply missed it. I had to go back and write additional code after I thought I was done programming. Overlooking a requirement is more than an embarrassment if it means that a customer isn't satisfied or a delivered product is missing a safety-critical function. At one level, requirements tracing provides a way to demonstrate compliance with a contract, specification, or regulation. At a more sophisticated level, requirements tracing can improve the quality of your products, reduce maintenance costs, and facilitate reuse (Ramesh 1998).

Tracing requirements is a manually intensive task that requires organizational commitment. Keeping the link information current as the system undergoes development and maintenance takes discipline. If the traceability information becomes obsolete, you'll probably never reconstruct it. Obsolete traceability data wastes time by sending developers and maintainers down the wrong path. Because of these realities, you should adopt requirements traceability for the right reasons (Ramesh et al. 1995). Following are some potential benefits of implementing requirements traceability:

- **Certification**   You can use traceability information when certifying a safety-critical product to demonstrate that all requirements were implemented—although it doesn't confirm that they were implemented correctly or completely! Of course, if the requirements are incorrect or key requirements are absent, even the best traceability data won't help you.

- **Change impact analysis**   Without traceability information, there's a high probability of overlooking a system element that would be affected if you add, delete, or modify a particular requirement.

- **Maintenance**   Reliable traceability information facilitates making changes correctly and completely during maintenance, which improves your productivity. When corporate policies or government regulations change, software applications often require updating. A table that shows where each applicable business rule was implemented in the functional requirements, designs, and code makes it easier to make the necessary changes properly.

- **Project tracking**   If you diligently record the traceability data during development, you'll have an accurate record of the implementation status of planned functionality. Missing links indicate work products that have not yet been created.

- **Reengineering**   You can list the functions in a legacy system you're replacing and record where they were addressed in the new system's requirements and software components. Defining traceability links is a way to capture some of what you learn through reverse engineering of an existing system.

- **Reuse**   Traceability information facilitates reusing product components by identifying packages of related requirements, designs, code, and tests.

- **Risk reduction**   Documenting the component interconnections reduces the risk if a key team member with essential knowledge about the system leaves the project (Ambler 1999).

- **Testing**   When a test yields an unexpected result, the links between tests, requirements, and code point you toward likely parts of the code to examine for a defect. Knowing which tests verify which requirements can save time by letting you eliminate redundant tests.

Many of these are long-term benefits, reducing overall product life cycle costs but increasing the development cost by the effort expended to accumulate and manage the traceability information. View requirements tracing as an investment that increases your chances of delivering a maintainable product that satisfies all the stated customer requirements. Although difficult to quantify, this investment will pay dividends anytime you have to modify, extend, or replace the product. Defining traceability links is not much work if you collect the information as development proceeds, but it's tedious and expensive to do on a completed system.

The Requirements Traceability Matrix

The most common way to represent the links between requirements and other system elements is in a *requirements traceability matrix*, also called a *requirements trace matrix* or a *traceability table* (Sommerville and Sawyer 1997). Table 20-1 illustrates a portion of one such matrix, drawn from the Chemical Tracking System. When I've set up such matrices in the past, I made a copy of the baselined SRS and deleted everything except the labels for the functional requirements. Then I set up a table formatted like Table 20-1 with only the Functional

Requirement column populated. As fellow team members and I worked on the project, we gradually filled in the blank cells in the matrix.

Table 20-1   One Kind of Requirements Traceability Matrix

User Requirement	Functional Requirement	Design Element	Code Module	Test Case
UC-28	catalog.query.sort	Class catalog	catalog.sort()	search.7 search.8
UC-29	catalog.query.import	Class catalog	catalog.import() catalog.validate()	search.12 search.13 search.14

Table 20-1 shows how each functional requirement is linked backward to a specific use case and forward to one or more design, code, and test elements. Design elements can be objects in analysis models such as data flow diagrams, tables in a relational data model, or object classes. Code references can be class methods, stored procedures, source code filenames, or procedures or functions within the source file. You can add more columns to extend the links to other work products, such as online help documentation. Including more traceability detail takes more work, but it gives you the precise locations of the related software elements, which can save time during change impact analysis and maintenance.

Fill in the information as the work gets done, not as it gets planned. That is, enter "catalog.sort()" in the Code Module column of the first row in Table 20-1 only when the code in that function has been written, has passed its unit tests, and has been integrated into the source code baseline for the product. This way a reader knows that populated cells in the requirements traceability matrix indicate work that's been completed. Note that listing the test cases for each requirement does *not* indicate that the software has passed those tests. It simply indicates that certain tests have been written to verify the requirement at the appropriate time. Tracking testing status is a separate matter.

Nonfunctional requirements such as performance goals and quality attributes don't always trace directly into code. A response-time requirement might dictate the use of certain hardware, algorithms, database structures, or architectural choices. A portability requirement could restrict the language features that the programmer uses but might not result in specific code segments that enable portability. Other quality attributes are indeed implemented in code. Integrity requirements for user authentication lead to derived functional requirements that are implemented through, say, passwords or biometrics functionality. In those cases, trace the corresponding functional requirements backward to their parent nonfunctional requirement and forward into downstream deliverables as usual. Figure 20-3 illustrates a possible traceability chain involving nonfunctional requirements.

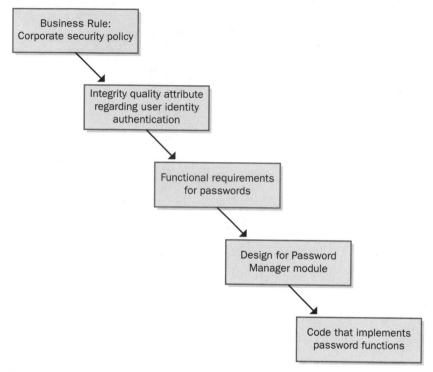

Figure 20-3   Sample traceability chain for requirements dealing with application security.

Traceability links can define one-to-one, one-to-many, or many-to-many relationships between system elements. The format in Table 20-1 accommodates these cardinalities by letting you enter several items in each table cell. Here are some examples of the possible link cardinalities:

- **One-to-one**   One design element is implemented in one code module.

- **One-to-many**   One functional requirement is verified by multiple test cases.

- **Many-to-many**   Each use case leads to multiple functional requirements, and certain functional requirements are common to several use cases. Similarly, a shared or repeated design element might satisfy a number of functional requirements. Ideally, you'll capture all these interconnections, but in practice, many-to-many traceability relationships can become complex and difficult to manage.

Another way to represent traceability information is through a set of matrices that define links between pairs of system elements, such as these:

- One type of requirement to other requirements of that same type

- One type of requirement to requirements of another type

- One type of requirement to test cases

You can use these matrices to define various relationships that are possible between pairs of requirements, such as "specifies/is specified by," "depends on," "is parent of," and "constrains/is constrained by" (Sommerville and Sawyer 1997). Table 20-2 illustrates a two-way traceability matrix. Most cells in the matrix are empty. Each cell at the intersection of two linked components is marked to indicate the connection. You can use different symbols in the cells to explicitly indicate "traced-to" and "traced-from" or other relationships. Table 20-2 uses an arrow to indicate that a certain functional requirement is traced from a particular use case. These matrices are more amenable to automated tool support than is the single traceability table illustrated in Table 20-1.

Table 20-2   Requirements Traceability Matrix Showing Links Between Use Cases and Functional Requirements

Functional Requirement	Use Case			
	UC-1	UC-2	UC-3	UC-4
FR-1	↵			
FR-2	↵			
FR-3			↵	
FR-4			↵	
FR-5		↵		↵
FR-6			↵	

Traceability links should be defined by whoever has the appropriate information available. Table 20-3 identifies some typical sources of knowledge about links between various types of source and target objects. Determine the roles and individuals who should supply each type of traceability information for your project. Expect some pushback from busy people whom the analyst or project manager asks to provide this data. Those practitioners are entitled to an explanation of what requirements tracing is, why it adds value, and why they're being asked to contribute to the process. Point out that the incremental cost of capturing traceability information at the time the work is done is small; it's primarily a matter of habit and discipline.

> **Trap** Gathering and managing requirements traceability data must be made the explicit responsibility of certain individuals or it won't happen. Typically, a requirements analyst or a quality assurance engineer collects, stores, and reports on the traceability information.

Table 20-3 Likely Sources of Traceability Link Information

Link Source Object Type	Link Target Object Type	Information Source
System requirement	Software requirement	System engineer
Use case	Functional requirement	Requirements analyst
Functional requirement	Functional requirement	Requirements analyst
Functional requirement	Test case	Test engineer
Functional requirement	Software architecture element	Software architect
Functional requirement	Other design elements	Designer or Developer
Design element	Code	Developer
Business rule	Functional requirement	Requirements analyst

Tools for Requirements Tracing

Chapter 21, "Tools for Requirements Management," describes several commercial requirements management tools that have strong requirements-tracing capabilities. You can store requirements and other information in a tool's database and define links between the various types of stored objects, including peer links between two requirements of the same kind. Some tools let you differentiate "traced-to" and "traced-from" relationships, automatically defining the complementary links. That is, if you indicate that requirement R is traced to test case T, the tool will also show the symmetrical relationship in which T is traced from R.

Some tools automatically flag a link as *suspect* whenever the object on either end of the link is modified. A suspect link has a visual indicator (such as a red question mark or a diagonal red line) in the corresponding cell in the requirements traceability matrix. For example, if you changed use case 3, the requirements traceability matrix in Table 20-2 might look like Table 20-4 the next time you see it. The suspect link indicators (in this case, question marks) tell you to check whether functional requirements 3, 4, and 6 need to be changed to remain consistent with the modified UC-3. After making any necessary changes, you clear the suspect link indicators manually. This process helps ensure that you've accounted for the known ripple effects of a change.

The tools also let you define cross-project or cross-subsystem links. I know of one large software product that had 20 major subsystems, with certain high-level product requirements apportioned among multiple subsystems. In some cases, a requirement that was allocated to one subsystem was actually implemented through a service that another subsystem provided. This project used a requirements management tool to successfully track these complex traceability relationships.

Table 20-4   Suspect Links in a Requirements Traceability Matrix

Functional Requirement	Use Case			
	UC-1	**UC-2**	**UC-3**	**UC-4**
FR-1	↵			
FR-2	↵			
FR-3			↵?	
FR-4			↵?	
FR-5		↵		↵
FR-6			↵?	

It's impossible to perform requirements tracing manually for any but very small applications. You can use a spreadsheet to maintain traceability data for up to a couple hundred requirements, but larger systems demand a more robust solution. Requirements tracing can't be fully automated because the knowledge of the links originates in the development team members' minds. However, once you've identified the links, tools can help you manage the vast quantity of traceability information.

Requirements Traceability Procedure

Consider following this sequence of steps when you begin to implement requirements traceability on a specific project:

1. Select the link relationships you want to define from the possibilities shown in Figure 20-2.

2. Choose the type of traceability matrix you want to use: the single matrix shown in Table 20-1 or several of the matrices illustrated in Table 20-2. Select a mechanism for storing the data: a table in a text document, a spreadsheet, or a requirements management tool.

3. Identify the parts of the product for which you want to maintain traceability information. Start with the critical core functions, the high-risk portions, or the portions that you expect to undergo the most maintenance and evolution over the product's life.

4. Modify your development procedures and checklists to remind developers to update the links after implementing a requirement or an approved change. The traceability data should be updated as soon as someone completes a task that creates or changes a link in the requirements chain.

5. Define the tagging conventions you will use to uniquely identify all system elements so that they can be linked together (Song et al. 1998). If necessary, write scripts that will parse the system files to construct and update the traceability matrices.

6. Identify the individuals who will supply each type of link information and the person who will coordinate the traceability activities and manage the data.

7. Educate the team about the concepts and importance of requirements tracing, your objectives for this activity, where the traceability data is stored, and the techniques for defining the links (for example, by using the traceability feature of a requirements management tool). Make sure all participants commit to their responsibilities.

8. As development proceeds, have each participant provide the requested traceability information as they complete small bodies of

work. Stress the need for ongoing creation of the traceability data, rather than for attempts to reconstruct it at a major milestone or at the end of the project.

9. Audit the traceability information periodically to make sure it's being kept current. If a requirement is reported as implemented and verified yet its traceability data is incomplete or inaccurate, your requirements tracing process isn't working as intended.

I've described this procedure as though you were starting to collect traceability information at the outset of a new project. If you're maintaining a legacy system, the odds are good that you don't have traceability data available, but there's no time like the present to begin accumulating this useful information. The next time you add an enhancement or make a modification, write down what you discover about connections between code, tests, designs, and requirements. Build the recording of traceability data into your procedure for modifying an existing software component. You'll never reconstruct a complete requirements traceability matrix, but this small amount of effort might make it easier the next time someone needs to work on that same part of the system.

Is Requirements Traceability Feasible? Is It Necessary?

You might conclude that creating a requirements traceability matrix is more expensive than it's worth or that it's not feasible for your big project, but consider the following counterexample. A conference attendee who worked at an aircraft manufacturer told me that the SRS for his team's part of the company's latest jetliner was a stack of paper six feet thick. They had a complete requirements traceability matrix. I've flown on that very model of airplane, and I was happy to hear that the developers had managed their software requirements so carefully. Managing traceability on a huge product with many interrelated subsystems is a lot of work. This aircraft manufacturer knows it is essential; the Federal Aviation Administration agrees.

Even if your products won't cause loss to life or limb if they fail, you should take requirements tracing seriously. The CEO of a major corporation who was present when I described traceability at a seminar asked, "Why *wouldn't* you create a requirements traceability matrix for your strategic business systems?" That's an excellent question. You should decide to use any improved requirements engineering practice based on both the costs of applying the technique and the risks of *not* using it. As with all software processes, make an economic decision to invest your valuable time where you expect the greatest payback.

Next Steps

■ Set up a traceability matrix for 15 or 20 requirements from an important portion of the system you're currently developing. Try the approaches shown in both Table 20-1 and Table 20-2 (on pages 359 and 361, respectively). Populate the matrix as development progresses for a few weeks. Evaluate which method seems most effective and what procedures for collecting and storing traceability information will work for your team.

■ The next time you perform maintenance on a poorly documented system, record what you learn from your reverse-engineering analysis of the part of the product you are modifying. Build a fragment of a traceability matrix for the piece of the puzzle you're manipulating so that the next time someone has to work on it they have a head start. Grow the traceability matrix as your team continues to maintain the product.

21

Tools for Requirements Management

In earlier chapters, I discussed the creation of a natural-language software requirements specification to contain the functional and nonfunctional requirements and the creation of documents that contain the business requirements and use-case descriptions. A document-based approach to storing requirements has numerous limitations, including the following:

- It's difficult to keep the documents current and synchronized.

- Communicating changes to all affected team members is a manual process.

- It's not easy to store supplementary information (attributes) about each requirement.

- It's hard to define links between functional requirements and other system elements.

- Tracking requirements status is cumbersome.

- Concurrently managing sets of requirements that are planned for different releases or for related products is difficult. When a requirement is deferred from one release to another, an analyst needs to move it from one requirements specification to the other.

- Reusing a requirement means that the analyst must copy the text from the original SRS into the SRS for each other system or product where the requirement is to be used.

- It's difficult for multiple project participants to modify the requirements, particularly if the participants are geographically separated.

- There's no convenient place to store proposed requirements that were rejected and requirements that were deleted from a baseline.

A requirements management tool that stores information in a multiuser database provides a robust solution to these restrictions. Small projects can use spreadsheets or simple databases to manage their requirements, storing both the requirements text and several attributes of each requirement. Larger projects will benefit from commercial requirements management tools. Such products let users import requirements from source documents, define attribute values, filter and display the database contents, export requirements in various formats, define traceability links, and connect requirements to items stored in other software development tools.

> **Trap**   Avoid the temptation to develop your own requirements management tool or to cobble together general-purpose office automation products in an attempt to mimic the commercial products. This initially looks like an easy solution, but it can quickly overwhelm a team that doesn't have the resources to build the tool it really wants.

Note that I classify these products as requirements *management* tools, not requirements *development* tools. They won't help you identify your prospective users or gather the right requirements for your project. However, they provide a lot of flexibility in managing changes to those requirements and using the requirements as the foundation for design, testing, and project management. These tools don't replace a defined process that your team members follow to elicit and manage its requirements. Use a tool when you already have an approach that works but that requires greater efficiency; don't expect a tool to compensate for a lack of process, discipline, experience, or understanding.

This chapter presents several benefits of using a requirements management tool and identifies some general capabilities you can expect to find in such a product. Table 21-1 lists several of the requirements management tools presently available. This chapter doesn't contain a feature-by-feature tool comparison because these products are still evolving and their capabilities change with each release. The prices, supported platforms, and even vendors of software development tools also change frequently, so use the Web addresses in Table 21-1 to get current information about the products (recognizing that Web addresses themselves are subject to change if, say, one tool vendor acquires another, as happened two weeks prior to this writing). You can find detailed feature comparisons of these and many other tools at the Web site for the International Council on Systems Engineering (*http://www.incose.org/toc.html*), along with guidance on how to select a requirements management tool (Jones et al. 1995).

Table 21-1   Some Commercial Requirements Management Tools

Tool	Vendor	Database- or Document-Centric
Active! Focus	Xapware Technologies, *http://www.xapware.com*	Database
CaliberRM	Borland Software Corporation, *http://www.borland.com*	Database
C.A.R.E.	SOPHIST Group, *http://www.sophist.de*	Database
DOORS	Telelogic, *http://www.telelogic.com*	Database
RequisitePro	Rational Software Corporation, *http://www.rational.com*	Document
RMTrak	RBC, Inc., *http://www2.rbccorp.com*	Document
RTM Workshop	Integrated Chipware, Inc., *http://www.chipware.com*	Database
Slate	EDS, *http://www.eds.com*	Database
Vital Link	Compliance Automation, Inc., *http://www.complianceautomation.com*	Document

One distinction between the tools is whether they are database-centric or document-centric. Database-centric products store all requirements, attributes, and traceability information in a database. Depending on the product, the database is either commercial or proprietary, relational or object-oriented. Requirements can be imported from various source documents, but they then reside in the database. In most respects, the textual description of a requirement is treated simply as a required attribute. Some products let you link individual requirements to external files (such as Microsoft Word files, Microsoft Excel files, graphics files, and so on) that provide supplementary information to augment the contents of the requirements repository.

The document-centric approach treats a document created using a word-processing program (such as Microsoft Word or Adobe FrameMaker) as the primary container for the requirements. RequisitePro lets you select text strings in a Word document to be stored as discrete requirements in a database. Once the requirements are in the database, you can define attributes and traceability links, just as you can with the database-centric products. Mechanisms are provided to synchronize the database and document contents. RTM Workshop straddles both paradigms by being primarily database-centric but also letting you maintain requirements in a Microsoft Word document.

These tools aren't cheap, but the high cost of requirements-related problems can justify your investment in them. Recognize that the cost of a tool is not simply what you pay for the initial license. The cost also includes the host computer, annual maintenance fees and periodic upgrades, and the costs of installing the software, performing administration, obtaining vendor support and consulting, and training your users. Your cost-benefit analysis should take into account these additional expenses before you make a purchase decision.

Benefits of Using a Requirements Management Tool

Even if you do a magnificent job gathering your project's requirements, automated assistance can help you work with these requirements as development progresses. A requirements management tool becomes most beneficial as time passes and the team's memory of the requirements details fades. The following sections describe some of the tasks such a tool can help you perform.

Manage versions and changes   Your project should define a requirements baseline, a specific collection of requirements allocated to a particular release. Some requirements management tools provide flexible baselining functions. The tools also maintain a history of the changes made to every requirement. You can record the rationale behind each change decision and revert to a previous version of a requirement if necessary. Some of the tools, including Active! Focus and DOORS, contain a simple, built-in change-proposal system that links change requests directly to the affected requirements.

Store requirements attributes   You should record several descriptive attributes for each requirement, as discussed in Chapter 18. Everyone working on the project must be able to view the attributes, and selected individuals will be permitted to update attribute values. Requirements management tools generate several system-defined attributes, such as the date a requirement was created and its current version number, and they let you define additional attributes of various data types. Thoughtful definition of attributes allows stakeholders to view subsets of the requirements based on specific combinations of attribute values. You might ask to see a list of all the requirements originating from a specific business rule so that you can judge the consequences of a change in that rule. One way to keep track of the requirements that are allocated to the baselines for various releases is by using a Release Number attribute.

Facilitate impact analysis   The tools enable requirements tracing by letting you define links between different types of requirements, between requirements in different subsystems, and between individual requirements and related system components (for example, designs, code modules, tests, and user documentation). These links help you analyze the impact that a proposed change will have on a specific requirement by identifying other system elements the change might affect. It's also a good idea to trace each functional requirement back to its origin or parent so that you know where every requirement came from.

> **More Info**   Chapter 19 describes impact analysis, and Chapter 20 addresses requirements tracing.

Track requirements status   Collecting requirements in a database lets you know how many discrete requirements you've specified for the product. Tracking the status of each requirement during development supports the overall status tracking of the project. A project manager has good insight into project status if he knows that 55 percent of the requirements committed to the next release have been verified, 28 percent have been implemented but not verified, and 17 percent are not yet fully implemented.

Control access   The requirements management tools let you define access permissions for individuals or groups of users and share information with a geographically dispersed team through a Web interface to the database. The databases use requirement-level locking to permit multiple users to update the database contents concurrently.

Communicate with stakeholders   Some tools permit team members to discuss requirements issues electronically through threaded conversations. Automatically triggered e-mail messages notify affected individuals when a new discussion entry is made or when a specific requirement is modified. Making the requirements accessible on line can save travel costs and reduce document proliferation.

Reuse requirements   Storing requirements in a database facilitates reusing them in multiple projects or subprojects. Requirements that logically fit into multiple parts of the product description can be stored once and referenced whenever necessary to avoid duplicating requirements.

Requirements Management Tool Capabilities

Commercial requirements management tools let you define different requirement types (or classes), such as business requirements, use cases, functional requirements, hardware requirements, and constraints. This lets you differentiate individual objects that you want to treat as requirements from other useful information contained in the SRS. All the tools provide strong capabilities for defining attributes for each requirement type, which is a great advantage over the typical document-based SRS approach.

Most requirements management tools integrate with Microsoft Word to some degree, typically adding a tool-specific menu to the Microsoft Word menu bar. Vital Link is based on Adobe FrameMaker, and Slate integrates with both FrameMaker and Word. The higher-end tools support a rich variety of import and export file formats. Several of the tools let you mark text in a Word document to be treated as a discrete requirement. The tool highlights the requirement and inserts Word bookmarks and hidden text into the document. The tools can also parse documents in various fashions to extract individual requirements. The parsing from a word-processed document will be imperfect unless you were diligent about using text styles or keywords such as "shall" when you created the document.

The tools support hierarchical numeric requirement labels, in addition to maintaining a unique internal identifier for each requirement. These identifiers typically consist of a short text prefix that indicates the requirement type—such as UR for a user requirement—followed by a unique integer. Some tools provide efficient Microsoft Windows Explorer–like displays to let you manipulate the hierarchical requirements tree. One view of the requirements display in DOORS looks like a hierarchically structured SRS.

Output capabilities from the tools include the ability to generate a requirements document, either in a user-specified format or as a tabular report. CaliberRM has a powerful "Document Factory" feature that lets you define an SRS template in Word by using simple directives to indicate page layout, boilerplate text, attributes to extract from the database, and the text styles to use. The Document Factory populates this template with information it selects from the database according to user-defined query criteria to produce a customized specification document. An SRS, therefore, is essentially a report generated from selected database contents.

All the tools have robust traceability features. For example, in RTM Workshop, each project defines a class schema resembling an entity-relationship diagram for all the stored object types. Traceability is handled by defining links between objects in two classes (or within the same class), based on the class relationships defined in the schema.

Other features include the ability to set up user groups and define permissions for selected users or groups to create, read, update, and delete projects, requirements, attributes, and attribute values. Several of the products let you incorporate nontextual objects such as graphics and spreadsheets into the requirements repository. The tools also include learning aids, such as tutorials or sample projects, to help users get up to speed.

These products show a trend toward increasing integration with other tools used in application development, as illustrated in Figure 21-1. When you select a requirements management product, determine whether it can exchange data with the other tools you use. Here are just a few examples of the tool interconnections that these products exhibit today:

- You can link requirements in RequisitePro to use cases modeled in Rational Rose and to test cases stored in Rational TeamTest.

- DOORS lets you trace requirements to individual design elements stored in Rational Rose, Telelogic Tau, and other design modeling tools.

- RequisitePro and DOORS can link individual requirements to project tasks in Microsoft Project.

- CaliberRM has a central communications framework that lets you link requirements to use-case, class, or process design elements stored in TogetherSoft Control Center, to source code stored in Borland's StarTeam, and to test elements stored in Mercury Interactive's TestDirector. You can then access those linked elements directly from the requirements stored in CaliberRM's database.

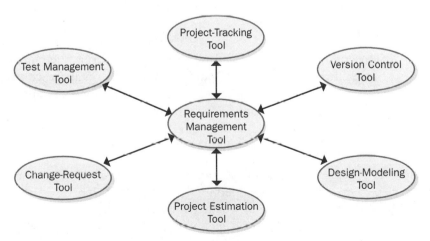

Figure 21-1 Requirements management tools integrate with other kinds of software tools.

When evaluating tools, think about how you'll take advantage of these product integrations as you perform your requirements engineering, testing, project tracking, and other processes. For example, consider how you would publish a baselined set of requirements into a version control tool and how you would define traceability links between functional requirements and specific design or code elements.

Implementing Requirements Management Automation

Any of these products will move your requirements management practices to a higher plane of sophistication and capability. However, the diligence of the tools' users remains a critical success factor. Dedicated, disciplined, and knowledgeable people will make progress even with mediocre tools, whereas the best tools won't pay for themselves in the hands of unmotivated or ill-trained users. Don't write a check for a requirements management tool unless you're willing to respect the learning curve and make the time investment. Because you can't expect instantaneous results, don't base a project's success on a tool you're using for the first time. Gain some experience working with the tool on a pilot project before you employ it on a high-stakes project.

> **More Info**   Chapter 22, "Improving Your Requirements Processes," describes the learning curve associated with adopting new tools and techniques.

Selecting a Tool

Select a tool based on the combination of platform, pricing, access modes, and requirements paradigm—document-centric or database-centric—that best fits your development environment and culture. Some companies contract tool evaluations to consultants, who can assess a company's needs comprehensively and make recommendations from the available tool candidates. If you do the evaluation yourself, the following procedure can help you select the right tool:

1.   First, define your organization's requirements for a requirements management tool. Identify the capabilities that are most significant to you, the other tools with which you'd like the product to integrate, and whether issues such as remote data access through the Web are important. Decide whether you want to continue using documents to contain some of your requirements information or whether you prefer to store all the information in a database.

2. List 10 to 15 factors that will influence your selection decision. Include subjective categories such as tailorability, as well as the efficiency and effectiveness of the user interface. Cost will be a selection factor, but evaluate the tools initially without considering their cost.

3. Distribute 100 points among the selection factors that you listed in step 2, giving more points to the more important factors.

4. Obtain current information about the available requirements management tools, and rate the candidates against each of your selection factors. Scores for the subjective factors will have to wait until you can actually work with each tool. A vendor demonstration can fill in some of the blanks, but the demo will likely be biased toward the tool's strengths. A demo isn't a substitute for using the product yourself for several hours.

5. Calculate the score for each candidate based on the weight you gave each factor to see which products appear to best fit your needs.

6. Solicit experience reports from other users of each candidate product, perhaps by posting queries in online discussion forums, to supplement your own evaluation and the vendor's literature, demo, and sales pitch.

7. Obtain evaluation copies from the vendors of your top-rated tools. Define an evaluation process before you install the candidates to make sure you get the information you need to make a good decision.

8. Evaluate the tools by using a real project, not just the tutorial project that comes with the product. After you complete your evaluations, adjust your rating scores if necessary and see which tool now ranks highest.

9. To make a decision, combine the ratings, licensing costs, and ongoing costs with information on vendor support, input from current users, and your team's subjective impressions of the products.

Changing the Culture

Buying a tool is easy; changing your culture and processes to accept the tool and take best advantage of it is much harder. Most organizations already have a comfort level with storing their requirements in word-processing documents. Changing to an online approach requires a different way of thinking. A tool makes the requirements visible to any stakeholder who has access to the database. Some stakeholders interpret this visibility as reducing the control they have over the requirements, the requirements-engineering process, or both.

Some people prefer not to share an incomplete or imperfect SRS with the world, yet the database contents are there for all to see. Keeping the requirements private until they're "done" means you miss an opportunity to have many pairs of eyes scan the requirements frequently for possible problems.

There's little point in using a requirements management tool if you don't take advantage of its capabilities. I encountered one project team that had diligently stored all its requirements in a commercial tool but hadn't defined any requirements attributes or traceability links. Nor did they provide online access for all the stakeholders. The fact that the requirements were stored in a different form didn't really provide significant benefits, although it consumed the effort needed to get the requirements into the tool. Another team stored hundreds of requirements in a tool and defined many traceability links. Their only use of the information was to generate massive printed traceability reports that were supposed to be reviewed manually for problems. No one really studied the reports, and no one regarded the database as the authoritative repository of the project's requirements. Neither of these organizations reaped the full benefits of their considerable investments of time and money in the requirements management tools.

Consider the following cultural and process issues as you strive to maximize your return on investment from a commercial requirements management tool:

- Don't even pilot the use of a tool until your organization can create a reasonable software requirements specification on paper. If your biggest problems are with gathering and writing clear, high-quality requirements, these tools won't help you.

- Don't try to capture requirements directly in the tool during the early elicitation workshops. As the requirements begin to stabilize, though, storing them in the tool makes them visible to the workshop participants for refinement.

- Use the tool as a groupware support aid to facilitate communication with project stakeholders in various locations. Set the access and change privileges to permit sufficient input to the requirements by various people without giving everyone complete freedom to change everything in the database.

- Think carefully about the various requirement types that you define. Don't treat every section of your current SRS template as a separate requirement type, but don't simply stuff all the SRS contents into a single requirement type either. The tools let you create different attributes for each requirement type you define, so selecting appropriate attributes will help you determine how many different types of requirement to define.

- Define an owner for each requirement type, who will have the primary responsibility for managing the database contents of that type.

- Use business, not IT, terminology when defining new data fields or requirements attributes.

- Don't define traceability links until the requirements stabilize. Otherwise, you can count on doing a lot of work to revise the links as requirements continue to change.

- To accelerate the movement from a document-based paradigm to the use of the tool, set a date after which the tool's database will be regarded as the definitive repository of the project's requirements. After that date, requirements residing only in word-processing documents won't be recognized as valid requirements.

- Instead of expecting to freeze the requirements early in the project, get in the habit of baselining a set of requirements for a particular release. Dynamically shift requirements from the baseline for one release to another as necessary.

> **More Info**   Chapter 18 discussed using requirement attributes to manage requirements destined for different releases.

As the use of a requirements management tool becomes ingrained in your culture, project stakeholders will begin to regard requirements as life cycle assets, just as they do code. The team will discover ways to use the tool to speed up the process of documenting requirements, communicating them, and managing changes to them. Remember, though: even the best tool can't compensate for an ineffective requirements development process. The tool won't help you scope your project, identify users, talk to the right users, or collect the right requirements. And it doesn't matter how well you manage poor requirements.

Making Requirements Management Tools Work for You

For the smoothest transition, assign a tool advocate, a local enthusiast who learns the tool's ins and outs, mentors other users, and sees that it gets employed as intended. Begin with a pilot application of the tool on a noncritical project. This will help the organization learn how much effort it takes to administer and support the tool. The initial tool advocate will manage its use in the pilot, and then he'll train and mentor others to support the tool as other projects adopt it. Your team members are smart, but it's better to train them than to expect them to figure out how best to use the tool on their own. They can undoubtedly deduce the basic operations, but they won't learn about the full set of tool capabilities and how to exploit them efficiently.

Recognize that it will take effort to load a project's requirements into the database, define attributes and traceability links, keep the database's contents current, define access groups and their privileges, and train users. Management must allocate the resources needed for these operations. Make an organization-wide commitment to actually use the product you select, instead of letting it become expensive shelfware.

Provided you remember that a tool can't overcome process deficiencies, you're likely to find that commercial requirements management tools enhance the control you have over your software requirements. Once you've made a requirements database work for you, you'll never go back to plain paper.

Next Steps

- Analyze shortcomings in your current requirements management process to see whether a requirements management tool is likely to provide sufficient value to justify the investment. Make sure you understand the causes of your current shortcomings; don't simply assume that a tool will correct them.

- Before launching a comparative evaluation, assess your team's readiness for adopting a tool. Reflect on previous attempts to incorporate new tools into your development process. Understand why they succeeded or failed so that you can position yourselves for success this time.

IV

Implementing Requirements Engineering

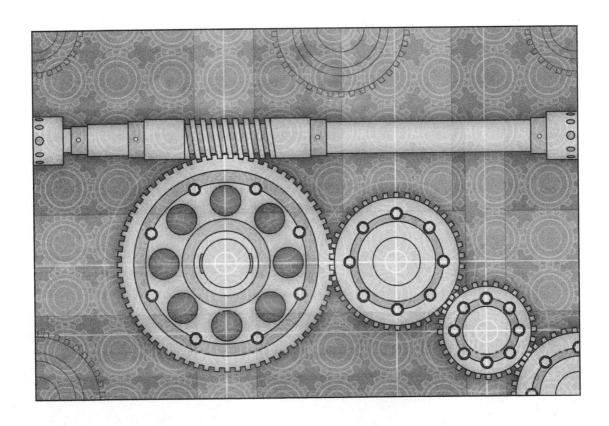

22

Improving Your Requirements Processes

Previous chapters have described several dozen requirements engineering "good practices" for you to consider applying in your software organization. Putting better practices into action is the essence of software process improvement. In a nutshell, process improvement consists of using more of the approaches that work well for us and avoiding those that have given us headaches in the past. However, the path to improved performance is paved with false starts, resistance from those who are affected, and the frustration of having too little time to handle current tasks, let alone improvement programs.

The ultimate objective of software process improvement is to reduce the cost of creating and maintaining software. There are several ways to accomplish this:

- Correcting problems encountered on previous or current projects that arose from process shortcomings

- Anticipating and preventing problems that you might encounter on future projects

- Adopting practices that are more efficient than the practices currently being used

If your team's current methods seem to work well—or if people insist that they do despite evidence to the contrary—people might not see the need to change their approach. However, even successful software organizations can struggle when confronted with larger projects, different customers, long-distance collaborations, tighter schedules, or new application domains. Approaches that worked for a team of five people with a single customer don't scale up to 125 people located in two different time zones who are serving 40 corporate customers. At the least, you should be aware of other approaches to requirements engineering that could be valuable additions to your software engineering tool kit.

This chapter describes how requirements relate to various key project processes and stakeholders. I'll present some basic concepts about software process improvement and a suggested process improvement cycle. I'll also list several useful requirements "process assets" that your organization should have available. The chapter concludes by describing a process improvement road map for implementing improved requirements engineering practices.

How Requirements Relate to Other Project Processes

Requirements lie at the heart of every well-run software project, supporting the other technical and management activities. Changes that you make in your requirements development and management approaches will affect these other processes, and vice versa. Figure 22-1 illustrates some connections between requirements and other processes; the sections that follow briefly describe these process interfaces.

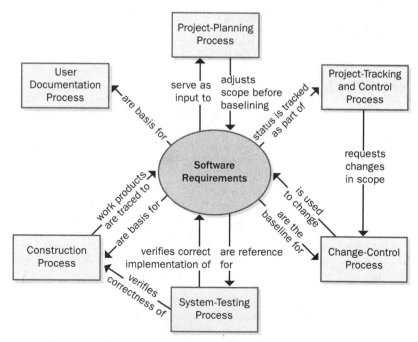

Figure 22-1 Relationship of requirements to other project processes.

Project planning   Requirements are the foundation of the project-planning process. The planners select an appropriate software development life cycle and develop resource and schedule estimates based on the requirements. Project planning might indicate that it's not possible to deliver the entire desired feature set within the available bounds of resources and time. The planning process can lead to reductions in the project scope or to the selection of an incremental or staged-release approach to deliver functionality in phases.

Project tracking and control   Project tracking includes monitoring the status of each requirement so that the project manager can see whether construction and verification are proceeding as intended. If not, management might need to request a scope reduction through the change-control process.

Change control   After a set of requirements has been baselined, all subsequent changes should be made through a defined change-control process. This process helps ensure that

- The impact of a proposed change is understood.

- The appropriate people make informed decisions to accept changes.

- All people who are affected by a change are made aware of it.

- Resources and commitments are adjusted as needed.

- The requirements documentation is kept current and accurate.

System testing   User requirements and functional requirements are essential inputs to system testing. If the expected behavior of the software under various conditions isn't clearly specified, the testers will be hard-pressed to identify defects and to verify that all planned functionality has been implemented as intended.

Construction   Although executable software is the ultimate deliverable of a software project, requirements form the foundation for the design and implementation work and they tie together the various construction work products. Use design reviews to ensure that the designs correctly address all of the requirements. Unit testing can determine whether the code satisfies the design specifications and the pertinent requirements. Requirements tracing lets you document the specific software design and code elements that were derived from each requirement.

 User documentation   I once worked in an office area that also housed the technical writers who prepared user documentation for complex software products. I asked one of the writers why they worked such long hours. "We're at the end of the food chain," she replied. "We have to respond to the final changes in user interface displays and the features that got dropped or added at the last minute." The product's requirements provide input to the user documentation process, so poorly written or late requirements will lead to documentation problems. It's not surprising that the long-suffering people at the end of the requirements chain, such as technical writers and testers, are often enthusiastic supporters of improved requirements engineering practices.

Requirements and Various Stakeholder Groups

Figure 22-2 shows some of the project stakeholders who can interface with a software development group and some of the contributions they make to a project's requirements engineering activities. Explain to your contact people in each functional area the information and contributions you need from them if the product development effort is to succeed. Agree on the form and content of key communication interfaces between development and other functional areas, such as a system requirements specification or a market requirements document. Too often, important project documents are written from the author's point of view without full consideration of the information that the readers of those documents need.

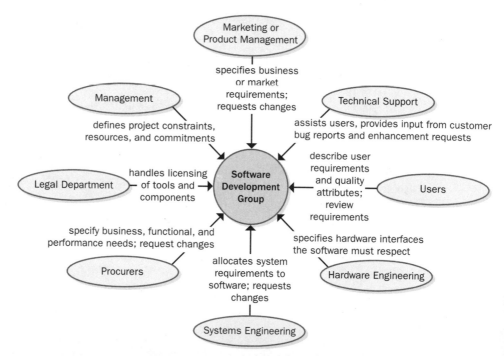

Figure 22-2 Requirements-related interfaces between software development and other stakeholders.

On the flip side, ask the other organizations what they need from the development group to make their jobs easier. What input about technical feasibility will help marketing plan their product concepts better? What requirements status reports will give management adequate visibility into project progress? What collaboration with system engineering will ensure that system requirements are properly partitioned among software and hardware subsystems? Strive to build collaborative relationships between development and the other stakeholders of the requirements process.

When the software development group changes its requirements processes, the interfaces it presents to other project stakeholder communities also change. People don't like to be forced out of their comfort zone, so expect some resistance to your proposed requirements process changes. Understand the origin of the resistance so that you can both respect it and defuse it. Much resistance comes from fear of the unknown. To reduce the fear, communicate your process improvement rationale and intentions to your counterparts in other areas. Explain the benefits that these other groups will receive from the new process. When seeking collaboration on process improvement, begin from this viewpoint: "Here are the problems we've all experienced. We think that these process changes will help solve those problems. Here's what we plan to do, this is the help we'll need from you, and this is how our work will help us both." Following are some forms of resistance that you might encounter:

- A change-control process might be viewed as a barrier thrown up by development to make it harder to get changes made. In reality, a change-control process is a structure, not a barrier. It permits well-informed people to make good business decisions. The software team is responsible for ensuring that the change process really does work. If new processes don't yield better results, people will find ways to work around them—and they probably should.

- Some developers view writing and reviewing requirements documents as bureaucratic time-wasters that prevent them from doing their "real" work of writing code. If you can explain the high cost of continually rewriting the code while the team tries to figure out what the system should do, developers and managers will better appreciate the need for good requirements.

- If customer-support costs aren't linked to the development process, the development team might not be motivated to change how they work because they don't suffer the consequences of poor product quality.

■   If one objective of improved requirements processes is to reduce support costs by creating higher-quality products, the support manager might feel threatened. Who wants to see his empire shrink?

■   Busy customers sometimes claim that they don't have time to spend working on the requirements. Remind them of earlier projects that delivered unsatisfactory systems and the high cost of responding to customer input after delivery.

Anytime people are asked to change the way they work, the natural reaction is to ask, "What's in it for me?" However, process changes don't always result in fabulous, immediate benefits for every individual involved. A better question—and one that any process improvement leader must be able to answer convincingly—is, "What's in it for *us*?" Every process change should offer the prospect of clear benefits to the project team, the development organization, the company, the customer, or the universe. You can often sell these benefits in terms of correcting the known shortcomings of the current ways of working that lead to less than desirable business outcomes.

Fundamentals of Software Process Improvement

You're reading this book presumably because you intend to change some of the current approaches your organization uses for requirements engineering. As you begin your quest for excellent requirements, keep the following four principles of software process improvement in mind (Wiegers 1996a):

1.   **Process improvement should be evolutionary, continuous, and cyclical.**   Don't expect to improve all your processes at once, and accept that you won't get everything right the first time you try to make changes. Instead of aiming for perfection, develop a few improved templates and procedures and get started with implementation. Adjust your approaches as your team gains experience with the new techniques. Sometimes simple and easy changes can lead to substantial gains, so look for the low-hanging fruit.

2.   **People and organizations change only when they have an incentive to do so.**   The strongest incentive for change is pain. I don't mean artificially induced pain, such as management-imposed schedule pressure intended to make developers work harder, but rather the very real pain you've experienced on previous projects. Following are some examples of problems that can provide compelling drivers for changing your requirements processes:

❑   The project missed deadlines because the requirements were more extensive and complicated than expected.

❑   Developers worked a lot of overtime because misunderstood or ambiguous requirements were addressed late in development.

❑   System test effort was wasted because the testers didn't understand what the product was supposed to do.

❑   The right functionality was present, but users were dissatisfied because of sluggish performance, poor usability, or other quality shortcomings.

❑   The organization experienced high maintenance costs because customers requested many enhancements that should have been identified during requirements elicitation.

❑   The development organization acquired a reputation for delivering software that customers don't want.

3.   **Process changes should be goal-oriented.**   Before you begin the journey to superior processes, make sure that you know where you're headed (Potter and Sakry 2002). Do you want to reduce the amount of work that is redone because of requirements problems? Do you want better schedule predictability? Do you want to stop overlooking requirements during implementation? A road map that defines pathways to your business objectives greatly improves your chances of successful process improvement.

4.   **Treat your improvement activities as miniprojects.**   Many improvement initiatives founder because they're poorly planned or because resources never materialize. Include process improvement resources and tasks in your project's overall plans. Perform the planning, tracking, measurement, and reporting that you'd do for any project, scaled down for the size of the improvement project. Write an action plan for each process improvement area you tackle. Track the time the participants spend executing the action plan to check whether you're getting the level of effort you expected and to know how much the improvement work is costing.

> **Trap**   The single biggest threat to a software process improvement program is lack of management commitment, followed closely by reorganizations that shuffle the program's participants and priorities.

All team members have the opportunity—and the responsibility—to actively improve how they do their work. Professional software practitioners don't need permission from their managers to better themselves and their teams. Grass-roots improvement programs that grow out of frustration with the status quo or are galvanized by a charismatic leader can be quite successful. However, a broad process improvement effort can succeed only if management is motivated to commit resources, set expectations, and hold team members accountable for their contributions to the change initiative.

Process Improvement One-Liners

The experienced software process improvement leader accumulates a list of short, pithy observations about this difficult domain. Here are some that I've picked up over the years:

- Take chewable bites. (If you bite into too large a process change, the team will likely choke on it.)

- Take a lot of satisfaction from small victories. (You won't have many big victories.)

- Use gentle pressure, relentlessly applied. (The process improvement leaders and committed managers steer the team toward a better future by keeping the change initiative visible and continually chipping away at it.)

- Focus, focus, focus. (A busy software team can work on only three, or two, or perhaps just one improvement initiative at a time. But never work on fewer than one.)

- Look for allies. (Every team has its early adopters who will try out new templates and procedures and give the improvement leaders feedback. Cultivate them. Thank them. Reward them.)

- Action plans that don't turn into actions are not useful. (It's easy to do a process assessment and to write an action plan. It's hard to get people to work in new ways that hold the promise of better results, yet that's the only useful outcome of process improvement.)

The Process Improvement Cycle

Figure 22-3 illustrates a process improvement cycle I've found to be effective. This cycle reflects the importance of knowing where you are before you take off for someplace else, the need to chart your course, and the value of learning from your experiences as part of continuous process improvement.

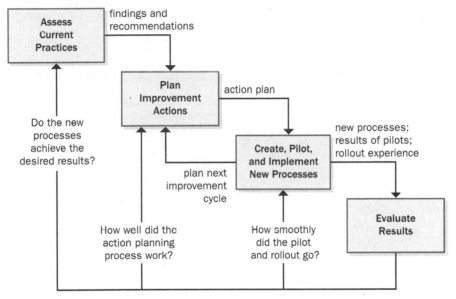

Figure 22-3   The software process improvement cycle.

Assess Current Practices

Step 1 of any improvement activity is to assess the practices currently being used in an organization and to identify their strengths and shortcomings. An assessment does not in itself provide any improvement—it provides information. The assessment lays the foundation for making the right choices about the changes you should make. It also brings visibility to the processes actually being used in the organization, which are frequently different from the stated or documented processes. And you'll find that different team members typically have very different perspectives as to what processes the team is using.

You can evaluate your current processes in several ways. If you tried any of the Next Steps at the end of previous chapters, you've already begun an informal evaluation of your requirements practices and their results. Structured questionnaires provide a more systematic approach, which can reveal insights about your current processes at low cost. Interviews and discussions with team members provide a more accurate and comprehensive understanding.

You can use the questionnaire in Appendix A to calibrate your organization's current requirements engineering practices.[1] This self-assessment helps you decide which of your requirements processes are most in need of improvement. Just because you give yourself a low rating on a particular question isn't reason enough to address it immediately or perhaps at all. Focus your energy on improving those practice areas that are causing your projects the most difficulties and those that pose risks to the success of your future projects.

A more thorough approach is to have an outside consultant evaluate your current software processes. The most comprehensive process assessments are based on an established process improvement framework, such as the Capability Maturity Model for Software (SW-CMM) developed by the Software Engineering Institute (Paulk et al. 1995). Outside assessors typically examine many of your software development and management processes, not just the requirements activities. The deliverables from a formal assessment include a list of findings—statements of both strengths and weaknesses in the current processes—and recommendations for addressing the improvement opportunities. Select an assessment approach that aligns with the business goals you want to achieve through your process improvement activities, and don't worry too much about satisfying the requirements of the SW-CMM or any other specific model. Appendix B, "Requirements and Process Improvement Models," describes how requirements fit into the SW-CMM and the newer CMM Integration model, the CMMI-SE/SW.

Plan Improvement Actions

In keeping with the philosophy of treating process improvement activities as projects, write an action plan following your assessment (Potter and Sakry

---

1. Motorola developed a similar "Software Requirements Quality Model" for requirements process assessment (Smith 1998).

2002). A strategic plan describes your organization's overall software process improvement initiative. Tactical action plans target specific improvement areas, such as the way you gather requirements or your prioritization procedure. Each action plan should state the goals of the improvement activities, the participants, and the individual action items that must be completed to implement the plan. Without a plan, it's easy to overlook important tasks. The plan also provides a way to monitor progress as you track the completion of individual action items.

Figure 22-4 illustrates a process improvement action plan template I've used many times. Include no more than 10 items in each action plan, scoped such that the plan can be completed in two to three months. As an example, I saw a plan for requirements management improvements that included these action items:

1. Draft a requirements change-control procedure.

2. Review and revise the change-control procedure.

3. Pilot the change-control procedure with Project A.

4. Revise the change-control procedure based on feedback from the pilot.

5. Evaluate problem-tracking tools, and select one to support the change-control procedure.

6. Procure the problem-tracking tool, and customize it to support the change-control procedure.

7. Roll out the new change-control procedure and tool to the organization.

Assign each action item to a specific individual owner who is responsible for seeing that the item is completed. Don't assign "the team" as an action item owner. Teams don't do work; individuals do.

If you need more than about 10 action items, focus the initial activity cycle on the most important issues and address the rest later in a separate action plan; remember, change is cyclical. The process improvement road map described later in this chapter illustrates how you can group multiple improvement actions into an overall software process improvement plan.

Action Plan for Requirements Process Improvement

Project   **Date:**
<your project name here>   *<date plan was written>*

Goals:
<State a few goals you wish to accomplish by successfully executing this plan. State the goals in terms of business value, not in terms of process changes.>

Measures of Success:
<Describe how you will determine if the process changes have had the desired effects on the project.>

Scope of Organizational Impact:
<Describe the breadth of impact of the process changes described in this plan.>

Staffing and Participants:
<Identify the individuals who will implement this plan, their roles, and their time commitment on an hours per week or percentage basis.>

Tracking and Reporting Process:
<Describe how progress on the action items in this plan will be tracked and to whom status, results, and issues will be reported.>

Dependencies, Risks, and Constraints:
<Identify any external factors that might be required for this plan to succeed or that could prevent successful implementation of the plan.>

Estimated Completion Date for All Activities:
<When do you expect this plan to be fully implemented?>

ACTION ITEMS:
<Write 3 to 10 action items for each action plan.>

Action Item	Owner	Due Date	Purpose	Description of Activities	Deliverables	Resources Needed
<Sequence number>	*<Responsible individual>*	*<Target date>*	*<Objective of this action item>*	*<Activities that will be performed to implement this action item>*	*<Procedures, templates, or other process assets that will be created>*	*<Any external resources needed, including materials, tools, documents, or other people>*

Figure 22-4   Action plan template for software process improvement.

Create, Pilot, and Implement New Processes

So far, you've evaluated your current requirements practices and crafted a plan for addressing the process areas that you think are most likely to yield benefits. Now comes the hard part: implementing the plan. Many process improvement initiatives stumble when they try to turn action plans into actions.

Implementing an action plan means developing processes that you believe will yield better results than your current ways of working do. Don't expect to get the new processes perfect on the first try. Many approaches that seem like a good idea in the abstract turn out to be less pragmatic or less effective than anticipated. Therefore, plan a process *pilot* for most of the new procedures or document templates you create. Use the knowledge gained from the pilot to adjust the new process. This improves the chance that it will be effective and well received when you roll it out to the affected community. Keep the following suggestions in mind for the process pilots you conduct:

- Select pilot participants who will give the new approaches a fair try and provide helpful feedback. These participants could be either allies or skeptics, but they shouldn't strongly oppose the improvement effort.

- To make the outcome easy to interpret, quantify the criteria the team will use to evaluate the pilot.

- Identify the stakeholders who need to be kept informed of what the pilot is about and why it is being performed.

- Consider piloting portions of the new processes on different projects. This engages more people in trying new approaches, which increases awareness, feedback, and buy-in.

- As part of the evaluation, ask pilot participants how they would feel if they had to go back to their former ways of working.

Even motivated and receptive teams have a limited capacity to absorb change, so don't place too many new expectations on a project team at once. Write a roll-out plan that defines how you'll distribute the new methods and materials to the project team, and provide sufficient training and assistance. Also consider how management will communicate their expectations about the new processes, perhaps through a formal requirements engineering policy.

Evaluate Results

The final step of a process improvement cycle is to evaluate the activities performed and the results achieved. This evaluation will help the team do an even better job on future improvement activities. Assess how smoothly the pilots ran and how effective they were in resolving the uncertainties about the new processes. Would you change anything the next time you conduct a process pilot?

Consider how well the general rollout of the new processes went. Was the availability of the new processes or templates communicated effectively to everyone? Did participants understand and successfully apply the new processes? Would you change anything about how you handle the next rollout?

A critical step is to evaluate whether the newly implemented processes are yielding the desired results. Some new technical and management practices deliver visible improvements quickly, but others take time to demonstrate their full value. For example, you should be able to tell quickly whether a new process for dealing with requirement changes facilitates incorporating changes into the project in a less chaotic way. However, a new software requirements specification template can take some time to prove its worth as analysts and customers get used to the discipline of documenting requirements in a particular format. Give new approaches adequate time to work, and select measures that will demonstrate the success of each process change.

Accept the reality of the learning curve—that is, the productivity drop that takes place as practitioners take time to assimilate new ways of working, as illustrated in Figure 22-5. This short-term productivity drop—sometimes called the "valley of despair"—is part of the investment your organization is making in process improvement. People who don't understand this might be tempted to abandon the process improvement effort before it begins to pay off, thereby achieving a zero return on their investment. Educate your managers and peers about the learning curve, and commit to seeing the change initiative through. The team *will* achieve superior project and business results with the help of superior requirements processes.

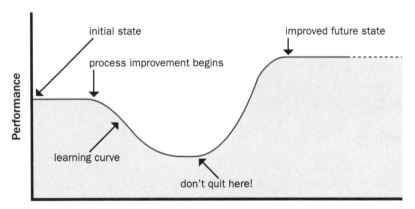

Figure 22-5   The learning curve is an unavoidable part of process improvement.

Requirements Engineering Process Assets

High-performance projects have effective processes for all of the requirements engineering components: elicitation, analysis, specification, validation, and management. To facilitate the performance of these processes, every organization needs a collection of *process assets* (Wiegers 1998c). A process encompasses the actions you take and the deliverables you produce; process assets help the team members perform processes consistently and effectively. These process assets will help those involved in the project understand the steps they should follow and the work products they're expected to create. Process assets include the types of documents described in Table 22-1.

Table 22-1   Process Asset Documents

Type	Description
checklist	A list that enumerates activities, deliverables, or other items to be noted or verified. Checklists are memory joggers. They help ensure that busy people don't overlook important details.
example	A representative of a specific type of work product. Accumulate good examples as your project teams create them.
plan	An outline of how an objective will be accomplished and what is needed to accomplish it.
policy	A guiding principle that sets a management expectation of behaviors, actions, and deliverables. Processes should enable satisfaction of the policies.
procedure	A step-by-step description of the sequence of tasks that accomplishes an activity. Describe the tasks to be performed and identify the project roles that perform them. Don't include tutorial information in a procedure. Guidance documents can support a process or procedure with tutorial information and helpful tips.
process description	A documented definition of a set of activities performed for some purpose. A process description might include the process objective, key milestones, participants, communication steps, input and output data, artifacts associated with the process, and ways to tailor the process to different project situations (Caputo 1998).
template	A pattern to be used as a guide for producing a complete work product. Templates for key project documents remind you to ask questions that you might otherwise overlook. A well-structured template provides many "slots" for capturing and organizing information. Guidance text embedded in the template will help the document author use it effectively.

Figure 22-6 identifies some valuable process assets for requirements engineering. No software process rule book says that you need all of these items, but they will all assist your requirements-related activities. The procedures listed in Figure 22-6 should be no longer than they need to be to let team members consistently perform the procedures effectively. They need not be separate documents; an overall requirements management process could include the change-control procedure, status-tracking procedure, and impact analysis checklist. Many of the process assets in Figure 22-6 are available at *http://www.processimpact.com/goodies.shtml.*

Requirements Development Process Assets	Requirements Management Process Assets
• Requirements Development Process • Requirements Allocation Procedure • Requirements Prioritization Procedure • Vision and Scope Template • Use-Case Template • Software Requirements Specification Template • SRS and Use-Case Defect Checklists	• Requirements Management Process • Change-Control Process • Requirements Status-Tracking Procedure • Requirements Traceability Procedure • Change Control Board Charter • Requirements Change Impact Analysis Checklist and Template

Figure 22-6   Key process assets for requirements development and requirements management.

Following are brief descriptions of each of the process assets listed in Figure 22-6, along with references to the chapters where they are discussed in detail. Keep in mind that each project should tailor the organization's assets to best suit its needs.

Requirements Development Process Assets

Requirements development process   This process describes how to identify stakeholders, user classes, and product champions in your domain. It should address how to plan the elicitation activities, including selecting appropriate elicitation techniques, identifying participants, and estimating the effort and calendar time required for elicitation. The process also describes the various requirements documents and models your project is expected to create and points the reader toward appropriate templates. The requirements development process also should identify the steps the project should perform for requirements analysis and validation.

Requirements allocation procedure   Allocating high-level product requirements to specific subsystems, including people, is necessary when developing systems that include both hardware and software components or complex products that contain multiple software subsystems (Nelsen 1990). Allocation takes place after the system-level requirements are specified and the system architecture has been defined. This procedure describes how to perform these allocations to ensure that functionality is assigned to the appropriate components. It also describes how allocated requirements will be traced back to their parent system requirements and to related requirements in other subsystems.

Requirements prioritization procedure   To sensibly reduce scope or to accommodate added requirements within a fixed schedule, we need to know which planned system capabilities have the lowest priority. Chapter 14, "Setting Requirement Priorities," describes a spreadsheet tool for prioritization that incorporates the value provided to the customer, the relative technical risk, and the relative cost of implementation for each feature, use case, or functional requirement.

Vision and scope template   The vision and scope document is a concise, high-level description of the new product's business requirements. It provides a reference for making decisions about requirements priorities and changes. Chapter 5, "Establishing the Product Vision and Project Scope," recommends a template for this document.

Use-case template   The use-case template provides a standard format for describing tasks that users need to perform with a software system. A use-case definition includes a brief description of the task, descriptions of alternative behaviors and known exceptions that must be handled, and additional information about the task. Chapter 8, "Understanding User Requirements," proposes a use-case template.

Software requirements specification template   The SRS template provides a structured, consistent way to organize the product's functional and nonfunctional requirements. Consider adopting more than one template to accommodate the different types or sizes of projects your organization undertakes. This can reduce the frustration that arises when a "one size fits all" template or procedure isn't suitable for your project. Chapter 10, "Documenting the Requirements," describes a sample SRS template.

SRS and use-case defect checklists   Formal inspection of requirements documents is a powerful software quality technique. An inspection defect checklist identifies many of the errors commonly found in requirements documents. Use the checklist during the inspection's preparation stage to focus your attention on common problem areas. Chapter 15, "Validating the Requirements," contains sample SRS and use-case defect checklists.

Requirements Management Process Assets

Requirements management process   This process describes the actions a project team takes to deal with changes, distinguish versions of the requirements documentation, track and report on requirements status, and accumulate traceability information. The process should list the attributes to include for each requirement, such as priority, predicted stability, and planned release number. It should also describe the steps required to approve the SRS and establish the requirements baseline. For an example of a requirements management process description, see Appendix J of *CMM Implementation Guide* (Caputo 1998).

Change-control process   A practical change-control process can reduce the chaos inflicted by endless, uncontrolled requirements changes. The change-control process defines the way that a new requirement or a modification to an existing requirement is proposed, communicated, evaluated, and resolved. A problem-tracking tool facilitates change control, but remember that a tool is not a substitute for a process. Chapter 19, "Change Happens," describes a change-control process in detail.

Requirements status tracking procedure   Requirements management includes monitoring and reporting the status of each functional requirement. You'll need to use a database or a commercial requirements management tool to track the status of the many requirements in a large system. This procedure also describes the reports you can generate to view the status of the collected requirements at any time. See Chapter 18, "Requirements Management Principles and Practices," for more about requirements status tracking.

Change control board charter   The change control board (CCB) is the body of stakeholders that decides which proposed requirements changes to approve, which to reject, and in which product release each approved change will be incorporated. As described in Chapter 19, the CCB charter describes the composition, function, and operating procedures of the CCB.

Requirements change impact analysis checklist and template   Estimating the cost and other impacts of a proposed requirement change is a key step in determining whether to approve the change. Impact analysis helps the CCB make smart decisions. As illustrated in Chapter 19, an impact analysis checklist helps you contemplate the possible tasks, side effects, and risks associated with implementing a specific requirement change. An accompanying worksheet provides a simple way to estimate the labor for the tasks. A sample template for presenting the results of an impact analysis also appears in Chapter 19.

Requirements traceability procedure   The requirements traceability matrix lists all the functional requirements, the design components and code modules that address each requirement, and the test cases that verify its correct implementation. The traceability matrix should also identify the parent system requirement, use case, business rule, or other source from which each functional requirement was derived. This procedure describes who provides the traceability data, who collects and manages it, and where it is stored. Chapter 20, "Links in the Requirements Chain," addresses requirements traceability.

Requirements Process Improvement Road Map

Haphazard approaches to process improvement rarely lead to sustainable success. Rather than just diving in, develop a road map for implementing improved requirements practices in your organization. This road map is part of your strategic process improvement plan. If you tried one of the requirements process assessment approaches described in this chapter, you have some ideas about the practices or process assets that would be most helpful to your team. The process improvement road map sequences improvement actions in a way that will yield the greatest benefits with the smallest investment.

Because every situation is different, I can't give you a one-size-fits-all road map. Formulaic approaches to process improvement don't replace careful thinking and common sense. Figure 22-7 illustrates one organization's road map for improving its requirements processes. The desired business goals are shown in the boxes on the right side of the figure, and the major improvement activities are shown in the other boxes. The circles indicate intermediate milestones along the paths to achieving the business goals. (*M1* means *milestone 1.*) Implement each set of improvement activities from left to right. Once you've created a road map, give ownership of each milestone to an individual, who can then write an action plan for achieving that milestone. Then turn those action plans into actions!

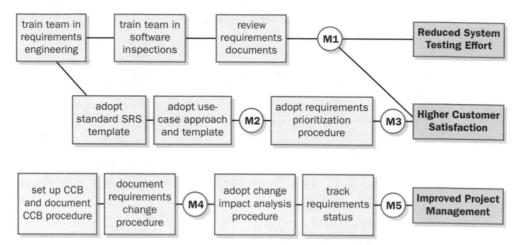

Figure 22-7   Sample requirements process improvement road map.

 Next Steps

- Complete the Current Requirements Practice Self-Assessment in Appendix A. Identify your top three improvement opportunities for requirements practices, based on the consequences of shortcomings in your current practices.

- Determine which of the requirements engineering process assets listed in Figure 22-6 (on page 396) are not presently available in your organization but would be useful to have.

- Based on the two preceding steps, develop a requirements process improvement road map patterned after that shown in Figure 22-7 (on this page). Persuade someone in your organization to take responsibility for each milestone. Have each milestone owner use the template in Figure 22-4 (on page 392) to write an action plan for implementing the recommendations leading up to his or her milestone. Track the progress of the action items in the plan as they are implemented.

23

Software Requirements and Risk Management

Dave, the project manager for the Chemical Tracking System at Contoso Pharmaceuticals, is meeting with his lead programmer, Helen, and the lead tester, Ramesh. All are excited about the new project, but they remember the problems they ran into on an earlier project called the Pharm-Simulator.

"Remember how we didn't find out that the users hated the Simulator's user interface until beta testing?" Helen asked. "It took us four weeks to rebuild it and retest it. I sure don't want to go through that death march again."

"That wasn't fun," Dave agreed. "It was also annoying that the users we talked to swore they needed a lot of features that no one has used so far. That drug interaction modeling feature took three times longer to code than we expected, and we wound up throwing it out anyway. What a waste!"

"We really had to rush on the Simulator and didn't have time to write detailed requirements," Ramesh remembered. "Half the time the testers had to ask a programmer how some feature was supposed to work so they could test it. Then it turned out that some of the functions the programmers implemented didn't do what the users needed anyway."

"I was really annoyed that the manager who requested the Pharm-Simulator signed off on the requirements without even looking at them," Dave added. "Then remember the constant stream of change requests from people in her department? It's no surprise the project came in five months late and cost almost twice what they budgeted. If that happens again, I'll probably get fired."

Ramesh had a suggestion. "Maybe we should make a list of these problems from the Simulator so we can try to avoid them on the Chemical Tracking System. I read an article on software risk management that said we should identify risks up front and figure out how to prevent them from hurting the project."

"I don't know about that," Dave protested. "We learned a lot from the Simulator, so we probably won't have those problems again. This project isn't big enough to need risk management. If we write down things that could go wrong on the Chemical Tracking System, it'll look like I don't know how to run a software project. I don't want any negative thinkers on this project. We have to plan for success!"

As Dave's final comments suggest, software engineers are eternal optimists. We often expect our next project to run smoothly, despite the history of problems on earlier projects. The reality is that dozens of potential pitfalls can delay or derail a software project. Contrary to Dave's beliefs, software project managers *must* identify and control their project risks, beginning with requirements-related risks.

A *risk* is a condition that could cause some loss or otherwise threaten the success of a project. This condition hasn't actually caused a problem yet, and you'd like to keep it that way. These potential problems might have an adverse impact on the project's cost, schedule, or technical success, the product's quality, or team effectiveness. Risk management—a software industry best practice (Brown 1996)—is the process of identifying, evaluating, and controlling risks before they damage your project. If something untoward has already happened on your project, it's an issue, not a risk. Deal with current problems and issues through your project's ongoing status tracking and corrective action processes.

Because no one can predict the future with certainty, risk management is a way to minimize the likelihood or impact of potential problems. Risk management means dealing with a concern before it becomes a crisis. This improves the chance of project success and reduces the financial or other consequences of those risks that you can't avoid. Risks that lie outside the team's sphere of control should be directed to the appropriate level of management.

Because requirements play such a central role in software projects, the prudent project manager will identify requirements-related risks early and control them aggressively. Typical requirements risks include misunderstanding the requirements, inadequate user involvement, uncertain or changing project scope and objectives, and continually changing requirements. Project managers can control requirements risks only through collaboration with customers or their representatives. Jointly documenting requirements risks and planning mitigation actions reinforces the customer-development partnership that was discussed in Chapter 2, "Requirements from the Customer's Perspective."

Simply knowing about the risks doesn't make them go away, so this chapter presents a brief tutorial on software risk management (Wiegers 1998b). Later in the chapter, I'll also describe a number of risk factors that can raise their ugly heads during requirements engineering activities. Use this information to launch an attack on your requirements risks before they attack your project.

Fundamentals of Software Risk Management

Projects face many kinds of risks besides those related to project scope and requirements. Dependence on an external entity, such as a subcontractor or another project providing components to be reused, is a common source of risk. Project management is fraught with risks caused by poor estimation, rejection of accurate estimates by managers, insufficient visibility into project status, and staff turnover. Technology risks threaten highly complex and leading-edge development projects. Lack of knowledge is another source of risk, as with practitioners who have insufficient experience with the technologies being used or with the application domain. And ever-changing, imposed government regulations can disrupt the best-laid project plans.

Scary! This is why all projects need to take risk management seriously. Risk management involves scanning the horizon for icebergs, rather than steaming full speed ahead with great confidence that your ship is unsinkable. As with other processes, scale your risk management activities to your project's size. Small projects can get by with a simple risk list, but formal risk management planning is a key element of a successful large-scale project.

Elements of Risk Management

Risk management is the application of tools and procedures to contain project risk within acceptable limits. Risk management provides a standard approach to identify and document risk factors, evaluate their potential severity, and propose strategies for mitigating them (Williams, Walker, and Dorofee 1997). Risk management includes the activities shown in Figure 23-1.[1]

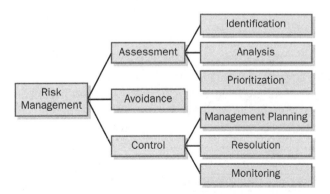

Figure 23-1   Elements of risk management.

---

1. Adapted from McConnell, Steve. 1996. *Rapid Development: Taming Wild Software Schedules.* Redmond, Wash.: Microsoft Press.

Risk assessment is the process of examining a project to identify areas of potential risk. Facilitate *risk identification* with lists of common risk factors for software projects, including the requirements risk factors described in the "Requirements-Related Risks" section later in this chapter (Carr et al. 1993; McConnell 1996). During *risk analysis*, you'll examine the potential consequences of specific risks to your project. *Risk prioritization* helps you focus on the most severe risks by assessing the potential *risk exposure* from each. Risk exposure is a function of both the probability of incurring a loss due to the risk and the potential magnitude of that loss.

Risk avoidance is one way to deal with a risk: don't do the risky thing. You can avoid risks by not undertaking certain projects, by relying on proven rather than cutting-edge technologies, or by excluding features that will be especially difficult to implement correctly. Software development is intrinsically risky, though, so avoiding risk also means losing an opportunity.

Most of the time, you'll have to perform *risk control* activities to manage the top-priority risks you identified. *Risk management planning* produces a plan for dealing with each significant risk, including mitigation approaches, contingency plans, owners, and timelines. Mitigation actions try either to prevent the risk from becoming a problem at all or to reduce the adverse impact if it does. The risks won't control themselves, so *risk resolution* involves executing the plans for mitigating each risk. Finally, track your progress toward resolving each risk item through *risk monitoring*, which should become part of your routine project status tracking. Monitor how well your risk mitigation actions are working, look for new risks that have popped up, retire risks whose threat has passed, and update the priorities of your risk list periodically.

Documenting Project Risks

It's not enough to simply recognize the risks that face your project. You need to manage them in a way that lets you communicate risk issues and status to stakeholders throughout the project's duration. Figure 23-2 shows a template for documenting an individual risk statement. You might find it more convenient to store this information in tabular form in a spreadsheet, which makes it easy to sort the list of risks. Rather than embedding it in your project management plan or software requirements specification, keep the risk list as a stand-alone document so that it's easy to update throughout the project's duration.

ID:
<sequence number>

Date Opened:
<date the risk was identified>

Date Closed:
<date the risk was closed out>

Description:
<description of the risk in the form "condition–consequence">

Probability:
<the likelihood of this risk becoming a problem>

Impact:
<the potential damage if the risk does become a problem>

Exposure:
<probability multiplied by impact>

Mitigation Plan:
<one or more approaches to control, avoid, minimize, or otherwise mitigate the risk>

Owner:
<individual responsible for resolving the risk>

Date Due:
<date by which the mitigation actions are to be implemented>

Figure 23-2   Risk item tracking template.

Use a *condition-consequence* format when you document risk statements. That is, state the risk condition that you are concerned about, followed by the potential adverse outcome—the consequence—from that condition. Often, people who suggest risks state only the condition ("the customers don't agree on the product requirements") or the consequence ("we can satisfy only one of our major customers"). Pull these statements together into the condition-consequence structure: "The customers don't agree on the product requirements, so we will only be able to satisfy one of our major customers." One condition might lead to several consequences, and several conditions can result in the same consequence.

The template provides locations to record the probability of a risk materializing into a problem, the negative impact on the project as a result of that problem, and the overall risk exposure. I estimate the probability on a scale from 0.1 (highly unlikely) to 1.0 (certain to happen), and the impact on a relative scale of 1 (no sweat) to 10 (deep tapioca). Even better, try to rate the potential impact in units of lost time or money. Multiply the probability by the impact to estimate the exposure from each risk.

Don't try to quantify risks too precisely. Your goal is to differentiate the most threatening risks from those you don't need to tackle immediately. You might find it easier simply to estimate both probability and impact as high, medium, or low. Those items that have at least one *high* rating demand your early attention.

Use the Mitigation Plan field to identify the actions you intend to take to control the risk. Some mitigation strategies try to reduce the risk probability, and others reduce the impact. Consider the cost of mitigation when planning. It doesn't make sense to spend $20,000 to control a risk that could cost you only $10,000. You might also devise contingency plans for the most severe risks to anticipate what actions to take if, despite your efforts, the risk does affect your project. Assign every risk that you're going to control to an individual owner, and set a target date for completing the mitigation actions. Long-term or complex risks might require a multistep mitigation strategy with multiple milestones.

Figure 23-3 illustrates a risk that the Chemical Tracking System team leaders discussed at the beginning of this chapter. The team estimated the probability and impact on the basis of their previous experience. Until they evaluate other risk factors, they won't know how serious a risk exposure of 4.2 is. The first two mitigation approaches reduce the probability of this risk becoming a problem by increasing user involvement in the requirements process. Prototyping reduces the potential impact by seeking early feedback on the user interface.

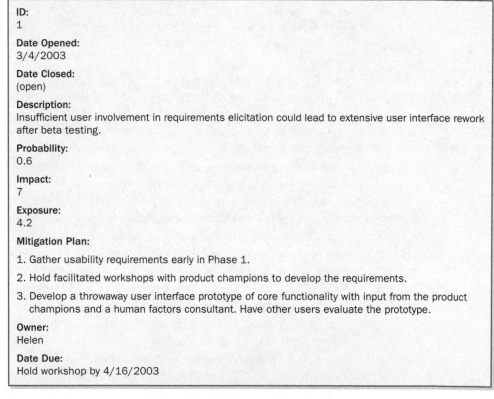

ID:
1

Date Opened:
3/4/2003

Date Closed:
(open)

Description:
Insufficient user involvement in requirements elicitation could lead to extensive user interface rework after beta testing.

Probability:
0.6

Impact:
7

Exposure:
4.2

Mitigation Plan:

1. Gather usability requirements early in Phase 1.

2. Hold facilitated workshops with product champions to develop the requirements.

3. Develop a throwaway user interface prototype of core functionality with input from the product champions and a human factors consultant. Have other users evaluate the prototype.

Owner:
Helen

Date Due:
Hold workshop by 4/16/2003

Figure 23-3 Sample risk item from the Chemical Tracking System.

Planning for Risk Management

A risk list is not the same as a risk management plan. For a small project, you can include your plans for controlling risks in the software project management plan. A large project should write a separate risk management plan that spells out the approaches it intends to take to identify, evaluate, document, and track risks. This plan should include the roles and responsibilities for the risk management activities. A risk management plan template is available from *http://www.processimpact.com/goodies.shtml*. Many projects appoint a project risk manager to be responsible for staying on top of the things that could go wrong. One company dubbed their risk manager "Eeyore," after the gloomy Winnie-the-Pooh character who constantly bemoaned how bad things could become.

> **Trap**   Don't assume that risks are under control just because you identified them and selected mitigation actions. Follow through on the risk management actions. Include enough time for risk management in the project schedule so that you don't waste your investment in risk planning. Include risk mitigation activities, risk status reporting, and updating of the risk list in your project's task list.

Establish a rhythm of periodic risk monitoring. Keep the ten or so risks that have the highest risk exposure highly visible, and track the effectiveness of your mitigation approaches regularly. When a mitigation action is completed, reevaluate the probability and impact for that risk item and then update the risk list and any other pending mitigation plans accordingly. A risk is not necessarily under control simply because the mitigation actions have been completed. You need to judge whether your mitigation approaches have reduced the exposure to an acceptable level or whether the opportunity for a specific risk to become a problem has passed.

Out of Control

A project manager once asked me what to do if the same items remained on his top five risk list week after week. This suggests that the mitigation actions for those risks either aren't being implemented or aren't effective. If your mitigation actions are doing the trick, the exposure from risks that you are actively attempting to control will decrease. This lets other risks

(continued)

> **Out of Control**   *(continued)*
>
> ---
>
> that were less threatening than the initial top five float up the risk list and engage your attention. Periodically reassess the probability of each risk materializing and the potential loss if it does to see whether your risk mitigation activities are getting the job done.

Requirements-Related Risks

The risk factors described on the following pages are organized by the requirements engineering subdisciplines of elicitation, analysis, specification, validation, and management. Techniques are suggested that can reduce the risk's probability or impact. This list is just a starting point; accumulate your own list of risk factors and mitigation strategies, based on the lessons you learn from each project. Leishman and Cook (2002) describe additional risks related to software requirements. Use the items here to prompt your thinking when identifying requirements risks. Be sure to write your risk statements in the condition-consequence format.

Requirements Elicitation

Product vision and project scope   Scope creep is more likely if the stakeholders lack a clear, shared understanding of what the product is supposed to be (and not be) and do. Early in the project, write a vision and scope document that contains your business requirements, and use it to guide decisions about new or modified requirements.

Time spent on requirements development   Tight project schedules often pressure managers and customers into glossing over the requirements because they believe that if the programmers don't start coding immediately, they won't finish on time. Projects vary widely depending on their size and application class (such as information systems, systems software, commercial, or military), but a rough guideline is to spend about 10 to 15 percent of your project effort on requirements development activities (Rubin 1999). Record how much effort you actually spend on requirements development for each project so that you can judge whether it was sufficient and improve your planning for future projects.

Completeness and correctness of requirements specifications   To ensure that the requirements specify what the customer really needs, apply the use-case technique to elicit requirements by focusing on user tasks. Devise specific usage scenarios, write test cases from the requirements, and have customers develop their acceptance criteria. Create prototypes to make the requirements more meaningful for users and to elicit specific feedback from them. Enlist customer representatives to inspect the requirements specifications and analysis models.

Requirements for highly innovative products   It's easy to misgauge market response to products that are the first of their kind. Emphasize market research, build prototypes, and use customer focus groups to obtain early and frequent feedback about your innovative product visions.

Defining nonfunctional requirements   Because of the natural emphasis on product functionality, it's easy to neglect nonfunctional requirements. Query customers about quality characteristics such as performance, usability, integrity, and reliability. Document these nonfunctional requirements and their acceptance criteria as precisely as you can in the SRS.

Customer agreement on product requirements   If the diverse customers for your product don't agree on what you should build, someone will be unhappy with the result. Determine who the primary customers are, and use the product champion approach to get adequate customer representation and involvement. Make sure you're relying on the right people for decision-making authority on the requirements.

Unstated requirements   Customers often hold implicit expectations that are not communicated or documented. Try to identify any assumptions the customers might be making. Use open-ended questions to encourage customers to share more of their thoughts, wishes, ideas, information, and concerns than you might otherwise hear.

Existing product used as the requirements baseline   Requirements development might not be deemed important on next-generation or reengineering projects. Developers are sometimes told to use the existing product as their source for requirements, with a list of changes and additions. This forces the developer to glean the bulk of the requirements through reverse engineering of the current product. However, reverse engineering is an inefficient and incomplete way to discover requirements, and no one should be surprised if the new system has some of the same shortcomings as the legacy system.

Document the requirements that you discover through reverse engineering, and have customers review those requirements to ensure that they are correct and still relevant.

Solutions presented as needs   User-proposed solutions can mask the users' actual needs, lead to automating ineffective business processes, and pressure developers into making poor design decisions. The analyst must drill down to understand the intent behind a solution the customer has presented.

Requirements Analysis

Requirements prioritization   Ensure that every functional requirement, feature, or use case is prioritized and allocated to a specific system release or iteration. Evaluate the priority of every new requirement against the body of work remaining to be done so that you can make smart trade-off decisions.

Technically difficult features   Evaluate the feasibility of each requirement to identify those that might take longer than anticipated to implement. Success always seems just around the corner, so use your project status tracking to watch for requirements that are falling behind their implementation schedule. Take corrective action as early as possible.

Unfamiliar technologies, methods, languages, tools, or hardware   Don't underestimate the learning curve of getting up to speed with new techniques that are needed to satisfy certain requirements. Identify those high-risk requirements early on, and allow sufficient time for false starts, learning, experimentation, and prototyping.

Requirements Specification

Requirements understanding   Different interpretations of the requirements by developers and customers lead to expectation gaps, in which the delivered product fails to satisfy customer needs. Formal inspections of requirements documents by teams that include developers, testers, and customers can mitigate this risk. Trained and experienced requirements analysts will ask the right questions of customers and write high-quality specifications. Models and prototypes that represent the requirements from multiple perspectives will also reveal fuzzy, ambiguous requirements.

Time pressure to proceed despite TBDs   It is a good idea to mark areas of the SRS that need further work with TBD (to be determined), but it's risky to proceed with construction if these TBDs haven't been resolved. Record the name of the person responsible for closing each TBD and the target date for resolution.

Ambiguous terminology   Create a glossary to define business and technical terms that might be interpreted differently by different readers. In particular, define any terms that have both common and technical or domain-specific meanings. Create a data dictionary that defines the data items and structures. SRS reviews can help participants reach a common understanding of key terms and concepts.

Design included in requirements   Designs that are included in the SRS place unnecessary constraints on the options available to developers. Unnecessary constraints inhibit the creation of optimal designs. Review the requirements to make sure they emphasize what needs to be done to solve the business problem, rather than stating how it will be solved.

Requirements Validation

Unvalidated requirements   The prospect of inspecting a lengthy SRS is daunting, as is the idea of writing test cases very early in the development process. However, if you confirm the correctness and quality of the requirements before construction begins, you can avoid considerable expensive rework later in the project. Include time and resources for these quality activities in the project plan. Gain commitment from your customer representatives to participate in requirements inspections, because only customers can judge whether the stated requirements will meet their needs. Also, perform incremental, informal reviews to find problems as early and cheaply as possible.

Inspection proficiency   If inspectors do not know how to properly inspect requirements documents and how to contribute to effective inspections, they might miss serious defects. Train all team members who will participate in inspections of requirements documents. Invite an experienced inspector from your organization or an outside consultant to observe, and perhaps to moderate, your early inspections to coach the participants.

Requirements Management

Changing requirements   You can reduce scope creep by using a vision and scope document as the benchmark for approving changes. A collaborative requirements elicitation process with extensive user involvement can cut requirements creep nearly in half (Jones 1996a). Quality-control practices that detect requirements errors early reduce the number of modifications requested later on. To reduce the impact of changing requirements, defer implementation of those requirements that are most likely to change until they're pinned down, and design the system for easy modifiability.

Requirements change process   Risks related to the way changes to requirements are handled include not having a defined change process, using an ineffective change mechanism, and incorporating changes that bypass the process. It takes time to develop a culture and discipline of change management. A requirements change process that includes impact analysis of proposed changes, a change control board to make decisions, and a tool to support the defined procedure is an important starting point.

Unimplemented requirements   The requirements traceability matrix helps to avoid overlooking any requirements during design, construction, or testing.

Expanding project scope   If requirements are poorly defined initially, further definition can expand the scope of the project. Vaguely specified areas of the product will consume more effort than anticipated. The project resources that were allocated according to the initial incomplete requirements might be insufficient to implement the full scope of user needs. To mitigate this risk, plan on a phased or incremental delivery life cycle. Implement the core functionality in the initial release, and elaborate the system's capabilities in later iterations.

Risk Management Is Your Friend

A project manager can use risk management to raise the awareness of conditions that could cause the project to suffer. Consider the manager of a new project who's concerned about getting appropriate users involved in requirements elicitation. The astute manager will realize that this condition poses a risk and will document it in the risk list, estimating the probability and impact based on previous experience. If time passes and users still are not involved, the risk exposure for this item will increase, perhaps to the point where it compromises the project's success. I've been able to convince managers to postpone a project that could not engage sufficient user representatives by arguing that we shouldn't waste the company's money on a doomed project.

Periodic risk tracking keeps the project manager apprised of the threat from identified risks. Escalate risks that aren't adequately controlled to senior managers, who can either initiate corrective actions or make a conscious business decision to proceed despite the risks. Risk management helps you keep your eyes open and make informed decisions, even if you can't control every adversity your project might encounter.

Next Steps

■ Identify several requirements-related risks facing your current project. Don't identify current problems as risks, only things that haven't happened yet. Document the risk factors by using the template in Figure 23-2 (on page 405). Suggest at least one possible mitigation approach for each risk.

■ Hold a risk brainstorming session with key project stakeholders. Identify as many requirements-related risk factors as you can. Evaluate each factor for its probability of occurrence and relative impact, and multiply these together to calculate the risk exposure. Sort the risk list in descending order by risk exposure to identify your top five requirements-related risks. Assign each risk to an individual to implement mitigation actions.

Epilogue

Nothing is more important to a software project's success than understanding what problems need to be solved. Requirements provide the foundation for that success. If the development team and its customers don't agree on the product's capabilities and characteristics, the most likely outcome is one of those unpleasant software surprises that we'd all prefer to avoid. If your current requirements practices aren't giving you the results you need, selectively and thoughtfully apply the techniques presented in this book that you think might help. Key themes of effective requirements engineering include

- Engaging customer representatives early and extensively
- Developing requirements iteratively and incrementally
- Representing the requirements in various ways to make sure everyone understands them
- Assuring the requirements' completeness and correctness with all stakeholder groups
- Controlling the way that requirements changes are made

Changing the way a software development organization works is difficult. It's hard to acknowledge that your current approaches aren't working as well as you'd like and to figure out what to try next. It's hard to find the time to learn about new techniques, develop improved processes, pilot them and adjust them, and roll them out to the rest of the organization. And it can be difficult to convince the various stakeholders that change is needed. However, if you don't change the way you work, you have no reason to believe that the current project will go any better than the last project.

Success in software process improvement depends on

- Addressing clear points of pain in the organization
- Focusing on a few improvement areas at a time
- Setting clear goals and defining action plans for your improvement activities
- Addressing the human and cultural factors associated with organizational change

■   Persuading senior managers to view process improvement as a strategic investment in business success

Keep these process improvement principles in mind as you define a road map to improved requirements engineering practice and commence your journey. Stay grounded in practical approaches that are appropriate for your organization and team. If you actively apply known good practices and rely on common sense, you can significantly improve how you handle your project's requirements, with all the advantages and benefits that brings. And remember that without excellent requirements, software is like a box of chocolates: you never know what you're going to get.

Appendix A

Current Requirements Practice Self-Assessment

This appendix contains twenty questions that you can use to calibrate your current requirements engineering practices and to identify areas to reinforce. You can download a copy of this assessment and a spreadsheet to help you analyze the responses from *http://www.processimpact.com/goodies.shtml*. Select from the four possible responses for each question the one that most closely describes the way you currently deal with that requirements issue. If you want to quantify the self-assessment, give yourself zero points for each "a" response, 1 point for each "b," 3 points for each "c," and 5 points for each "d" response. The maximum possible score is 100 points. Each question refers you to the chapter that addresses the topic of the question.

Don't focus on achieving a high score, but use this self-assessment to spot opportunities to apply new practices that might benefit your organization. Some questions might not pertain to the kind of software your organization develops. Also, situations are different; not every project needs the most rigorous approaches. For example, highly innovative products with no precedent in the marketplace will have volatile requirements that evolve over time from a general product concept. Recognize, though, that informal approaches to requirements increase the likelihood of doing extensive rework. Most organizations will benefit from following the practices represented by the "c" and "d" responses.

The people you select to complete the assessment could influence the results. Watch out for respondents who, rather than describing what's really going on in the organization, might bias their responses based on politics or on what they think the "correct" answers should be.

1. How is the project's scope defined, communicated, and used? [Chapter 5]

    a. The person who conceives the product communicates telepathically or verbally with the development group.

    b. There's a project vision statement around here somewhere.

    c.   We write a vision and scope, project charter, or similar document according to a standard template. All project stakeholders have access to this document.

    d.   We evaluate all proposed product features and requirement changes to see whether they lie within the documented project scope.

2.   How are the customer communities for the product identified and characterized? [Chapter 6]

    a.   The developers guess who our customers will be.

    b.   Marketing believes that they know who the customers are.

    c.   Target customer groups and market segments are identified by management, from market research, and from our existing user base.

    d.   The project stakeholders identify distinct user classes, whose characteristics are summarized in the software requirements specification.

3.   How do you obtain user input on the requirements? [Chapter 7]

    a.   The developers already know what to build.

    b.   Marketing, product management, or the users' managers believe that they can provide the user perspective.

    c.   Focus groups of typical users are surveyed or interviewed.

    d.   Specific individuals who represent different user classes participate on the project, with agreed-upon responsibilities and authority.

4.   How well-trained and how experienced are your requirements analysts? [Chapter 4]

    a.   They are developers or former users who have little experience and no specific training in software requirements engineering.

    b.   Developers, experienced users, or project managers who have had some previous exposure to requirements engineering perform the analyst role.

    c.   The analysts have had several days of training and considerable experience in collaborating with users.

    d.   We have professional business analysts or requirements engineers who are trained and experienced in interviewing techniques, the facilitation of group sessions, and technical writing. They understand both the application domain and the software development process.

5. How are the system requirements allocated to the software portions of the product? [Chapter 17]

    a. Software is expected to overcome any shortcomings in the hardware.

    b. Software and hardware engineers discuss which subsystems should perform which functions.

    c. A system engineer or an architect analyzes the system requirements and decides which ones will be implemented in each software subsystem.

    d. Portions of the system requirements are allocated to software subsystems and traced into specific software requirements. Subsystem interfaces are explicitly defined and documented.

6. What techniques are used to understand the customer's problem? [Chapter 7]

    a. Our developers are smart; they understand the problem fine.

    b. We ask users what they want and then we build it.

    c. We talk with users about their business needs and their current systems and then we write a requirements specification.

    d. We watch users perform their tasks, model their current work processes, and learn what they need to do with the new system. This shows us how parts of their business process might be automated and gives us ideas about what software features would be most valuable.

7. What approaches are used to identify all specific software requirements? [Chapters 7 and 8]

    a. We begin with a general understanding, write some code, and modify the code until we're done.

    b. Management or marketing provides a product concept, and the developers write the requirements. Marketing tells development if they've missed anything. Sometimes marketing remembers to tell development when the product direction changes.

    c. Marketing or customer representatives tell development what features and functions the product should contain.

   d.   We hold structured requirements elicitation interviews or work-shops with representatives from the different user classes for the product. We employ use cases to understand the users' goals, and we derive functional requirements from the use cases.

8.   How are the software requirements documented? [Chapters 10 and 11]

   a.   We piece together oral history, e-mail and voice-mail messages, interview notes, and meeting notes.

   b.   We write unstructured narrative textual documents, or we draw use-case diagrams and class diagrams.

   c.   We write requirements in structured natural language at a consistent level of detail according to a standard SRS template. Sometimes we augment these requirements with graphical analysis models using standard notations.

   d.   We store our requirements in a database or a commercial requirements management tool, and we store our analysis models in a CASE tool. Several attributes are stored along with each requirement.

9.   How are nonfunctional requirements, such as software quality attributes, elicited and documented? [Chapter 12]

   a.   What are "software quality attributes"?

   b.   We do beta testing to get feedback about how the users like the product.

   c.   We document certain attributes, such as performance, usability, and security requirements.

   d.   We work with customers to identify the important quality attributes for each product, which we then document in a precise and verifiable way.

10.   How are the individual functional requirements labeled? [Chapter 10]

   a.   We write paragraphs of narrative text; specific requirements are not discretely identified.

   b.   We use bulleted and numbered lists.

   c.   We use a hierarchical numbering scheme, such as "3.1.2.4."

   d.   Every discrete requirement has a unique, meaningful label that is not disrupted when other requirements are added, moved, or deleted.

11. How are priorities for the requirements established? [Chapter 14]

    a. All of the requirements are important or we wouldn't have written them down in the first place.

    b. The customers tell us which requirements are most important to them.

    c. All requirements are labeled as high, medium, or low priority by customer consensus.

    d. To help us make priority decisions, we use an analytical process to rate the customer value, cost, and technical risk of each use case, feature, or functional requirement.

12. What techniques are used to prepare a partial solution and verify a mutual understanding of the problem? [Chapter 13]

    a. None. We just build the system.

    b. We build some simple prototypes and ask users for feedback. Sometimes we're pressured to deliver prototype code.

    c. We create prototypes for both user interface mock-ups and technical proofs-of-concept when appropriate.

    d. Our project plans include tasks to create electronic or paper throwaway prototypes to help us refine the requirements. Sometimes we build evolutionary prototypes. We use structured evaluation scripts to obtain customer feedback on our prototypes.

13. How are the requirements validated? [Chapter 15]

    a. We think our requirements are pretty good when we first write them.

    b. We pass the requirements specification around to people to get their feedback.

    c. The analyst and some stakeholders hold informal reviews.

    d. We inspect our requirements documents and models, with participants that include customers, developers, and testers. We write test cases against the requirements and use them to validate the SRS and models.

14. How are different versions of the requirements documents distinguished? [Chapter 18]

    a. The date the document is printed is generated automatically.

    b.   We use a sequence number—like 1.0, 1.1, and so on—for each document version.

    c.   We have a manual identification scheme that distinguishes draft versions from baselined versions and major revisions from minor revisions.

    d.   The requirements documents are stored under version control in a configuration management system, or requirements are stored in a requirements management tool that maintains a revision history for each requirement.

15. How are software requirements traced back to their origin? [Chapter 20]

    a.   They aren't.

    b.   We know where many of the requirements came from.

    c.   All requirements have an identified origin.

    d.   We have full two-way tracing between every software requirement and some voice-of-the-customer statement, system requirement, use case, business rule, architectural need, or other origin.

16. How are requirements used as the basis for developing project plans? [Chapter 17]

    a.   The delivery date is set before we begin gathering requirements. We can't change either the project schedule or the requirements.

    b.   We go through a rapid descoping phase to drop features just before the delivery date.

    c.   The first iteration of the project plan addresses the schedule needed to gather requirements. The rest of the project plan is developed after we have a preliminary understanding of the requirements. We can't really change the plan thereafter, however.

    d.   We base the schedules and plans on the estimated effort needed to implement the required functionality. These plans are updated as the requirements change. If we must drop features or adjust resources to meet schedule commitments, we do so as early as possible.

.**17.** How are the requirements used as a basis for design? [Chapter 17]

   a.   If we had written requirements, we would refer to them during programming.

   b.   The requirements documents describe the solution we intend to implement.

   c.   Each functional requirement is traced to a design element.

   d.   Designers inspect the SRS to make sure it can be used as the basis for design. We have full two-way traceability between individual functional requirements and design elements.

18. How are the requirements used as the basis for testing? [Chapter 17]

   a.   There's no direct relationship between testing and requirements.

   b.   The testers test what the developers said they implemented.

   c.   We write system test cases against the use cases and functional requirements.

   d.   Testers inspect the SRS to make sure the requirements are verifiable and to begin their test planning. We trace system tests to specific functional requirements. System testing progress is measured in part by requirements coverage.

19. How is a software requirements baseline defined and managed for each project? [Chapter 18]

   a.   What's a "baseline"?

   b.   The customers and managers sign off on the requirements, but development still gets a lot of changes and complaints.

   c.   We define an initial requirements baseline in an SRS, but we don't always keep it current as changes are made over time.

   d.   The requirements are stored in a database when an initial baseline is defined. The database and SRS are updated as requirements changes are approved. We maintain a change history for each requirement once it's baselined.

20. How are changes to the requirements managed? [Chapter 19]

   a.   Uncontrolled changes creep into the project whenever someone has a new idea or realizes that he or she forgot something.

b.   We discourage change by freezing the requirements after the requirements phase is complete, but informal change agreements are still made.

c.   We use a defined format for submitting change requests and a central submission point. The project manager decides which changes to incorporate.

d.   Changes are made according to our documented change-control process. We use a tool to collect, store, and communicate change requests. The impact of each change is evaluated before the change control board decides whether to approve it.

Appendix B

Requirements and Process Improvement Models

Many software development organizations have used the Capability Maturity Model for Software (SW-CMM) to guide their process improvement activities (Paulk et al. 1995). The SW-CMM was developed by the Software Engineering Institute (SEI), a part of Carnegie Mellon University. The SEI also developed a related Systems Engineering CMM (SE-CMM) for complex products containing multiple subsystems, often including both hardware and software.

In 2000, the SEI released the CMMI-SE/SW, an integrated model for improving both software and systems engineering capabilities (CMU/SEI 2000a; CMU/SMI 2000b). It has already replaced the Systems Engineering CMM and ultimately will replace the CMM for Software as well. Both the SW-CMM and the CMMI-SE/SW provide specific recommendations for developing and managing requirements. This appendix briefly describes these two process improvement frameworks and how requirements development and management fit into them.

The Capability Maturity Model for Software

The SW-CMM describes five *maturity levels* of increasing software process capability. Organizations at Level 1 typically conduct their projects in an informal and inconsistent fashion. They achieve success primarily through the heroic efforts of talented practitioners and managers. Organizations at higher maturity levels combine capable, creative, and trained people with appropriate software engineering and project management processes to consistently achieve software success.

To achieve Level 2 of the SW-CMM, an organization must demonstrate that it satisfies stated goals in six *key process areas* (KPAs) of software development and management (Table B-1). The SW-CMM describes several *key practices* that can help project teams achieve each set of goals, grouped into activities to be performed, prerequisite abilities to perform the work, indications of organizational commitment, and practices to verify and measure performance. Requirements management—highlighted in Table B-1—is one of the six Level 2 key process areas. It has two goals (Paulk et al. 1995):

■ System requirements allocated to software are controlled to establish a baseline for software engineering and management use.

■ Software plans, products, and activities are kept consistent with the system requirements allocated to software.

Table B-1   Structure of the Capability Maturity Model for Software

Maturity Level	Name	Key Process Areas
1	Initial	(none)
2	Repeatable	**Requirements Management**
		Software Project Planning
		Software Project Tracking and Oversight
		Software Subcontract Management
		Software Quality Assurance
		Software Configuration Management
3	Defined	Peer Reviews
		Intergroup Coordination
		Software Product Engineering
		Integrated Software Management
		Training Program
		Organization Process Focus
		Organization Process Definition
4	Managed	Software Quality Management
		Quantitative Process Management
5	Optimizing	Defect Prevention
		Process Change Management
		Technology Change Management

Whether or not they know or care about the SW-CMM, most software development organizations will benefit from achieving these two goals. The SW-CMM identifies several prerequisites and technical practices that enable an organization to consistently achieve these goals. However, it does not prescribe specific requirements management processes that the organization must follow.

The requirements management KPA doesn't address gathering and analyzing the project's requirements. It assumes that the software requirements have already been collected or that they were allocated from higher-level system requirements (hence the phrase "system requirements allocated to software"). This situation reflects the origin of the CMM as an aid to government organizations (principally the Department of Defense) that rely on contractors to provide complex systems containing hardware and software.

Once the requirements are in hand and documented, the software development group and any other affected groups—such as quality assurance and testing—review them. Identified problems are resolved with the customers or other sources of requirements. The project manager bases the software development plan on the approved requirements. The development group should agree to the requirements and identify any constraints, risks, contingencies, or assumptions before making commitments to customers, managers, or other stakeholders. You might be pressured to commit to requirements that are unrealistic for technical feasibility or scheduling reasons, but don't make commitments that you know you can't fulfill.

This KPA also recommends that requirements documents be managed through version-control and change-control practices. Version control ensures that the version of the requirements being used for development or planning is known at all times. Change control provides a way to incorporate requirements changes in a disciplined manner, based on good business and technical decisions to approve or reject proposed changes. As requirements are modified, added, or deleted during development, it's important to update the software development plan to be consistent with the new requirements. Plans that don't reflect the current reality cannot usefully guide your project.

Unlike requirements management, requirements development didn't warrant a KPA of its own in the SW-CMM. In my view, this is a major shortcoming of the model. Most organizations find it harder to discover and write good requirements than to manage whatever requirements they have. Requirements development is addressed through a single key practice in the Software Product Engineering KPA at Level 3 (also highlighted in Table B-1). Activity 2 of that KPA states that "The software requirements are developed, maintained, documented, and verified by systematically analyzing the allocated requirements according to the project's defined software process." This activity addresses the kinds of practices that this book has described for requirements development, including the following:

- Analyzing the requirements for feasibility and other desirable qualities

- Documenting the requirements

- Reviewing the requirements document with customer representatives

- Identifying how each requirement will be validated and verified

Requirements traceability is also addressed at Level 3 of the SW-CMM. Activity 10 of the Software Product Engineering KPA states, "Consistency is maintained across software work products, including the software plans, process descriptions, allocated requirements, software requirements, software design, code, test plans, and test procedures." Subpractices within this activity provide some specific recommendations for how an organization should handle requirements traceability.

Even if you're not using the SW-CMM to guide your software process improvements, the principles and practices outlined in the Requirements Management and Software Product Engineering KPAs make good sense. Every development organization can benefit from the thoughtful application of these approaches.

CMMI-SE/SW

The CMM Integration model combines processes for systems and software engineering. The CMMI-SE/SW comes in two forms. The *staged representation* is analogous to the structure of the SW-CMM, with five maturity levels that contain the 22 process areas shown in Table B-2 (CMU/SEI 2000a). An alternative form is the *continuous representation* (like the old SE-CMM), which groups the same 22 process areas into four categories: Process Management, Project Management, Engineering, and Support (CMU/SEI 2000b). The continuous representation does not define overall maturity levels. Instead, it defines six *capability levels* for each process area. The continuous representation lets each organization decide which level of capability is appropriate for it in each of the 22 process areas. For example, you might decide that you need to be at Level 4 (Quantitatively Managed) for requirements development and at Level 3 (Defined) for requirements management. The contents of the process areas are the same in both representations.

As with the CMM for Software, the CMMI-SE/SW has a process area at Level 2 called Requirements Management, but it also has a separate process area at Level 3 called Requirements Development. Placing requirements development at Level 3 does not imply that an organization's projects don't need to collect and document requirements until they've already achieved Level 2. Of course, every project must do this. Requirements management is viewed as a capability that helps an organization achieve more predictable and less chaotic projects, which is the essence of CMM Level 2. Once an organization has adopted the discipline of managing requirements changes and tracking status, it can focus more on developing high-quality requirements.

This is a reasonable argument, but in another sense, it doesn't matter how effectively you manage poor, erroneous, or nonexistent requirements. Software organizations that are serious about improving their effectiveness will work on those aspects of requirements development and management that are causing them the most problems, regardless of how a capability maturity model is structured.

Table B-2   Structure of the CMMI-SE/SW, Staged Representation

Maturity Level	Name	Process Areas
1	Initial	(none)
2	Managed	**Requirements Management**
		Project Planning
		Project Monitoring and Control
		Supplier Agreement Management
		Measurement and Analysis
		Process and Product Quality Assurance
		Configuration Management
3	Defined	**Requirements Development**
		Technical Solution
		Product Integration
		Verification
		Validation
		Organizational Process Focus
		Organizational Process Definition
		Organizational Training
		Integrated Project Management
		Risk Management
		Decision Analysis and Resolution
4	Quantitatively Managed	Organizational Process Performance
		Quantitative Project Management
5	Optimizing	Organizational Innovation and Deployment
		Causal Analysis and Resolution

Requirements Management Process Area

The requirements management process area in the CMMI-SE/SW is similar to the corresponding KPA in the SW-CMM. Key themes include having the development team gain an understanding of the requirements and resolve issues with the customer, gaining commitment to the requirements by project participants, and managing changes. Unlike the CMM for Software, requirements traceability is included in the Requirements Management process area. One of the five specific practices called out for requirements management is "Maintain Bi-directional Traceability of Requirements." The three aspects of traceability discussed are as follows:

- Ensuring that the source of lower-level or derived requirements is recorded

- Tracing each requirement downward into derived requirements and its allocation to functions, objects, processes, and people

- Establishing horizontal links from one requirement to another of the same type

Requirements Development Process Area

The CMMI-SE/SW describes three sets of requirements development practices:

- Practices that identify a complete set of customer requirements, which are then used to develop product requirements (elicit stakeholder needs; transform needs and constraints into customer requirements)

- Practices that define a complete set of product requirements (establish product components; allocate requirements to product components; identify interface requirements)

- Practices to derive child requirements, to understand the requirements, and to validate them (establish operational concepts and scenarios; define required system functionality; analyze derived requirements; evaluate product cost, schedule, and risk; validate requirements)

All CMMs state goals toward which a software-developing project or organization should strive in the various process areas. They also recommend technical practices that can achieve those goals. The "good practices" described in this book for software requirements engineering can help any organization achieve CMM goals in the Requirements Management and the Requirements Development process areas. Each organization needs to select appropriate practices and incorporate them into pragmatic processes that will help the organization's projects excel at requirements engineering.

The objective of process improvement isn't simply to accumulate processes to satisfy a reference model such as a CMM. The objective is to reduce the cost of building and maintaining software by integrating better ways of working into routine practice among the project team members. The members of the organization need to turn new, improved practices into habits, actions they take without having to think about them explicitly anymore. Achieving this goal requires management commitment, resources, plans, training, and monitoring to see whether new processes are being performed as intended and are yielding the desired results. To this end, both CMMs include practices to help institutionalize new processes into the way that an organization works.

Figure B-1 illustrates some connections between the Requirements Management, Requirements Development, and other process areas in the CMMI-SE/SW. This diagram clearly illustrates that requirements don't exist in a vacuum but have close relationships with a project's other processes and activities.

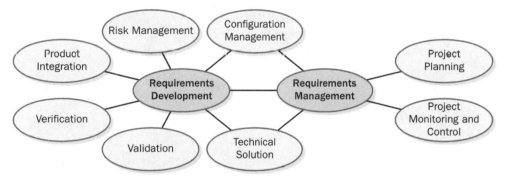

Figure B-1   Connections between Requirements Development, Requirements Management, and other process areas in the CMMI-SE/SW.

Appendix C

Requirements Troubleshooting Guide

With perseverance and the cooperation of the various stakeholders, you can successfully implement improved requirements development and management practices in your organization. You should select practices that will solve or prevent specific requirements-related problems that your projects experience. Once you've identified the most pressing issues, it's important to determine the root causes that contribute to each observed problem. Effective solutions confront the root cause, not just the superficially observed symptoms.

Table C-1, which begins on page 437 and closes this appendix, lists many symptoms of requirements engineering problems that you might encounter, grouped into several categories. The symptoms are accompanied by related possible root causes and suggestions for dealing with each problem. Of course, these aren't the only possible requirements-related problems, so extend this table with your own experiences as you encounter—and handle—symptoms that aren't listed here.

Unfortunately, there's no guarantee that a proposed solution will cure your specific symptom, especially if the underlying problems are political or cultural in nature or if the root causes lie outside the development team's sphere of control. And none of these solutions will work if you're dealing with unreasonable people.

To use this table, identify symptoms that suggest that requirements activities aren't going as well as you'd like on your project. Search the "Symptoms" column for something that resembles your observation. Next, study the "Possible Root Causes" column for that symptom to see which factors might be contributing to the problem in your environment. Then select practices and approaches from the "Possible Solutions" column that you think would effectively address those root causes, thereby—if all goes well—resolving the problem.

Root Cause Analysis

Root cause analysis seeks to identify the underlying factors that contribute to an observed problem, tracing the symptoms back to the fundamental conditions that you must address to fix the problem. Root cause analysis involves asking "why" the observed problem exists several times in succession, each time probing for the reason that underlies the answer to the previous "why" question.

Sometimes it's not clear which is the problem and which is the root cause. Certain symptoms and root causes chain together, with one symptom being the root cause of another symptom. For example, the elicitation symptom of "Necessary requirements are missed" in Table C-1 has as one possible root cause "Requirements analyst didn't ask the right questions." This root cause is itself one aspect of the process symptom "People performing analyst role don't know how to do it well."

A *cause and effect diagram*—also called a *fishbone chart* or *Ishikawa diagram*, after its inventor, Kaoru Ishikawa—is a useful way to depict the results of a root cause analysis. Figure C-1 illustrates a cause and effect diagram that partially analyzes a problem in which an organization's project teams repeatedly fail to complete projects on time. The "bones" in the diagram that branch off the main "backbone" show the answers to the question "Why don't teams finish projects on time?" Additional bones show the answers to subsequent "why" questions. Eventually this analysis reveals fundamental root causes in the most highly branched "bones."

You won't have to tackle every root cause you identify using this type of analysis. The Pareto principle states the familiar 80/20 rule, which suggests that perhaps 20 percent of the vital root causes lead to approximately 80 percent of the observed problems (Schulmeyer and McManus 1996). Even a simple root cause analysis will likely reveal the high-leverage causes that your requirements improvement actions should target.

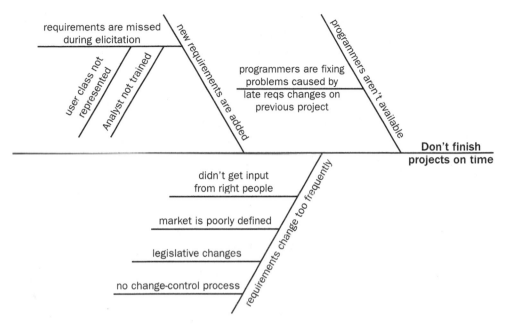

Figure C-1   A cause and effect diagram identifies root causes for identified problem symptoms.

Common Symptoms of Requirements Problems

Problems are conditions that lead to some negative impact on your project. Begin the root cause analysis with a symptom of some undesired outcome that you've experienced, and build a cause and effect diagram to understand the fundamental issues and to consider how to address them. Some of the common symptoms that arise from requirements problems are the following:

- Schedule and cost overruns

- A product that doesn't satisfy user needs or doesn't meet user expectations

- A product that requires corrections and patches immediately following release

- Team member frustration, loss of morale, demotivation, and staff turnover
- Extensive rework
- Duplication of effort
- Missed market window or delayed business benefit
- Loss of market share or revenue
- Product returns or market rejection of the product
- Reduced feature set delivered
- Software that isn't testable

Common Barriers to Implementing Solutions

Any attempt to change the way that people work or the way an organization operates encounters resistance. As you identify corrective actions that could address the root causes for your requirements problems, also think about the obstacles that might make it difficult to implement those actions and possible ways to get around those obstacles. Some common barriers to implementing requirements changes include these:

- Lack of time (everyone is already too busy); market pressure to deliver quickly
- Lack of management commitment to a requirements engineering process and to making the necessary investment
- General resistance to change
- Skepticism about the value of the requirements engineering process
- Reluctance to follow a new or more structured process
- Friction between stakeholders
- Politics and entrenched corporate culture
- Inadequately trained and skilled people
- Unclear project roles and responsibilities

- Lack of ownership and accountability for requirements activities
- Unavailability of qualified product champions
- Lack of recognition or acknowledgment of the problems that current requirements practices cause

Notice that these are people- and communication-oriented issues, not technical impediments. There are no easy ways to overcome most of these barriers, but the first step is to recognize the barriers.

Table C-1   Requirements Troubleshooting Guide

Process Issues

Symptoms	Possible Root Causes	Possible Solutions
■ Requirements processes and document templates are inconsistent across projects. ■ Requirements processes being used aren't effective.	■ Lack of common understanding of the requirements process. ■ Lack of management commitment to effective requirements processes. ■ No mechanism for sharing templates and process documents. ■ Lack of good examples of templates and requirements documents.	■ Document the current requirements process and create a proposed description of the desired process. ■ Train all team members in requirements engineering. ■ Adopt one or more standard templates for vision and scope document, use cases, and SRS. Provide guidance to help projects tailor the templates as appropriate. ■ Collect and share good examples of requirements documents. ■ Use defect correction metrics to let the team understand the costs of poor requirements. ■ Use project retrospectives to capture examples of current problems and their impact.

Table C-1   Requirements Troubleshooting Guide   *(continued)*

■ People performing analyst role don't know how to do it well.	■ Lack of education about requirements engineering and the requirements analyst role. ■ Management expecting that any developer can automatically be a good analyst.	■ Train prospective analysts in both requirements engineering and associated soft skills. ■ Write a job description and a skills list for your requirements analysts. ■ Set up a mentoring program for new analysts.
■ Requirements management tools are underutilized.	■ Lack of understanding of tool capabilities. ■ Processes and culture haven't been modified to take full advantage of tools. ■ No one's responsible for leading the use of the tool.	■ Send some analysts to a tool vendor training class. ■ Establish a tool advocate to administer the tool and mentor other tool users. ■ Identify and change the process and culture issues that impede fully exploiting the tool.

Product Issues

Symptoms	**Possible Root Causes**	**Possible Solutions**
■ Dissatisfied customers. ■ Customers reject the product when they see it. ■ Poor product reviews. ■ Low sales, loss of market share.	■ Inadequate user involvement in requirements development. ■ Unrealistic customer expectations. ■ Developers built what they thought customers wanted. ■ Customer is not aware of the capabilities and limitations of developers and technology. ■ Mismatch between customer's and developer's perception of requirements. ■ Insufficient market research.	■ Convene focus groups. ■ Define user classes. ■ Identify product champions. ■ Align customer expectations with business objectives. ■ Build prototypes and have users evaluate them. ■ Use collaborative requirements elicitation workshops. ■ Have customer representatives participate in requirements document inspections.

Table C-1 **Requirements Troubleshooting Guide** *(continued)*

Planning Issues

Symptoms	Possible Root Causes	Possible Solutions
■ Requirements are incomplete. ■ Requirements are insufficiently detailed. ■ Construction begins before the requirements for that increment are sufficiently understood.	■ Inadequate user involvement in requirements development. ■ Insufficient time spent on requirements development. ■ Release date set before requirements are defined, perhaps because of legislative or market pressures. ■ Key marketing or business stakeholders not engaged in requirements process. ■ Analysts are not sufficiently skilled and experienced. ■ Misconception that it's more productive to begin coding than to understand requirements. ■ Management or customers don't understand the need for requirements. ■ Analysts and developers don't agree on what constitutes adequate requirements.	■ Don't commit to a delivery schedule before requirements are sufficiently understood. ■ Involve technical staff early in the project to begin understanding requirements. ■ Define product vision and project scope carefully. ■ Educate stakeholders about the risks of hasty construction. ■ Build a collaborative relationship between analysts, developers, and business partners to set realistic goals. ■ Enhance the team's requirements analyst capability. ■ Use defect correction metrics to educate the team about the costs of poor requirements. ■ Use incremental development approaches to begin delivering customer value quickly. ■ Have developers assess requirements quality before they begin implementing them.

Table C-1   Requirements Troubleshooting Guide   *(continued)*

■ Major change in time constraint after project started but no scope reduction.	■ Stakeholders don't understand the impact of reduced time on achievable project scope.	■ Build a collaborative relationship between development and business partners to set realistic goals. ■ Negotiate trade-offs when project constraints change.
■ Gaps in requirements work being done. ■ Multiple people perform the same requirements activities.	■ Unclear definition of roles and responsibilities for requirements engineering activities. ■ No one is assigned responsibility for managing requirements.	■ Define roles and assign responsibilities for requirements development and management on each project. ■ Commit the necessary people needed for effective requirements development and management. ■ Build requirements activities into project plans and schedules.
■ More requirements are planned than can be implemented with available time and resources.	■ Schedule is set before requirements are defined. ■ Poorly defined project scope. ■ Uncontrolled scope growth. ■ Learning curve from use of unfamiliar technologies or tools isn't taken into account. ■ Insufficient staff allocated to project. ■ Unprioritized requirements. ■ Risk factors turn into problems. ■ Project is committed to before scope is accurately assessed. ■ Enthusiasm about exciting new technologies or challenges overrides realistic capability assessments.	■ Document product vision and project scope, aligned with business objectives, before making commitments. ■ Derive development schedule from requirements, perhaps through an initial requirements exploration phase. ■ Incorporate training time and learning curve time in schedule. ■ Separate technology exploration and product research from product development. ■ Prioritize requirements. ■ Practice proactive risk management. ■ Timebox development or deliver product features incrementally. ■ Adjust scope dynamically as project realities dictate.

Table C-1   Requirements Troubleshooting Guide   *(continued)*

■ Undocumented or poorly defined scope.	■ Lack of proper management sponsorship for project. ■ Haste to begin construction. ■ Lack of understanding of the importance of a scope statement. ■ Lack of agreement on scope among stakeholders. ■ Volatile market or rapidly changing business needs.	■ Educate managers about scope and sponsorship. ■ Write a vision and scope document and obtain buy-in from key stakeholders. ■ Don't begin a project with a poorly defined scope. ■ Cancel the project if sponsorship and scope definition are not achieved.

Communication Issues

Symptoms	**Possible Root Causes**	**Possible Solutions**
■ Duplication of effort as multiple people implement the same requirement.	■ Responsibilities for implementing requirements are not explicitly assigned. ■ Inadequate communication among subgroups working on parts of the project. ■ Geographical separation between development teams or between developers and customers.	■ Define clear roles and responsibilities for software implementation. ■ Provide visible status tracking of individual requirements.
■ Revisiting decisions made previously.	■ Lack of clear recognition and empowerment of appropriate decision makers.	■ Decide who the project's requirements decision makers are and define their decision-making process. ■ Identify product champions. ■ Document histories of why requirements were rejected, deferred, or canceled.
■ Project participants don't share the same vocabulary.	■ Assuming that everyone has the same and the correct interpretation of key terms.	■ Define terms in a glossary. ■ Define data items in a data dictionary. ■ Train development team in the business domain. ■ Train user representatives in requirements engineering.

Table C-1 **Requirements Troubleshooting Guide** *(continued)*

Elicitation Issues

Symptoms	Possible Root Causes	Possible Solutions
■ Insufficient customer involvement. ■ Developers make a lot of guesses about what to implement.	■ Customer representatives don't have enough time to participate in requirements development. ■ Customers don't understand the need for them to participate. ■ Customers don't know what analysts need from them. ■ Customers aren't committed to the project. ■ Customers think that developers should already know what the customers need. ■ Analysts don't know who the right customers are. ■ Analysts don't have access to actual customers. ■ Analysts don't know how to collaborate with customers. ■ Resistance to following a requirements development process.	■ Educate customers and managers on requirements and the need for their participation. ■ Describe the risks from insufficient user involvement to customers and managers. ■ Build a collaborative relationship between development and business partners. ■ Define user classes or market segments. ■ Identify product champions (users or suitable surrogates). ■ Develop skilled requirements analysts. ■ Obtain development and customer management commitment to an effective requirements process.
■ Wrong user representatives are involved.	■ Managers, marketing, or other surrogates try to speak for end users. ■ Managers don't make actual users available to analysts.	■ Define user classes. ■ Identify product champions. ■ Get input from other stakeholders besides direct users.
■ Users are uncertain about their needs.	■ Users don't understand or can't describe their business process well. ■ System is being built to support a new, incompletely defined business process. ■ Users aren't committed to the project, perhaps are threatened by it. ■ New system is being expected to drive development of the new business process.	■ Clarify the intended outcomes of a successful project for the stakeholders affected by it. ■ Model the user's business process. Identify product champions. ■ Develop use cases. ■ Build prototypes and have users evaluate them. ■ Use incremental development to clarify requirements a bit at a time.

Table C-1   Requirements Troubleshooting Guide   *(continued)*

■ Development doesn't know who the users are.	■ Ill-defined product vision. ■ Poorly understood market-place needs.	■ Create a product vision document. ■ Do market research. ■ Identify users of current or competing products. ■ Establish focus groups.
■ Too many people are involved in requirements elicitation.	■ Everyone wants to be represented for political reasons. ■ User classes aren't clearly defined. ■ Lack of delegation to specific user representatives. ■ There really are a lot of different user classes.	■ Define user classes. ■ Identify product champions. ■ Identify requirements decision makers. ■ Distinguish political priorities from business priorities and technical priorities. ■ Focus the project on the needs of the favored user classes.
■ Solutions are presented as needs and requirements have to be deduced from the presented solutions. ■ Implemented "requirements" don't meet user needs. ■ Requirements are overconstrained.	■ Customer requests solutions with which they are already familiar. ■ Requirements contain design constraints. ■ New software must conform to existing application standards and user interface. ■ Customers don't know what information constitutes "the requirements". ■ Requirements discussions focus on user interface design.	■ Ask "why" several times to understand the real user needs behind the presented requirements and to understand the rationale behind design constraints. ■ Develop use cases at the essential level before addressing user interface specifics. ■ Develop skilled analysts who can ask the right questions. ■ Educate customers about requirements engineering.

Table C-1   Requirements Troubleshooting Guide *(continued)*

■ Necessary requirements are missed.	■ Users don't know what they need. ■ Requirements analyst didn't ask the right questions. ■ Insufficient time was provided for elicitation. ■ Some user classes aren't represented. ■ Appropriate, knowledgeable user representatives did not participate in elicitation. ■ Analysts, developers, and customers make incorrect assumptions or fail to see inconsistencies in their requirements documentation. ■ Insufficient communication between development and customers.	■ Define user classes. ■ Identify product champions. ■ Develop skilled analysts who can ask the right questions. ■ Develop use cases. ■ Represent requirements in multiple ways (such as analysis models). ■ Inspect requirements documents. Use multiple, incremental reviews. ■ Educate customers about requirements engineering. ■ Analyze requirements using a CRUD matrix. ■ Build prototypes and have users evaluate them. ■ Build the product incrementally so that overlooked requirements can be incorporated in an upcoming release.
■ Requirements specified are incorrect or inappropriate. ■ Requirements are imposed by upper management or by an outside authority.	■ The wrong user representatives or inappropriate surrogates are involved. ■ User representatives speak for themselves, not for the communities they represent. ■ Analysts talk too much to managers and not enough to users. ■ Managers do not provide access to user representatives. ■ Lack of accountability or commitment on the part of the outside authority.	■ Determine what was wrong with the flawed requirements and why they were specified. ■ Define user classes. ■ Identify appropriate product champions, educate them, and empower them. ■ Have a multifunctional team inspect requirements documents. ■ Communicate the risks of inaccurate requirements to high-authority stakeholders.

Table C-1   **Requirements Troubleshooting Guide**   *(continued)*

Analysis Issues

Symptoms	Possible Root Causes	Possible Solutions
■ Unnecessary requirements are specified (gold plating). ■ Unexpected functionality becomes apparent during testing. ■ Functionality is specified and built, but not used.	■ Lack of controls on approving requirements. ■ Developers incorporate functionality without consulting with users. ■ Users request complex solutions instead of expressing business needs. ■ Elicitation focuses on system functions instead of user goals. ■ Developers and customers interpret requirements differently.	■ Record the origin and rationale for each requirement. ■ Employ use cases to focus on the users' business objectives instead of system functionality. Derive functional requirements from the use cases. ■ Prioritize requirements to deliver high-value functionality early. ■ Have a multifunctional team inspect requirements documentation.
■ Requirements aren't clear enough to write test cases.	■ Requirements are ambiguous, incomplete, or lack sufficient detail.	■ Have testers or quality assurance engineers inspect requirements for testability.
■ Requirements are not prioritized. All requirements seem to be equally important. ■ All requirements have top priority. ■ Analysts can't make informed trade-off decisions when new requirements come along. ■ Only customers provide input regarding priorities.	■ Fear that low-priority requirements will never be implemented. ■ Insufficient knowledge about the business and its needs. ■ Information on the value and cost of each requirement is not known, communicated, or discussed. ■ The product isn't usable unless a large, critical set of functionality is implemented. ■ Unreasonable customer or developer expectations.	■ Develop a collaborative process for prioritizing requirements. ■ Prioritize requirements early. Develop detailed specifications of high-priority requirements. ■ Use incremental development or staged releases to deliver maximum value as early as possible. ■ Recognize that priorities might shift radically as early releases get used.

Table C-1   Requirements Troubleshooting Guide *(continued)*

■ Changing requirements priorities.	■ Decision makers are not identified or empowered. ■ "Micro" goals conflict with "macro" goals. ■ Internal politics. ■ Unclear business objectives, or lack of agreement on business objectives. ■ External forces, such as regulatory or legislative issues. ■ Requirements and their priorities are not approved and baselined by appropriate people.	■ Document the project scope, objectives, and priorities. ■ Identify requirements decision makers. ■ Provide a clear assessment of the costs of accepting changes. ■ Track the impact of changes in terms of cost dollars, revenue dollars, and schedule slippage. ■ Keep requirements aligned with business objectives.
■ Conflicts about requirements priorities among stakeholders.	■ Different user classes have diverse needs. ■ Lack of discipline to adhere to the original vision. ■ Unclear business objectives, or lack of agreement on business objectives. ■ It's not clear who the requirements decision makers are.	■ Perform more market research. ■ Identify favored user classes or market segments. ■ Use product champions to represent different user classes. ■ Base priorities on vision, scope, and business objectives. ■ Identify requirements decision makers.
■ Rapid descoping late in the project.	■ Unrealistic optimism about developer productivity. ■ Insufficient early and periodic prioritization. ■ Not relying on priorities to define implementation sequence and to make controlled scope changes.	■ Define priorities early in the project. Use priorities to guide decisions about what to work on now and what to defer. ■ Reprioritize when new requirements are incorporated. ■ Make decisions to defer functionality periodically, not just late in the project.

Table C-1   Requirements Troubleshooting Guide   *(continued)*

■ Developers find requirements vague and ambiguous.	■ Analysts and customers don't understand the level of requirements detail that developers need.	■ Train analysts in writing good requirements. Avoid using subjective, ambiguous words in requirements specifications.
■ Developers have to track down missing information.	■ Customers don't know what they need or can't articulate it clearly.	■ Have developers review requirements early for clarity and appropriate detail.
■ Developers misinterpret requirements and have to redo their implementations.	■ Insufficient time is spent on requirements elicitation.	■ Model requirements to find missing requirements and missing information.
	■ Business rules aren't identified, communicated, or understood.	■ Build prototypes and have users evaluate them.
	■ Requirements contain many vague and ambiguous words.	■ Refine requirements in progressive levels of detail.
	■ Stakeholders interpret terms, concepts, and data definitions differently.	■ Document business rules.
		■ Define terms in a glossary.
	■ Customers assume that developers already know enough about the business domain and their needs.	■ Define data items in a data dictionary.
		■ Facilitate effective communication among all project participants.
	■ Analysts are afraid to appear ignorant of the business domain, so they don't ask user representatives for help.	■ Leverage the business domain knowledge held by user representatives.
■ Some requirements aren't technically feasible.	■ Requirements are not analyzed properly.	■ Perform feasibility analysis or vertical prototyping.
	■ Customers don't accept feasibility analysis results.	■ Conduct a separate research or exploratory mini-project to assess feasibility.
	■ Insufficient time is provided to evaluate feasibility.	
	■ Lack of understanding of new tools and technologies and their limitations.	

Table C-1   Requirements Troubleshooting Guide   *(continued)*

■ Requirements from different sources or user classes conflict. ■ Difficulty in reaching agreement on requirements among stakeholders.	■ Lack of unified product vision communicated from management to all stakeholders. ■ Requirements decision makers are not identified. ■ Departmental processes are not understood in the same way. ■ Politics drive requirements input. ■ Diverse user groups or market segments have differing needs, expectations, and business objectives. ■ Product isn't sufficiently focused on a specific target market. ■ Some user groups may already have a useful system in place that they're attached to, despite its shortcomings.	■ Develop, approve, and communicate a unified product vision and project scope. ■ Understand target market segments and user classes. ■ Identify favored user classes to resolve conflicts. ■ Identify product champions to resolve conflicts within each user class. ■ Identify requirements decision makers. ■ Focus on shared business interests instead of defending emotional and political positions.
■ Requirements contain TBDs and information gaps.	■ No one is assigned to resolve TBDs before requirements are delivered to the developers. ■ No time is available to resolve TBDs before beginning implementation.	■ Inspect requirements to identify information gaps. ■ Assign responsibility for resolving each TBD to an individual. ■ Track each TBD to closure.

Table C-1 Requirements Troubleshooting Guide *(continued)*

Specification Issues

Symptoms	Possible Root Causes	Possible Solutions
■ Requirements are not documented. ■ Developers provide the requirements to customers or marketing. ■ Customers provide requirements to developers verbally or through informal channels. ■ Developers do a lot of exploratory programming as they try to figure out what customers want.	■ No one is sure what to build. ■ Insufficient time is provided to elicit and document requirements. ■ The perception that writing requirements slows the project down. ■ Individuals responsible for documentation aren't clearly identified and committed. ■ People performing the analyst function don't know what to do. ■ No defined requirements development process or templates. ■ Development management doesn't understand, value, and expect requirements development. ■ Overconfident developers think they know what customers need.	■ Define and follow a requirements development process. ■ Establish team role definitions with management and obtain commitment from individuals. ■ Train requirements analysts. ■ Train other team members and customers in the requirements process. ■ Build requirements development effort, resources, and tasks into project plans and schedules.
■ Customers or developers assume that functionality present in the existing system will be duplicated in the new system.	■ Requirements for a new system are specified as differences from a poorly documented existing system.	■ Reverse engineer the existing system to understand its full capabilities. ■ Write a requirements specification that includes all the desired functionality for the new system.

Table C-1 **Requirements Troubleshooting Guide** *(continued)*

■ Requirements documentation doesn't accurately describe the system.	■ Changes are not incorporated in requirements documentation.	■ Follow a change-control process that includes updating requirements documentation when changes are accepted.
		■ Pass all change requests through the change control board.
		■ Meet with key stakeholders to review the modified requirements specifications.
■ Different, conflicting versions of the requirements documents exist.	■ Poor version control practices.	■ Define and follow good version control practices for requirements documents.
	■ Multiple "master" copies of requirements documents.	■ Store requirements in a requirements management tool. Generate requirements documents as reports from the tool's database contents.
		■ Assign a requirements manager to be responsible for making changes to specifications.

Validation Issues

Symptoms	Possible Root Causes	Possible Solutions
■ Product doesn't achieve business objectives or meet user expectations.	■ Customers didn't accurately present their needs.	■ Perform market research to understand market segments and their needs.
■ Customers have unstated, assumed, or implicit requirements that weren't satisfied.	■ Requirements analyst didn't ask the right questions.	■ Engage product champions representing each major user class throughout the duration of the project.
	■ Inadequate customer participation in requirements development.	■ Train analysts in how to ask the right questions.
	■ Wrong customer representatives involved, such as managers, developers, or other surrogates who don't represent the real users' real needs.	■ Develop use cases to make sure business tasks are understood.
	■ Novel, innovative product with uncertain requirements, and marketing or product management didn't assess market needs accurately.	■ Have customers participate in requirements document inspections, starting early in the requirements process.
	■ Project participants made inaccurate assumptions.	■ Build prototypes and have users evaluate them.
		■ Have users write acceptance tests and acceptance criteria.

Table C-1   **Requirements Troubleshooting Guide**   *(continued)*

▪ Quality attributes and performance goals are not specified. ▪ Product does not achieve performance goals or satisfy other quality expectations that users have.	▪ Performance goals and quality attributes were not discussed during elicitation. ▪ Stakeholders lack understanding of nonfunctional requirements and their importance. ▪ SRS template being used doesn't have sections for nonfunctional requirements. ▪ Users don't express their assumptions about the system's performance and quality characteristics. ▪ Performance goals and quality attributes weren't specified precisely enough to give all stakeholders the same understanding.	▪ Educate analysts and customers about nonfunctional requirements and how to specify them. ▪ Have analysts discuss nonfunctional requirements during elicitation. ▪ Use an SRS template that includes sections for nonfunctional requirements. ▪ Use Planguage to specify performance goals and quality attributes precisely.

Requirements Management Issues

Symptoms	Possible Root Causes	Possible Solutions
▪ Some planned requirements were not implemented.	▪ Developer didn't follow the SRS. ▪ SRS was not communicated to all developers. ▪ SRS was not kept current as changes were accepted. ▪ Changes were not communicated to all those affected. ▪ Requirements were accidentally overlooked during implementation. ▪ Responsibilities for implementing requirements are not explicitly assigned.	▪ Keep SRS current and make it available to whole team. ▪ Make sure change-control process includes communication to stakeholders. ▪ Store requirements in a requirements management tool. ▪ Track the status of individual requirements. ▪ Build and use a requirements traceability matrix. ▪ Define clear roles and responsibilities for software implementation.

Table C-1   Requirements Troubleshooting Guide   *(continued)*

Change Management Issues

Symptoms	Possible Root Causes	Possible Solutions
■ Requirements change frequently. ■ Many requirements changes are made late in the development process.	■ Customers don't understand what they need. ■ Changing business processes or market demands. ■ Not all the right people were involved in providing and approving the requirements. ■ Requirements weren't sufficiently well defined initially. ■ Requirements baseline wasn't defined or agreed to. ■ Technology changes. ■ External factors, such as the government, dictate changes. ■ Requirements contained many solution ideas, which did not satisfy the real needs. ■ Market needs weren't well understood. ■ Political issues drive changes.	■ Improve requirements elicitation practices. ■ Implement and follow a change-control process. ■ Establish a change control board to make decisions on proposed changes. ■ Perform change impact analysis before accepting changes. ■ Have stakeholders inspect requirements before baselining them. ■ Design software for maximum modifiability to accommodate change. ■ Include contingency buffers in the project schedule to accommodate some change. ■ Use incremental development approaches to respond quickly to changing requirements. ■ Become aware of local political issues and try to anticipate their impact on requirements.

Table C-1   Requirements Troubleshooting Guide   *(continued)*

■ New requirements frequently are added.	■ Requirements elicitation was incomplete. ■ Application domain is not well understood. ■ Stakeholders don't understand or respect project scope. ■ Project scope is growing in an uncontrolled way. ■ Management, marketing, or customers demand new features without considering their impact on the project. ■ Insufficient customer participation in requirements development.	■ Improve requirements elicitation practices. ■ Define and communicate scope. ■ Have the right people make explicit business decisions to change scope. ■ Perform root cause analysis to see where new requirements come from and why. ■ Perform change impact analysis before accepting new requirements and communicate the results broadly. ■ Include management in requirements elicitation activities. ■ Ensure that all user classes have provided input. ■ Include contingency buffers in the project schedule to accommodate some growth. ■ Use incremental development approaches to respond quickly to new requirements.
■ Requirements move in and out of scope.	■ Vision and scope are not clearly defined. ■ Business objectives are not clearly understood. ■ Scope is volatile, perhaps in response to changing market demands. ■ Requirements priorities are ill-defined. ■ Change control board members don't agree on project scope.	■ Clearly define the business objectives, vision, and scope. ■ Use the scope statement to decide whether proposed requirements are in or out of scope. ■ Record the rationale for rejecting a proposed requirement. ■ Align change control board members on project scope. ■ Ensure that the change control board has the appropriate members and authority. ■ Use incremental development to adapt flexibly to a changing scope boundary.

Table C-1   Requirements Troubleshooting Guide *(continued)*

■ Scope definition changes after development is underway.	■ Poorly defined, poorly understood, or changing business objectives. ■ Market segments and market needs aren't well understood. ■ Competing products become available. ■ Key stakeholders did not review and approve requirements.	■ Define business objectives and align vision and scope with them. ■ Identify decision-making stakeholders at business requirements level. ■ Have decision makers inspect vision and scope document. ■ Follow a change-control process to incorporate changes. ■ Include contingency buffers in project schedule to accommodate some scope growth. ■ Renegotiate schedules and resources when project direction changes.
■ Requirements changes aren't communicated to all affected stakeholders.	■ Requirements documents aren't updated when requirements change. ■ Customers request changes directly from developers. ■ Not everyone has easy access to the requirements documentation. ■ Informal, verbal communication pathways exclude some project participants. ■ It's not clear who all needs to be informed of changes. ■ No established change-control process. ■ Lack of understanding of interrelationships between requirements.	■ Have a defined owner for each requirement. ■ Define traceability links between requirements and other artifacts. ■ Include all affected areas in requirements communications. ■ Establish a change-control process that includes the communication mechanisms. ■ Use a requirements management tool to make current requirements available to stakeholders via the Web.

Table C-1   Requirements Troubleshooting Guide   *(continued)*

■ Proposed requirements changes are lost. ■ Status of change requests isn't known.	■ Ineffective change-control process. ■ Change-control process isn't followed.	■ Adopt a practical, effective change-control process and educate stakeholders about it. ■ Assign responsibilities for performing the change-control process steps. ■ Ensure that the change-control process is followed. ■ Use requirements management tools to track changes and track each requirement's status.
■ Stakeholders bypass the change-control process. ■ Customers request changes directly with developers.	■ Change-control process isn't practical and effective. ■ Change control board is ineffective. ■ Some stakeholders don't understand or accept the change-control process. ■ Management doesn't require that the change-control process be followed.	■ Ensure that the change-control process is practical, effective, efficient, understood, and accessible to all stakeholders. ■ Establish an appropriate change control board. ■ Enlist management to support and champion the change-control process. ■ Enforce a policy that requirements changes are made only through the change-control process.
■ Requirements changes take much more effort than planned. ■ Changes affect more system components than expected. ■ Changes compromise other requirements. ■ Changes hurt quality because of side effects.	■ Insufficient impact analysis of proposed requirements changes. ■ Hasty decisions are made to approve changes. ■ The wrong people make decisions to accept changes. ■ Team members are afraid to be honest about the impact of proposed changes.	■ Adopt a change impact analysis procedure and checklists. ■ Incorporate impact analysis into the change-control process. ■ Communicate changes to all affected stakeholders. ■ Use traceability information to evaluate the impact of proposed changes. ■ Renegotiate project commitments as needed and make necessary trade-offs when changes are proposed.

Appendix D

Sample Requirements Documents

This appendix illustrates some of the requirements documents and diagrams described in this book, using a small, hypothetical project called the Cafeteria Ordering System (COS). The artifacts included here are the following:

- A vision and scope document
- A list of use cases and several use-case descriptions
- A portion of a software requirements specification
- Some analysis models
- A partial data dictionary
- Several business rules

Because this is just an example, these requirements elements aren't intended to be complete. My objective here is to provide an idea of how the various types of requirements information relate to each other and to illustrate how you might write the contents of each document section. On a small project, it often makes sense to combine different requirements information into a single document, so you might not have a separate vision and scope document, use-case document, and SRS. The information in these documents could be organized in many other reasonable ways. Clarity, completeness, and usability of the requirements documents are the essential objectives.

The documents generally conform to the templates described in previous chapters, but because this is a small project, the templates have been simplified somewhat. In some cases, several sections have been combined to avoid duplicating information. Every project should consider how to adapt the organization's standard templates to best suit the size and nature of the project.

Vision and Scope Document

1. Business Requirements

1.1 Background, Business Opportunity, and Customer Needs

A majority of Process Impact employees presently spend an average of 60 minutes per day going to the cafeteria to select, purchase, and eat lunch. About 20 minutes of this time is spent walking to and from the cafeteria, selecting their meals, and paying for their meals by cash or credit card. When employees go out for lunch, they spend an average of 90 minutes off-site. Some employees phone the cafeteria in advance to order a meal to be ready for them to pick up. Employees don't always get the selections they want because the cafeteria runs out of certain items. The cafeteria wastes a significant quantity of food that is not purchased and must be thrown away. These same issues apply to breakfast and supper, although far fewer employees use the cafeteria for those meals than for lunch.

Many employees have requested a system that would permit a cafeteria user to order meals on-line, to be delivered to a designated company location at a specified time and date. Such a system would save those employees who use the service considerable time and it would increase the chance of them getting the food items they prefer. This would improve both their quality of work life and their productivity. Knowing what food items customers want in advance would reduce wastage in the cafeteria and would improve the efficiency of cafeteria staff. The future ability for employees to order meals for delivery from local restaurants would make a wider range of choices available to employees and provide the possibility of cost savings through volume purchase agreements with the restaurants. It might also permit Process Impact to have the cafeteria handle only individual lunches, relying on restaurants to fill orders for breakfasts, dinners, special events, and weekend meals.

1.2 Business Objectives and Success Criteria

BO-1: Reduce cafeteria food wastage by 50% within 6 months following initial release.[1]

Scale: Value of food thrown away each week by cafeteria staff

Meter: Examination of Cafeteria Inventory System logs

Past [2002, initial study]: 30%

Plan: Less than 15%

Must: Less than 20%

BO-2: Reduce cafeteria operating costs by 15% within 12 months following initial release.

---

1. This example shows the use of Planguage as a way to precisely state a business objective or other requirement.

BO-3: Increase average effective work time by 20 minutes per employee per day within 3 months following initial release.

SC-1: Have 75% of those employees who presently use the cafeteria use the Cafeteria Ordering System within 6 months following initial release.

SC-2: Achieve an increase in the average rating on the quarterly cafeteria satisfaction survey of 0.5 within 3 months following initial release and 1.0 within 12 months following initial release.

1.3 Business Risks

RI-1: The Cafeteria Employees Union might require that their contract be renegotiated to reflect the new employee roles and cafeteria hours of operation. (Probability = 0.6; Impact = 3)

RI-2: Too few employees might use the system, reducing the return on investment from the system development and the changes in cafeteria operating procedures. (Probability = 0.3; Impact = 9)

RI-3: Local restaurants might not agree to offer price reductions to justify employees using the system, which would reduce employee satisfaction with the system and possibly their usage of it. (Probability = 0.4; Impact = 3)

2. Vision of the Solution

2.1 Vision Statement

For employees who wish to order meals from the company cafeteria or from local restaurants on-line, the Cafeteria Ordering System is an Internet-based application that will accept individual or group meal orders, process payments, and trigger delivery of the prepared meals to a designated location on the Process Impact campus. Unlike the current telephone and manual ordering processes, employees who use the Cafeteria Ordering System will not have to go to the cafeteria to get their meals, which will save them time and will increase the food choices available to them.

2.2 Major Features

FE-1: Order meals from the cafeteria menu to be picked up or delivered

FE-2: Order meals from local restaurants to be delivered

FE-3: Create, view, modify, and delete meal service subscriptions

FE-4: Register for meal payment options

FE-5: Request meal delivery

FE-6: Create, view, modify, and delete cafeteria menus

FE-7: Order custom meals that aren't on the cafeteria menu

FE-8: Produce recipes and ingredient lists for custom meals from cafeteria

FE-9: Provide system access through corporate intranet or through outside Internet access by authorized employees

2.3 Assumptions and Dependencies

AS-1: Intranet-enabled computers and printers will be available in the cafeteria to permit cafeteria employees to process the expected volume of orders without missing any delivery time windows.

AS-2: Cafeteria staff and vehicles will be available to deliver all orders within 15 minutes of the requested delivery time.

DE-1: If a restaurant has its own on-line ordering system, the Cafeteria Ordering System must be able to communicate with it bidirectionally.

3. Scope and Limitations

3.1 Scope of Initial and Subsequent Releases

Feature	Release 1	Release 2	Release 3
FE-1	Standard meals from lunch menu only; delivery orders can be paid for only by payroll deduction	Accept orders for breakfasts and dinners, in addition to lunches; accept credit and debit card payments	
FE-2	Not implemented	Not implemented	Fully implemented
FE-3	Implemented if time permits (medium priority)	Fully implemented	
FE-4	Register for payroll deduction payments only	Register for credit card and debit card payments	
FE-5	Meals will be delivered only to company campus sites	Add delivery from cafeteria to selected off-site locations	
FE-6	Fully implemented		
FE-7	Not implemented	Not implemented	Fully implemented
FE-8	Not implemented	Fully implemented	
FE-9	Fully implemented		

3.2 Limitations and Exclusions

LI-1: Some food items that are available from the cafeteria will not be suitable for delivery, so the menus available to patrons of the Cafeteria Ordering System will be a subset of the full cafeteria menus.

LI-2:   The Cafeteria Ordering System shall be used only for the cafeteria at the main Process Impact campus in Clackamas, Oregon.

4. Business Context

4.1 Stakeholder Profiles

Stakeholder	Major Value	Attitudes	Major Interests	Constraints
Corporate Management	improved employee productivity; cost savings for cafeteria	strong commitment through release 2; support for release 3 contingent on earlier results	cost savings must exceed development and usage costs	none identified
Cafeteria Staff	more efficient use of staff time throughout the day; higher customer satisfaction	concern about union relationships and possible downsizing; otherwise receptive	job preservation	training for staff in Internet usage needed; delivery staff and vehicles needed
Patrons	better food selection; time savings; convenience	strong enthusiasm, but might not use it as much as expected because of social value of eating lunches in cafeteria and restaurants	simplicity of use; reliability of delivery; availability of food choices	access to corporate intranet is needed
Payroll Department	no benefit; needs to set up payroll deduction registration scheme	not happy about the software work needed, but recognizes the value to the company and employees	minimal changes in current payroll applications	no resources yet committed to make software changes
Restaurant Managers	increased sales; marketing exposure to generate new customers	receptive but cautious	minimal new technology needed; concern about resources and costs of delivering meals	might not have staff and capacity to handle order levels; might need to get Internet access

4.2 Project Priorities

Dimension	Driver	Constraint	Degree of Freedom
Schedule			release 1 planned to be available by 3/1/03, release 2 by 5/1/03; over-run of up to 3 weeks acceptable without sponsor review
Features		All features scheduled for release 1.0 must be fully operational	
Quality		95% of user acceptance tests must pass; all security tests must pass; compliance with corporate security standards must be demonstrated for all secure transactions	
Staff	projected team size is half-time project manager, 2 developers, and half-time tester; additional half-time developer and half-time tester will be available if necessary		
Cost			budget overrun up to 15% acceptable without sponsor review

Use Cases

The various user classes identified the following use cases and primary actors for the Cafeteria Ordering System:

Primary Actor	Use Cases	
Patron	**1.**	Order Meal
	2.	Change Meal Order
	3.	Cancel Meal Order
	4.	View Menu
	5.	Register for Payroll Deduction
	6.	Unregister for Payroll Deduction
	7.	Subscribe to Standard Meal
	8.	Modify Meal Subscription
	9.	Override Meal Subscription
Menu Manager	**10.**	Create Menu
	11.	Modify Menu
	12.	Define Meal Special
Cafeteria Staff	**13.**	Prepare Meal
	14.	Generate Payment Request
	15.	Request Delivery
	16.	Generate System Usage Reports
Meal Deliverer	**17.**	Deliver Meal
	18.	Record Meal Delivery
	19.	Print Delivery Instructions

Use Case ID:	**UC-1**		
Use Case Name:	Order Meal		
Created By:	Karl Wiegers	Last Updated By:	Jack McGillicutty
Date Created:	October 21, 2002	Date Last Updated:	November 7, 2002
Actors:	Patron		
Description:	A Patron accesses the Cafeteria Ordering System from the corporate intranet or from home, optionally views the menu for a specific date, selects food items, and places an order for a meal to be delivered to a specified location within a specified 15-minute time window.		
Preconditions:	1. Patron is logged into COS. 2. Patron is registered for meal payments by payroll deduction.		
Postconditions:	1. Meal order is stored in COS with a status of "Accepted". 2. Inventory of available food items is updated to reflect items in this order. 3. Remaining delivery capacity for the requested time window is updated to reflect this delivery request.		
Normal Course:	1.0 Order a Single Meal		

Normal Course (continued):

1.0 Order a Single Meal

1. Patron asks to view menu for a specified date.
2. System displays menu of available food items and the daily special.
3. Patron selects one or more food items from menu.
4. Patron indicates that meal order is complete.
5. System displays ordered menu items, individual prices, and total price, including any taxes and delivery charge.
6. Patron confirms meal order or requests to modify meal order (back to step 3).
7. System displays available delivery times for the delivery date.
8. Patron selects a delivery time and specifies the delivery location.
9. Patron specifies payment method.
10. System confirms acceptance of the order.
11. System sends Patron an e-mail confirming order details, price, and delivery instructions.
12. System stores order in database, sends e-mail to notify Cafeteria Staff, sends food item information to Cafeteria Inventory System, and updates available delivery times.

Alternative Courses:	1.1 Order multiple meals (branch after step 4)

1. Patron asks to order another meal.
2. Return to step 2.

1.2 Order multiple identical meals (after step 3)

1. Patron requests a specified number of identical meals.
2. Return to step 4.

1.3. Order the daily special (after step 2)

1. Patron orders the daily special from the menu.
2. Return to step 5.

Exceptions:	1.0.E.1 Current time is after order cutoff time (at step 1)

1. System informs Patron that it's too late to place an order for today.
2a. Patron cancels the meal order.
2b. System terminates use case.
3a. Patron requests to select another date.
3b. System restarts use case.

1.0.E.2 No delivery times left (at step 1)

1. System informs Patron that no delivery times are available for the meal date.
2a. Patron cancels the meal order.
2b. System terminates use case.
3. Patron requests to pick the order up at the cafeteria (skip steps 7–8).

1.2.E.1 Can't fulfill specified number of identical meals (at step 1)

1. System informs Patron of the maximum number of identical meals it can supply.
2. Patron changes number of identical meals ordered or cancels meal order.

Includes:	None
Priority:	High
Frequency of Use:	Approximately 400 users, average of one usage per day
Business Rules:	BR-1, BR-2, BR-3, BR-4, BR-8, BR-11, BR-12, BR-33
Special Requirements:	

1. Patron shall be able to cancel the meal order at any time prior to confirming the order.
2. Patron shall be able to view all meals he ordered within the previous six months and repeat one of those meals as the new order, provided that all food items are available on the menu for the requested delivery date.
    (Priority = medium)

Assumptions:	1. Assume that 30 percent of Patrons will order the daily special (source: previous six months of cafeteria data).
Notes and Issues:	1. The default date is the current date if the Patron is using the system before today's order cutoff time. Otherwise, the default date is the next day that the cafeteria is open.
	2. If Patron doesn't want to have the meal delivered, the precondition requiring registration for payroll deduction is not applicable.
	3. Peak usage load for this use case is between 8:00 A.M. and 10:00 A.M. local time.

Use Case ID:	**UC-5**		
Use Case Name:	Register for Payroll Deduction		
Created By:	Karl Wiegers	Last Updated By:	Chris Zambito
Date Created:	October 21, 2002	Date Last Updated:	October 31, 2002
Actors:	Patron, Payroll System		
Description:	Cafeteria patrons who use the Cafeteria Ordering System and have meals delivered must be registered for payroll deduction. For noncash purchases made through the COS, the cafeteria will issue a payment request to the Payroll System, which will deduct the meal costs from the next scheduled employee paycheck or payday direct deposit.		
Preconditions:	1. Patron is logged into COS.		
Postconditions:	1. Patron is registered for payroll deduction.		
Normal Course:	5.0 Register for Payroll Deduction		

5.0 Register for Payroll Deduction

1. Patron requests to register for payroll deduction.
2. System invokes Authenticate User's Identity use case.
3. System asks Payroll System if Patron is eligible to register for payroll deduction.
4. Payroll System confirms that Patron is eligible.
5. System informs Patron that he is eligible for payroll deduction.
6. System asks Patron to confirm his desire to register for payroll deduction.
7. Patron confirms desire to register for payroll deduction.
8. System asks Payroll System to establish payroll deduction for Patron.
9. Payroll System confirms that payroll deduction is established.
10. System informs Patron that payroll deduction is established and provides confirmation number of the registration transaction.

Alternative Courses:	None

Exceptions:	5.0.E.1 Patron identity authentication fails (at step 2)

1. System gives user two more opportunities for correct identity authentication.
2a. If authentication is successful, Patron proceeds with use case.
2b. If authentication fails after three tries, System notifies Patron, logs invalid authentication attempt, and terminates use case.

5.0.E.2 Patron is not eligible for payroll deduction (at step 4)

1. System informs Patron that he is not eligible for payroll deduction and gives the reason why.
2. System terminates use case.

5.0.E.3 Patron is already enrolled for payroll deduction (at step 4)

1. System informs Patron that he is already registered for payroll deduction.
2. System terminates use case.

Includes:	Authenticate User's Identity
Priority:	High
Frequency of Use:	Once per employee on average
Business Rules:	BR-86 and BR-88 govern an employee's eligibility to enroll for payroll deduction.
Special Requirements:	1. User authentication is performed per corporate standards for medium-security applications.
Assumptions:	None
Notes and Issues:	1. Expect high frequency of executing this use case within first 2 weeks after system is released.

Use Case ID:	**UC-11**	
Use Case Name:	Modify Menu	
Created By:	Karl Wiegers	Last Updated By:
Date Created:	October 21, 2002	Date Last Updated:
Actors:	Menu Manager	
Description:	The cafeteria Menu Manager may modify the menu of available food items and prices for a specified date to reflect changes in availability or prices or to define daily meal specials.	
Preconditions:	1. Menus already exist in the system.	
Postconditions:	1. Modified menu has been saved.	

Normal Course:	11.0 Edit Existing Menu

1. Menu Manager requests to view the menu for a specific date.
2. System displays the menu.
3. Menu Manager modifies the menu to add new food items, remove or change food items, create or change a meal special, or change prices.
4. Menu Manager requests to save the modified menu.
5. System saves modified menu.

Alternative Courses:	None
Exceptions:	11.0.E.1 No menu exists for specified date (at step 1)

1. System informs Menu Manager that no menu exists for the specified date.
2. System asks Menu Manager if he would like to create a menu for the specified date.

3a. Menu Manager says yes.

3b. System invokes Create Menu use case.

4a. Menu Manager says no.

4b. System terminates use case.

11.0.E.2 Date specified is in the past (at step 1)

1. System informs Menu Manager that the menu for the requested date cannot be modified.
2. System terminates use case.

Includes:	Create Menu
Priority:	High
Frequency of Use:	Approximately 20 times per week by one user
Business Rules:	BR-24
Special Requirements:	1. The Menu Manager may cancel out of the menu modification function at any time. If the menu has been changed, the system shall request confirmation of the cancellation.
Assumptions:	1. A menu will be created for every official Process Impact business day, including weekends and holidays in which employees are scheduled to be on site.
Notes and Issues:	1. Certain food items will not be deliverable, so the menu presented to the Patrons of the Cafeteria Ordering System for delivery will not always exactly match the menu available for pickup in the cafeteria. The menu shall indicate which items may not be delivered. The system shall not permit a Patron to order those items for delivery.

Software Requirements Specification

1. Introduction

1.1 Purpose
This SRS describes the software functional and nonfunctional requirements for release 1.0 of the Cafeteria Ordering System (COS). This document is intended to be used by the members of the project team that will implement and verify the correct functioning of the system. Unless otherwise noted, all requirements specified here are high priority and committed for release 1.0.

1.2 Project Scope and Product Features
The Cafeteria Ordering System will permit Process Impact employees to order meals from the company cafeteria on-line to be delivered to specified campus locations. A detailed project description is available in the *Cafeteria Ordering System Vision and Scope Document* [1]. The section in that document titled "Scope of Initial and Subsequent Releases" lists the features that are scheduled for full or partial implementation in this release.

1.3 References

1. Wiegers, Karl. *Cafeteria Ordering System Vision and Scope Document,* *www.processimpact.com/projects/COS/COS_vision_and_scope.doc*

2. Wiegers, Karl. *Process Impact Intranet Development Standard, Version 1.3, www.processimpact.com/corporate/standards/PI_intranet_ dev_std.doc*

3. Zambito, Christine. *Process Impact Business Rules Catalog, www.processimpact.com/corporate/policies/PI_business_rules.doc*

4. Zambito, Christine. *Process Impact Internet Application User Interface Standard, Version 2.0, www.processimpact.com/corporate/standards/PI_internet_ui_std.doc*

2. Overall Description

2.1 Product Perspective
The Cafeteria Ordering System is a new system that replaces the current manual and telephone processes for ordering and picking up lunches in the Process Impact cafeteria. The context diagram in Figure D-1 illustrates the external entities and system interfaces for release 1.0. The system is expected to evolve over several releases, ultimately connecting to the Internet ordering services for several local restaurants and to credit and debit card authorization services.

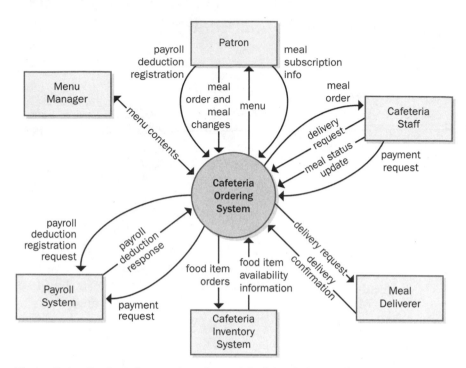

Figure D-1 Context diagram for release 1.0 of the Cafeteria Ordering System.

2.2 User Classes and Characteristics

User Class	Description
Patron (favored)	A Patron is a Process Impact employee at the corporate campus in Clackamas, Oregon, who wishes to order meals to be delivered from the company cafeteria. There are about 600 potential Patrons, of which an estimated 400 are expected to use the Cafeteria Ordering System an average of 4 times per week each (source: current cafeteria usage data). Patrons will sometimes order multiple meals for group events or guests. An estimated 90 percent of orders will be placed using the corporate Intranet, with 10 percent of orders being placed from home. All Patrons have Intranet access from their offices. Some Patrons will wish to set up meal subscriptions, either to have the same meal to be delivered every day or to have the day's meal special delivered automatically. A Patron must be able to override a subscription for a specific day.
Cafeteria Staff	The Process Impact cafeteria currently employs about 20 Cafeteria Staff, who will receive orders from the Cafeteria Ordering System, prepare meals, package them for delivery, print delivery instructions, and request delivery. Most of the Cafeteria Staff will need to be trained in the use of the computer, the Web browser, and the Cafeteria Ordering System.

User Class	Description
Menu Manager	The Menu Manager is a cafeteria employee, perhaps the cafeteria manager, who is responsible for establishing and maintaining daily menus of the food items available from the cafeteria and the times of day that each item is available. Some menu items may not be available for delivery. The Menu Manager will also define the cafeteria's daily specials. The Menu Manager will need to edit the menus periodically to reflect planned food items that are not available or price changes.
Meal Deliverer	As the Cafeteria Staff prepare orders for delivery, they will print delivery instructions and issue delivery requests to the Meal Deliverer, who is either another cafeteria employee or a contractor. The Meal Deliverer will pick up the food and delivery instructions for each meal and deliver it to the Patron. The Meal Deliverers' primary interactions with the system will be to reprint the delivery instructions on occasion and to confirm that a meal was (or was not) delivered.

2.3 Operating Environment

OE-1:   The Cafeteria Ordering System shall operate with the following Web browsers: Microsoft Internet Explorer versions 5.0 and 6.0, Netscape Communicator version 4.7, and Netscape versions 6 and 7.

OE-2:   The Cafeteria Ordering System shall operate on a server running the current corporate-approved versions of Red Hat Linux and Apache HTTP Server.

OE-3:   The Cafeteria Ordering System shall permit user access from the corporate Intranet and, if a user is authorized for outside access through the corporate firewall, from an Internet connection at the user's home.

2.4 Design and Implementation Constraints

CO-1:   The system's design, code, and maintenance documentation shall conform to the *Process Impact Intranet Development Standard, Version 1.3* [2].

CO-2:   The system shall use the current corporate standard Oracle database engine.

CO-3:   All HTML code shall conform to the HTML 4.0 standard.

CO-4:   All scripts shall be written in Perl.

2.5 User Documentation

UD-1:   The system shall provide an online hierarchical and cross-linked help system in HTML that describes and illustrates all system functions.

UD-2:   The first time a new user accesses the system and on user demand thereafter, the system shall provide an online tutorial to allow users to practice ordering meals using a static tutorial menu. The system shall not store meals ordered using this template in the database or place orders for such meals with the cafeteria.

2.6 Assumptions and Dependencies

AS-1:   The cafeteria is open for breakfast, lunch, and dinner every company business day in which employees are expected to be on site.

DE-1:   The operation of the COS depends on changes being made in the Payroll System to accept payment requests for meals ordered with the COS.

DE-2:   The operation of the COS depends on changes being made in the Cafeteria Inventory System to update the availability of food items as COS orders are accepted.

3. System Features

3.1 Order Meals

3.1.1 Description and Priority   A cafeteria Patron whose identity has been verified may order meals either to be delivered to a specified company location or to be picked up in the cafeteria. A Patron may cancel or change a meal order if it has not yet been prepared. Priority = High.

3.1.2 Stimulus/Response Sequences

Stimulus: Patron requests to place an order for one or more meals.

Response: System queries Patron for details of meal(s), payment, and delivery instructions.

Stimulus: Patron requests to change a meal order.

Response: If status is "Accepted," system allows user to edit a previous meal order.

Stimulus: Patron requests to cancel a meal order.

Response: If status is "Accepted," system cancels a meal order.

3.1.3 Functional Requirements

Order.Place:	The system shall let a Patron who is logged in to the Cafeteria Ordering System place an order for one or more meals.
Order.Place.Register:	The system shall confirm that the Patron is registered for payroll deduction to place an order.
Order.Place.Register.No:	If the Patron is not registered for payroll deduction, the system shall give the Patron options to register now and continue placing an order, to place an order for pickup in the cafeteria (not for delivery), or to exit from the COS.
Order.Place.Date:	The system shall prompt the Patron for the meal date (see BR-8).
Order.Place.Date.Cutoff:	If the meal date is the current date and the current time is after the order cutoff time, the system shall inform the patron that it's too late to place an order for today. The Patron may either change the meal date or cancel the order.

Order.Deliver.Select:	The Patron shall specify whether the order is to be picked up or delivered.
Order.Deliver.Location:	If the order is to be delivered and there are still available delivery times for the meal date, the Patron shall provide a valid delivery location.
Order.Deliver.Notimes:	The system shall notify the Patron if there are no available delivery times for the meal date. The Patron shall either cancel the order or indicate that the Patron will pick up the order in the cafeteria.
Order.Deliver.Times:	The system shall display the remaining available delivery times for the meal date. The system shall allow the Patron to request one of the delivery times shown, to change the order to be picked up in the cafeteria, or to cancel the order.
Order.Menu.Date:	The system shall display a menu for the specified date.
Order.Menu.Available:	The menu for the current date shall display only those food items for which at least one unit is available in the cafeteria's inventory.
Order.Units.Food:	The system shall allow the Patron to indicate the number of units of each menu item that he wishes to order.
Order.Units.Multiple:	The system shall permit the user to order multiple identical meals, up to the fewest available units of any menu item in the order.
Order.Units.TooMany:	If the Patron orders more units of a menu item than are presently in the cafeteria's inventory, the system shall inform the Patron of the maximum number of units of that food item that he can order.
Order.Units.Change:	If the available inventory cannot fulfill the number of units ordered, the Patron may change the number of units ordered, change the number of identical meals being ordered, or cancel the meal order.
Order.Confirm.Display:	When the Patron indicates that he does not wish to order any more food items, the system shall display the food items ordered, the individual food item prices, and the payment amount, calculated per BR-12.
Order.Confirm.Prompt:	The system shall prompt the Patron to confirm the meal order.
Order.Confirm.Not:	If the Patron does not confirm the meal order, the Patron may either edit or cancel the order.
Order.Confirm.More:	The system shall let the Patron order additional meals for the same or for different date. BR-3 and BR-4 pertain to multiple meals in a single order.

Order.Pay.Method:	When the Patron indicates that he is done placing orders, the system shall ask the user to select a payment method.
Order.Pay.Deliver:	See BR-11.
Order.Pay.Pickup:	If the meal is to be picked up in the cafeteria, the system shall let the Patron choose to pay by payroll deduction or by paying cash at the time of pickup.
Order.Pay.Details:	The system shall display the food items ordered, payment amount, payment method, and delivery instructions.
Order.Pay.Confirm:	The Patron shall either confirm the order, request to edit the order, or request to cancel the order.
Order.Pay.Confirm.Deduct:	If the Patron confirmed the order and selected payment by payroll deduction, the system shall issue a payment request to the Payroll System.
Order.Pay.Confirm.OK:	If the payment request is accepted, the system shall display a message confirming acceptance of the order with the payroll deduction transaction number.
Order.Pay.Confirm.NG:	If the payment request is rejected, the system shall display a message with the reason for the rejection. The Patron shall either cancel the order, or change the payment method to cash and request to pick up the order at the cafeteria.

Order.Done:	When the Patron has confirmed the order, the system shall do the following as a single transaction:
Order.Done.Store:	Assign the next available meal order number to the meal and store the meal order with an initial status of "Accepted."
Order.Done.Inventory:	Send a message to the Cafeteria Inventory System with the number of units of each food item in the order.
Order.Done.Menu:	Update the menu for the current order's order date to reflect any items that are now out of stock in the cafeteria inventory.
Order.Done.Times:	Update the remaining available delivery times for the date of this order.
Order.Done.Patron:	Send an e-mail message to the Patron with the meal order and meal payment information.
Order.Done.Cafeteria:	Send an e-mail message to the Cafeteria Staff with the meal order information.
Order.Done.Failure:	If any step of Order.Done fails, the system shall roll back the transaction and notify the user that the order was unsuccessful, along with the reason for failure.

Order.Previous.Period:	The system shall permit the Patron to view any meals he has ordered within the previous six months. [Priority = Medium]
Order.Previous.Reorder:	The Patron may reorder any meal he had ordered within the previous six months, provided that all food items in that order are available on the menu for the meal date. [Priority = Medium]

[functional requirements for changing and canceling meal orders are not provided in this example]

3.2 Create, View, Modify, and Delete Meal Subscriptions
[details not provided in this example]

3.3 Register for Meal Payment Options
[details not provided in this example]

3.4 Request Meal Delivery
[details not provided in this example]

3.5 Create, View, Modify, and Delete Cafeteria Menus
[details not provided in this example]

4. External Interface Requirements

4.1 User Interfaces
UI-1: The Cafeteria Ordering System screen displays shall conform to the *Process Impact Internet Application User Interface Standard, Version 2.0* [4].

UI-2: The system shall provide a help link from each displayed HTML page to explain how to use that page.

UI-3: The Web pages shall permit complete navigation and food item selection using the keyboard alone, in addition to using mouse and keyboard combinations.

4.2 Hardware Interfaces
No hardware interfaces have been identified.

4.3 Software Interfaces

SI-1:   Cafeteria Inventory System

SI-1.1:   The COS shall transmit the quantities of food items ordered to the Cafeteria Inventory System through a programmatic interface.

SI-1.2:   The COS shall poll the Cafeteria Inventory System to determine whether a requested food item is available.

SI-1.3:   When the Cafeteria Inventory System notifies the COS that a specific food item is no longer available, the COS shall remove that food item from the menu for the current date.

SI-2:   Payroll System
             The COS shall communicate with the Payroll System through a programmatic interface for the following operations:

SI-2.1:   To allow a Patron to register for payroll deduction.

SI-2.2:   To allow a Patron to unregister for payroll deduction.

SI-2.3:   To check whether a patron is registered for payroll deduction.

SI-2.4:   To submit a payment request for a purchased meal.

SI-2.5:   To reverse all or part of a previous charge because a patron rejected a meal or wasn't satisfied with it, or because the meal was not delivered per the confirmed delivery instructions.

4.4 Communications Interfaces

CI-1:   The Cafeteria Ordering System shall send an e-mail message to the Patron to confirm acceptance of an order, price, and delivery instructions.

CI-2:   The Cafeteria Ordering System shall send an e-mail message to the Patron to report any problems with the meal order or delivery after the order is accepted.

5. Other Nonfunctional Requirements

5.1 Performance Requirements

PE-1:   The system shall accommodate 400 users during the peak usage time window of 8:00 A.M. to 10:00 A.M. local time, with an estimated average session duration of 8 minutes.

PE-2:   All Web pages generated by the system shall be fully downloadable in no more than 10 seconds over a 40 KBps modem connection.

PE-3:   Responses to queries shall take no longer than 7 seconds to load onto the screen after the user submits the query.

PE-4:   The system shall display confirmation messages to users within 4 seconds after the user submits information to the system.

5.2 Safety Requirements

No safety requirements have been identified.

5.3 Security Requirements

SE-1:   All network transactions that involve financial information or personally identifiable information shall be encrypted per BR-33.

SE-2:   Users shall be required to log in to the Cafeteria Ordering System for all operations except viewing a menu.

SE-3:   Patrons shall log in according to the restricted computer system access policy per BR-35.

SE-4:   The system shall permit only cafeteria staff members who are on the list of authorized Menu Managers to create or edit menus, per BR-24.

SE-5:   Only users who have been authorized for home access to the corporate Intranet may use the COS from non-company locations.

SE-6:   The system shall permit Patrons to view only their own previously placed orders, not orders placed by other patrons.

5.4 Software Quality Attributes

Availability-1:   The Cafeteria Ordering System shall be available to users on the corporate Intranet and to dial-in users 99.9% of the time between 5:00 A.M. and midnight local time and 95% of the time between midnight and 5:00 A.M. local time.

Robustness-1:   If the connection between the user and the system is broken prior to an order being either confirmed or canceled, the Cafeteria Ordering System shall enable the user to recover an incomplete order.

Appendix A: Data Dictionary and Data Model

delivery instruction	=	patron name
	+	patron phone number
	+	meal date
	+	delivery location
	+	delivery time window

| delivery location | = | * building and room to which an ordered meal is to be delivered * |

| delivery time window | = | * 15-minute range during which an ordered meal is to be delivered; must begin and end on quarter-hour intervals * |

| employee ID | = | * company ID number of the employee who placed a meal order; 6-character numeric string * |

| food item description | – | * text description of a food item on a menu; maximum 100 characters * |

food item price	=	* pre-tax cost of a single unit of a menu food item, in dollars and cents *
meal date	=	* the date the meal is to be delivered or picked up; format MM/DD/YYYY; default = current date if the current time is before the order cutoff time, else the next day; may not be prior to the current date *
meal order	=	meal order number
	+	order date
	+	meal date
	+	1:m{ordered food item}
	+	delivery instruction
	+	meal order status
meal order number	=	* a unique, sequential integer that the system assigns to each accepted meal order; initial value is 1 *
meal order status	=	[incomplete | accepted | prepared | pending delivery | delivered | canceled] * see state-transition diagram in Figure D-3 *
meal payment	=	payment amount
	+	payment method
	+	(payroll deduction transaction number)
menu	=	menu date
	+	1:m{menu food item}
	+	0:1{special}
menu date	=	* the date for which a specific menu of food items is available; format MM/DD/YYYY *
menu food item	=	food item description
	+	food item price
order cutoff time	=	* the time of day before which all orders for that date must be placed *
order date	=	* the date on which a patron placed a meal order; format MM/DD/YYYY *

ordered food item	=	menu food item
	+	quantity ordered

patron	=	patron name
	+	employee ID
	+	patron phone number
	+	patron location
	+	patron e-mail

patron e-mail = * e-mail address of the employee who placed a meal order; 50-character alphanumeric *

patron location = * building and room numbers of the employee who placed a meal order; 50-character alphanumeric *

patron name = * name of the employee who placed a meal order; 30-character alphanumeric *

patron phone number = * telephone number of the employee who placed a meal order; format AAA-EEE-NNNN xXXXX for area code, exchange, number, and extension *

payment amount = * total price of an order in dollars and cents, calculated per BR-12 *

payment method = [payroll deduction | cash] * others to be added beginning with release 2 *

payroll deduction transaction number = * 8-digit sequential integer number that the Payroll System assigns to each payroll deduction transaction that it accepts *

quantity ordered = * the number of units of each food item that the Patron is ordering; default = 1; maximum = quantity presently in inventory *

special	=	special description
	+	special price

* the Menu Manager may define one or more special meals for each menu, with a particular combination of food items at a reduced price *

special description = * text description of a daily special meal; maximum 100 characters *

special price = * cost of a single unit of a daily special meal, in dollars and cents *

Figure D-2 is a partial data model for release 1.0 of the Cafeteria Ordering System, showing the entities described in the data dictionary and the relationships between them.

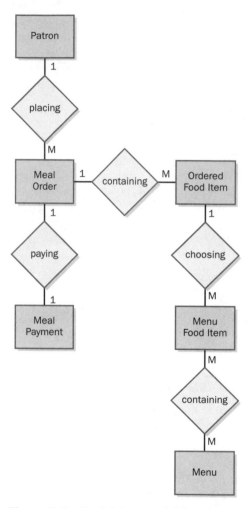

Figure D-2   Partial data model for release 1.0 of the Cafeteria Ordering System.

Appendix B: Analysis Models

Figure D-3 is a state-transition diagram that shows the possible meal order status and the allowed changes in status.

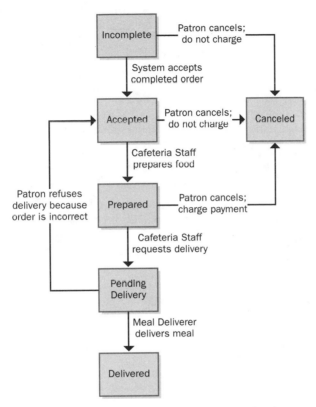

Figure D-3   State-transition diagram for meal order status.

Business Rules

[the following is a sample of a separate business rules catalog]

ID	Rule Definition	Type of Rule	Static or Dynamic	Source
BR-1	Delivery time windows are 15 minutes, beginning on each quarter hour.	Fact	Static	Cafeteria Manager
BR-2	Deliveries must be completed between 10:00 A.M. and 2:00 P.M. local time.	Constraint	Dynamic	Cafeteria Manager
BR-3	All meals in a single order must be delivered to the same location.	Constraint	Static	Cafeteria Manager
BR-4	All meals in a single order must be paid for using the same payment method.	Constraint	Static	Cafeteria Manager
BR-8	Meals must be ordered within 14 calendar days of the meal date.	Constraint	Dynamic	Cafeteria Manager
BR-11	If an order is to be delivered, the patron must pay by payroll deduction.	Constraint	Dynamic	Cafeteria Manager
BR-12	Order price is calculated as the sum of each food item price times the quantity of that food item ordered, plus applicable sales tax, plus a delivery charge if a meal is delivered outside the free delivery zone.	Computation	Dynamic	cafeteria policy; state tax code
BR-24	Only cafeteria employees who are designated as Menu Managers by the Cafeteria Manager may create, modify, or delete cafeteria menus.	Constraint	Static	cafeteria policy
BR-33	Network transmissions that involve financial information or personally identifiable information require 128-bit encryption.	Constraint	Static	corporate security policy
BR-35	*[details about restricted computer system access policy would go here]*	Constraint	Static	corporate security policy
BR-86	Only permanent employees may register for payroll deduction for any company purchase.	Constraint	Static	Corporate Accounting Manager
BR-88	An employee may register for payroll deduction payment of cafeteria meals if no more than 40 percent of his gross pay is currently being deducted for other reasons.	Constraint	Dynamic	Corporate Accounting Manager

Glossary

acceptance criteria   Conditions that a software product must satisfy to be accepted by a user, customer, or other stakeholder.

activity diagram   An analysis model that shows a dynamic view of a system by depicting the flow from one activity to another. Similar to a flowchart.

actor   A person playing a specific role, a software system, or a hardware device that interacts with a system to achieve a useful goal. Also called a *user role*.

allocation   See *requirements allocation*.

alternative course   A path through a use case that leads to success (accomplishing the actor's goal) but which involves a variation from the normal course in the specifics of the task or of the actor's interaction with the system.

analysis, requirements   The process of classifying requirements information into various categories, evaluating requirements for desirable qualities, representing requirements in different forms, deriving detailed requirements from high-level requirements, negotiating priorities, and so on.

analyst   See *requirements analyst*.

architecture   The structure of a software-containing system, including the software and hardware components that make up the system, the interfaces and relationships between those components, and the component behaviors that are visible to other components.

assumption   A statement that is believed to be true in the absence of proof or definitive knowledge.

attribute, requirement   See *requirement attribute*.

baseline, requirements   A snapshot in time representing the current agreed-upon, reviewed, and approved set of requirements for a specific product release.

business analyst   See *requirements analyst*.

business requirement   A high-level business objective of the organization that builds a product or of a customer who procures it.

business rule   A policy, guideline, standard, or regulation that defines or constrains some aspect of the business.

cardinality   The number of instances of a given object or data entity that logically relates to an instance of another object or entity. Examples are one-to-one, one-to-many, and many-to-many.

change control board   The group of people responsible for making decisions to accept or reject proposed changes in software requirements.

class   A description of a set of objects having common properties and behaviors, which typically correspond to real-world items (persons, places, or things) in the business or problem domain.

class diagram   An analysis model that shows a set of system or problem domain classes and their relationships.

constraint   A restriction that is imposed on the choices available to the developer for the design and construction of a product.

context diagram   An analysis model that depicts a system at a high level of abstraction. The context diagram identifies objects outside the system that interact with it, but it shows nothing about the system's internal structure or behavior.

COTS (commercial off-the-shelf) product   A software package purchased from a vendor and either used as a self-contained solution to a problem or integrated, customized, and extended to satisfy local customer needs.

CRUD matrix   A table that correlates system actions with data entities to show where each data item is created, read, updated, and deleted.

customer   A project stakeholder who requests, pays for, selects, specifies, uses, or receives the output generated by a product.

data dictionary   A collection of definitions for the data elements, structures, and attributes that are important to the problem domain.

data flow diagram   An analysis model that depicts the processes, data collections, terminators, and flows among them that characterize the behavior of a business process or of a software system.

decision rule   An agreed-upon way by which a body of people arrives at a decision.

decision table   A table that shows all combinations of values for a set of factors that influence a portion of a system's behavior and indicates the expected system action in response to each combination.

decision tree   An analysis model that graphically shows a system's actions in response to all combinations of a set of factors that influence a portion of the system's behavior.

dependency   A reliance that a project has on an external factor, event, or group outside its control.

dialog map   An analysis model that depicts a user interface architecture, showing the display elements and the navigations permitted between them.

elicitation, requirements   The process of identifying software or system requirements from various sources through interviews, workshops, workflow and task analysis, document analysis, and other mechanisms.

entity   An item in the business domain about which data will be collected and stored.

entity-relationship diagram   An analysis model that identifies the logical relationships between pairs of entities.

essential   Devoid of implementation specifics and constraints. An essential model depicts information at a conceptual level, independent of how it might be implemented in a system.

event   A trigger or stimulus that takes place in a system's environment that leads to a system response, such as a functional behavior or a change in state.

event-response table   A list of the external or time-triggered events that could affect the system and a description of how the system is to respond to each event.

evolutionary prototype   A fully functional prototype created as a skeleton or an initial increment of the final product, which is fleshed out and extended incrementally as requirements become clear and ready for implementation.

exception   A condition that can prevent a use case from successfully concluding. Unless some recovery mechanism is possible, the use case's postconditions are not reached and the actor's goal is not satisfied.

extends relationship   A construct in which an alternative course in a use case branches off from the normal sequence of steps. The steps that the actor follows when executing the alternative course can be packaged into an extension use case that is invoked to perform the alternative action. The process flow then rejoins the normal course for completion.

external interface requirement   A description of an interface between a software system and a user, another software system, or a hardware device.

Extreme Programming   An "agile" software development methodology characterized by face-to-face collaboration between developers and an on-site customer representative, limited documentation of requirements in the form of "user stories," and rapid and frequent delivery of small increments of useful functionality.

facilitator   A person who is responsible for planning and leading a group activity, such as a requirements elicitation workshop.

feature   A set of logically related functional requirements that provides a capability to the user and enables the satisfaction of a business objective.

flowchart   A model that shows the processing steps and decision points in the logic of a process or of a program. Similar to an activity diagram.

function point   A measure of software size, based on the number and complexity of internal logical files, external interface files, external inputs, outputs, and queries.

functional requirement   A statement of a piece of required functionality or a behavior that a system will exhibit under specific conditions.

gold plating   Unnecessary or excessively complex functionality that is specified or built into a product.

horizontal prototype   A partial or possible implementation of a user interface for a software system. Used to evaluate usability and to assess the completeness and correctness of requirements. Also called a *behavioral prototype* or a *mock-up*.

IEEE   The Institute of Electrical and Electronics Engineers. A professional society that maintains a set of standards for managing and executing software and systems engineering projects.

includes relationship   A construct in which several steps that recur in multiple use cases are factored out into a separate sub-use case, which the higher-level (or "calling") use cases then invoke when needed.

inspection   A type of peer review that involves a trained team of individuals who follow a well-defined and rigorous process to examine a work product carefully for defects.

navigation map   See *dialog map*.

nonfunctional requirement   A description of a property or characteristic that a software system must exhibit or a constraint that it must respect, other than an observable system behavior.

normal course   The default sequence of steps in a use case, which leads to satisfying the use case's postconditions and letting the user achieve his goal. Also known as the *basic course, main course, normal sequence, flow of events, main success scenario,* and *happy path*.

object   A specific instance of a class for which a set of data attributes and a list of operations that can be performed on those attributes can be collected. For example, "Mary Jones" is a specific instance of the class "Customer."

operational profile   A suite of scenarios that represent the expected usage patterns of a software product.

paper prototype   A nonexecutable mock-up of a software system's user interface using inexpensive, low-tech screen sketches.

peer review   An activity in which one or more persons other than the author of a work product examine that product with the intent of finding defects and improvement opportunities.

pilot   A controlled execution of a new process with the objective of evaluating the new process under real project conditions to assess its readiness for general deployment.

Planguage   A keyword-oriented language developed by Tom Gilb that permits precise and quantitative specification of requirements.

postcondition   A condition that describes the state of a system after a use case is successfully completed.

precondition   A condition that must be satisfied or a state the system must be in before a use case may begin.

procedure   A step-by-step description of a course of action to be taken to perform a given activity, describing how the activity is to be accomplished.

process   A sequence of activities performed for a given purpose. A *process description* is a documented definition of those activities. A process can contain one or more procedures.

process assets   Documents such as templates, forms, checklists, policies, procedures, process descriptions, and sample work products that are collected to assist an organization's effective application of improved software development practices.

product champion   A designated representative of a specific user class who supplies the user requirements for the group that he or she represents.

prototype   A partial, preliminary, or possible implementation of a program. Used to explore and validate requirements and design approaches. Types of prototypes include *evolutionary, throwaway, paper, horizontal,* and *vertical.* These can be combined, as in an evolutionary vertical prototype.

quality attribute   A kind of nonfunctional requirement that describes a quality or property of a system. Examples include usability, portability, maintainability, integrity, efficiency, reliability, and robustness. Quality attribute requirements describe the extent to which a software product demonstrates desired characteristics, not what the product does.

requirement   A statement of a customer need or objective, or of a condition or capability that a product must possess to satisfy such a need or objective. A property that a product must have to provide value to a stakeholder.

requirement attribute   Descriptive information about a requirement that enriches its definition beyond the statement of intended functionality. Examples include origin, rationale, priority, owner, release number, and version number.

requirements allocation   The process of apportioning system requirements among various architectural subsystems and components.

requirements analyst   The role on a project team that has lead responsibility for working with stakeholder representatives to elicit, analyze, specify, validate, and manage the project's requirements. Also called a *business analyst, system analyst, requirements engineer,* and simply *analyst.*

requirements development   The process of defining a project's scope, identifying user classes and user representatives, and eliciting, analyzing, specifying, and validating requirements. The product of requirements development is a requirements baseline that defines the product to be built.

requirements engineering   The domain that encompasses all project life cycle activities associated with understanding a product's necessary capabilities and attributes. Includes requirements development and requirements management. A subdiscipline of system engineering and software engineering.

requirements management   The process of working with a defined set of product requirements throughout the product's development process and its operational life. Includes tracking requirements status, managing changes to requirements and versions of requirements specifications, and tracing individual requirements to other project phases and work products.

requirements specification   See *software requirements specification* and *specification, requirements.*

requirements traceability matrix   A table that illustrates logical links between individual functional requirements and other system artifacts, including other functional requirements, use cases, architecture and design elements, code modules, test cases, and business rules.

retrospective   A review in which project participants reflect on the project's activities and outcomes with the intent of identifying ways to make the next project be even more successful.

risk   A condition that could cause some loss or otherwise threaten the success of a project.

root cause analysis   An activity that seeks to understand the underlying factors that contribute to an observed problem.

scenario   A description of a specific interaction between a user and a system to accomplish some goal. An instance of usage of the system. A specific path through a use case. Often presented in the form of a story.

scope   The portion of the ultimate product vision that the current project will address. The scope draws the boundary between what's in and what's out for the project.

scope creep   A condition in which the scope of a project continues to increase, typically in an uncontrolled fashion, throughout the development process.

sequence diagram   An analysis model that shows the order in which messages pass between objects or components in a system to accomplish an activity.

software development life cycle   A sequence of activities by which a software product is defined, designed, built, and verified.

software requirements specification   A collection of the functional and nonfunctional requirements for a software product.

specification, requirements   The process of documenting a system's requirements in a structured, shareable, and manageable form. Also, the product from this process (see *software requirements specification*).

stakeholder   A person, group, or organization that is actively involved in a project, is affected by its outcome, or can influence its outcome.

statechart diagram   An analysis model that shows the sequence of states that an object in a system goes through during its lifetime in response to specific events that take place, or that shows the possible states of the system as a whole. Similar to a state-transition diagram.

state-transition diagram   An analysis model that shows the various states that a system can be in, or the statuses that an object in the system can have, and the permitted transitions that can take place between states. Similar to a statechart diagram.

subject matter expert   An individual who has extensive experience and knowledge in a domain and who is recognized as an authoritative source of information about the domain.

system requirement   A top-level requirement for a product that contains multiple subsystems, which could be all-software or software and hardware.

template   A pattern to be used as a guide for producing a complete document or other item.

terminator   An object on a context diagram or a data flow diagram that represents a user class, actor, software system, or hardware device that is external to the system being described but interfaces to it in some fashion. Also called an *external entity*.

throwaway prototype   A prototype that is created with the express intent of discarding it after it has served its purpose of clarifying and validating requirements and design alternatives.

tracing (also **traceability**)   The process of defining logical links between one system element (use case, functional requirement, business rule, design component, code module, test case, and the like) and another.

usage scenario   See *scenario*.

use case   A description of a set of logically related possible interactions between an actor and a system that results in an outcome that provides value to the actor. Can encompass multiple scenarios.

use-case diagram   An analysis model that identifies the actors who can interact with a system to accomplish valuable goals and the various use cases that each actor will perform.

user   A customer who will interact with a system either directly or indirectly (for example, using outputs from the system but not generating those outputs personally). Also called *end user*.

user class   A group of users for a system who have similar characteristics and requirements for the system. Members of a user class function as *actors* when interacting with the system.

user requirement   User goals or tasks that users must be able to perform with a system, or statements of the user's expectations of system quality.

user role   See *actor*.

validation   The process of evaluating a work product to determine whether it satisfies customer requirements.

verification   The process of evaluating a work product to determine whether it satisfies the specifications and conditions imposed on it at the beginning of the development phase during which it was created.

vertical prototype   A partial implementation of a software-containing system that slices through all layers of the architecture. Used to evaluate technical feasibility and performance. Also called a *structural prototype* or *proof of concept*.

vision   A long-term strategic concept of the ultimate purpose and form of a new system.

vision and scope document   A document that presents the business requirements for a new system, including a product vision statement and a project scope description.

waterfall development life cycle   A model of the software development process in which the various activities of requirements, design, coding, testing, and deployment are performed sequentially with little overlap or iteration.

References

Abran, Alain, and James W. Moore, eds. 2001. *Guide to the Software Engineering Body of Knowledge, Trial Version*. Los Alamitos, CA: IEEE Computer Society Press.

Alexander, Ian F., and Richard Stevens. 2002. *Writing Better Requirements*. London: Addison-Wesley.

Ambler, Scott. 1995. "Reduce Development Costs with Use-Case Scenario Testing." *Software Development* 3(7):53–61.

———. 1999. "Trace Your Design." *Software Development* 7(4):48–55.

Andriole, Stephen J. 1996. *Managing Systems Requirements: Methods, Tools, and Cases*. New York: McGraw-Hill.

Arlow, Jim. 1998. "Use Cases, UML Visual Modeling and the Trivialisation of Business Requirements." *Requirements Engineering* 3(2):150–152.

Armour, Frank, and Granville Miller. 2001. *Advanced Use Case Modeling: Software Systems*. Boston, MA: Addison-Wesley.

Arnold, Robert S., and Shawn A. Bohner. 1996. *Software Change Impact Analysis*. Los Alamitos, CA: IEEE Computer Society Press.

Bass, Len, Paul Clements, and Rick Kazman. 1998. *Software Architecture in Practice*. Reading, MA: Addison-Wesley.

Beck, Kent. 2000. *Extreme Programming Explained: Embrace Change*. Boston, MA: Addison-Wesley.

Beizer, Boris. 1990. *Software Testing Techniques*, 2d ed. New York: Van Nostrand Reinhold.

———. 1999. "Best and Worst Testing Practices: A Baker's Dozen." *Cutter IT Journal* 12(2):32–38.

Beyer, Hugh, and Karen Holtzblatt. 1998. *Contextual Design: Defining Customer-Centered Systems*. San Francisco, CA: Morgan Kaufmann Publishers, Inc.

Blackburn, Joseph D., Gary D. Scudder, and Luk N. Van Wassenhove. 1996. "Improving Speed and Productivity of Software Development: A Global Survey of Software Developers." *IEEE Transactions on Software Engineering* 22(12):875-885.

Boehm, Barry W. 1981. *Software Engineering Economics.* Englewood Cliffs, NJ: Prentice Hall.

———. 1988. "A Spiral Model of Software Development and Enhancement." *IEEE Computer* 21(5):61–72.

———. 2000. "Requirements that Handle IKIWISI, COTS, and Rapid Change." *IEEE Computer* 33(7):99-102.

Boehm, Barry W., and Philip N. Papaccio. 1988. "Understanding and Controlling Software Costs." *IEEE Transactions on Software Engineering* 14(10):1462–1476.

Boehm, Barry, J. R. Brown, and M. Lipow. 1976. "Quantitative Evaluation of Software Quality." *Second IEEE International Conference on Software Engineering,* 592-605. Los Alamitos, CA: IEEE Computer Society Press.

Boehm, Barry W., et al. 2000. *Software Cost Estimation with Cocomo II.* Upper Saddle River, NJ: Prentice Hall PTR.

Booch, Grady, James Rumbaugh, and Ivar Jacobson. 1999. *The Unified Modeling Language User Guide.* Reading, MA: Addison-Wesley.

Brooks, Frederick P., Jr. 1987. "No Silver Bullet: Essence and Accidents of Software Engineering." *Computer* 20(4):10–19.

Brown, Norm. 1996. "Industrial-Strength Management Strategies." *IEEE Software* 13(4):94–103.

———. 1999. "High-Leverage Best Practices: What Hot Companies Are Doing to Stay Ahead." *Cutter IT Journal* 12(9):4–9.

Business Rules Group. 1993. "Defining Business Rules: What Are They Really?" *http://www.businessrulesgroup.org.*

Caputo, Kim. 1998. *CMM Implementation Guide: Choreographing Software Process Improvement.* Reading, MA: Addison-Wesley.

Carnegie Mellon University/Software Engineering Institute. 2000a. "CMMI for Systems Engineering/Software Engineering, Version 1.02: Staged Representation." *Technical Report CMU/SEI-2000-TR-018.* Pittsburgh, PA: Carnegie Mellon University/Software Engineering Institute.

————. 2000b. "CMMI for Systems Engineering/Software Engineering, Version 1.02: Continuous Representation." *Technical Report CMU/SEI-2000-TR-029*. Pittsburgh, PA: Carnegie Mellon University/Software Engineering Institute.

Carr, Marvin J., Suresh L. Konda, Ira Monarch, F. Carol Ulrich, and Clay F. Walker. 1993. *Taxonomy-Based Risk Identification* (CMU/SEI-93-TR-6). Pittsburgh, PA: Software Engineering Institute, Carnegie Mellon University.

Cavano, J. P., and J. A. McCall. 1978. "A Framework for the Measurement of Software Quality." *ACM SIGSOFT Software Engineering Notes* 3(5):133-139.

Charette, Robert N. 1990. *Applications Strategies for Risk Analysis*. New York: McGraw-Hill.

Christel, Michael G., and Kyo C. Kang. 1992. *Issues in Requirements Elicitation* (CMU/SEI-92-TR-12). Pittsburgh, PA: Software Engineering Institute, Carnegie Mellon University.

Cockburn, Alistair. 2001. *Writing Effective Use Cases*. Boston, MA: Addison-Wesley.

————. 2002. *Agile Software Development*. Boston, MA: Addison-Wesley.

Cohen, Lou. 1995. *Quality Function Deployment: How to Make QFD Work for You*. Reading, MA: Addison-Wesley.

Collard, Ross. 1999. "Test Design." *Software Testing & Quality Engineering* 1(4):30–37.

Constantine, Larry. 1998. "Prototyping from the User's Viewpoint." *Software Development* 6(11):51–57.

Constantine, Larry L., and Lucy A. D. Lockwood. 1999. *Software for Use: A Practical Guide to the Models and Methods of Usage-Centered Design*. Reading, MA: Addison-Wesley.

Cooper, Alan. 1999. *The Inmates Are Running the Asylum: Why High Tech Products Drive Us Crazy and How To Restore the Sanity*. Indianapolis, IN: Sams.

Covey, Stephen R. 1989. *The 7 Habits of Highly Effective People*. New York: Simon & Schuster.

Davis, Alan M. 1993. *Software Requirements: Objects, Functions, and States*. Englewood Cliffs, NJ: Prentice Hall PTR.

————. 1995. *201 Principles of Software Development*. New York: McGraw-Hill.

DeGrace, Peter, and Leslie Hulet Stahl. 1993. *The Olduvai Imperative: CASE and the State of Software Engineering Practice*. Englewood Cliffs, NJ: Yourdon Press/Prentice Hall.

DeMarco, Tom. 1979. *Structured Analysis and System Specification*. Englewood Cliffs, NJ: Prentice Hall.

DeMarco, Tom, and Timothy Lister. 1999. *Peopleware: Productive Projects and Teams*, 2d ed. New York: Dorset House Publishing.

Drabick, Rodger D. 1999. "On-Track Requirements." *Software Testing & Quality Engineering* 1(3):54–60.

Dutta, Soumitra, Michael Lee, and Luk Van Wassenhove. 1999. "Software Engineering in Europe: A Study of Best Practices." *IEEE Software* 16(3):82–90.

ESPITI. 1995. European Software Process Improvement Training Initiative. *User Survey Report*.

Fagan, Michael E. 1976. "Design and Code Inspections to Reduce Errors in Program Development." *IBM Systems Journal* 15(3):182–211.

Ferdinandi, Patricia L. 2002. *A Requirements Pattern: Succeeding in the Internet Economy*. Boston, MA: Addison-Wesley.

Fisher, Roger, William Ury, and Bruce Patton. 1991. *Getting to Yes: Negotiating Agreement Without Giving In*. New York: Penguin USA.

Florence, Al. 2002. "Reducing Risks Through Proper Specification of Software Requirements." *CrossTalk* 15(4):13-15.

Fowler, Floyd J. 1995. *Improving Survey Questions: Design and Evaluation*. Thousand Oaks, CA: Sage Publications.

Fowler, Martin. 1999. *Refactoring: Improving the Design of Existing Code*. Boston, MA: Addison-Wesley.

Freedman, Daniel P., and Gerald M. Weinberg. 1990. *Handbook of Walkthroughs, Inspections, and Technical Reviews: Evaluating Programs, Projects, and Products*, 3d ed. New York: Dorset House Publishing.

Gainer, Jeff. 1999. *The Cutter IT E-Mail Advisor*, August 11, 1999.

Gause, Donald C., and Brian Lawrence. 1999. "User-Driven Design." *Software Testing & Quality Engineering* 1(1):22–28.

Gause, Donald C., and Gerald M. Weinberg. 1989. *Exploring Requirements: Quality Before Design*. New York: Dorset House Publishing.

Gilb, Tom. 1988. *Principles of Software Engineering Management.* Harlow, England: Addison- Wesley.

———. 1997. "Quantifying the Qualitative: How to Avoid Vague Requirements by Clear Specification Language." *Requirenautics Quarterly* 12:9-13.

Gilb, Tom, and Dorothy Graham. 1993. *Software Inspection.* Wokingham, England: Addison-Wesley.

Glass, Robert L. 1992. *Building Quality Software.* Englewood Cliffs, NJ: Prentice Hall.

———. 1999. "Inspections—Some Surprising Findings." *Communications of the ACM* 42(4):17–19.

Gotel, O., and A. Finkelstein. 1994. "An Analysis of the Requirements Traceability Problem." In *Proceedings of the First International Conference on Requirements Engineering*, 94–101. Los Alamitos, CA: IEEE Computer Society Press.

Gottesdiener, Ellen. 2001. "Decide How to Decide." *Software Development* 9(1):65-70.

———. *Requirements by Collaboration: Workshops for Defining Needs.* Boston, MA: Addison-Wesley.

Grady, Robert B. 1999. "An Economic Release Decision Model: Insights into Software Project Management." In *Proceedings of the Applications of Software Measurement Conference*, 227–239. Orange Park, FL: Software Quality Engineering.

Grady, Robert B., and Tom Van Slack. 1994. "Key Lessons in Achieving Widespread Inspection Use." *IEEE Software* 11(4):46–57.

Graham, Dorothy. 2002. "Requirements and Testing: Seven Missing-Link Myths." *IEEE Software* 19(5):15-17.

Ham, Gary A. 1998. "Four Roads to Use Case Discovery: There Is a Use (and a Case) for Each One." *CrossTalk* 11(12):17–19.

Hatley, Derek, Peter Hruschka, and Imtiaz Pirbhai. 2000. *Process for System Architecture and Requirements Engineering.* New York: Dorset House Publishing.

Highsmith, James A., III. 2000. *Adaptive Software Development: A Collaborative Approach to Managing Complex Systems.* New York: Dorset House Publishing.

Hofmann, Hubert F., and Franz Lehner. 2001. "Requirements Engineering as a Success Factor in Software Projects." *IEEE Software* 18(4):58-66.

Hohmann, Luke. 1997. "Managing Highly Usable Graphical User Interface Development Efforts." *http://members.aol.com/lhohmann/papers.htm.*

Hooks, Ivy F., and Kristin A. Farry. 2001. *Customer-Centered Products: Creating Successful Products Through Smart Requirements Management.* New York: AMACOM.

Hsia, Pei, David Kung, and Chris Sell. 1997. "Software Requirements and Acceptance Testing." In *Annals of Software Engineering*, Nancy R. Mead, ed. 3:291–317.

Humphrey, Watts S. 1989. *Managing the Software Process.* Reading, MA: Addison-Wesley.

_____. 1997. *Managing Technical People: Innovation, Teamwork, and the Software Process.* Reading, MA: Addison-Wesley.

IEEE. 1990. IEEE Std 610.12-1990: "IEEE Standard Glossary of Software Engineering Terminology." Los Alamitos, CA: IEEE Computer Society Press.

———. 1992. IEEE Std 1061-1992: "IEEE Standard for a Software Quality Metrics Methodology." Los Alamitos, CA: IEEE Computer Society Press.

———. 1998a. IEEE Std 1362-1998: "IEEE Guide for Information Technology— System Definition—Concept of Operations (ConOps) Document." Los Alamitos, CA: IEEE Computer Society Press.

———. 1998b. IEEE Std 830-1998: "IEEE Recommended Practice for Software Requirements Specifications." Los Alamitos, CA: IEEE Computer Society Press.

———. 1998c. IEEE Std 1233-1998: "IEEE Guide for Developing System Requirements Specifications." Los Alamitos, CA: IEEE Computer Society Press.

International Function Point Users Group. 2002. *Function Point Counting Practices Manual, Version 4.1.1.* Princeton Junction, NJ: International Function Point Users Group.

Jackson, Michael. 1995. *Software Requirements & Specifications: A Lexicon of Practice, Principles, and Prejudices.* Harlow, England: Addison-Wesley.

Jacobson, Ivar, Magnus Christerson, Patrik Jonsson, and Gunnar Övergaard. 1992. *Object-Oriented Software Engineering: A Use Case Driven Approach.* Harlow, England: Addison-Wesley.

Jacobson, Ivar, Grady Booch, and James Rumbaugh. 1999. *The Unified Software Development Process*. Reading, MA: Addison-Wesley.

Jarke, Matthias. 1998. "Requirements Tracing." *Communications of the ACM* 41(12):32–36.

Jeffries, Ron, Ann Anderson, and Chet Hendrickson. 2001. *Extreme Programming Installed*. Boston, MA: Addison-Wesley.

Jones, Capers. 1994. *Assessment and Control of Software Risks*. Englewood Cliffs, NJ: Prentice Hall PTR.

———. 1996a. "Strategies for Managing Requirements Creep." *IEEE Computer* 29(6):92–94.

———. 1996b. *Applied Software Measurement*, 2d ed. New York: McGraw-Hill.

———. 1997. *Software Quality: Analysis and Guidelines for Success*. Boston, MA: International Thomson Computer Press.

Jones, David A., Donald M. York, John F. Nallon, and Joseph Simpson. 1995. "Factors Influencing Requirement Management Toolset Selection." In *Proceedings of the Fifth Annual Symposium of the National Council on Systems Engineering*, vol. 2, 33-58. Seattle, WA: International Council on Systems Engineering.

Jung, Ho-Won. 1998. "Optimizing Value and Cost in Requirements Analysis." *IEEE Software* 15(4):74–78.

Karlsson, Joachim, and Kevin Ryan. 1997. "A Cost-Value Approach for Prioritizing Requirements." *IEEE Software* 14(5):67–74.

Keil, Mark, and Erran Carmel. 1995. "Customer-Developer Links in Software Development." *Communications of the ACM* 38(5):33–44.

Kelly, John C., Joseph S. Sherif, and Jonathon Hops. 1992. "An Analysis of Defect Densities Found During Software Inspections." *Journal of Systems and Software* 17(2):111–117.

Kerth, Norman L. 2001. *Project Retrospectives: A Handbook for Team Reviews*. New York: Dorset House Publishing.

Kosman, Robert J. 1997. "A Two-Step Methodology to Reduce Requirement Defects." In *Annals of Software Engineering*, Nancy R. Mead, ed. 3:477–494.

Kovitz, Benjamin L. 1999. *Practical Software Requirements: A Manual of Content and Style*. Greenwich, CT: Manning Publications Co.

Kruchten, Philippe. 1996. "A Rational Development Process." *CrossTalk* 9(7):11–16.

Kulak, Daryl, and Eamonn Guiney. 2000. *Use Cases: Requirements in Context*. New York: ACM Press.

Larman, Craig. 1998. "The Use Case Model: What Are the Processes?" *Java Report* 3(8):62–72.

Lauesen, Soren. 2002. *Software Requirements: Styles and Techniques*. London: Addison-Wesley.

Lawlis, Patricia K., Kathryn E. Mark, Deborah A. Thomas, and Terry Courtheyn. 2001. "A Formal Process for Evaluating COTS Software Products." *IEEE Computer* 34(5):58-63.

Lawrence, Brian. 1996. "Unresolved Ambiguity." *American Programmer* 9(5):17–22.

———. 1997. "Requirements Happens…" *American Programmer* 10(4):3-9.

Leffingwell, Dean. 1997. "Calculating the Return on Investment from More Effective Requirements Management." *American Programmer* 10(4):13–16.

Leffingwell, Dean, and Don Widrig. 2000. *Managing Software Requirements: A Unified Approach*. Reading, MA: Addison-Wesley.

Leishman, Theron R., and David A. Cook. 2002. "Requirements Risks Can Drown Software Projects." *CrossTalk* 15(4):4-8.

Leveson, Nancy. 1995. *Safeware: System Safety and Computers*. Reading, MA: Addison-Wesley.

Lilly, Susan. 2000. "How to Avoid Use-Case Pitfalls." *Software Development* 8(1):40-44.

Martin, James. 1991. *Rapid Application Development*. New York: Macmillan Publishing.

Martin, Johnny, and W. T. Tsai. 1990. "N-fold Inspection: A Requirements Analysis Technique." *Communications of the ACM* 33(2):225–232.

McCabe, Thomas J. 1982. *Structured Testing: A Software Testing Methodology Using the Cyclomatic Complexity Metric*. National Bureau of Standards Special Publication 500-599.

McConnell, Steve. 1993. *Code Complete: A Practical Handbook of Software Construction*. Redmond, WA: Microsoft Press.

————. 1996. *Rapid Development: Taming Wild Software Schedules*. Redmond, WA: Microsoft Press.

————. 1998. *Software Project Survival Guide*. Redmond, WA: Microsoft Press.

McGraw, Karen L., and Karan Harbison. 1997. *User-Centered Requirements: The Scenario-Based Engineering Process*. Mahwah, NJ: Lawrence Erlbaum Associates.

McMenamin, Stephen M., and John F. Palmer. 1984. *Essential Systems Analysis*. Englewood Cliffs, NJ: Prentice Hall.

Moore, Geoffrey A. 1991. *Crossing the Chasm: Marketing and Selling High-Tech Products to Mainstream Customers*. New York: HarperBusiness.

Morgan, Tony. 2002. *Business Rules and Information Systems: Aligning IT with Business Goals*. Boston, MA: Addison-Wesley.

Musa, John D. 1996. "Software-Reliability-Engineered Testing." *IEEE Computer* 29(11):61-68.

Musa, John, Anthony Iannino, and Kazuhira Okumoto. 1987. *Software Reliability: Measurement, Prediction, Application*. New York: McGraw-Hill.

Myers, Glenford J. 1979. *The Art of Software Testing*. New York: John Wiley & Sons.

Nejmeh, Brian A., and Ian Thomas. "Business-Driven Product Planning Using Feature Vectors and Increments." *IEEE Software* 19(6):34-42.

Nelsen, E. Dale. 1990. "System Engineering and Requirement Allocation." In *System and Software Requirements Engineering*, Richard H. Thayer and Merlin Dorfman, eds. Los Alamitos, CA: IEEE Computer Society Press.

Nielsen, Jakob. 2000. *Designing Web Usability*. Indianapolis, IN: New Riders Publishing.

Pardee, William J. 1996. *To Satisfy & Delight Your Customer: How to Manage for Customer Value*. New York: Dorset House Publishing.

Paulk, Mark, et al. 1995. *The Capability Maturity Model: Guidelines for Improving the Software Process*. Reading, MA: Addison-Wesley.

Pfleeger, Shari Lawrence. 2001. *Software Engineering: Theory and Practice*, 2d ed. Englewood Cliffs, NJ: Prentice Hall.

Porter, Adam A., Lawrence G. Votta, Jr., and Victor R. Basili. 1995. "Comparing Detection Methods for Software Requirements Inspections: A Replicated Experiment." *IEEE Transactions on Software Engineering* 21(6):563–575.

Porter-Roth, Bud. 2002. *Request for Proposal: A Guide to Effective RFP Development*. Boston, MA: Addison-Wesley.

Poston, Robert M. 1996. *Automating Specification-Based Software Testing*. Los Alamitos, CA: IEEE Computer Society Press.

Potter, Neil S., and Mary E. Sakry. 2002. *Making Process Improvement Work: A Concise Action Guide for Software Managers and Practitioners*. Boston, MA: Addison-Wesley.

Project Management Institute. 2000. *A Guide to the Project Management Body of Knowledge, 2000 Edition*. Newtown Square, PA: Project Management Institute.

Putnam, Lawrence H., and Ware Myers. 1997. *Industrial Strength Software: Effective Management Using Measurement*. Los Alamitos, CA: IEEE Computer Society Press.

Radice, Ronald A. 2002. *High Quality Low Cost Software Inspections*. Andover, MA: Paradoxicon Publishing.

Ramesh, Bala, Curtis Stubbs, Timothy Powers, and Michael Edwards. 1995. "Lessons Learned from Implementing Requirements Traceability." *CrossTalk* 8(4):11–15, 20.

Ramesh, Balasubramaniam. 1998. "Factors Influencing Requirements Traceability Practice." *Communications of the ACM* 41(12):37–44.

Rettig, Marc. 1994. "Prototyping for Tiny Fingers." *Communications of the ACM* 37(4):21–27.

Robertson, James. 2002. "Eureka! Why Analysts Should Invent Requirements." *IEEE Software* 19(4):20-22.

Robertson, James, and Suzanne Robertson. 1994. *Complete Systems Analysis: The Workbook, The Textbook, The Answers*. New York: Dorset House Publishing.

———. 1997. "Requirements: Made to Measure." *American Programmer* 10(8):27–32.

Robertson, Suzanne, and James Robertson. 1999. *Mastering the Requirements Process*. Harlow, England: Addison-Wesley.

Ross, Ronald G. 1997. *The Business Rule Book: Classifying, Defining, and Modeling Rules, Version 4.0*, 2d ed. Houston: Business Rule Solutions, LLC.

———. 2001. "The Business Rules Classification Scheme." *DataToKnowledge Newsletter* 29(5).

Rothman, Johanna. 2000. *Reflections Newsletter* 3(1).

Rubin, Howard. 1999. "The *1999 Worldwide Benchmark Report*: Software Engineering and IT Findings for 1998 and 1999, Part II." *IT Metrics Strategies* 5(3):1-13.

Schneider, G. Michael, Johnny Martin, and W. T. Tsai. 1992. "An Experimental Study of Fault Detection in User Requirements Documents." *ACM Transactions on Software Engineering and Methodology* 1(2):188–204.

Schneider, Geri, and Jason P. Winters. 1998. *Applying Use Cases: A Practical Guide*. Reading, MA: Addison-Wesley.

Schulmeyer, G. Gordon, and James I. McManus, eds. 1996. *Total Quality Management for Software*. London: International Thomson Computer Press.

Sibbet, David. 1994. *Effective Facilitation*. San Francisco, CA: The Grove Consultants International.

Simmons, Erik. 2001. "From Requirements to Release Criteria: Specifying, Demonstrating, and Monitoring Product Quality." In *Proceedings of the 2001 Pacific Northwest Software Quality Conference*, 155-165. Portland, OR: Pacific Northwest Software Quality Conference.

Smith, Larry W. 2000. "Project Clarity Through Stakeholder Analysis." *CrossTalk* 13(12):4-9.

Smith, R. Craig. 1998. "Using a Quality Model Framework to Strengthen the Requirements Bridge." In *Proceedings of the Third International Conference on Requirements Engineering*, 118–125. Los Alamitos, CA: IEEE Computer Society Press.

Sommerville, Ian, and Pete Sawyer. 1997. *Requirements Engineering: A Good Practice Guide*. Chichester, England: John Wiley & Sons.

Sommerville, Ian, and Gerald Kotonya. 1998. *Requirements Engineering: Processes and Techniques*. Chichester, England: John Wiley & Sons.

Song, Xiping, Bill Hasling, Gaurav Mangla, and Bill Sherman. 1998. "Lessons Learned from Building a Web-Based Requirements Tracing System." In *Proceedings of the Third International Conference on Requirements Engineering*, 41–50. Los Alamitos, CA: IEEE Computer Society Press.

Sorensen, Reed. 1999. "CCB—An Acronym for 'Chocolate Chip Brownies'? A Tutorial on Control Boards." *CrossTalk* 12(3):3–6.

The Standish Group. 1995. *The CHAOS Report*. Dennis, MA: The Standish Group International, Inc.

Steven, John. 2002. "Putting Software Terminology to the Test." *IEEE Software* 19(3):88-89.

Stevens, Richard, Peter Brook, Ken Jackson, and Stuart Arnold. 1998. *Systems Engineering: Coping with Complexity*. London: Prentice Hall.

Thayer, Richard H. 2002. "Software System Engineering: A Tutorial." *IEEE Computer* 35(4):68-73.

Thayer, Richard H., and Merlin Dorfman, eds. 1997. *Software Requirements Engineering*, 2d ed. Los Alamitos, CA: IEEE Computer Society Press.

Thompson, Bruce, and Karl Wiegers. 1995. "Creative Client/Server for Evolving Enterprises." *Software Development* 3(2):34–44.

Voas, Jeffrey. 1999. "Protecting Against What? The Achilles Heel of Information Assurance." *IEEE Software* 16(1):28–29.

von Halle, Barbara. 2002. *Business Rules Applied: Building Better Systems Using the Business Rules Approach*. New York: John Wiley & Sons.

Votta, Lawrence G., Jr. 1993. "Does Every Inspection Need a Meeting?" In *Proceedings of the First ACM SIGSOFT Symposium on Software Development Engineering*, 107–114. New York: ACM Press.

Wallace, Dolores R., and Laura M. Ippolito. 1997. "Verifying and Validating Software Requirements Specifications." In *Software Requirements Engineering*, 2d ed., Richard H. Thayer and Merlin Dorfman, eds., 389–404. Los Alamitos, CA: IEEE Computer Society Press.

Wasserman, Anthony I. 1985. "Extending State Transition Diagrams for the Specification of Human-Computer Interaction." *IEEE Transactions on Software Engineering* SE-11(8):699-713.

Weinberg, Gerald M. 1995. "Just Say No! Improving the Requirements Process." *American Programmer* 8(10):19–23.

Whitmire, Scott A. 1995. "An Introduction to 3D Function Points." *Software Development* 3(4):43–53.

———. 1997. *Object-Oriented Design Measurement*. New York: John Wiley & Sons.

Wiegers, Karl E. 1996a. *Creating a Software Engineering Culture*. New York: Dorset House Publishing.

———. 1996b. "Reducing Maintenance with Design Abstraction." *Software Development* 4(4):47–50.

———. 1998a. "The Seven Deadly Sins of Software Reviews." *Software Development* 6(3):44–47.

———. 1998b. "Know Your Enemy: Software Risk Management." *Software Development* 6(10):38-42.

———. 1998c. "Improve Your Process With Online 'Good Practices'." *Software Development* 6(12):45-50.

———. 1999a. "A Software Metrics Primer." *Software Development* 7(7):39-42.

———. 1999b. "Software Process Improvement in Web Time." *IEEE Software* 15(4):78-86.

———. 2000. "The Habits of Effective Analysts." *Software Development* 8(10):62–65.

———. 2001. "Requirements When the Field Isn't Green." *STQE* 3(3):30-37.

———. 2002a. *Peer Reviews in Software: A Practical Guide*. Boston, MA: Addison-Wesley.

———. 2002b. "Promises, Promises." *The Rational Edge* 2(1) (*http://www.therationaledge.com*).

———. 2002c. "Success Criteria Breed Success." *The Rational Edge* 2(2) (*http://www.therationaledge.com*).

———. 2002d. "Saving for a Rainy Day." *The Rational Edge* 2(4) (*http://www.therationaledge.com*).

———. 2003. "See You In Court." *Software Development* 11(1):36-40.

Wiegers, Karl, and Johanna Rothman. 2001. "Looking Back, Looking Ahead." *Software Development* 9(2):65-69.

Wieringa, R. J. 1996. *Requirements Engineering: Frameworks for Understanding*. Chichester, England: John Wiley & Sons.

Wiley, Bill. 2000. *Essential System Requirements: A Practical Guide to Event-Driven Methods*. Reading, MA: Addison-Wesley.

Williams, Ray C., Julie A. Walker, and Audrey J. Dorofee. 1997. "Putting Risk Management into Practice." *IEEE Software* 14(3):75-82.

Wilson, Peter B. 1995. "Testable Requirements—An Alternative Sizing Measure." *The Journal of the Quality Assurance Institute* 9(4):3–11.

Wirfs-Brock, Rebecca. 1993. "Designing Scenarios: Making the Case for a Use Case Framework." *Smalltalk Report* 3(3).

Wood, David P., and Kyo C. Kang. 1992. *A Classification and Bibliography of Software Prototyping* (CMU/SEI-92-TR-013). Pittsburgh, PA: Software Engineering Institute, Carnegie Mellon University.

Wood, Jane, and Denise Silver. 1995. *Joint Application Development*, 2d ed. New York: John Wiley & Sons.

Young, Ralph R. 2001. *Effective Requirements Practices*. Boston, MA: Addison-Wesley.

Zultner, Richard E. 1993. "TQM for Technical Teams." *Communications of the ACM* 36(10):79–91.

Index

Karl E. Wiegers

Karl E. Wiegers is principal consultant at Process Impact, a software process consulting and education company based in Portland, Oregon. He has consulted and presented training seminars at dozens of companies worldwide. Previously, Karl spent 18 years at Eastman Kodak Company, where he held positions as a photographic research scientist, software developer, software manager, and software process and quality improvement leader. Karl received a B.S. in chemistry from Boise State College, and an M.S. and a Ph.D. in organic chemistry from the University of Illinois. He is a member of the IEEE, IEEE Computer Society, and ACM.

Karl is the author of *Peer Reviews in Software: A Practical Guide* (Addison-Wesley, 2002) and the *Software Development* Productivity Award–winning book *Creating a Software Engineering Culture* (Dorset House, 1996). He has also written some 160 articles on many aspects of computing, chemistry, and military history. Karl has served as a contributing editor for *Software Development* magazine and on the editorial board for *IEEE Software* magazine.

When he isn't in front of the computer or the classroom, Karl enjoys playing his Gibson Les Paul, Fender Stratocaster, and Guild D40 guitars, riding his Suzuki VX800 motorcycle, studying military history, cooking, and sipping wine with his wife, Chris Zambito. You can contact Karl through *http://www.processimpact.com*.

The manuscript for this book was prepared and galleyed using Microsoft Word. Pages were composed by Microsoft Press using Adobe FrameMaker+SGML for Windows, with text in Garamond and display type in Helvetica Condensed. Composed pages were delivered to the printer as electronic prepress files.

Cover Designers:	Patricia Bradbury, Design; Todd Daman, Illustration
Interior Graphic Designer:	James D. Kramer
Principal Compositor:	Gina Cassill
Interior Artist:	Michael Kloepfer
Principal Copy Editor:	Sandi Resnick
Proofreader:	nSight, Inc.
Indexer:	Julie Kawabata

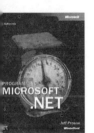
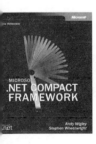

Get a **Free**
*e-mail newsletter, updates,
special offers, links to related books,
and more when you*

register on line!

Register your Microsoft Press® title on our Web site and you'll get a FREE subscription to our e-mail newsletter, *Microsoft Press Book Connections.* You'll find out about newly released and upcoming books and learning tools, online events, software downloads, special offers and coupons for Microsoft Press customers, and information about major Microsoft® product releases. You can also read useful additional information about all the titles we publish, such as detailed book descriptions, tables of contents and indexes, sample chapters, links to related books and book series, author biographies, and reviews by other customers.

Registration is easy. Just visit this Web page and fill in your information:

http://www.microsoft.com/mspress/register

Microsoft®

Proof of Purchase

Use this page as proof of purchase if participating in a promotion or rebate offer on this title. Proof of purchase must be used in conjunction with other proof(s) of payment such as your dated sales receipt—see offer details.

Software Requirements, Second Edition
0-7356-1879-8

CUSTOMER NAME

Microsoft Press, PO Box 97017, Redmond, WA 98073-9830